D1266511

History of the General Federation of Trade Unions, 1899–1980

History of the General Federation of Trade Unions, 1899–1980

ALICE PROCHASKA

London
GEORGE ALLEN & UNWIN
Boston   Sydney

George Allen & Unwin (Publishers) Ltd,
40 Museum Street, London WC1A 1LU, UK

338.0941
P96h

George Allen & Unwin (Publishers) Ltd,
Park Lane, Hemel Hempstead, Herts HP2 4TE, UK

Allen & Unwin Inc.,
9 Winchester Terrace, Winchester, Mass. 01890, USA

George Allen & Unwin Australia Pty Ltd,
8 Napier Street, North Sydney, NSW 2060, Australia

First published in 1982

British Library Cataloguing in Publication Data

Prochaska, Alice
    History of the General Federation of Trade Unions, 1899–1980.
1. General Federation of Trade Unions – History.
I. Title.
331.88′06′041   HD8383.G/
ISBN 0-04-331087-7

Library of Congress Cataloging in Publication Data

Prochaska, Alice.
    History of the General Federation of Trade Unions, 1899–1980.
1. General Federation of Trade Unions – History.
I. Title
HD8383.G4P76 1982   331.88′0941   82–11495
ISBN 0-04-331087-7

Set in 10 on 11 point Times by Fotographics (Bedford) Ltd
and printed in Great Britain by Biddles Ltd, Guildford, Surrey

Contents

Preface   *page*   ix
List of Abbreviations   xiii
1   The Beginnings of the General Federation of
    Trade Unions, 1890–1900   1
2   Growth: Internal Affairs, 1900–10   34
3   The General Federation in a Wider World, 1900–10   70
4   A Turbulent Decade. The Challenges of Syndicalism
    and War, 1910–20   101
5   International Affairs and the Exclusion of the General
    Federation from British Representation, 1913–22   142
6   Between the Wars   169
7   From the 1940s to the 1970s   206
Appendix   250
Sources and Select Bibliography   254
Index   262

Preface

The General Federation of Trade Unions came into being in 1899 incorporating the highest and most visionary hopes of many leading trade unionists in Great Britain. They wanted to forge an instrument of unity among all trade unions in the country, through which common action might be attained towards the betterment of all working people's lives. It was hoped that a nationwide federation of trade unions might transcend the sectional interests which necessarily made up the daily business of the multitude of separate unions in the country. Some hoped that with a solid enough financial basis for federation this new organisation could overcome the mixture of feuding and inertia so often displayed at the Trades Union Congress in the 1890s. It might become the industrial arm of the labour movement whose separate political identity was affirmed in the foundation of the Labour Representation Committee (later the Labour Party) in the following year.

After more than eighty years of sometimes turbulent history, the General Federation of Trade Unions in the 1980s is a modest but prosperous organisation catering for some forty unions (almost all also affiliated to the TUC) whose membership ranges in size from less than 100 to over 100,000. The great majority of its gross aggregate membership of over 490,000 do skilled manual work, with a high concentration in the textile and garment industries and a significant proportion also in specialised engineering, furniture making and the ceramic industry. Its small headquarters staff of four full-time officials including the general secretary provides a range of services which most affiliated unions could not provide for themselves: research, educational courses, publications on general industrial problems, and legal advice. It does not compete with but complements the services offered by the TUC, gearing its own services to the needs of its own small and medium-sized affiliated unions and providing an atmosphere at its courses and meetings where the members and officials of these unions can feel especially at home.

If we were to judge from published writings on labour history, the history of the General Federation of Trade Unions would seem a study in obscurity, buried with few traces in the corporate past of trade unions and the broader labour movement. The General Federation appears from time to time in a few pages of works on the labour movement in the early years of this century, but hardly ever gets a mention in any work dealing with a period later than 1920. Its early history is seen as something of a blind alley, or at best a path that trade unions as a whole decided not to follow, and therefore of little interest. After the decline of the General Federation as a force in national trade unionism, round about 1920–3, its very existence is seldom acknowledged. Its continuation and gradual renaissance in the 1960s and 1970s are facts of which many active participants in and students of the labour movement are ignorant. But the GFTU, far from dwindling into insignificance, has turned itself into a highly useful representative of small and medium-sized trade unions. Many of these enjoy a record of success in industrial relations which might be the envy of more prominent organisations and provide services for their members which in some instances are superior to those offered by the giant unions to workers in the same or closely related industries. The GFTU in the late twentieth century is a very different organisation from what its founders in 1899 hoped it might become, and more modest by far than the vocal national representative of labour that its early management committee wanted it to be. In both its early and its present form, however, it holds a significant place in the history of British trade unionism, and the vicissitudes it has suffered in all its eighty years and more shed much light on the history of labour relations and working-class organisation in this country as a whole.

It is my aim in this book to draw attention to the unduly neglected past and present of the GFTU and to provide a framework within which its contribution to the history of British labour in the twentieth century may be understood. Several hundred separate trade unions have belonged to the General Federation at different times, and its activities have impinged on many different aspects of national industrial life, from the nuts and bolts of wage bargaining in particular industries to the principles of social insurance, international labour relations and the higher philosophy of syndicalism and the class struggle. It has not been possible in a limited time and space to provide anything like a comprehensive history. Much still remains to be discovered about the General Federation and its past, and I have left many sources untapped. I hope that other students of British labour may be stimulated by this book to probe further, and that in the meantime members of the GFTU, other trade unionists and more general readers may find matter here to interest and perhaps surprise them.

I owe a debt of gratitude to various organisations and to individuals, above all to the General Federation of Trade Unions itself for commissioning me to do this work and giving me the freedom to produce an honest portrait. The general secretary when I was commissioned at the end of 1976 was the late Leslie Hodgson, whose personal kindness was a great encouragement. The chairman of the Management Committee in 1976–7 was Mrs. Margaret Fenwick, who recently retired as general secretary of the Union of Jute, Flax and Kindred Textile Operatives (now the Jute, Flax Branch of the National Union of Dyers, Bleachers and Textile Workers). She and her successors as chairmen each year have been unstintingly generous with time, information and hospitality. My visits to them and my contacts with many others as the guest of the General Federation at the annual general council meetings in Edinburgh in 1977 and Torquay in 1978 formed the basis for this book and gave purpose and meaning to the documentary research. Without these personal contacts and all the reminiscences and verbal guidance that I received, it would have been very difficult to approach an understanding of the GFTU. I only wish time had permitted me to visit all of the unions now affiliated. The list of individuals who have helped me in this way would be very extensive, so I hope they will not feel slighted by this general note of thanks. The names of some of them will be found in the text and notes and in the notes on sources and bibliography. I must, however, thank by name the present general secretary of the GFTU, Peter Potts; the two research officers, Rod Smith and Roger Sutton, and the education officer, Nigel Knowles. I am indebted also to the several secretaries at General Federation headquarters, who have joined in helping me and making me feel welcome.

Others whose connection with this history is more detached have given very valuable help. Roger Rideout, Professor of Law at University College, London, who has long been associated with the GFTU as informal legal adviser and as a lecturer at the federation's courses, has read this book in typescript and made many invaluable comments. Parts of it also have been read by Logie Barrow of Bremen University, Arthur Marsh of St Edmund Hall, Oxford University, and Noelle Whiteside of Bristol University. For general discussion and advice I am indebted to Sir Harold Emmerson, formerly Permanent Secretary at the Ministry of Labour, to John Edwards, Certification Officer for Trade Unions and Employers' Associations, John Halmos of the TUC, John Hughes, Principal of Ruskin College, Oxford, Rodney Lowe of Bristol University and to several friends and colleagues at the Institute of Historical Research, University of London, and at the Public Record Office. I am particularly grateful to the Keeper of Public Records for granting me six months' leave of absence in order to work on the book, to the Social Science Research Council for supporting me financially, and to the Director and Secretary of the Institute of Historical Research, University of London, for advice and many kindnesses while I was attached to the Institute during that time. The Twenty-Seven Foundation generously made a grant towards the cost of typing and photocopying the manuscript. I would also like to thank the many individuals in libraries who have lightened my task, especially in the British Library, the British Library of Political and Economic Science, Darlington Public Library and the Public Record Office. Thanks, finally, to Frank Prochaska, whose advice, criticism and moral support have been indispensable. For the imperfections that remain after all these kindnesses I am myself alone responsible.

ALICE PROCHASKA

List of abbreviations used in text and notes

agcm	annual general council meeting
AEU	Amalgamated Engineering Union
AFOfL	American Federation of Labor
ASE	Amalgamated Society of Engineers
ASRS	Amalgamated Society of Railway Servants
ASTMS	Association of Scientific, Technical and Managerial Staffs
ATWU	Amalgamated Textile Workers' Union
AUEW	Amalgamated Union of Engineering Workers
BL	British Library
BLPES	British Library of Political and Economic Science
CATU	Ceramic and Allied Trades Union
CGT	Confédération Générale de Travail
CUB	Central (Unemployed) Body for London
ETU	Electrical Trades Union
FTAT	Furniture, Timber and Allied Trades Union
GFTU	General Federation of Trade Unions
GMWU	General and Municipal Workers' Union
IFTU	International Federation of Trade Unions
ILP	Independent Labour Party
JIC	Joint Industrial Council
LRC	Labour Representation Committee
LTC	London Trades Council
NAUL	National Amalgamated Union of Labour
NSMM	National Society of Metal Mechanics
NUFSO	National Union of Funeral Service Operatives
NULMW	National Union of Lock and Metal Workers
NUT&GW	National Union of Tailors and Garment Workers
PRO	Public Record Office
SDF	Social Democratic Federation
SLADE	Society of Lithographic Artists, Designers, Engravers and Process Workers
TGWU	Transport and General Workers' Union
TUC	Trades Union Congress
TURU	Trade Union Research Unit
USE	United Society of Engravers
UTWFA	United Textile Workers' Factory Association

VAF	Variety Artistes' Federation
WEA	Workers' Educational Association
WEWNC	War Emergency: Workers' National Committee

1

The Beginnings of the General Federation of Trade Unions, 1890-1900

Industrial Relations in Britain in the 1890s

Industrial relations in Great Britain today inherit a tradition that stretches back unbroken to the 1820s. In 1824, with the repeal of the Combination Acts of 1799 and 1800 which had forbidden the existence of 'combinations of workmen', some unions which already existed in defiance of the law became free to organise openly and others soon developed. As continuous associations of working people, they sought to maintain and improve the conditions of their working lives.[1] But the law scarcely bestowed freedom on their organisations. In 1825, barely a year after legalising the existence of trade unions, Parliament passed some much more restrictive legislation. The celebrated case of the 'Tolpuddle Martyrs' in 1834 showed just how oppressively the law could work, when six farm labourers from Dorset were sentenced to transportation for the crime of swearing an illegal oath for a seditious purpose, because they had sworn to work together to obtain higher wages.[2]

The Tolpuddle case coincided with the end of the first well-documented upsurge of trade union activity. The next great landmark in working people's industrial organisation came after the failure of Chartism, the movement for working-class political rights, in the 1840s: this was the formation of the Amalgamated Society of Engineers in 1851, the first of what the Webbs, pioneering historians of trade unionism, called the 'new model' unions of highly organised skilled workers in major industries. In 1868, with the foundation of the Trades Union Congress, trade unionism in Great Britain reached another watershed, the beginnings of a permanent working-class organisation on a national scale. By the 1890s the picture of British trade unionism was highly complicated. Some industries, like coal-mining and cotton textile manufacturing, were relatively well organised into amalgamations or federations of unions with tens of thousands of members and boasting considerable strength *vis-à-vis* the employers. Other important industries like engineering (despite the dominant ASE) and woollen textiles were much more divided. In some, the division fell between unorganised labourers and multiple organisations of skilled craftsmen, while in other industries rival unions competed for the membership of very much the same sorts of workers, and divided along regional lines. Relative newcomers on the scene were the general unions, which catered for a shifting population of unskilled or casual labour. In spite of the great diversity and the large number of unions, however, not more than about a quarter of Britain's working population belonged to any trade union. Although the strength of trade unionism as a whole had grown enormously since about 1850, the scene in the 1890s was still volatile and swiftly changing, and the membership both of individual unions and of the movement as a whole fluctuated widely. Many unions, moreover, owed their existence mainly to the driving force of a particular leader, like W. J. Davies of the brassworkers, John Ward, the founder of the navvies' union, or Ben Tillett, the leader of the London dockers. Throughout the trade union world and in the TUC itself the personalities of the leading officials were profoundly influential.

The great dockers' strike of 1889 was widely thought to signal an era of 'new unionism'. Workers who previously had been little organised were joining unions which, unlike the older-established organisations in such industries as textiles and mining, required few or no qualifications for membership and offered the simple benefits of strike pay and solidarity in return for low contributions. They were led by some of the most daring and eye-catching of trade union leaders, men like Ben Tillett of the dockers, Will Thorne of the gas-workers and John Burns, the engineers' leader who had helped Tillett and Tom Mann to lead the dockers to victory. These men's militant rhetoric and qualities of leadership brought a new flavour to the Trades Union Congress. On the other hand, older societies too were organising in new ways to deal with the problems of the 1890s. In the Lancashire textile industry, seat of pioneering trade unionism and of some of the most fiercely guarded traditional crafts, the weavers' amalgamation was displaying a new militancy on behalf of both skilled and unskilled labour. Unions founded to protect the skilled crafts of heavy engineering, like the United Society of Boilermakers and Iron and Steel Shipbuilders, or the Friendly Society of Iron-founders, were devising schemes for greater unity within their trades. The Miners' Federation of Great Britain, formed in 1888, drew together the miners of several districts to fight for a legally compulsory 8-hour day rather than the sliding scale of payments on which the more conservative miners' organisations still centred their negotiations. The Miners' Federation was rapidly to become one of the strongest and most distinctive trade union groups (it was still by no means a single union) in the history of British industrial relations. Membership of the TUC rose dramatically with the influx of new unionists in 1890, and although it dwindled during the trade recession of the early 1890s, by 1896 a steady rise was again in progress.[3]

Increased numbers of organisations with a greater numerical strength and new methods were far from being the preserve of the unions alone. As early as 1873, five years after the first meeting of the TUC, the National Federated Association of Employers of Labour came into being to combat the 'extraordinary development – oppressive action – far-reaching, but openly-avowed designs – and elaborate organisation of the Trade Unions'.[4] In the 1890s more federations of employers were founded in particular industries and the National Free Labour Association, formed in 1893 to provide a pool of blackleg labour for employers whose workers were on strike, presented the unions with another unwelcome example of the power of 'scientific organisation'.[5] Workers in many industries felt the impact of their employers' renewed organisation. In the gas industry this took a relatively benign form when the South Metropolitan Gas Company in London attempted to wean its employees away from the union with schemes of profit-sharing and co-partnership. But in the docks the Shipping Federation established 'free labour registries' in 1893 and provoked a major strike in Hull. Other examples of the employers' anti-union organisation were to be found in mining, where the coal owners locked out the miners and tried to impose wage cuts of 25 per cent in 1893; and among cotton manufacturers and railway companies.

It was the engineers who engaged in the most fiercely fought of all the industrial battles of the 1890s.[6] The Amalgamated Society of Engineers in that decade was gathering new strength and beginning to change direction. In 1892 supporters of Tom Mann, who had stood unsuccessfully for the post of general secretary in the previous year, succeeded in replacing the old local executive councils of the ASE with one central council. The new system put seventeen full-time central officials in the place of the previous four, and at the same time the society broadened its base to give full membership for the first time to workers in some of the newer processes, like electrical engineering. In 1896 George Barnes, who had stood for Rochdale as an Independent Labour Party parliamentary candidate in 1895, became general secretary. Barnes wanted direct political representation in Parliament for the ASE (which in fact was already paying £100 a year to John Burns, the former engineer who was Liberal MP for Battersea). He also wanted a more militant industrial policy which would include a federation of all the unions in engineering and kindred trades; and he sought greater authority for the general secretary within the ASE. The engineering employers regarded the ASE under its new management as a threat. But at the same time they were looking for an opportunity to impose a national system of bargaining on an industry which, however centralised its main union might become, would always retain strong local diversity and independence.

Early in 1897 the London committees of the main engineering unions together with a number of smaller ones formed an Eight Hours Committee to campaign for an 8-hour day throughout the industry, the same cause that the Miners' Federation had already made the kingpin of its policy. As far as the ASE was concerned, there were other things to fight for, too. In parts of Scotland and the north of England, for example, the 'machine question' was the burning issue: employers who had introduced new machinery were using 'handymen' instead of 'labourers' to operate it, an intermediate grade not recognised by the ASE, which threatened the jobs of skilled labourers whose skills in any case were becoming obsolete. The London Eight Hours Committee had some success in negotiations with employers in London, but meanwhile the Employers' Federation of Engineering Associations, under the new leadership of Colonel Dyer of Armstrong-Whitworth, was preparing to resist the engineers' demands nationally. In March 1897 the ASE called for a levy of 9d per member and prepared for battle. In June a London branch of the employers' federation was formed, and the Eight Hours Committee refused to recognise it, threatening at the same time to call a strike against any employer who did not grant the 8-hour day. The employers' federation retaliated with a progressive lockout of engineers throughout the country (25 per cent of employees in each federated firm were locked out each week). In the minds of some of its members at least, the federation's resolve was to 'get rid of trade unionism altogether'.[7]

The national lockout of engineers lasted for nearly seven months. During the course of it the ASE found itself bearing some other unions' expenses as well as its own, and some of the other large unions involved, like the boilermakers and the patternmakers in areas outside London, caused permanent bitterness by negotiating separately with the employers. Energetic campaigns in the labour press, notably the *Clarion*, brought in thousands of pounds for the engineers' funds, as did special football matches and concerts and a huge demonstration in Hyde Park. Through the agency of Eleanor Marx, who did so much to help British trade unions during her short life, foreign trade unionists, especially in Germany, contributed generously. The TUC, however, had done pathetically little to muster support. In January 1898, with its own funds close to exhaustion and with waning support from other unions, the ASE finally negotiated terms with the employers. Although the agreement that ended the lockout did set up machinery for the settlement of future disputes, it really represented humiliating defeat for the ASE: no 8-hour day, no agreement on the machinery question and no right to negotiate for non-unionists; let alone any approach to the closed shop, which the ASE in some areas had virtually achieved before the lockout. This complex and embittered struggle was the epic of the 1890s as far as most British trade unionists were concerned. It helped to convince many of them that there was an urgent need for some form of systematic joint action in the trade union movement.

Against this industrial background, trade unionists were increasingly uneasy about the attitudes of the legal and parliamentary establishment in general. Now that most working men had the vote under the Parliamentary Reform Acts of 1867 and 1884, growing numbers of them wanted to use their political power independently. Within trade union ranks there was a groundswell of dissatisfaction with the Liberal policies of Henry Broadhurst (secretary to the TUC Parliamentary Committee, 1875–90) and the other long-established leaders. Many working men were attracted to the socialist ideas put forward by H. M. Hyndman's Social Democratic Federation and, more important, to those of Keir Hardie, the Ayrshire miner and founder of the Scottish Labour Party. Hardie became effectively the leader of the Independent Labour Party after its formation on a national basis at the Bradford conference of 1893. The Liberal Party under Gladstone and then under the patrician Lord Rosebery, held little hope for a sustained representation of working men's interest in Parliament. Moreover, a series of important judgements in the courts in this last decade of the century was undermining the legal protection for trade unions' activities embodied in the Trade Union Act 1871, and union leaders rightly judged that nothing short of major legislation would be needed to reverse this trend. Three decisions in 1893, 1895 and 1896 severely restricted the freedom of unions to carry out peaceable industrial action including picketing. Then the decision of Mr Justice Farwell and subsequently of the House of Lords in the Taff Vale case (1900–2) laid open union funds to common law actions for restraint of trade, a crippling disability from which the Trade Union Act 1871 was supposed to have freed them.*

* Liability for restraint of trade before 1871 was a criminal and not a civil one, which made it all the more oppressive. The Taff Vale case itself did not involve a common law action for restraint of trade, but the decision paved the way for such actions. See R. Y. Hedges and A. Winterbottom, *The Legal History of Trade Unionism* (London: Longman, 1930).

During these years of ferment and realignment in the world of British labour, leaders of the working-class movement were looking for a formula that would bring them greater unity and strength. The idea of a federation that would unite trade unions and so create an irresistible weapon in the workers' struggle against capital had been in the air since the creation of the Trades Union Congress in 1868 and even before that. The notion finally bore fruit just one year before the birth of the Labour Representation Committee, or Labour Party, as it was to become. Like the Labour Party, the General Federation of Trade Unions was the outcome of several different schemes and of some heated disagreements. Although its subsequent history was to be very different indeed from that of the Labour Party, its origins in the British working-class movement in the 1890s shed much light on the possibilities that existed then.

The Campaigns for Trade Union Federation

Federation was a 'hardy annual' at the TUC in the early 1890s.[8] The Parliamentary Committee had drawn up a constitution for federation in 1890, the Congresses of 1893 and 1894 had both considered the question, and in September 1895 yet another scheme, devised by a committee appointed at the Norwich Congress the previous year, was placed before the Congress at Cardiff. The stumbling block of previous plans had been their failure to secure any agreement on a financial underpinning for the proposed federation, and the 1895 plan avoided this problem by simply omitting financial arrangements altogether. Financial benefits, claimed the framers of the scheme, would come from saving expenditure on disputes that the federation would settle at an early stage through mediation. Any financial assistance required by a union that did get to the stage of a strike or lockout would be easier to obtain through the auspices of the new federation than it had been previously. This was spineless stuff. But there were two more constructive features of the scheme: its reliance on mediation and its proposal that overall federation should be preceded by the federation of unions in kindred trades into groups which would then be represented in a general council and as equally as possible on the central executive committee which the general council would set up. The constitution was to be as democratic as possible, leaving full autonomy to the affiliated unions, and a subsidiary constitution was suggested for the industrial groups, which provided for the approval of any dispute by all unions in the group before sympathetic action could be taken, and for courts of conciliation and arbitration which would be set up by the group in case of disputes between its members. The preamble to the scheme contained this singularly tame sentence:

> The aim of the Federation is the avoidance of all unnecessary friction between employers and operatives, by affording ample facilities for the adjustment of industrial difficulties through the agency of *mediation* or some such means.[9]

A heated scene followed the presentation of the report. Alexander Wilkie of the Associated Shipwrights, chairman of the committee responsible for the scheme, was supported by most of the speakers who followed him, and a show of hands gave a majority of 108 delegates to 68 in favour of forming the federation. Squabbling and booing accompanied the vote and after two card votes and much wrangling a majority of 133,000 against federation was recorded.[10] This was the Congress where the Parliamentary Committee had obtained a change in standing orders giving full weight to the numerical strength of the big unions and so diminishing the influence of the smaller (and often older) unions. A card vote took precedence over a show of hands in the new system and it was this issue that mainly accounted for the anger over the vote on federation. The episode was not auspicious for the future unity of the trade union movement, all the less so for having become entangled with the opportunist manœuvres of the Parliamentary Committee over the TUC's own rules.[11]

Congress was not to be allowed to forget the idea of federation, however unprepared it had shown itself for putting together a workable or acceptable scheme. In 1896 an obscure trade union organiser named P. J. King approached Robert Blatchford, editor of the *Clarion* newspaper, with a comprehensive scheme for a national and international federation of trade unions.[12] For more than two years Blatchford gave much space and full editorial support to King's articles on the subject. The *Clarion* was a lively and highly influential socialist newspaper. For a penny a week it offered its huge readership a mixture of practical politics and readable journalism on all sorts of subjects. The *Clarion* Cycling Clubs were among its most successful offshoots, combining healthy and sociable weekends with the inculcation of good socialist ideas for thousands of readers all over the country. Blatchford's views were influenced to some extent by those of the Social Democratic Federation (SDF) but still more by his own hatred of industrial competitiveness and his non-political vision of the right of all people to lead a decent, healthy life. He intensely disliked anything he saw as political intrigue and was a fervent campaigner for socialist unity. His most famous writing, *Merrie*

England, was first serialised in the *Clarion.* From 1894 it then sold more than 2 million copies in book form and is said to have converted more people to socialism in Britain than any other written work.[13] Although Blatchford said that he espoused King's scheme of federation not because it was socialist (he did not think it was) but because it offered some practical benefit to working people,[14] there was much more of socialism and the class war in this scheme than in any that the TUC had considered to date. By comparison with the proposals put forward in Cardiff in 1895, it was revolutionary.

King's plan for a federation of trade unions was ambitious and comprehensive. He based it upon equal payments, equal benefits and equal representation: each affiliated union would make a fixed contribution per week per head of its membership and it would then be entitled to exactly as much dispute benefit from each of the other affiliated unions (or in practice, from the federation funds) as it had paid in contributions; its voting strength in the federation would be proportioned exactly to the size of its contribution. The executive committee would consist of representatives of every affiliated union and would be required to vote its approval of any dispute before benefit could be paid. In the case of small disputes, affiliated unions would be free to conduct their own affairs without applying to the federation for benefit, and King made much of the fact that their autonomy would be unimpaired. A guarantee fund was to be formed consisting of the first year's contributions from each union, and no union could draw benefit until a year after entering the federation. Should any union wish to leave the federation, it would be entitled to withdraw with interest any money that it had paid in for a period of one year or more during which it had not received any benefits. The proposed level of contributions was 6*d* per week per union member. Benefits would be paid out at the same rate, but only in cases where a whole union or separately affiliated branch was involved in the dispute. No benefit at all was payable for disputes affecting only part of an affiliated union or branch. Estimating a potential aggregate membership of up to 2 million workers, King worked out that each one would receive about £4 per week in benefits while on strike or locked out. This figure, he conceded, was probably unnecessarily high and he proposed therefore that a maximum of 30 shillings per week might be given to each member, the remainder to be placed to the union's account in the federation funds.[15]

The *Clarion* scheme gathered formidable support from various sources. The Amalgamated Society of Railway Servants framed a resolution for the 1897 Congress (one of several resolutions on federation that year) which adopted King's proposals in outline.[16] The Scottish TUC, having put forward their own proposal at first, dropped it in favour of the *Clarion*'s.[17] The Wharton Hall branch of the Lancashire and Cheshire Miners' Federation proposed at the federation's meeting in Wigan in August 1897 that 'the time has arrived when all trades should amalgamate in one federation' and that 12,000 copies of the Clarion Pamphlet on the subject should be bought for distribution among the miners. This was in direct opposition to the views of Thomas Ashton, general secretary of the Lancashire and Cheshire Miners' Federation, and tended to support the *Clarion*'s claim that federation had the backing of rank-and-file trade unionists even if it went against the vested institutional interests of their paid officials.[18] Further demonstrations of support from trade unionists at meetings throughout the country, and most notably from the railway workers,[19] were reported in the pages of the *Clarion* for 1897 and 1898 and, equally telling, support flowed in from some of the most respected leaders of the labour movement. John Burns wrote, 'Your scheme of Federation is theoretically comprehensive, financially practicable and tactically adaptable.' But he added, 'you have not allowed sufficient for the personal and official elements that in labour movements are sometimes inimical to progress as the bureaucracy often have been to the growth of Democracy within the State, whose paid servants they are'.[20] Blatchford subsequently pressed John Burns to head the new federation, but Burns's enthusiasm stopped short of that.[21] Henry Broadhurst, whom the TUC's new rules had excluded because he was no longer either a full-time official or an active worker in industry, also lent his support in the *Clarion*'s pages. 'The present union of unions requires a thorough overhauling and modernising' he wrote.[22] Further testimonials came in the pages of other labour journals. Keir Hardie backed the *Clarion* scheme in the *Labour Leader*,[23] an article in the SDF organ *Justice* approved,[24] and Bruce Glasier commended the scheme to the ILP as a model for its own constitution.[25]

As the *Clarion*'s campaign for federation progressed, its arguments gained force from the plight of the Amalgamated Society of Engineers. In 1896 employers in the engineering industry had formed a federation to combat the growing militancy of the ASE. The following year, the employers' federation intervened when engineers in the London area struck for an 8-hour day and forced a national lockout. It was the first national strike or lockout on such a scale in British history. After six months' struggle the engineers had to return to work without having gained the 8-hour day and under humiliating terms which included giving the employers the right to determine whether skilled or unskilled men worked on new machinery. The lockout aroused prolonged discussion in the national press and helped to convince many trade unionists of the need both for a federation of

trade unions and for concerted political action. The engineers' leader
was George Barnes, a member of the ILP and politically sympathetic
to the advanced ideas of Tom Mann. From mid-1897, when the
disputes began, his letters appeared in most issues of the *Clarion*,
together with progress reports on the lockout and lists of subscribers
to the engineers' cause.

On 1 January 1898, with the engineers still locked out, the London
Trades Council held a conference to consider the best means of helping them. Robert Blatchford reported the proceedings with approval.
Although the London Trades Council had produced a rival and
slightly different scheme of federation, there was a great deal of
common ground between its politics and Blatchford's.[26] The
conference began by recommending a universal levy among trade
unionists of 3*d* per head to form a fighting fund for the engineers. It
then proceeded to condemn the Parliamentary Committee of the
TUC. James Sexton of the Liverpool dockers moved, and Pete Curran
of the gasworkers seconded, a motion deploring the apathy of the
Parliamentary Committee. 'Most people were beginning to think',
said Pete Curran, 'that the only function of a Parliamentary
Committee was to buttonhole capitalist members of Parliament in
the House of Commons with a request for support for labour
measures.'[27] Robert Blatchford added his own gloss:

[The Parliamentary Committee] should be at once abolished I
do hope that this clique of belated and enervated amateur statesmen
will soon be put upon the retired list . . . . If only the rank and file of
the unions will learn to distrust paid leaders, to watch permanent
officials, and to attend zealously and systematically to their own
affairs, the tactics of Colonel Dyer [of the Employers' Federation of
Engineering Associations] and his staff will prove entirely futile.[28]

By this time a committee set up by the 1897 Congress in Birmingham
was at work on an official scheme of federation to be considered at the
next Congress in Bristol. Blatchford and King, however, decided to
pre-empt these deliberations, which they expected to be valueless.
They called a 'Federal Labour Parliament' to meet at Co-operative
Hall, Manchester, on 18–20 July 1898,[29] and here they achieved a
large attendance. One interesting feature of the meeting was the
support that it gained from unions which refused to join the General
Federation of Trade Unions in the following year. The president of
the parliament was Robert Smillie, the Scottish miners' leader, and
vice-president J. Toyn came from the Cleveland miners. Ben Turner
of the Yorkshire textile workers, later a supporter of the GFTU, acted
as treasurer and T. Wilson of the Scottish bakers (who did join the

General Federation in 1900) acted as secretary. Among the 136 delegates was one from the Amalgamated Society of Railway Servants, which along with the Miners' Federation was later one of the most important unions to cold-shoulder the TUC's official scheme. The size and nature of the unions represented, with an aggregate membership of some 750,000, ranged from the ASE to the Amalgamated Society of Billposters, the Jewish Tailors and the Bolton Spindle and Fly Makers. The meeting agreed to an initial levy of 10 shillings per 1,000 members from each union represented there, and adopted the *Clarion* scheme of federation. P. J. King became secretary of the 'National and International General Federation of Trade and Labour Unions', which was to be governed by annual parliaments elected by the membership of the affiliated trade unions.

This, as it turned out, was the peak of King's success. Some of the unions in his federation, including the very important ASE, became founder members of the General Federation in 1899. Little was heard of the National and International General Federation after its first parliament. In 1902 King resigned from the secretaryship, and by about 1906 it had fizzled out.[30] Although a Clarion Pamphlet published by King in 1899 lambasted the TUC's official scheme of federation, Blatchford's columns in the *Clarion* newspaper itself were not so hostile to the TUC after the beginning of 1899. He appeared to be prepared to accept any workable scheme for the closer unity of the trade union movement, even though he wished to see King's efforts rewarded.[31] Why, when this scheme had made all the going for two years, when it had pushed the TUC into taking seriously the question of federation, when apparently it had gathered such strong support among both rank-and-file trade unionists and their leaders, why did it fail so quickly?

The reasons lie partly, no doubt, in the fact that the *Clarion* scheme opposed the TUC. Quite explicitly King's federation was designed to replace the Parliamentary Committee for which he and Blatchford avowed the deepest contempt.[32] Whatever traces of justice there may have been in the *Clarion*'s charges of apathy, aloofness and personal vanity, the fact remained that the TUC and its officials embodied such unity as the working classes then possessed. Few trade unionists would be prepared in practice to do away with the body that had represented their interests nationally since 1868, however superior the new institution might promise to be in theory. There was, further, a strong sectionalism among trade unions in Britain. Despite King's claim that federations of unions in kindred trades were simply accumulations of weakness, liable all to be involved in a dispute at one time and therefore powerless to help each other,[33] this was not always the experience of those trades that were federating in the

1890s. The merger or federation of unions into something approaching one industrial union for each industry was a trend that the TUC
federation scheme of 1895 had been designed to encourage; and from
a purely industrial point of view the trend towards federation of
kindred trades must have weakened the impetus to any more general
federation. The miners in particular were building their federation
into a great power within the trade union world; and especially after
the changes in TUC rules in 1895 which favoured large unions, few of
their leaders were prepared to give away part of their strength to a
common pool.[34]

Another interesting aspect of the *Clarion* scheme of federation, and
one that also played a part in its eventual failure, was that it was so
thoroughgoing. P. J. King wanted to weld the whole trade union
movement into a fighting force. The political theory that lay behind
his plans was close to what later came to be called 'syndicalism'. This
school of thought became especially influential in the USA and France
after the turn of the century and had some following in Britain,
especially in the Social Democratic Federation.[35] It rejected intervention by the state, as then preached by many socialists, in favour of
workers taking over the arrangement of society through the trade
unions (for which the French word, origin of the wider term, is
'syndicat'). Conciliation and class co-operation play no part in such
theories which at their most developed give a recipe for total
working-class revolution. Notions like this are not traditionally
associated with the gradualism that has prevailed in British politics,
although the presence of syndicalist influences in Britain in the early
twentieth century has not been ignored.[36] It is worthy of note that part
of the British trade union movement in the late 1890s, before
syndicalism had really developed in its more recognised centres, was
open and responsive to such ideas; and never more so than when it
turned its collective mind to the question of federation. One mark of
this school of thought as it later developed was to suspect all
institutions and leadership, even within the working class. King and
Blatchford repeatedly claimed that the *Clarion* scheme had the
support of the rank and file and warned against the paid trade union
official who 'likes to be a personage'.[37] They objected to the TUC's
schemes of federation because they introduced distinctions between
large and small unions;[38] and they warned against 'all predatory
unemployed heroes' and 'what John Burns calls "Bounders on the
Bounce" '.[39] The language of class warfare flowed easily from King's
pen: under his scheme, trade unionism would be ready for 'swift and
decisive attack'.[40] It was equally prepared for a defensive war, and in
the face of collective action by the employers only collective action
by the workers would do. There was no reason to pay out dispute

benefits for partial strikes, for instance, as the ironfounders suggested, for such strikes were useless.[41] At times the scheme took flight altogether, departed from the limited realms of wage bargaining and working conditions, and held out the lure of whole sections of the economy run by and for the working people. Looking forward to a federation of trade unions with an income of as much as £3 million per year, King invoked the examples of the Co-operative Movement and the Prudential Insurance Company to show that he was not being utopian. In fact, he continued, why should not a strong federation of trade unions found an insurance company of its own? It could also rival the Co-operative Movement and 'become its own universal provider'.[42] Turning to the problem of the employers importing blackleg labour (from which the engineers were suffering as he wrote), he argued that a strong federation could bring out on strike progressively the whole of an industry throughout the country until it had exhausted the supply of blacklegs. Suppose this were to happen in a bakery strike, for instance, when the strike had reached an acute stage and no more bread was being produced, the federation would quietly open its own bakeries. Behold, the workers would have taken over the means of production in a whole industry.[43] When elsewhere King suggested that a maximum of 30 shillings per head per week should be paid in dispute benefit, the remaining entitlement to be paid into the common fund,[44] he clearly had in mind that such co-operative enterprises could be financed with the surplus. Schemes like this, though inspiring in theory, went far beyond what most trade unionists meant by federation. The movement towards more positive representation of labour in Parliament offered a much more appealing alternative to those who did not share King's scorn for existing institutions.[45]

While it is certain that large numbers of trade unionists supported King's plan for federation, it is also likely that many of them, practical people as they were, suspected it more than somewhat when it departed from hard financial detail. The detail too left some questions unanswered, although the scheme was probably the most watertight of those put forward for federation in the 1890s. One problem was that until the federation had built up strength, the arrangements for proportional benefits to be assessed out of the contributions of each affiliated union only encouraged the larger unions to hold back. A further difficulty arose from the insistence that only strikes by a complete union or affiliated branch should be eligible for strike benefit. Industrial unions were still rare in Britain and the 'new unionism' in fact was producing affiliations of workers in many different industries, often organised into branches along geographical rather than industrial lines. In the Gasworkers' and

General Labourers' Union, for example, it must have been difficult to guarantee a solid strike even of one branch, so that for practical purposes King's federation would have been almost useless to them.[46]

In considering why the *Clarion* scheme for a federation of trade unions failed in the end, we should not forget that it did succeed in pushing the question of federation to the forefront of the TUC, at a time when the Parliamentary Committee seemed to have given it up. Without the propaganda of Blatchford and King, it is doubtful whether the General Federation of Trade Unions would have come into being. And when it did, its organisation and some of the ideas it embodied were not altogether different from those of the *Clarion* scheme.

Motion number 40 at the Trades Union Congress in Birmingham in 1897 proposed:

> That the trade-unionists of the United Kingdom form one federation to render mutual assistance in disputes, strikes and lock-outs affecting any trade unions affiliated to the federation, the representation to be proportional, and a scale of benefits to correspond to the scale of payments. Further, that a committee of thirteen be elected from this Congress for the purpose of taking into consideration the best means of federating the trade unions . . . .[47]

This motion, clearly inspired by the *Clarion* scheme, was proposed by A. Clarke of the Railway Workers' General Union and seconded by A. T. Dipper, from the Clyde-based National Amalgamated Union of Labour. The Miners' Federation delegation, led by Ben Pickard, MP, objected to the question of federation even being discussed and took no part in the vote; but apart from them there was only one dissentient. Cracks appeared in this picture of general harmony when it came to appointing a committee to draw up the scheme of federation. Congress had voted to allow not more than one representative of each trade on the committee but its first list was found to include four representatives of the general labourers. After an unruly scene when John Ward of the navvies' union protested his right to remain on the committee, he, McCarthy and Clynes were removed from the list, leaving Dipper alone to represent the general unions.[48] The whole question of federation seemed to be dogged by such scenes. The committee on federation was slow to complete its work and appears to have suffered itself from internal dissensions: for although it eventually managed to produce a scheme for Congress to consider in 1898, not all the unions it represented later joined the General Federation. Nevertheless, the formation of a general federation of trade unions had now become an accepted prospect. It was no longer a question of whether it should be formed but when and in precisely what form.

At the Bristol Congress of 1898 Councillor James O'Grady of the cabinetmakers gave the presidential address. O'Grady was a respected figure, already distinguished in local politics and with an eminent career in Parliament and ultimately in the commonwealth ahead of him.[49] His address to Congress placed federation firmly at the head of a list of priorities which set the tone for momentous events in the world of labour over the next few years. The subjects placed before Congress in 1898 including the half-time system and child labour, the need to extend the Workmen's Compensation Act of 1897 to cover all workers, the aftermath of the engineers' dispute, taxation of land values and the nationalisation of the railways and of mining royalties. O'Grady wove these themes into a grand design for labour. The first task for that Congress was to form a federation sound in finance and organisation and as 'scientific' as any of the employers' organisations now arraigned against working men. 'The whole brain of our movement must be concentrated upon the best way to checkmate the latest manifestations of the capitalist force that has threatened the very existence of our trade organisations.' But this would not be enough. The trend of modern industry and society was towards collectivism, and trade unions must recognise this fact if they were to be a force in shaping industrial and social life in Britain. 'Just as trades federation is a matter of vital necessity to our industrial organisations, so also will a scheme of political action be of vital necessity if we wish Parliament to faithfully register the effect of the industrial revolution on our social life.' The TUC ought to form a political fund based on a levy from all the unions. O'Grady ended with a long quotation from William Morris, and sat down amid thunderous applause. This was the first time that a main speaker at the TUC had called so clearly for separate labour representation in politics, or spelled out with such force the connection between political and industrial action. To many among his hearers it must have seemed like a new dawn.[50]

At the end of the third day of the Congress, 31 August 1898, the delegates adjourned, leaving the question of federation to be discussed on the following day. But during the night a fire started in Clarke's clothing factory next door to the Colston Halls and by morning it had destroyed the large hall, with all the TUC minutes and some papers and personal possessions of the delegates. Meeting in the lesser Colston Hall afterwards, Congress addressed itself briefly to the question of forming a federation and decided to call a special congress at Manchester not later than the following January. Their mood was subdued but they listened with general approval to the report of

Robert Knight of the boilermakers on behalf of the federation committee, followed by H. Johnson of the carpenters, secretary to the committee, whose own union had given an unfavourable verdict on the committee's scheme.[51] Congress adjourned that year with the question of federation postponed yet again.

The Formation of the General Federation of Trade Unions

In Manchester in January 1899 it was finally settled. There the special congress that had been arranged after the fire at Bristol met for three days and agreed, with some amendments, on the rules drawn up by the TUC's federation committee under the chairmanship of Robert Knight. The Parliamentary Committee of the TUC constituted itself a provisional executive committee but decided to hand over responsibility to a management committee to be elected by delegates from all the unions that had federated, at a special 'general council meeting' in the following July.

The declared objectives of the new General Federation of Trade Unions were:

> to uphold the right of combination of labour, to improve in every direction the general economic position and status of the workers by the inauguration of a policy that shall secure to them the power to determine the economic and social conditions under which they shall work and live, and to secure unity of action amongst all societies forming the Federation.[52]

The means by which the federation would promote these objects were emphatically peaceable and moderate. It would work for industrial peace and seek to prevent strikes and lockouts. Where disputes did arise, the federation would 'assist in their settlement by just and equitable methods' which were to include mediation and conciliation and the establishment of permanent boards. In other words, moderate voices on the federation committee had determined the inaugural tone of the new organisation but those who favoured the creation of a strong, centralised body had also won a victory by including an interventionist policy amongst its main objectives.

The last object listed in the preamble to the General Federation's rules was 'to establish a Fund for mutual assistance and support and for carrying out the foregoing objects'. This defensive insurance against costly strikes and lockouts became the characteristic for which the GFTU is now best known. But in the beginning, even though the need to build up a sound financial base determined much of the federation's earliest policy, the fighting fund was only one of its features. In the minds of several founders it was important principally as an earnest of the good intentions of those unions which affiliated.

Much detailed policy of the General Federation of Trade Unions would be worked out by the Management Committee but in outline its first rules set the pattern for the future.[53] Each union was to affiliate to the federation in respect of 90 per cent of its membership, paying an entrance fee of 1*d* per member. Contributions could be made on a higher scale of 6*d* per member per quarter or a lower scale of 3*d*, with corresponding entitlement to benefit of 5 shillings or 2*s* 6*d* per week per member. No benefit was payable to any union until after it had paid one year's subscription. Unions affiliating after July 1899 (this time limit was extended later) were to be charged an entrance fee amounting to 10 per cent of the average worth per member of the unions already affiliated on the higher or lower scale, as appropriate. Affiliated unions would be allowed three months' grace in which to pay arrears of subscriptions. Representation at the general council was proportioned to the size of the unions, and both the rules for eligibility and the voting system closely followed those of the TUC itself. Only active working men or full-time trade union officials could become delegates to the annual general council meeting. Voting by show of hands was to yield in any case of doubt or dispute to a card vote, as at the TUC. A Management Committee of fifteen members plus secretary was to be elected at each annual general council meeting. Payment of benefit was to be at the discretion of the Management Committee, who would scrutinise the background to any dispute for which benefit had been requested before deciding whether to pay.

The new federation rapidly came under fire from the secretary of the rival federation, P. J. King. In a *Clarion* Pamphlet published in 1899 he delivered a blistering onslaught against the financial unsoundness of the scheme.[54] Of the 900,000 trade union members represented at the special congress in Manchester, he claimed that well over half belonged to unions like the Miners' Federation who were implacably opposed to any scheme of general federation. Their delegates had blocked any discussion of the *Clarion* scheme and ensured, so he claimed, that it would be in the financial interests of the larger unions to hold aloof from the federation at least until it had accumulated several years' worth of contributions from smaller unions. The voting system, he objected, meanwhile favoured the larger unions within the federation. A further object of ridicule for King was the period of grace allowed to unions whose contributions were in arrears. Had the GFTU existed at the time of the engineers' lockout, it would have collapsed in one week: 'How the masters must admire the gigantic intellects that devised such a scheme – smashed up in one week!'[55] King's pleasure in belittling his opponents' intelligence may help to explain why his own scheme of federation faded so soon; but whatever the weight of intellectual superiority behind them, his predictions were not fulfilled. The General Federation of Trade Unions grew with painful slowness but its founding members included several of the largest unions; and one of its earliest distinguishing features turned out to be a financial caution, even cheeseparing,. which has helped it to survive for more than eighty years.

The first general council meeting of the General Federation of Trade Unions was held on Wednesday 19 July 1899 in the Westminster Palace Hotel, London. Fifty-eight delegates attended from the forty-four unions that had affiliated since the previous January. Altogether they represented 310,437 members, that is, 90 per cent of the total membership of their unions, according to the federation's rules. The smallest of the unions was the Sheffield Table Blade Grinders, affiliated in respect of ninety-six members and contributing an entrance fee of 8 shillings. The largest was the Amalgamated Society of Engineers, which brought 72,000 members into the federation and paid an entrance fee of £300. A total of £1,276 7s 2d in entrance fees constituted the modest beginning of the federation's fighting fund.[56]

About two-thirds of the founding membership was concentrated in five large unions: the ASE (total membership 85,000), the Gasworkers' and General Labourers' Union (48,000), the National Union of Boot and Shoe Operatives (22,000) and the National Amalgamated Union of Labour (22,000). In addition to these the Friendly Society of Ironfounders (about 19,000 members altogether), the tailors, the shipwrights and the two main dockers' unions added strength to the federation in both numbers and influence.[57]

The total founding membership of the GFTU was rather less than a quarter of the total TUC membership, but it was by no means a concentration of weakness. On the debit side, the federation was unquestionably damaged by the failure of other large unions to affiliate. The Miners' Federation, despite some of its officers' interest in joining a general federation of some sort, remained obdurately aloof, as did the Amalgamated Society of Railway Servants, who had shown strong interest in the *Clarion* scheme.[58] The Boilermakers and Amalgamated Weavers, two of the strongest craft unions, numbering some of the most able trade unionists in the country among their leaders, also decided against affiliating at first but eventually joined the General Federation in 1906 and 1907 respectively.[59]

For the first six months of the General Federation's existence the Parliamentary Committee of the TUC had acted for it in place of a Management Committee, but on 19 July at the general council meeting a new Management Committee was elected and the Parliamentary Committee handed over to it all responsibility for the GFTU. The proceedings of the general council were very brief, beginning at noon and leaving time in the afternoon for the Management Committee to hold its first meeting.[60] Fifteen members were present including the chairman, Pete Curran, national organiser of the gasworkers, and Isaac Mitchell, Scottish organiser of the ASE, who was the federation's first secretary. These two men were to guide the General Federation through its first eight years.

Pete Curran, then aged 39, had helped to form the Gasworkers' and General Labourers' Union and was a well-known spokesman for the 'new unionism' at the TUC.[61] A committed socialist and member at one time of both the Social Democratic Federation and the Fabian Society, he had already stood as an Independent Labour Party candidate in two elections, although he finally entered Parliament only in 1907 as MP for Jarrow. His Irish parentage seems to have given him a special eloquence. During the debate on federation at Manchester in January 1899 he had combated the sectionalism of many delegates with a typically idealistic call to unity: 'they should not consider rich and poor organisations, or large and small organisations, but the noble scheme of uniting under a national banner for the purpose of getting a national war-chest to meet all contingencies.'[62] At the TUC in September the same year he moved a resolution demanding the abolition of child labour in such terms that some delegates objected to the extreme language of the motion. Eventually it was passed in Curran's words: 'that the time has come for Great Britain to cease building its empire on children's hearts, to give up coining its wealth out of children's wasted lives.'[63]

Curran had made no secret of his contempt for the TUC Parliamentary Committee at the time of the engineers' lockout[64] and was probably among those who hoped that the GFTU might supersede it. He was also deeply involved in parliamentary politics. He helped to set up the Labour Representation Committee in 1900 and became one of its seven trade union representatives; in 1903 he moved the successful resolution calling for a separate and distinct Labour Party. He remained chairman of the GFTU until his untimely death in February 1910; in many ways an ideal person for the job, for there was no question about his great abilities or his standing among fellow trade unionists. His sociable, courteous nature must have helped him to smooth over differences among his fellow members of the Management Committee. Publicly known as a fiery orator and an impassioned fighter for working-class causes, in private he was respected even by his opponents for always fighting fair. Curran's commitment to the LRC, later the Labour Party, could have detracted from his contribution to the General Federation, but in his mind the two organisations shared the same fundamental aims, and he had energy to give to both. His part in setting up the Joint Board of the TUC, Labour Party and GFTU in 1905 was to open the period of the General Federation's greatest influence.

Isaac Mitchell shared some of Pete Curran's political tendencies, though he was a very different personality. Seven years younger than Curran, Mitchell was born in Roxburghshire, the son of border Scottish parents, in 1867.[65] He was educated at a church school and stayed there as a pupil teacher for years after less fortunate boys would have left to learn a trade. Eventually he did become apprenticed to an engineer and millwright, and moved to the Newcastle area when he was 20. Here he first came into contact with trade unions and socialism, and embarked on a swift ascent through the ranks of labour. From 1887 to 1892 he represented the Gateshead branch of the ASE on Newcastle Trades Council. In 1890 with John Burns and other socialists, he was involved in the Scottish Railway Servants' strike for recognition.[66] Two years or so after this formative experience he went to work as a millwright in New York for a year or more, and there joined Daniel de Leon's Socialist Labour Party and, rather incongruously, the Theosophical Society of New York. Returning to Scotland in 1894 he worked as a millwright in a woollen mill and devoted his leisure to his continuing studies of social and political questions, somehow also finding time to found the Galashiels Independent Labour Party. By 1896 he was in Glasgow and in 1897 attended the TUC for the first time as the ASE's Scottish delegate. That year he became a member of the lockout committee in Glasgow and at the end of the lockout was elected Glasgow district secretary of the ASE. In 1898, aged 30 or 31, Mitchell became one of the few members of the Independent Labour Party ever to win a place on the Parliamentary Committee of the TUC.[67]

Mitchell was a good foil to Curran's more exuberant personality, perhaps all the more so because they shared a background of socialist politics and of organising in a large and militant trade union. Where Curran was decisive, energetic, hard-hitting, Mitchell could be cautious and discreet. The language of the GFTU reports during his eight years' tenure of office is measured and occasionally rather didactic. By contrast with his successor, William Appleton, Isaac Mitchell does not appear to have been particularly interested in stamping his personality on the federation. That he did so nevertheless, in his quiet way, can be assumed from the evidence of his constant activity that appears in the minutes of Management Committee meetings and in the GFTU reports. He was indefatigable in pursuing the Management Committee's policy of positive intervention and conciliation in disputes involving its affiliated unions, and he must have been personally responsible for many of the new affiliations that added steadily to the federation's strength while he was secretary. When the Joint Board was founded Mitchell was as much involved as Curran. He became joint secretary in a triumvirate whose other members were Ramsay MacDonald for the Labour Party and W. C. Steadman for the Parliamentary Committee, and was given full organising responsibility. Outside the realm of trade union affairs, Mitchell was a respected Progressive member of the London County Council, a champion of temperance, an executive member of the National Temperance Legue and a founder of the Labour Temperance Fellowship.[68] The young William Beveridge got to know him as a fellow member of the Central (Unemployed) Body for London and later at the Board of Trade, and respected his capacity for involving his fellow trade unionists in constructive talks.[69] When in 1907 he left the GFTU to become a labour adviser at the Board of Trade, the appointment was a tribute to his recognised skills as a conciliator.[70]

During Mitchell's year on the Parliamentary Committee his union became involved in an acrimonious dispute which led to its secession in July 1899. The Co-operative Smiths' Society, a craft union with less than 1,000 members, accused members of the ASE of having acted as blacklegs during a strike called by the smiths. The Parliamentary Committee upheld their complaint and called on the ASE to withdraw its members from the jobs in dispute. This the engineers were too proud to consider, preferring instead to disaffiliate from the TUC.[71] With so momentous a quarrel hanging over his head, Mitchell must have been deeply relieved to accept the post of general secretary of the GFTU in July 1899, at the very moment when his union made its break with the TUC.[72] The ASE had not made itself popular by its arrogant behaviour towards smaller unions and in particular by refusing to join the Federation of Engineering and Shipbuilding Trades, so the TUC may have been glad to teach it a lesson. The engineers for their part had plenty of reason to pick a quarrel with the Parliamentary Committee, which they had censured at Congress for its failure to help during the great lockout of 1897–8; and the Federation of Engineering and Shipbuilding Trades had also failed to give them support during their struggle. It was unfortunate that the birth of the GFTU should have been associated, however indirectly, with the rift between the TUC and one of the largest and most influential unions in the country. Isaac Mitchell's position was invidious, but he was careful not to let it impair the relationship between the two organisations

The Management Committee of the GFTU faced a difficult first year. The TUC washed its hands of all responsibility for the new organisation from the date of the inaugural general council meeting, and so succeeded in ridding itself finally of the problem of federation, with all the sectional quarrels that had bedevilled it. It may be questioned whether this was an act of wise policy rather than simple necessity.[73] Necessary it certainly was, for it is difficult to imagine how any close relationship could have worked for long while Sam Woods, the miners' leader and convinced opponent of federation, remained secretary to the Parliamentary Committee. Moreover, the change in voting procedure enacted at the 1895 Congress appeared to have built in a permanent large opposition to federation at the TUC, for the new procedure gave great strength to the large memberships of the Miners' Federation and the Weavers' Amalgamation, then both equally opposed to the existence of any general federation. The separation of the TUC from the GFTU, however, not only lifted an albatross from the shoulders of the TUC but paved the way for jealousies to arise between the two organisations.

In 1900, with the formation of the equally separate Labour Representation Committee, the TUC disposed of another troublesome issue, one also bedevilled by the independent stance of miners and textile workers, the vexed question of labour representation in Parliament and the relationship between the Liberal Party and working-class MPs.[74] The General Federation was at pains both in 1900 and at subsequent Congresses, to emphasise its own intention of concentrating on industrial questions alone, leaving politics to the TUC.[75] But although in 1900 the separation of the TUC from the LRC was by no means as clear-cut as that between the TUC and the General Federation, the question arose: if the federation were to become a great success on the industrial scene and the LRC on the political what precisely would be left for the TUC to do?[76] Although in retrospect the GFTU is generally regarded as having been set up to provide insurance against the financial drain of strikes and lockouts,[77] this was only one of its objectives and not considered by any means the paramount one. It had before it a clear field not only in industrial insurance but in conciliation and arbitration between unions and in establishing links with the international trade union movement, all aspects of potential development which the TUC shunned.[78]

The General Federation's First Year

The Management Committee that met for the first time in London on 19 July 1899 formed a disparate group. The mercurial Ben Tillett was to find himself working on delegations with the Yorkshire textile workers' leader, Allen Gee of Huddersfield: Tillett, the socialist organiser of that quintessentially casual workforce, the Dock, Wharf, Riverside and General Workers' Union; Gee, the more moderate journalist, craftsman and civic dignitary.[79] Two elder statesmen of the General Federation who had both played leading parts in its formation were the Lib-Lab craft union leaders W. J. Davis and Alexander Wilkie; but it was Davis who, as chairman of the special TUC at Manchester, had refused to be nominated himself for chairman of the General Federation and had proposed the socialist Pete Curran instead.[80]

The nature of the unions represented on the Management Committee was as various as the personalities themselves. Curran's gasworkers, Tillett's London dockers and J. N. Bell's National Amalgamated Union of Labour were all relatively new general unions with a socialist background although Bell's personal opinions did not altogether reflect the political complexion of his union.[81] Among the craft union representatives were Thomas Mallalieu of the Amalgamated Society of Journeymen Felt Hatters, Davis of the National Society of Amalgamated Brassworkers, Wilkie of the Associated Society of Shipwrights, James Holmes of the National Hosiery Federation, Gee of the Yorkshire Textile Workers' Federation, Matthew Arrandale of the United Machine Workers and Joseph Maddison of the Friendly Society of Ironfounders. Several of these were, however, practitioners of the methods associated with 'new unionism'. So were Tom Ashton's Amalgamated Operative Cotton Spinners, those aristocrats of the cotton trade, and H. Newell's Decorators and Painters, a union whose methods and membership defy classification among either 'craft' or 'general' unions.[82] Another craft-based union with a dynamic policy and socialist inclinations was the National Union of Boot and Shoe Operatives, represented on the first GFTU Management Committee by the Lib-Lab W. B. Hornidge who was to be president of the TUC in 1903.[83] Finally, in January 1900 James Crinion of the Amalgamated Association of Card and Blowing Room Operatives joined his fellow Lancashire textile representative Tom Ashton on the committee, apparently replacing Gregory of the Amalgamated Gasworkers', Brickmakers' and General Labourers' Union.[84]

The one characteristic shared by all the unions represented on the GFTU Management Committee in 1900 was that they were relatively large. Their average total membership was over 13,000 whereas that of all the unions in the General Federation was around 6,500.[85] If we include the secretary Isaac Mitchell as a representative of the ASE,[86] the disparity between Management Committee unions and the rest becomes even greater. This did not cause the committee any qualms. Indeed, in their first annual report they commented that the GFTU included 'a large portion of the best and strongest organisations' because the average membership of its affiliated unions was high. At the Trades Union Congress in 1900 Mitchell used the same figures to illustrate the 'calibre' of the unions that had joined the General Federation. It was a matter for pride that while nearly a quarter of all trade unionists in the country were affiliated, they came from less than one-twentieth of the total number of unions.[87] One of the hall-marks of GFTU policy in its early years was its concern over the large number of small unions and its repeated attempts to bring unions in kindred trades together in federations or, preferably, amalgamations.

The first year of the federation's existence gave its Management Committee plenty of time to consider policy in the abstract, for rule 5 clause 2 of the rules drawn up by the Manchester Congress stipulated that no union was eligible for dispute benefit until it had been affiliated for twelve months and had paid a year's contributions in full. The minutes of the committee meeting of 19 July 1899 suggest an absence of urgent business: the chairman, secretary and treasurer (Joseph Maddison) formed a subcommittee to search for office premises at a rent of up to £50 a year and to buy stationery, books, furniture and so on. They decided that all their printing would be done by the Co-operative Printers and then 'consideration was given to the purchasing of a typewriter, when after some discussion it was agreed to allow the matter to stand over meanwhile'.[88] Among other early decisions was the choice of 'Wellwisher, London' as their telegraphic address.

A little later,[89] they commissioned the socialist artist Walter Crane to design a device which was to appear on all of the General Federation's printed reports for many years, above the motto 'Unity is strength'. Crane's device drew on the ancient fable handed down by Aesop which is still one of the best illustrations of that motto. The story goes that a man had several sons who were so quarrelsome that they could never agree with each other. So he called them together and had a bundle of sticks brought. 'Now, boys,' he said, 'take this bundle and let me see which of you can break it.' Each son tried his hardest but the sticks were so closely bound together they would not break. Then the father untied the bundle and gave one stick to each boy, telling him to break it. 'Oh that is quite easy, father' they said. 'You see, my boys,' replied the father, 'you are like the bundle of sticks. While you keep together and agree, none can hurt you. When you fall apart, anyone may do you harm.' This fable greatly appealed to Tom Mann when ten years later he called on the GFTU to live up to the meaning of its emblem.[90]

The committee met again in September during the TUC meeting in Plymouth and in December at its new headquarters at 40 Bridge House, 181 Queen Victoria Street, in the City of London, deciding at this third meeting that the time had come to buy a typewriter.[91] By then, business of more moment was in progress. Rule 4 provided for the establishment of district committees. Given an initial membership of only forty-four unions, it may have been optimistic for the new federation to plan such a complex structure; and in fact the scheme was abandoned within three years. But a system of local committees with two members from each of the unions represented in the locality provided a good starting point for some of the federation's more ambitious plans. If, as rule 9 laid down, it was to arbitrate in cases of dispute between its members, this work could best be founded on a system of local contacts. The same applied to any attempts at mediation between employers and unions affiliated to the GFTU. District committees could be invaluable, too, in the work of persuading other unions to affiliate. In this respect the recruiting experience of several unions already in the GFTU, notably the ASE, demonstrated the benefits of setting up what amounted to autonomous branches all over the country. Not only were these committees likely to provide two-way channels of communication between the Management Committee and the wider trade union scene, they were also an instrument of democracy. The careful thought given to their constitution, both when rule 4 was formulated and in Management Committee meetings, suggests that the plan of forming district committees had originated with those enthusiasts for federation who wanted to involve the rank and file more closely in national trade union activity.

The district committee scheme drawn up by Curran and Mitchell and amended by the Management Committee consisted of eight districts centred on London, Bristol, Birmingham, Manchester, Leeds, Newcastle, Glasgow and Belfast. Each committee was to have an annually elected chairman, vice-chairman and secretary from three different unions. At the Management Committee's request they would report on disputes to GFTU headquarters. Local meetings could be arranged at their discretion. By March 1900 the committees were being formed, and members of the Management Committee were assigned to attend the inaugural meeting of each one. If, as they planned, all the inaugural meetings took place in May, the secretary had a busy programme. He was detailed to deal with London, Bristol, Leeds, Glasgow and Belfast in addition to visiting, sometime between March and early June, the Printing Machine Managers' Society, the Consolidated Bookbinders, and the slaters of Scotland, all of which unions were thinking of affiliating to the federation.[92]

The failure of the district committee system, which was abolished at the annual general council meeting in Leicester in 1902, was a severe blow to the Management Committee's hopes of building a strong, well-founded structure and a setback to its efforts to bring about amalgamations of small unions which operated within the same areas as each other. Without these lines of communication, the federation would have to rely on the reports of officers of individual unions, which it generally received only when a particular dispute was pending or in progress, involving the union which reported it. A possible threat to the complete autonomy of affiliated unions was removed, but at the cost of undermining the potential strength of the GFTU.

The system's quick demise reflected the wider difficulties of holding the federation together. In April 1901 Pete Curran's National Union of Gasworkers and General Labourers held a special conference to consider disaffiliating, largely because its members could see little financial benefit for themselves in federation. It took all the efforts of their general secretary, Will Thorne, to muster a majority of 20 votes to 11 in favour of remaining in the federation, despite the fact that their national organiser was its chairman.[93] Similar rumblings were to be heard among the membership of the ASE whose delegates found themselves being outvoted by combinations of smaller unions, a position they had found intolerable in the TUC in 1899, but one that the largest union in the country would have to put up with if it was not to exile itself altogether from the movement.[94] With the ASE as with the gasworkers, the standing within the union of its own representative at the GFTU did not appear to be affected, for in 1903 the ASE agreed to sponsor Isaac Mitchell as its parliamentary candidate for Darlington whenever the next election should take place.[95] The reports of the GFTU are scattered from the earliest years with comments on the selfishness of trade unions, usually large ones, which do not perceive the wider benefits of unity within the trade union movement and which either forget the financial benefits they themselves have already received from the federation or are too short-sighted to foresee the time when they will need its help. Sectionalism, in other words, remained as difficult to subdue within the General Federation of Trade Unions as it had been during the many attempts to get a federation established. Moreover, the early years of the GFTU coincided with a period of stagnation and in many cases decline in union membership, which seemed all the worse because it followed the enormous increases of the 1890s.[96] In these circumstances the district committees fell victim to a scarcity of both team spirit and finance, and their small claim on the funds of the federation and individual unions was begrudged.[97]

Apart from these matters of structure and the organisation of its headquarters, the Management Committee decided two questions of policy during the first year along lines that the federation would follow in the future. James Sexton of the Liverpool dockers wrote asking leave to move a resolution at the 1900 annual general council meeting that would deal with the Workman's Compensation Act. He was told that this would be 'inexpedient' and the Management Committee agreed that the proper body to deal with the question would be the Parliamentary Committee of the TUC.[98] That year at the TUC Isaac Mitchell took pains to reassure the delegates that the GFTU intended to leave politics alone;[99] and although some of its activities in succeeding years were to impinge on politics, the federation continued to emphasise its function as the purely industrial arm of the trade union movement. Even more characteristic of its future policy was a decision to limit the payment of dispute benefits more narrowly than the rules defined. Tom Ashton and Matthew Arrandale wanted affiliated unions to be eligible for benefits on behalf of all their members involved in a dispute even if their membership had increased during the year, provided that they had notified the GFTU Management Committee of the increase. Thomas Mallalieu and J. N. Bell moved an amendment 'that this federation recognise no claim for benefit on increased membership on the returns given until the contributions of the increased membership have been paid to the federation for twelve months'.[100] The committee passed their amendment by 6 votes to 4, a slender but decisive vote in favour of parsimony.

The federation's first annual report was almost euphoric. In contrast to the dry details of Management Committee meetings, this was an occasion for setting out the philosophy of federation and for broadcasting high hopes. The chairman and secretary let themselves go:[101] 'We have . . . so much faith in the basis upon which the GFTU is founded that we await with perfect confidence the time when the Trade Unions as a whole will be enrolled under the one banner.' The federation would preserve the independence and distinctive character of each union. 'Without violating the traditions of any, it hopes to increase the common interests of all.' Membership was inexpensive enough to permit every union in the country to join. 'One of [the federation's] chief objects is to promote peace, and [it] believes that such peace can best be obtained by organisation.' Most specific and most ambitious of all: 'it believes that a central authority, to systemise the many questions affecting Trade Unionism[,] should be established, and hopes to fill that position, supply information and be a means of communication between Unions all over the world.' The only discordant note was sounded by the exclusion of two unions, the United Association of Carters and the Amalgamated Society of Tailors, because they could not pay their dues. The case of the tailors, a large and prestigious union which ought to have managed its affairs better, occasioned particular sorrow and demonstrated to the Management Committee that 'the need for a central authority amongst the Trade Unions has been too long delayed'.

This report was laid before the delegates to the second annual general council meeting which took place in Nottingham in July 1900. Here two issues arose which were to illustrate the constraints on the General Federation more clearly than any decisions of the previous year. An attempt to amend the rules so that the Management Committee rather than the assembled general council would have power to increase contributions was narrowly defeated on a card vote. So much for 'central authority'. Then J. R. Clynes of the gas-workers raised the big question. Under rule 8, he observed, the general council or the Management Committee must approve any dispute before benefit could be granted 'to the societies implicated'. What did the word 'implicated' mean? He quoted the case of some ironmoulders' labourers represented by his own union, who were likely to be suspended because of a strike by the moulders (who belonged to their own relatively exclusive craft union). They had applied to the General Federation for benefit and the Management Committee had refused to consider their case. W. B. Hornidge pointed out that the GFTU would have to increase contributions very greatly if it was to pay out benefit to workers affected by strikes other than their own. Alexander Wilkie, supporting Hornidge, asked whether the GFTU was to be held responsible for its members losing work through all disputes, whether or not these originally involved members of the federation. 'In his own experience the shipwrights had been laid idle through a strike of Durham miners, and even a strike on the Delaware in America had been the means of stopping work in this country.' Later in the meeting a new rule was proposed by the National Amalgamated Society of Enginemen, Cranemen, Firemen and Boilermen and the UK Society of Amalgamated Smiths and Strikers, which would have removed this weakness in the federation's defences. They wanted to rule that where a dispute involved one federated society, all members of other federated societies in the same shop must stop work also. G. N. Barnes, general secretary of the ASE, spoke against the proposal which, as he must have known, his own members almost certainly would have disregarded, and the motion was lost. In effect the GFTU had decided against supporting the sympathetic strike.

It was ironic that the chief instrument and symbol of solidarity in the trade unions' arsenal should have been rejected so soon in the life of the federation designed to bring them closer together. Ironic but not surprising. P. J. King, promoting his *Clarion* scheme of federation, had claimed that the TUC's plans for the General Federation were pathetically weak and contained no proper financial or structural basis for concerted action. The history of the GFTU, however, was to show that even its relatively modest demands upon its members were difficult to enforce and that its policies depended upon a very fitful sense of unity among an extremely individualistic membership. At least it represented British trade unionism as a whole more faithfully, for this reason, than King's highly political and centralised body could have done and more so, too, than the 'central authority' that Pete Curran and Isaac Mitchell dreamed of. It would be a great mistake to suppose that these internal weaknesses doomed it to impotence. On the contrary, the Management Committee saw the building up of a strong financial reserve (a matter for pride in each succeeding annual report) as a prerequisite for the positive force in British industrial relations that it meant to become. If its members were conservative in the matter of supporting strikes, this was because they saw it as their business to avoid strikes and to promote industrial peace. The object of the federation described in rule 1 spelled out this theme with emphasis and made it clear that the reserve fund was to be used to this end; time and again the annual and quarterly reports of the GFTU hammered home the message. Organisation, to be sure, was the key to both strength and peace. Where disputes arose, the GFTU would do what it could to help settle them. But the positive intervention that this implied also involved taking measures to prevent trouble in the future. If only the quarrymen of North Wales had been organised in a nationwide union, for instance, they might have had the strength to overcome Lord Penrhyn's determination to stamp out the workers' organisation in his quarries.[102] The GFTU nevertheless supported what was clearly a just fight by the union, even while drawing a suitable moral from it. Later it intervened successfully to prevent a large-scale strike in the pottery industry, and used its influence afterwards to steer the unions towards amalgamation.[103] Beyond the constant flow of strikes and lockouts that called for its attention, the aim of closer unity within labour's ranks both at home and abroad guided an energetic and far from unadventurous policy. The work of the General Federation in its first full decade can best be assessed if we divide it into the spheres of internal and external affairs, taking first the internal, that is, matters which involved principally or wholly the GFTU and its affiliated unions or where the federation acted alone, and turning afterwards to its place in the wider industrial and political scene.

Notes: Chapter 1

1   This definition of nineteenth-century trade unionism is paraphrased from Sidney and Beatrice Webb, *The History of Trade Unionism* (London: Longman, 1920), p. 1.

2   In fact they were sentenced under a statute of 1797, not that of 1825.

3   B. C. Roberts, *The Trades Union Congress 1868–1921* (London: Allen & Unwin, 1958), pp. 126, 133.

4   British Library of Political and Economic Science, Webb Collection B, vol. 23; also quoted in Roberts, op. cit.

5   This theme recurred in the TUC's debates on federation during the 1890s. See, for example, the presidential address by James O'Grady, TUC, *Report*, 1898, pp. 28–38.

6   The account that follows is based largely on James B. Jefferys, *The Story of the Engineers, 1800–1945* (London: Amalgamated Engineering Union, 1946).

7   Jefferys, *Story of the Engineers*, p. 145.

8   As the writer Arthur Withy observed in an article subtitled 'Do the Trade Unions "mean business"?' in the *Westminster Review*, December 1897, pp. 597–603.

9   TUC, *Report*, 1895, pp. 64–7.

10 ibid., p. 53.

11 Roberts, *The TUC*, pp. 143–52.

12 *Clarion*, 8 January 1898.

13 See article on Blatchford in John Saville and Joyce Bellamy (eds), *Dictionary of Labour Biography*, Vol. IV (London: Macmillan, 1972– . A very full treatment of Blatchford's thought is to be found in Logie Barrow, 'The Socialism of Robert Blatchford and the *Clarion*', PhD thesis, London University, 1975. See also Judith P. Fincher, 'The *Clarion* movement: an attempt to implement the co-operative commonwealth in England', MA thesis, Manchester University, 1971.

14 *Clarion*, 8 January 1898.

15 This sketch of King's scheme is based on articles in the *Clarion*, 1897–8, and on Robert Blatchford and P. J. King, *Trades Federation*, Clarion Pamphlet 17 (London: Clarion, 1897), P. J. King, *Good and Bad Federation*, Clarion Pamphlet 24 (London: Clarion, 1898), *Federation in a Nutshell*, Clarion Pamphlet 28 (London: Clarion, 1898), and *Trades Federation. The Official Scheme. A Crushing Criticism*, Clarion Pamphlet 33 (London: Clarion, 1899).

16 TUC, *Report*, 1897, pp. 47–8; *Clarion*, 14 August 1897, p. 261, col. entitled 'Gleanings'.

17 *Clarion*, 4 September 1897, pp. 284–5, article by 'Agitator'; King, *Good and Bad Federation*.

18 *Clarion*, 14 August 1897, pp. 284–5.

19 See also *Railway Review*, 23 July 1897.

20 *Clarion*, 4 September 1897, pp. 284–5.

21 John Burns papers, British Library Add. MS 46287, f. 202, Blatchford to Burns, 9 May 1898.

22 *Clarion*, 4 September 1897, pp. 284–5.

23 For example, *Labour Leader*, 5 February 1898, pp. 44–5.

24 *Justice*, 7 August 1897.

25 *Clarion*, 4 September 1897, pp. 284–5.

26 At the January 1898 meeting James Macdonald, secretary of the LTC, announced that no scheme of federation would be put forward then because the TUC Parliamentary Committee was about to circulate a draft scheme. LTC, *Report of*

the National Trade Union Conference Held on Saturday 1 January 1898 (London: LTC, 1898).

27 *Clarion*, 8 January 1898.
28 ibid.
29 *Clarion*, 23 and 30 July 1898.
30 See article on Blatchford in Saville and Bellamy, *Dictionary of Labour Biography*, Vol. IV.
31 *Clarion*, 1899, *passim*. The issues following the inauguration of the GFTU in July 1899, however, made no mention of it.
32 *Clarion*, 8 January and 17 September 1898; King, *Trades Federation . . .* , p. 7.
33 Blatchford and King, *Trades Federation*, pp. 31–2.
34 On the miners' independent line in this period see R. Page Arnot, *The Miners, Vol. 1: A History of the Miners' Federation of Great Britain, 1889–1910* (London: Allen & Unwin, 1949). Sam Woods, secretary to the TUC Parliamentary Committee, was one of the majority of miners' leaders who did not think federation was either workable or timely.
35 See Bob Holton, *British Syndicalism 1900–1914: Myths and Realities* (London: Pluto Press, 1976), for some consideration of its roots in the 1890s. Tom Mann, *Tom Mann's Memoirs* (London: Labour Publishing, 1923), pp. 251–4, gives a good account of how the term 'syndicalism' came to be misused by the British press to describe a particular form of revolutionary activity undertaken by some French trade unions during the period of the Paris Commune, 1871.
36 Holton, op. cit., introduction and references, considers the literature.
37 *Clarion*, 8 January 1898.
38 Blatchford and King, *Trades Federation*; King, *Trades Federation . . .* , *passim*.
39 Blatchford and King, *Trades Federation*, p. 34.
40 ibid.
41 *Clarion*, 24 December 1897, p. 422.
42 Blatchford and King, *Trades Federation*, pp. 27–8.
43 ibid., p. 32.
44 See above, p. 8
45 Barrow, 'The Socialism of Robert Blatchford', pp. 344–66, also places King's scheme in a wider context of theory.
46 See E. J. Hobsbawm, 'British gas-workers, 1873–1914', in his *Labouring Men* (London: Weidenfeld & Nicolson, 1964), pp. 158–78, for an explanation of the gasworkers' organisation. H. A. Clegg, in *The System of Industrial Relations in Great Britain*, 3rd edn (Oxford: Blackwell, 1976), pp. 52–3, observes that throughout the 1890s the general unions were still too weak to have resisted rational restructuring of trade unions as a whole, had anyone attempted it systematically.
47 TUC, *Report of the 30th Annual TUC*, pp. 47–8 (day 5, 10 September 1897).
48 ibid.
49 See article on James O'Grady in Saville and Bellamy, *Dictionary of Labour Biography*, Vol. II, pp. 286–9.
50 TUC, *Report of the 31st Annual TUC*, pp. 28–38 (day 2, 30 August 1898).
51 ibid., pp. 61–5.
52 *Code of Rules Adopted by the Special TUC* (1899). Also quoted in Roberts, *The TUC*, pp. 163–4.
53 *Code of Rules Adopted by the Special TUC* (1899).
54 King, *Trades Federation . . .*
55 ibid., p. 7.
56 TUC, *Report*, 1899, pp. 21–2.
57 ibid.
58 See above, p. 8.

59 Historians tend, when they mention the GFTU at all, to follow Roberts, *The TUC*, p. 163, in dismissing its membership as drawn mainly from small and financially weak unions from the beginning. More considered treatment of the early years of the GFTU, however, is to be found in E. H. Phelps Brown, *The Growth of British Industrial Relations. A Study from the Standpoint of 1906–14* (London: Macmillan, 1959), ch. 5, and in H. A. Clegg, A. Fox and A. F. Thompson, *A History of British Trade Unions since 1889, Vol. 1: 1889–1910* (London: Oxford University Press, 1964), pp. 355–7.

60 TUC, *Report*, 1899, p. 21; GFTU MS minute book, report of meeting on 19 July 1899.

61 See article on Curran in Bellamy and Saville, *Dictionary of Labour Biography*, Vol. IV, pp. 65–9.

62 *The Times*, 25 January 1899, p. 7, col. *d*.

63 TUC, *Report*, 1899, pp. 71–3.

64 See above, p. 10.

65 This account of Mitchell's career is based on the biographical note in a pamphlet issued by Darlington LRC in 1903, *Report of a Meeting Held in the Assembly Hall, Darlington, on April 8th 1903, and an Address Delivered by Mr Isaac H. Mitchell* (copy in Darlington Public Library) and on Lord Beveridge, *Power and Influence. An Autobiography* (London: Hodder & Stoughton, 1953), pp. 62, 84, 438.

66 See Clegg, Fox and Thompson, *History of British Trade Unions*, Vol. 1, pp. 232–3.

67 Clegg, Fox and Thompson, op. cit., p. 262 n, and Phelps Brown, *Growth of British Industrial Relations*, p. 375, incorrectly give the date of Mitchell's membership as 1897–8. See TUC, *Report*, 1897, p. 52; 1898, p. 73; and 1899, pp. 35–8, 84.

68 GFTU, *Quarterly Report*, September 1906.

69 Beveridge, *Power and Influence*, pp. 62, 84.

70 See below, Chapter 2, pp. 47–8.

71 The date of receipt of Barnes's letter withdrawing his union from the TUC was 20 July, the day after the GFTU council meeting (TUC, *Report* 1899, pp. 35–8).

72 ibid., and Jefferys, *The Story of the Engineers*, p. 163.

73 For a contrary view, see Roberts, *The TUC*, pp. 169–70. In support of this view, see Ben Turner, *About Myself 1863–1930* (London: Cayme Press, 1930), p. 143.

74 For the role played by trade unionists in the LRC, see Roberts, *The TUC*, pp. 165–70; Clegg, Fox and Thompson, *History of British Trade Unions*, Vol. 1 ch. 10.

75 Roberts, *The TUC*, p. 170; TUC, *Reports*, 1900–5, *passim*, for example, 1900, pp. 40–1; 1904, pp. 77, 100.

76 This point was made with bitter force by W. A. Appleton in an article in the *Observer*, reprinted as a pamphlet on *The Future of Trade Unionism* in 1916, when relations between the TUC and GFTU were reaching their nadir. The idea was already current, however, in the early years of the federation. See the article by J. N. Bell on 'The confusion of labour interests', GFTU, *Quarterly Report*, September 1902.

77 For example, see Webb, *History of Trade Unionism*, p. 554: 'The GFTU was designed exclusively as a mutual reinsurance agency'.

78 See Phelps Brown, *Growth of British Industrial Relations*, p. 258ff.

79 Saville and Bellamy, *Dictionary of Labour Biography*, Vol. III, pp. 81–4.

80 W. J. Davis, *The British Trades Union Congress, History and Reflections*, 2 vols (London: Co-operative Printing Society, 1910 and 1916), Vol. 2, p. 156.

81 See Clegg, Fox and Thompson, *History of British Trade Unions*, Vol. 1, pp. 294–5, for socialism in these three unions.

82 The difficulties of changing names among trade unions are a special problem in the case of Newell's union. It is unclear which decorators' union he represented.

83 Clegg, Fox and Thompson, *History of British Trade Unions*, Vol. 1, p. 295.

84 GFTU MS minute book, meeting of 18 January 1900 where Crinion's first appearance is noted but no reason for it given.

85 The membership figures appearing in the GFTU reports are not always reliable, nor is it clear in all cases whether they refer to total membership of a union or the 90 per cent on which it had affiliated.

86 Mitchell's position in the first year was anomalous because he was technically still an elected representative of the ASE. This was put right at the first annual general council meeting.

87 GFTU, first *Annual Report*, 1899–1900, p. 5; TUC, *Report*, 1900, pp. 40–1.

88 GFTU, MS minute book, 19 July 1899.

89 ibid., meetings of 1 March and 5 July 1900.

90 The version given here is taken almost verbatim from Tom Mann's *Industrial Syndicalist*, vol. 1, no. 1 (July 1910), p. 24.

91 GFTU MS minute book, meetings of 29 September and 1 December 1899.

92 ibid., meetings of 1 December 1899, 1 March and 24 May 1900. The three recruiting visits turned out to be thankless chores. Not one of the unions affiliated.

93 H. A. Clegg, *General Union in a Changing Society. A Short History of the National Union of General and Municipal Workers, 1889–1964* (Oxford: Blackwell, 1964), p. 48.

94 Jefferys, *The Story of the Engineers*, p. 162.

95 GFTU, *Quarterly Report*, March 1903, p. 7.

96 Clegg, Fox and Thompson, *History of British Trade Unions*, Vol. 1, pp. 466, 468; Webb, *History of Trade Unionism*, app. VI, pp. 744–50.

97 Rule 5, clause 4, of the *Code of Rules* (1899) provided for officers' fees and the rent of the committee room to be paid from GFTU funds. The expenses of delegates on the committees were to be met by their unions. The GFTU quarterly balance sheet for 30 June 1901 shows an expenditure of £58 12s 6d on salaries to the eight district secretaries for their first full year, at a time when the federation's reserve fund stood at just over £47,000.

98 GFTU MS minute book, meeting of 18 January 1900.

99 TUC, *Report*, 1900, p. 80: 'The Federation's determination to confine itself to purely trade matters and leave political questions outside its work, precludes the danger of the two organisations overlapping'.

100 GFTU MS minute book, meeting of 1 December 1899.

101 This report was signed by both Pete Curran and Isaac Mitchell, in contrast to all later reports which were signed by the secretary only, on behalf of the Management Committee.

102 GFTU, ninth *Quarterly Report*, September 1901.

103 See below, pp. 42–3.

2
Growth: Internal Affairs, 1900–10

The General Federation of Trade Unions did not believe in obtruding itself. It waited to be invited to intervene in disputes and when it took positive steps to amalgamate unions or settle differences between them, it usually did so when one of the unions was thinking of becoming affiliated to the federation. It is difficult, therefore, to measure its work in bringing about settlements or mergers or in strengthening the tools of 'collective bargaining' and 'joint regulation'.* But it is beyond doubt that the federation made a significant contribution in this direction and that it regarded this as its main work. J. R. Clynes observed in 1907 that relations between craftsmen and general labourers had improved greatly since the beginning of the 'new unionism' and went on to say: 'In this department of organisation the Federation of Trade Unions has undoubtedly been the greatest instrument, fostering and improving better relationship[s] between the tradesman and the labourer, who formerly lived and worked with little in common.'[1] Such a tribute, appearing in the pages of the federation's own reports, has to be set against the judgement of historians who, working largely from the records of the TUC and of other trade unions, have found few traces of the work of the GFTU. The views of the Webbs have been noted above.[2] A more recent, authoritative, history of British trade unionism in this period asserts that: 'The Federation intervened in a major dispute for the first and only time when it burned its fingers in the cotton stoppage [of 1908] and withdrew, never again to take part

---

* The term 'collective bargaining' was coined by the Webbs to describe a procedure which, as Allan Flanders has pointed out, would better be described as 'joint regulation'. It involves not only the haggling of the market place that is implied in the word 'bargaining' but also the arrival at joint rules and agreements, which is a social and political process just as much as an economic one. 'Collective bargaining', however, is too well rooted in the vocabulary of industrial relations to be replaced now. Wherever the phrase is used in this study it is meant to include joint regulation. (See Allan Flanders, 'Collective bargaining – a theoretical analysis', *British Journal of Industrial Relations*, vol. 6, no. 1 (1968), pp. 1–26.)

in industrial negotiations of any importance.'[3] Another authority, while noting the GFTU's very positive role in mediation, has concluded that 'as a practical force in industrial relations it was negligible'.[4] The historian of the TUC, whose mistaken statement that the large unions did not join the General Federation has been followed in other works, also misconstrues its true objectives and so dismisses it because 'without the necessary power at the centre it was hamstrung . . . as a militant body aimed at directing the entire trade union movement against the employers'.[5] On the other side are to be found such comments as these: '. . . prior to the first world war, the General Federation of Trade Unions . . . was of greater importance than the TUC',[6] and 'for nearly two decades it cut a considerable figure in the trade union movement, even on occasion challenging the leadership of Congress'.[7] In the face of such differing opinions, the work of the federation as reflected in its own records deserves close study. In this chapter I propose to survey the first ten years of the GFTU's internal work and policy in general and then to focus on one particular year, 1908–9, for which the Management Committee minutes record in detail a mass of important work.

The Work of the Decade

The staple diet of each month's Management Committee meeting was requests for payment of dispute benefit and notifications of 'movements' which were likely to lead to strikes or lockouts. Although the general council had already decided against sympathetic strikes and the Management Committee had taken its first steps in the direction of extreme financial conservatism, these were not invariable principles. In July 1900 the committee issued a circular to all affiliated unions pleading for help on the dockers' behalf in a dispute for which, had it arisen after the end of the federation's first full year, the federation itself would have paid. W. B. Hornidge, who had been absent when this decision was taken, protested that 'this appeal is a violation of the very basis of the Federation'[8] but he was alone in this ungenerous attitude. Six years later, in an important strike against sweating among Jewish tailors in the East End of London, the Management Committee advanced £1,000 to the Amalgamated Society of Tailors (by then reaffiliated) to enable it to disburse benefits without delay and so to keep the strike going.[9]

An early dispute involving the federation in great expense was that of the North Wales Quarrymen's Union, fighting Lord Penrhyn's attempt to reduce piece rates and squeeze the union out of existence at his quarries in Bethesda. For three years running the quarrymen's general secretary appeared at the annual general council meeting of the GFTU to plead for an extension of support, and each time it was granted. On several occasions members of the Management Committee visited Bethesda and tried to negotiate with the quarry manager. An historical sketch of the union appeared in a federation report: the stark portrait of an isolated community of workers, mostly monoglot Welsh-speakers, with an intermittent record of organisation over the previous three decades. Eventually, in 1903, after the GFTU had spent over £9,000 in benefit, the firm of North Wales Quarries Ltd was established to employ the Penrhyn strikers, with the aid of a fund collected from trade unionists and other sympathisers.[10] The Penrhyn case, a *cause célèbre* in the trade union world in the late 1890s and early 1900s, helped to persuade several members of the GFTU Management Committee of the merits of government arbitration. Not only had their own efforts failed, but the Board of Trade conciliators had admitted defeat. Lord Penrhyn undoubtedly was determined to stamp out trade unionism among his employees. Even if he did not represent the spearhead of a general attack upon trade unions, as some feared, something more effective than the Conciliation Act of 1896 was needed to deal with employers like him. The GFTU annual report for 1901, while rejecting compulsory arbitration, criticised the Board of Trade for not making more use of its existing powers, and at the TUC in 1903 James Holmes, a member of the Management Committee, moved a resolution in favour of establishing a national conciliation board.[11]

Another dispute that absorbed a great deal of the Management Committee's time and resulted in what the minutes described as a 'somewhat heated discussion' was that of the Huddersfield ironfounders in 1900–1.[12] The Friendly Society of Ironfounders was a craft union operating a typically complex set of rules designed to regulate entry into the trade. As with so many crafts, changes in their industry were threatening the closely knit structure that they had achieved in the nineteenth century. This was particularly true in Huddersfield, where one of the few firms that recognised their closed shop took on a non-union man aged 42. According to the union's district by-laws, anyone over 40 was too old to join, but such a man could continue at his job provided he paid an 'acknowledgement' fee of 1 shilling per week. This particular individual objected that 6*d* would be quite enough, and the members of the ironfounders' society working in that factory promptly left work. Joseph Maddison, the ironfounders' secretary, put the case to his fellow members of the GFTU Management Committee at a special meeting in Huddersfield. In his support the craft unionists Arrandale and Davis urged that if the federation refused benefit to the strikers in this case they would be encouraging employers to employ non-unionists. Crinion and George Barnes[13] rejected this argument, and Maddison's plea for help was turned down by 7 votes to 5. The matter did not end there by any means. A subcommittee consisting of Ben Tillett, Allen Gee and James Holmes interviewed some of the strikers and the employer, and concluded that the workers had been too hasty in circumstances where they could only hope to maintain their position by diplomacy and tact. The Management Committee then voted 9 to 3 against supporting the strike, and the Friendly Society of Ironfounders proceeded to appeal against this decision at the annual general council meeting in 1901. There Maddison, treasurer of the GFTU though he was, delivered a spirited challenge to its policy which Mitchell as secretary then defended. Eventually the delegates decided that in appropriate circumstances they would support strikes in favour of closed shops, but they backed up the Management Committee's right to investigate the circumstances by rejecting the particular case of the ironfounders. The episode had not resulted in any decisive change of policy, but it is interesting for what it reveals of the federation's methods. It was ready to take immense pains, it seems, over disputes that were often quite trivial. (At Huddersfield about twenty men were involved.) Members of the Management Committee were very ready to pronounce judgement on their colleagues' methods, and the mixture of craft and general union representation on the committee could be as much a source of friction as it was a symbol of unity.

The great majority of disputes supported by the federation were indeed on a very small scale. The quarterly reports giving numbers of workmen affected in each dispute show that in most cases fewer than 100 people were involved. It was greeted as an important principle when the federation decided that it could support strikes involving only one individual, if need arose.[14] This accorded fully with the policy 'of narrowing down disputes to their smallest possible limits' and seeking settlements wherever possible.[15] The federation was prepared to commit considerable time and money to peace-keeping and, as the early case of the ironfounders shows, deprecated hasty action by its member unions. Its record of mediation in disputes involving important principles contrasts strongly with the small-scale and local nature of most of the disputes that it supported financially. A glance at the federation's published reports shows that this impression was deliberately fostered. The ambitious language of national strikes and all-out industrial warfare was not a suitable weapon for an organisation that promoted industrial peace and explicitly sought to represent the trade union movement as mature, responsible and dignified in its aims and methods.[16] Thus the list of disputes in the GFTU reports more often than not includes several which are listed separately but involve the same union fighting the same issue in different localities. This was the case with the iron-founders in 1900–1, when the Huddersfield strike was only one of three disputes in which the union was involved at the same time.[17] The prevailing attitude can be summed up by the almost audible sigh with which Isaac Mitchell wrote in the quarterly report for December 1906: 'It seems almost impossible to protect Labour conditions without occasional stoppages .... The great factor towards the settlement of all disputes is to keep negotiating.'

At least one historian has remarked on the General Federation's positive role in conciliation and has observed that it could have developed along similar lines to trade unionism in Scandinavia, where federation officials help to work out a common wage policy among unions, conducting negotiations industry by industry.[18] The GFTU Management Committee members certainly saw themselves in this role, a view expressed both in their references to the federation as a 'central authority' and in their general approach to mediation and their attempts to draw unions together within industries. They compared themselves with the national trade union federations of America and Europe and avowed particular admiration for the Danish federation, whose general secretary, J. Jensen, addressed the annual general council meeting in Glasgow in 1901.[19] The first decade of the GFTU's existence provides many examples of both successful and unsucessful attempts at conciliation. Two may be added here to those already cited.

The quarterly report for March 1907 includes a photograph of the Music Hall Dispute Conciliation Board with the rotund figure of Isaac Mitchell seated next to his friend W. C. Steadman, secretary of the TUC.[20] Mitchell had been called in to act on behalf of the artistes, musicians and stage hands. Their three separate, recently formed trade unions had formed 'the Alliance' and issued a 'Charter' calling for a closed shop in music hall orchestras for the Musicians' Union and demanding payment for matinée performances and a general minimum wage, together with various other rights. The dispute had begun in December 1906 at the Brixton Hippodrome, owned by Walter Gibbons, where the performers objected to being moved without consultation from one to another of Gibbons's music halls. Gibbons did reach agreement with his employees at one stage, but in an atmosphere of mounting distrust the Alliance demanded that he sign his assent to their charter and, when he refused to do so, sent pickets out to stop the performances at each of his six halls. The strike spread and late in January 1907 the music hall proprietors formed their own London Entertainments Protection Association. Their representatives met Mitchell, Steadman and the TUC's counsel, Edmund Browne, and worked out terms of agreement in February, but the Alliance repudiated their work and petitioned the Board of Trade to appoint the independent George Askwith as arbitrator. A star-studded performance at the Scala Theatre raised money for their more impoverished members, and the national press followed the dispute with fascination.

It was George Askwith, not Mitchell and Steadman, who was treated to an interview with the histrionic Marie Lloyd, summoned in the middle of the morning from her beauty sleep. And eventually it was Askwith's award, giving union recognition and a minimum wage but not authorising the closed shop, that brought peace of a sort to the music halls.[21] Mitchell recorded privately, after his attempts at mediation, that he had 'found the artistes quite in the wrong'.[22] In the GFTU quarterly report for March 1907 he praised the conciliation and arbitration powers of the Board of Trade (whose staff he would be invited to join very soon afterwards) and commented with approval on the growth of trade unionism in such professions as acting and journalism. No hint appears that the temperate Scotsman felt any distaste for the ribald, toping life of the music halls, but then business was business,[23] and the Musicians' Union had just affiliated to the General Federation. The episode shows Mitchell typically co-operating with both the Board of Trade and the TUC when asked to do so by the workers involved in the dispute. This was the way that he spent much of his time as secretary of the General Federation. In this particular case his role in the dispute might have seemed thankless enough on the face of it. But it resulted in the affiliation of both the Variety Artistes' Federation and the Theatrical Employees' Association. It was Mitchell's successor, W. A. Appleton, who was to discover just how troublesome they could be. The minutes of Management Committee meetings for the next two years and inter-mittently thereafter abound with disputes involving musicians, artistes and stage hands. Members of the committee spent a consider-able amount of time interviewing theatre managers and trade unionists, arranging for arbitration and incurring public odium for their pains. 'Trade Union principles do not apply to the artistes' profession, and if they had not been mixed up with the Federation of Trade Unions in the last strike the VAF would have got all it wanted in twenty-four hours,' declared the president of the Variety Artistes' Federation in the *Morning Leader* in January 1909.[24] The VAF then seceded from the General Federation but rejoined later and was still a member after the First World War, by which time the Musicians' Union in its turn had seceded.

A far bigger dispute, which involved the GFTU in protracted negotiations, was the battle for weekly rather than fortnightly pay in the shipbuilding industry on the Clyde. The payment of weekly wages was prevailing but by no means universal practice in manufacturing industry by then and the GFTU became involved in several struggles to extend it.[25] The Federation of Engineering and Shipbuilding Trades, founded in 1890 by Robert Knight, the boilermakers' secretary, had been attempting to establish weekly pay on the Clyde since the late 1890s. In 1898 the employers had agreed to a twelve months' trial of weekly pay, on the understanding that if timekeeping in the industry deteriorated or failed to improve as a result, they would call a conference with the unions, show proof of their complaints and then revert to paying their workforce fortnightly. A meeting was held in 1900 but the unions claimed that the employers did not then offer any proof of poor timekeeping before they unilaterally reverted to fortnightly pay, giving only about three days' notice. Intermittent disputes arose over the issue in the next few years and in 1905 the GFTU was asked by some of its affiliated unions to intervene. The position of the Federation of Engineering and Shipbuilding Trades had been undermined by the ASE's refusal to join them; but in 1905 the engineers finally entered[26] and with the help of the GFTU, represented by Pete Curran and Isaac Mitchell, the twenty-one unions involved were able to reopen negotiations with the North-West Coast Engineering Trades Employers' Association and the Clyde Shipbuilders' Association.[27] It took at least five meetings between representatives of the two sides between October 1905 and June 1906, before the employers' associations finally conceded on weekly pay. During the course of negotiations the unions held a ballot which resulted in a large majority in favour of a full-scale strike. Under a difficult balloting system which required the members to call in at their union branches during office hours to record their votes, at least 30 per cent voted out of a total membership of over 40,000, a larger proportion than any of the unions were used to getting in other elections. The employers quibbled at length over what seemed to them a small and unrepresentative vote, but at the end of an acrimonious meeting the union leaders agreed to stay their hand until the employers gave them a final answer on weekly pay. The displeasure of their members at this further delay turned out to have been worth risking, for by the autumn of 1906 members of most unions in the Clyde shipyards were receiving their pay weekly. The role of Mitchell and Curran in this outcome was that of moderators. When the discussion degenerated into squabbles over detail, one or other of them intervened to bring it back to the main business, pinning down the employers on dates and facts. After an exhausting

series of meetings they could justly congratulate themselves on an
important settlement.

Ten thousand boilermakers and some 700 members of the
National Amalgamated Union of Labour, however, were still
involved in disputes that lingered on, in some yards, for several years.
The boilermakers, one of the most important unions hitherto
unaffiliated, had finally joined the GFTU at the beginning of 1906
much to the pleasure, we can assume, of Pete Curran who had been
exhorting them to join for years.[28] When they brought 10,000
members out on strike on the Clyde in September 1906, after offering
to go to arbitration which the employers refused, they received the
General Federation's enthusiastic endorsement. Once again a clear
moral could be drawn:

> It is not difficult to foresee what will be the outcome of refusal to
> settle differences by conciliatory methods. The trade unionists
> themselves have, it is true, again and again declared against
> compulsory arbitration, but the best arguments in favour of that
> proposal are supplied by employers who refuse conciliation.[29]

In the case of weekly pay on the Clyde, the joint committee of the
GFTU and the Federation of Engineering and Shipbuilding Trades
could claim to have proved their point. They had shown a for-
bearance, a commitment to patient negotiating and, above all, a unity
of purpose among many very diverse trade unions, which showed
what federation could achieve. On the other hand, the continuance of
disputes over pay and conditions on the Clyde, with much disagreement between the boilermakers and some of the smaller unions,
illustrated depressingly how tenuous such success could be and how
persistent the internal difficulties of the federation.[30]

To the leaders of the GFTU it was quite clear that the solution to
these difficulties lay in forming a system of industrial unions (with the
general labourers' unions accounting for a separate section) within
the General Federation. The plans for federation that had preceded
the formation of the GFTU had included one calling for the formation
of smaller federations industry by industry as the basis of a general
federal organisation for all trade unions in the country.[31] This ideal
remained at the forefront of the General Federation's policy in an era
when both employers and workers were forming an increasing
number of such associations. The last decade of the nineteenth
century and the first of the twentieth witnessed a growth of collective
bargaining which laid foundations for the national agreements within
particular industries which first really took hold during the national
emergency of the First World War and which characterise much of

industrial relations in Britain today.[32] Before 1914 the path towards
national collective bargaining was perhaps most clearly marked in
coal, cotton, some branches of engineering and in those industries
(such as boot and shoe making) which were heavily concentrated in
one region of the country. The role of the General Federation of
Trade Unions in these developments was a positive one and has not
been explored. Its first annual report proclaimed that the federation
'hopes to strengthen itself and the Trade Union movement by first
strengthening the various unions'. It emphasised the federation's
objective of industrial peace, which ought to include a fusion of
unions competing for workers within the same industry. 'Competition in industry we believe to be bad, in Trade Unionism we know it
to be suicidal.'[33] Isaac Mitchell lent an historical perspective to the
same theme in the second annual report: 'if history is worth anything
it is valuable as a guide to future action. . . . British Trade Unions
have grown up from small local unions, gradually developing into a
national organisation, amalgamating the various sections of one
trade under one executive.'[34] Following this lead, W. A. Appleton
pointed out in 1908 under the heading 'Closer union of kindred
trades' that 'capitalism has frankly built up defensive and offensive
alliances which, in the nature of things, can be more easily directed
than can the alliances of labour, and amongst the workers the sense of
discipline and trust must needs be strong if hardly won positions are
to be maintained'.[35]

When the Jet and Rockingham Workmen's Association, founded
only in 1899, applied to join the GFTU in 1900, the Management
Committee turned it down until its efforts to unite the makers of jet
ware with other pottery workers had failed.[36] The jet ware workers
proved adamant and so the federation admitted their association,
hoping to bring about an amalgamation later on. (Within two years,
in fact, this particular association quietly faded out.)[37] In 1902 the
GFTU was asked to intervene in a dispute in the pottery industry
which it helped towards a settlement and thereafter a close watch was
kept on the pottery unions for signs of incipient unity.[38] In 1906–7 the
federation's services were needed again, this time in a strike over the
annual adjustment of piece rates that involved 600 workers.[39] Before
this strike it had persuaded three of the unions to discuss
amalgamation. The resulting National Amalgamated Society of
Male and Female Pottery Workers started life in 1906 with 3,000
members, rising to over 7,000 in two years.[40] Its amalgamated
structure replaced some of the old branch divisions within the
industry with a complicated system of lodges, some based on regional
membership and others on the membership of particular specialist
trades. This system, combined with the development of pricing

committees within each plant and presided over by a strong central-ised organisation, helped to solve the sectional problems that bedevilled industrial relations in any industry paying its workers by piece rate.

The GFTU's involvement in the pottery industry did not end with the formation of an amalgamated union, however. In 1907 a major dispute threatened to grow out of the strike over piece rates in the sanitary ware sector. Some 16,000 workers were given notice by their employers and, in the words of the GFTU's new secretary, W. A. Appleton, 'the greatest tact and patience was necessary to secure a settlement without a strike. The conditions in this industry were chaotic, and the erection of machinery for the gradual evolution of a uniform system of counts, sizes and prices had become essential if the industry was to thrive.'[41] Members of the Management Committee visited the Potteries to help form a board of conciliation and arbitra-tion. This achieved some improvements in pay and working conditions and survived until 1911. It foundered on the shoals of the 'good from oven' principle, whereby many pottery workers were not paid for any work which emerged imperfect at the end of the firing process, irrespective of whether it had entered the ovens 'good from hand'.[42] The early history of the National Society of Pottery Workers, as it later became, was not by any means one of uninterrupted progress but the GFTU could congratulate itself on having forwarded the cause of systematic bargaining in a singularly ill-organised industry.

The pottery workers' unions were far from being the only ones coaxed into amalgamation or closer unity by officers of the GFTU. The federation's reports record with satisfaction a steady trickle of amalgamations and newly formed federations, some fostered by itself and others created without its help.[43] Among craft unions there was plenty of scope for this work. In the strike-ridden year 1907–8, in addition to building and strengthening the new pottery workers' amalgamation, the federation succeeded in bringing together unions in the silver trade, called a conference of glassworkers' trade unions which then formed a federation, and witnessed amongst its affiliates the mergers of two hammermen's unions and of two very small leatherworkers' societies.[44] In cases where federation or amalgama-tion was preceded by a formal conference, the GFTU was always ready to deal with unaffiliated unions, presumably hoping that a successful conclusion to the conference would induce the outsiders to affiliate, as often happened when the federation had been instrumental in settling a dispute with employers.[45]

The most notable of these conferences and by far the most important in its outcome was that of general labour unions, summoned on the initiative of the GFTU in 1907. The immediate impetus for the conference came from the formation of the Municipal Employees' Association which was threatening the membership of the gasworkers and other general unions and, as the other unions complained, dividing workers in the same industry from each other on the basis of whether they were employed by a private firm or a municipal corporation. This issue was taken up with vigour not only by the GFTU but by the TUC and the Joint Board. Credit for the movement bringing together the existing general unions, however, belongs more specifically to the GFTU. It was the General Federation's Management Committee which summoned the original conference at which the general unions decided to form the General Labourers' National Council, and GFTU officials piloted the scheme through its early stages.[46]

J. N. Bell of the National Amalgamated Union of Labour and J. R. Clynes of the gasworkers outlined the objects of the new council in the GFTU quarterly report for March 1907. Clynes described the fundamental difference between skilled and general labour which made it desirable that one union alone should represent all general labourers, liable as they were to change their jobs many times, unlike the craftsmen whose settled employment made it appropriate for them to be represented by more specialist unions. He wrote with eloquence of the working people he represented:

Manual labour is entitled to better treatment and pay than it now receives, because those who perform it have to bear the greatest displeasures which arise from personal service. Labourers have to face the greatest dangers and risks of accidents, and, in addition to these things, the fact remains that common manual labour is an inseparable feature of the efforts which must be rendered to provide the necessities and pleasures of human existence. The fact that men who follow the occupation of labourers are not trained in the principles of Trade Unionism by a period of apprenticeship ... only increases the necessity for making the lesson of organisation as simple and conclusive as possible.

J. N. Bell foresaw that eventually an amalgamation of all general unions might be possible. In the meantime he wanted to see:

(1)   a systematic means of exchanging information, possibly including a monthly journal;
(2)   an agreement that no two general unions would attempt to cater for the same body of men;

(3) provision for general unions to recognise each other's membership cards in order to permit temporary employment of
individuals alongside the members of other general unions;
(4) mutual assistance in recruitment; and
(5) closer co-operation in disputes involving general unions and
employers.

The final agreement signed in April 1908 embodied most of Bell's
suggestions. The members of the General Labourers' National
Council agreed to recognise each other's cards and to facilitate
transfers of membership, subject to certain conditions. They also
entered into an agreement against poaching each other's members
and agreed to act jointly in any disputes involving firms where more
than one of the general unions already had members. The council's
constitution provided for arbitration in cases of dispute and for an
executive consisting of one representative from each union.[47]

In a letter forwarding a copy of the agreement to Appleton,
J. N. Bell gave credit to the General Federation for having brought it
about.[48] This was a useful achievement. The General Labourers'
National Council proved to be a strong force for unity at a time when
general unions were rather in the doldrums. In 1917 it formed itself
into the National Federation of General Workers, with an aggregate
membership of 800,000 compared with the 100,000 or so that it
represented in 1908. It might have become subsequently the single
general union envisaged by Bell and Clynes, had it not been for the
personalities involved in forming the Transport and General
Workers' Union and, no, doubt, for other forces at work in the swiftly
changing trade union world after the First World War.[49]

The formation of the General Labourers' National Council brings
us near to the year 1908–9, to which we will turn our attention more
closely below. What was left of the decade after that was taken up
mainly with unemployment policy and this subject, entangled as it
was with local and national government and the other national
institutions of labour, belongs more properly to Chapter 3, on the
GFTU's external affairs before 1910. But the general picture of the
federation's internal affairs in its first crowded decade is not complete
without a glance at the change of secretaries in 1907, when William
Appleton, general secretary of the Amalgamated Operative Lacemakers' Union, took over from Isaac Mitchell.

Mitchell had experienced some of the privileges of a 'labour
aristocracy' but his experiences in the engineers' union and in
America had made him a socialist with a strong belief that working
people must bring about their salvation independently of the other
classes of society. His firm espousal of the trade union side in the

debates within the Independent Labour Party and his preference for a party in which only active working men and trade union officials could participate suggest that a tincture of early syndicalism lingered with him from his days in the Socialist Labour Party of Daniel de Leon in New York. Within the context of British labour politics this meant that, in his words,

> The Trade Unionist has an entirely different interest in politics from the Socialist, and particularly from that type of Socialist peculiar to Britain who desires the organisation to be open to all who accept a theoretical collectivism as its basis. The economic organisation of Labour (Trade Unionism) is confined to those labourers who have a common economic interest. . . . Why, this being so, should the political organisation be different?[50]

As a trade unionist first and foremost, Mitchell was also a pragmatist, a negotiator and inevitably also therefore a master of compromise. In the labour politics of Britain in the first decade of the twentieth century, men like him began to find themselves more at home outside the ILP and eventually outside the Labour Party as a whole. In Mitchell's case as in others, this had the effect of pulling them towards the right of the labour spectrum as defined in Britain. The attraction was towards 'practical' politics, to things that could be done here and now, and away from the more theoretical climate of the Labour Party. Thus the Webbs with their dinner parties where 'it [was] always round some project that the conversation rage[d]'[51] must have delighted Mitchell, who first got to know them in about 1902 and became in 1903 a colleague of Sidney Webb among the Progressives on the London County Council. Certainly he pleased the Webbs. Beatrice first mentioned him in her diary as 'one of the ablest of the younger trade union officials'.[52] And more than four years later, when George Lansbury and Ramsay MacDonald both agreed in their dislike of Mitchell's politics, Lansbury lamented that Beatrice Webb, by far the ablest member of the new Royal Commission on the Poor Laws, nevertheless was 'not . . . very well informed from the un-employed side of our enquiry, and appears to me to be largely dominated by the Isaac Mitchell and John Burns school'.[53]

This was at once to damn Mitchell from the Labour Party point of view and to place him in exalted company. His political career, such as it was, will be considered in the next chapter. From the standpoint of the GFTU it meant that by 1907 the federation may have been perceived already, at least by some members of the Labour Party, as tending towards the Lib-Lab camp just when the last of the important unions that had held aloof were being drawn into the Labour Party fold.[54] But Mitchell and Pete Curran differed over labour politics, as they did in one important respect over industrial organisation. Where Mitchell, in keeping again with his de Leonite past, believed in the formation of industrial unions and then went on to make them the basis for his ideal of labour political organisation,[55] Curran, the national organiser of the first of the great general labour unions, could not agree. Curran's life's work was to bring together different sections of the working class in one organisation, and the full weight of his industrial experience lay behind his conviction that 'we [must] cast aside entirely petty jealousies, sectional and personal animosities, and those minor economic differences which can be unravelled in the days to come'.[56] Their differences nevertheless did not stop Curran and Mitchell working together effectively in the GFTU. Indeed it is difficult to perceive the effect of Mitchell's personal political views within the GFTU. He was careful not to let them intrude into federation business and when he expressed opinions of his own in the GFTU *Proceedings and Reports* he did so in separate, signed articles. From these it appears that next to trade unionism the cause he cared for most was temperance. He was on the executive of the National Temperance League and helped to found the Trade Union and Labour Officials' Temperance Fellowship. One of the policies he urged on his fellow trade unionists was that of ceasing to hold union meetings in public houses and investing in trade halls as meeting places instead.[57] The reception of this idea in the GFTU was lukewarm at best, and with Mitchell's departure the issue more or less disappeared from its proceedings.

Mitchell's great strength was as a negotiator. He and Curran together played an important part, for instance, in the negotiations for weekly pay in the Clyde shipbuilding industry. The steady rise in membership of the federation while he was secretary was due in no small part to his visits to unions all over the country. He was, as Beveridge recognised,[58] patient, hardworking and discreet. When after eight years' work for the GFTU he was offered a post at the Board of Trade, both his talents and his opinions suited him for it. In common with Ben Tillett[59] and, we may assume, other members of the federation Management Committee, he had believed for a long time in the merits of arbitration by the government. His practical experience of mediation, the frustration he must have felt often at the tangible proofs of the employers' superior strength *vis-à-vis* the unions,[60] counterbalanced any earlier influences that would have made him suspicious of interference by the state. The Webbs and their circle were probably decisive influences cutting him off from any real links with his more radical past. At all events, the GFTU reports during Mitchell's secretaryship often berated the Board of

Trade for its poor record in arbitration and conciliation. This, when the Board of Trade began to pursue a more active policy in that direction, qualified Mitchell well for a job as a full-time conciliator.

Following his appointment as 'labour correspondent' in the summer of 1907, he won golden opinions for his negotiating skills. By August 1908 the permanent secretary at the Board of Trade, Sir Hubert Llewellyn Smith, was pressing the Treasury to raise Mitchell's salary to £400, the maximum of the scale.

> Mr Mitchell has shown conspicuous ability in connection with difficult . . . negotiations relating to labour disputes. . . . Having regard to these services and to the arduous nature of the work, which entails much travelling and frequent employment outside office hours, Mr Mitchell is inadequately remunerated.[61]

During the height of the 'labour unrest' of 1910-12, he came to the notice of the Cabinet for his highly respected opinions and recommendations on industrial relations, and very probably influenced the opinion put forward by Sydney Buxton as president of the Board of Trade, that the increases in pay which the trade union militants had wrested from the employers were 'fully justified'.[62] Both then and later, he worked closely with the doyen of industrial conciliation, George Askwith (by then Sir George and later Lord Askwith), who wrote that Mitchell's loyal and able assistance could not be overrated.[63]

On entering the commercial, statistical and labour department of the Board of Trade, Isaac Mitchell was 40 years old. He remained there and in its successor, the Ministry of Labour, until his retirement as chief conciliator in 1932. But unlike some trade unionists (most notably, Sir David Shackleton) who became disillusioned with labour politics and entered government service, the best of Mitchell's career lay behind him. The impression he made in middle age upon at least one young colleague was that of a mediocrity or at best a spent force. He became known by his middle name of Haig rather than Isaac as his colleagues in the trade union world called him; he grew a little gingery beard which he used to stroke when asked for an opinion, remarking sagely, 'Aye, indeed . . . '. And it was thought by impatient younger members of the ministry that he always played too safe.[64] Such a view almost certainly does him less than justice, even as he was in his later career, but it does suggest a man who, however hardworking and whatever his flair for conciliation, lacked qualities of leadership. As far as the GFTU was concerned, any such weakness on the part of its secretary did not matter much while Pete Curran continued to play an extremely active part as chairman. But in July 1907 Curran became MP for Jarrow, the news of his election victory arriving dramatically while the GFTU's annual general council meeting was in session; and thereafter the time at his disposal for the federation's business was unavoidably less. The man who succeeded Isaac Mitchell as secretary was only too ready to fill the gap.

William Archibald Appleton, eight years older than Mitchell, had been general secretary of the Amalgamated Operative Lacemakers' Society since 1896. He succeeded to that post after the union sacked its previous officials for fraud, and his first action was to reform the accounting system.[65] The Lacemakers' Society, with 3,080 members when Appleton left it,[66] was the leading union in a fragmented and under-organised industry. It was a craft union *par excellence*. Entry into the society could cost as much as £15, with a correspondingly high rate of weekly contributions, and it offered a range of benefits more suited to a mediaeval guild than to a modern trade union.[67] It is said that in Nottingham, centre of the English lacemaking industry and headquarters of the union, the lacemakers had saloons reserved for their use in two public houses from where on Saturday mornings they would be fetched in hansom cabs and driven to their place of work to collect their pay.[68] Although strikes in the industry were not unknown the union enjoyed a cosy or at least ambivalent relationship with the managerial echelons; twisthands were entitled to keep their society membership if they became owners of a machine and the society would even lend them up to £200 for this purpose.[69] Appleton's regime did nothing to change this state of affairs and it explains much about his rather elitist approach to trade unionism. He was, however, an enterprising and energetic general secretary. He spoke regularly at the TUC, usually on educational matters, and attempted more than once to get elected to the Parliamentary Committee.[70] In 1900 he and his fellow lacemakers' delegates opposed the constitutional change whereby the president of Congress would always be that year's president of the Parliamentary Committee, because this reduced still further the powers of small trade unions. Also in 1900, he formed an international federation of lace trade unions with the Scottish and French lacemakers. As president of Nottingham Trades Council for four years between 1901 and 1907 he pressed for reforms in housing and education. Meanwhile, the lacemakers having affiliated to the GFTU in 1901, Appleton had proceeded to make himself as well known in the federation's councils as he wished to be at the TUC. He joined the Management Committee in 1903 and contributed articles on education and on 'the causes and consequences of war' to the quarterly reports.[71]

Appleton replaced Mitchell in a ballot between five candidates in which he was the only member of the Management Committee and received 120,714 votes more than all his opponents put together.[72]

He refrained from issuing any statement of policy on the grounds that policy was the business of the Management Committee.[73] But he soon made his presence felt. In going through the federation's papers with Mitchell when he took over, he discovered that an important document was missing: the bond for a loan of £100,000 to Sunderland Corporation. Although the federation had a receipt for its money which was perfectly safe and continuing to receive interest, the bond itself was nowhere to be found. The inquiries that followed revealed that Mitchell, honest and trustworthy though he was, had been astonishingly unbusinesslike in his office procedure, keeping bonds and other important documents hugger-mugger in the top of his roll-top desk. One of Appleton's first duties at the GFTU therefore, as it had been at the Lacemakers' Society, was to tighten up procedure and invest in a new safe.[74]

Ironically, the lacemakers were embarking at the same time on a lawsuit against Appleton himself. On leaving the union he had rather improperly held on to his post as treasurer of the International Lacemakers' Federation, a post that carried with it payment of a commission on affiliated membership. The lacemakers objected both to this and to the fact that they were no longer represented amongst the international federation's officials although they contributed two-thirds of its funds. Their action in the Chancery division of the High Court, heard in 1910, revealed that Appleton had kept the international federation's account in a loose and unbusinesslike fashion, with no cash book or register of members. By this time he had already been expelled from the Lacemakers' Society, which now withdrew from, and so broke up, the international federation. The lacemakers were unable to recover any funds on the grounds that according to its rules the officials of the International Lacemakers' Federation were elected for life. Appleton now faced an investigation by a subcommittee of the GFTU, formed by Tillett, Ward and Wilkie.[75] They found nothing 'detrimental to his character'; but they may have reflected wrily on the apparent efficiency with which he had wielded his new broom in the General Federation's affairs; and they might have taken warning from the fact that the federation of laceworkers' unions which he had founded gave life tenure to its officials. As it turned out, Appleton clung on to the general secretaryship of the GFTU until his 80th year.

The Work of a Year: July 1908 to July 1909

Appleton officially took office as general secretary of the GFTU in the autumn of 1907, but he had been acting as secretary since Mitchell's rather hasty departure in August. The year beginning with the annual general council meeting of 1908 was thus virtually his second full year in office. He looked back on it in 1909 as 'the most exciting period of the General Federation's existence'.[76]

The years 1908 and 1909 were bad ones for strikes, and between 31 March 1908 and 31 March 1909 the federation dealt with 638 disputes involving nearly 55,000 workers, and disbursed in benefits alone £122,819 14s. The three previous years had seen exceptional growth, including the affiliation of the boilermakers and the weavers' amalgamation, two of the largest unions in the country. In 1908–9, a second successive year of high unemployment, the number of new affiliations fell off very markedly. Although trade union membership in Britain was declining slightly just then whereas that of the GFTU continued to rise slightly, the federation still had an aggregate membership of only a little over one-quarter of all trade unionists, scarcely more than the proportion it boasted in its first year.[77] Thanks to the fact that the annual general council meeting of 1905 had voted to cut contributions by one-third, its finances were in a parlous state: by the end of March 1909, the federation's reserve fund had sunk below £75,000 in a year when expenditure had totalled well over £125,000.[78] Fortunately the annual general council meeting in July 1908 at least removed one of the disabilities inflicted in 1905, that part of rule 6 which limited the payments of any union to an accumulated total of 10 shillings per member, or 5 shillings on the lower scale.[79] The Management Committee had it in its power to increase contributions but in 1909 it refrained from doing so because the very circumstances that made it desirable were those in which the unions were least able to pay.[80] This was a difficult and challenging year, therefore, and one in which the members of the Management Committee devoted a great deal of time to their duties as federation officials. The minutes of their meetings between the annual general council meetings of 1908 and 1909 demonstrate what they conceived those duties to be.

The federation's new year began on 1 July 1908 with a report from Mallalieu (the felt hatters' leader and a founder member of the Management Committee) on the spinners' dispute at Monton Mill which he had visited.[81] The committee extended benefit payments for another two weeks only after hearing his report, heard the secretary report on the number of disputes registered and the payments made in the last quarter, and then proceeded to grant benefit in seventeen new cases. A claim from the National Amalgamated Union of Labour on behalf of one member on the north-east coast was adjourned until more information was available, this item being followed rather incongruously by the extension of benefit to 4,250 members of the ASE on the north-east coast. Other extensions included several involving the shipbuilding strike in the north-east. The committee voted cordial thanks to Joseph Maddison of the ironfounders, their retiring treasurer. A complaint from one union about the way the Salvation Army ran the Hanbury Street joinery works in London was referred to the Joint Board, the decision of the beamers, twisters and drawers to affiliate was noted and the committee wound up the meeting by appointing Appleton as the federation's fraternal delegate to the forthcoming Trades Union Congress. All of this was routine enough. Under rule 7 it was common for the committee to investigate disputes where the unions involved had applied for an extension of benefit payments beyond the twelfth week; and in addition to receiving the union's own report which had to be submitted before the end of the tenth week it frequently appointed one or more of its number to visit the scene of the dispute.

Between this and the next full Management Committee meeting on 30 July, two subcommittees met. The first dealt with financial matters, mainly tightening up office procedures. At the second a number of claims for benefit and extension of benefit were granted and the meeting heard a report from Appleton on his visit with Alderman Gee of the Yorkshire textile workers, to investigate the dockers' dispute in Dublin. This was likely to involve about 4,000 members of the National Union of Dock Labourers, and on receiving the union's request for help in negotiations Appleton had not waited for a committee meeting but immediately consulted Pete Curran, as chairman, and travelled to Dublin with Allen Gee to meet Lord Macdonnell (permanent under secretary of state for Ireland) and representatives of the firms involved. A very long conference had ended with tentative agreement and another meeting was to be held at the Irish Office the following week. There was extensive further business at this subcommittee meeting. A letter from Ben Tillett recorded his union's demand for a labour representative at the Board of Control for the Port of London, and for 'an exhaustive investigation into the harsh conditions imposed upon the docker'. Tillett, who in fact was present at the meeting, had got himself re-elected on to the Management Committee that year by the narrowest of margins, after a period of absence in Australia. His contributions during the year would make clear his intention to use the GFTU as a political platform. On this occasion as on others, his proposal was referred to the Joint Board.[82] Next it was learned that the Associated Ironmoulders of Scotland and the Central Ironmoulders had agreed to meet under the federation's auspices in Glasgow to discuss their differences. The Welsh ironfounders, meanwhile, were to be offered assistance in their general movement for an extra 2 shillings a week. The Sheffield silversmiths had asked for help in their dispute at Messrs Fenton Bros and Appleton and James Holmes (of the National Hosiery Federation) were deputed to visit them. The Associated Shipwrights wanted help in their difficulties with the Shipwrights' Provident Union of London, to whom Appleton had written already to ask them to 'take steps'. He was deputed also to help the textile workers at Newmilnes, where they had asked the federation to intervene in a dispute at a lace weaving firm. The minutes record several other pieces of business including the new affiliation of two unions, the forwarding to the Home Secretary of the general council's resolution against British blacklegs being sent abroad by the Shipping Federation and the receipt of 'a large number of other letters'.

Nine days later the full Management Committee considered the business referred to it from the earlier meeting. A subcommittee consisting of Appleton, Tillett, John Ward (of the navvies' union) and David Gardner (of the ASE) was to investigate the importation of blackleg labour with a view to referring the question eventually to the Joint Board. The meeting decided against a further such reference to the case of the engineers' dispute on the north-east coast, however, and Appleton, Ward and James O'Grady (of the Furnishing Trades Association) formed a deputation to make 'the usual enquiries' on behalf of the GFTU alone. There followed no fewer than six separate reports on deputations made by members of the Management Committee in July. The Dublin meetings had been noted already. In addition to those, Appleton and Mallalieu had been to the conference in Manchester which finally set up the Glassworkers' Federation. Appleton and Holmes had made some headway in the Sheffield silversmiths' dispute which centred on the firm's attempt to substitute day rates for piece work and their employment of one woman finisher. Mallalieu and Matthew Arrandale (of the United Machine Workers) had visited the french polishers on strike over working conditions in Leeds, attempted to negotiate with the firm, but 'saw no reason to advise a surrender'. Mallalieu had addressed the annual meeting of the Operative Mule and Ring Spindle Makers' Society on the merits of joining the federation, and persuaded them to affiliate. And James Crinion of the cardroom amalgamation and Thomas Ashton of the spinners, soon to be involved in a bitter dispute between their two unions, had been to Oldham together to try to settle the musicians' dispute over working in the theatres without pay on Christmas Day and Good Friday. Contrary to the publicly non-political stance of the GFTU, some discussion of the Old Age Pensions Act then ensued, and the MPs on the committee[83] were instructed to see Lloyd George about the desirability of labour representation on the administering authority. The meeting concluded by granting a large number of claims for benefit and the extension of benefit.

In August 1908 the subcommittees dealing respectively with finance and with grants of benefit met again before the meeting of the full committee at the end of the month. Here,[84] seven reports on different disputes were under consideration. Richards, Gardner and Appleton had visited the french polishers at Glasgow, where members of two unions, the Furnishing Trades Association and the Amalgamated Society of French Polishers, were resisting the terms of an arbitration award which allowed french polishers to work up to 20 hours' overtime per week on any one boat. The men wanted to limit overtime to a maximum of 10 hours, and to ban it altogether so long as any french polishers remained unemployed in the district; but after careful thought the Management Committee urged the men to accept the award, which simply recognised established local conditions. The same deputation also presided over a meeting in Glasgow between the Associated and the Central Ironmoulders of Scotland, where it seemed clear that their differences could be overcome by an amalgamation between the two societies, a course that the Management Committee urged upon them. Appleton had only been back from Glasgow for a week before he joined Ward and O'Grady in a deputation to Newcastle to investigate the engineer's dispute which was then still raging on the north-east coast. Although between 5,000 and 6,000 members of the ASE were on strike the chances of a favourable settlement seemed good and the Management Committee extended payment of benefit for a further four weeks in order not to prejudice the strikers' position. From Newcastle, Appleton had gone on to investigate a strike of fifteen Scottish textile workers at Darvel, where he found them hopeful of success in resisting a wage cut of up to 22½ per cent in one firm. Meanwhile James Holmes had revisited the Sheffield silversmiths and obtained agreement on the points of dispute, 'all but the woman question, and even this difficulty may be surmounted'. Ashton and Crinion had good progress to report in the Oldham musicians' strike. Arrandale had been looking into a strike of woodturners and sawyers for more pay in a firm that had not implemented the increase agreed by the employers' association; and here the committee agreed that Appleton should ask to meet the employers concerned, meanwhile continuing to pay benefit to the union. He and Gee were deputed also to make further investigations into the Dublin dock strike.

Another of Appleton's duties in the following month was to join a deputation representing British workmen, which was to present a message of peace and goodwill to German workmen meeting in Berlin. The August committee meeting followed this decision with further grants of dispute benefit, dominated this month by continuing strikes on the north-east coast and by boot and shoe workers fighting in various parts of the country to maintain recognised minimum rates and in London to obtain adequate workshop accommodation. Preliminary arrangements were made at this meeting for two conferences aimed at bringing together unions in kindred trades, one for the shipwrights and one for the Coach Makers' Society and the Furnishing Trades Association. The annual general council meeting had encouraged such efforts at bringing kindred societies together; and to this end the Management Committee divided the country into districts, assigning a member of the committee to each district, each man charged with helping unions in his district to convene conferences with each other. The old system of district committees had returned in less formal guise. This constructive note, however, did not end the meeting, for the spinners and the cardroom workers had to report that 58,000 of their members altogether had received notice of a 5 per cent reduction in pay, the early rumblings of a major crisis for workers in the cotton industry.

The high level of strikes affecting the General Federation of Trade Unions abated somewhat in early September 1908, but the crisis in the cotton industry was coming to a head and Appleton was instructed to transfer all the money from the federation's deposit to its current account in readiness for the claims that were expected. He and Gee meanwhile had paid another visit to Dublin where it was clear that all was not well within the National Union of Dock Labourers. The union had enjoyed spectacular successes in recruitment during the past few years, and in 1907–8 particularly, thanks to the efforts of its new organiser, the revolutionary Jim Larkin. A turbulent strike by carters in Belfast in 1907 had brought the city to a standstill and resulted in violent riots before it was settled with the help of G. R. Askwith's mediation, and James Sexton, the secretary, negotiated the union's recognition. In 1908 its chief scene of activity was in Dublin but the previous year's strike had almost wiped out its financial reserves. Relations between Sexton and Larkin had deteriorated and within a few months Larkin would be suspended from office, facing a libel action brought by Sexton and about to go to gaol for embezzling the union's funds. Two typically reticent entries in the minutes of the GFTU Management Committee recorded that they had decided to defer publication of Appleton's and Gee's report on the union, but that they would press for repayment of £78 10s 6d that had been overclaimed from federation funds.[85]

At a full meeting of the Management Committee on 1 October, the main item of business was to receive a report on unemployment which had been written in the previous two weeks by Appleton, Tillett and Gee for presentation to the Joint Board. Holmes had wound up his involvement in the Sheffield silversmiths' dispute and there were two other successful delegations to report. Curran, Appleton and Gardner had drawn up an agreement between the United Kingdom Society of Coach Builders and the National Amalgamated Furnishing Trades Association whereby neither union would poach the members or undercut the rates of pay of the other. A similar basis of agreement had been devised between the Associated Shipwrights and the Shipwrights' Provident Union which was to include the formation of a standing joint committee and which in fact formed part of the process of rationalisation among shipwrights' unions which resulted in their re-formation as the Ship-constructive and Shipwrights' Association. The Scottish textile workers whose dispute at a lacemaking factory at Newmilnes had taken up quite a bit of Appleton's time now reported that the employer refused to negotiate with the General Federation but was accepting the mediation of the Scottish Co-operative Wholesale Society, a rebuff which Appleton accepted with grace.

The scene now shifted to Manchester where the Management Committee held four special meetings between 3 and 17 October, in an attempt to agree a common policy in the cotton crisis. The main unions in the cotton industry had been winning advances for their members in recent years, and a policy of co-operation between the cardroom workers and the spinners had paid off. In 1908, however, there was a recession in the industry and the employers asked the unions to accept a 5 per cent reduction in pay, or face a lockout. The spinners reluctantly signed an agreement to accept a reduction from 1 January 1909, having failed to persuade the employers to reconsider the state of trade at that date before enforcing the reduction. But the cardroom workers decided to hold out. On 19 September they stopped work, putting the spinners out of work as well; altogether some 120,000 workers were affected, and federation benefit was claimed on behalf of all the unions involved. The cardroom workers, aggrieved at the spinners' action, objected to their being granted benefit and the first of the special Management Committee meetings was called specifically to consider the spinners' case in the presence of representatives from both unions. Following a fairly heated discussion it was agreed that the executives of the two unions would go away to try to find some common ground, returning to meet under the auspices of the GFTU a week later. During that week Ashton of the spinners and Crinion of the cardroom amalgamation published in the press conflicting accounts of their dealings, and when next they met Pete Curran took them both sternly to task for forgetting their position as representatives of the federation. At this second meeting a more conciliatory mood seemed to prevail and at a third meeting the next day Crinion for the cardroom workers and Gill for the spinners, nudged on by Curran, W. J. Davis and Tillett, managed to arrive at a common formula. A joint ballot of membership in both unions would be taken on the proposition that all cotton operatives should resume work in November or earlier, accepting a 5 per cent reduction in pay on the understanding that the employers would reconsider the position three months later. (This proposal, had it succeeded, would have paralleled the events of 1905 when the employers granted a provisional 5 per cent increase to all workers in the industry, which they withdrew after twelve weeks because of a downturn in trade.) Appleton was instructed to inform the employers' federation of the proposal and, on receiving a favourable reply, to make arrangements immediately for the ballot. If the Federation of Cotton Spinners' Associations had accepted the proposal, enormous costs would have been avoided on all sides and the GFTU could have taken the credit for a very important settlement.

Unfortunately the employers were not interested. At a time of slack trade, their saving on wages counterbalanced the loss of production; they had succeeded in dividing two of the most important unions among their employees and it must have seemed to be in their interests to exploit that fact. The fourth special meeting called by the GFTU included the reelers and winders, members of the weavers' amalgamation, who had objected to not being invited earlier in their own right. Crinion seized upon their presence as a reason for accusing the General Federation of unwarranted interference. His chief objection was that the reelers' and winders' union was in financial straits which would make it ready to give in to the employers and so isolate the cardroom workers still further. From the spirit of *bonhomie* that had graced the last meeting the tone degenerated rapidly into one of real animosity; and it became clear that there was little more the federation could do. It did, however, summon a special general council meeting at Caxton Hall in London to discuss the original issue of whether to pay benefit to the spinners and what could be done to strengthen the federation's finances. On this occasion the Management Committee won considerable support for its actions, and the payment of dispute benefit to the spinners was approved, although not for the whole period covered by the dispute. The financial problems of the federation predictably remained unresolved. Meanwhile the mayors of the Lancashire cotton towns were having better luck at solving the dispute. Under their auspices both employers and unions finally agreed to reopen the mills and to implement a 5 per cent reduction in pay from the following March. After eight weeks of an immensely costly stoppage, work began again on 16 November.

The GFTU's failure to bring about a settlement in the cotton crisis must have been a severe blow to those of the Management Committee who had spent so much effort on it. The fact that two of the principal actors in the affair, Thomas Ashton and James Crinion, were also members of the Management Committee must have strained relationships severely. Nor can the irony have been ignored that these two men had been collaborating effectively in recent months to mediate in the disputes of other unions. Why was it so difficult for them to accept the intervention of the GFTU when they themselves were actively committed to its policies?

To judge from the record we may acquit Thomas Ashton of wrecking tactics on this occasion. James Crinion seems to have been more intractable. His Amalgamated Union of Card and Blowing Room Operatives was more than twice the size of Ashton's Amalgamated Operative Cotton Spinners (almost 45,000 members in 1909, compared with the spinners' 20,000); but the spinners were the aristocrats of the cotton industry, in contrast to the cardroom workers and the weavers whose members included a large proportion of low-paid women and who could not claim the same order of skill as the basis of their work. Such jealousies apart, it must have been extremely frustrating for Crinion and his colleagues to lack the spinners' support just when they jointly faced the most serious threat to their members' interests since the Brooklands Agreement of 1902 had laid the basis of joint bargaining in the industry. The General Federation of Trade Unions seemed, by being prepared to pay benefit to the spinners, to be acknowledging their parity in a struggle which the cardroom workers had undertaken alone. Yet despite Crinion's bitterness, the spinners were caught up in the fight willy-nilly once the cardroom workers' strike had closed the mills. Crinion and his union, indeed, were ready to acknowledge this in the interests of obtaining a settlement. If the employers had accepted the terms which Appleton put to them after the third special meeting in Manchester, the whole story would have been different. But when their proposals failed, Crinion could contain his frustration no longer. The inclusion of the reelers and winders in negotiations was more than he could bear; he clearly felt that the General Federation was placing obstacles in the path of his own union's chances of success by introducing the other unions that were affected into the negotiations, as of course it was bound to do. In the end it was far easier to negotiate through the mayor of Salford and the other Lancashire mayors, whose involvement was purely temporary and implied no threat whatever to the autonomy of the unions. No doubt the financial weakness of the General Federation also weakened its authority, for there was all too clear a limit to the length of time that it might support a strike on this scale. The fact that it had other unions to consider whose heart was not in the strike would give it an excuse to withdraw support and made the federation seem a positive menace to any hopes of long-term solidarity in this particular struggle.

Although the mere payment of dispute benefit was not the GFTU's primary function, it was this which gave it the authority to intervene in a dispute without being invited (as in the case of the cotton crisis) and which encouraged unions to invite its intervention. If it was the General Federation's mission to bring about unity and conciliation in the trade union world and to foster collective bargaining, only its financial operations gave it the authority with its members to further this mission. The members, especially the larger unions among them, were not prepared to pay contributions that would enable the federation to support really large or protracted strikes. So long as a dispute did not reach the stage of a strike or lockout, that did not necessarily matter, for the GFTU had funds and ability to sponsor any number of conferences and negotiations. But even here, the knowledge that if negotiations reached deadlock the federation could do relatively little to help finance a strike inevitably weakened it even at the negotiating stage. The cotton crisis exposed the dilemma.

The full Management Committee next met on 26 November. Before then a subcommittee had already heard details of another troublesome dispute, that between the Variety Artistes' Federation and several music hall proprietors over payment of 10 per cent commission to agents at the expense of the artistes. The proprietors were deducting the 10 per cent from their employees' pay and the VAF claimed that in fact they split this percentage with the agents. Further consultations were still going on at the end of November, so the Management Committee left the dispute to one side. The french polishers on the Clyde were still refusing to abide by the award permitting 20 hours' overtime per man per boat. Appleton was instructed to advise them to conform 'and to suggest that any alteration of the Award under which the district worked should be made by all the parties interested and not by one society'. The ship-wrights' unions were still debating their differences and the committee made plans for a further meeting between them. Also in dispute with each other were the Friendly Society of Ironfounders and the Amalgamated Society of Plate and Machine Moulders; Mallalieu and Arrandale were deputed to make investigations and Appleton was instructed to arrange a conference between the two sides. Yet another inter-union dispute, this time between the roller-makers and the machine workers, was to be investigated by Gardner, Mallalieu and Crinion. Several questions arose in the aftermath of the cotton strike. The spinners' formal protest against having had their benefit docked by three weeks at the special general council meeting was entered in the minutes. John Ward had written alleging that the cardroom union had not paid to all its members the full amount of money received on their behalf from the GFTU, and several members of the committee suggested that the rules must be amended to prevent any such abuse in future. The union also admitted that it had claimed benefit for about 600 members who in fact had been at work for up to 27½ hours per week; such members, the committee resolved, were not entitled to dispute benefit from the federation.

The main business of December 1908 concerned the variety artistes who had still not settled their differences with the music hall owners and were loath to take their case to arbitration again. At a meeting at the GFTU's new offices in Adam Street, off the Strand, on Christmas Eve they gave examples of how the music hall owners had repeatedly broken the terms of the previous award. They objected strongly to the legal costs of attempting to maintain the position awarded by the arbitrator. Nevertheless, pressed by the GFTU, they finally agreed to another arbitration, and the GFTU promised to support them if the agents turned this down. There were three pairs of squabbling unions whose differences the federation tried to solve in that month: the rollermakers and the machine workers, the iron-founders and the plate and machine moulders, and the Associated Shipwrights and London Provident Shipwrights. The first two had gone away to consider the terms of a working agreement for amalgamation suggested by the GFTU. The ironfounders' dispute was a classic illustration of the changing world in which the craft unions now found themselves. When the process of plate moulding was first introduced, they had turned it down as being unskilled and had helped the moulders to organise separately; but now when a firm in Bury adopted plate moulding for the first time and took on a member of the moulders' union at the ironfounders' rate of 40 shillings per week, the members of the Friendly Society of Ironfounders at the firm had gone on strike in protest against the employment of 'non-union' labour. The GFTU firmly refused benefit to the ironfounders. In the case of the shipwrights, the patient policy of supervising a long series of meetings had borne fruit and Gardner, Mallalieu and Appleton were able to record a formal agreement between the two unions who had set up a joint committee to govern all work by their members in shipyards on the Thames. Among other business in December, Appleton and Gee were instructed to meet a member of one of the textile employers' associations who had telegraphed that he would be calling on them in connection with a dispute in Huddersfield and the Colne Valley.

In January 1909 the variety artistes again dominated the regular monthly meeting of the Management Committee. The VAF had eventually rejected the General Federation's insistence on arbitration, baulking over the question of whether an artiste could also act as an agent. They had published a series of adverse comments on the General Federation in the press. Curran and Appleton reported that in the end the VAF, negotiating directly with the theatrical agents, had accepted terms more stringent than those which they had refused indignantly when submitted through the General Federation. Appleton had concluded the sad affair by writing to demand the withdrawal of the opprobrious statements, but he had to wait until the following month for a reply. Apart from the row with the variety artistes, the early months of 1909 were considerably less troubled than the first half of the federation year. In February Appleton was appointed as one of three arbitrators for the National Council of General Labourers' Unions (the other two being representatives of the TUC and the Labour Party). He also attended the Labour Party conference and assiduously canvassed the merits of the General Federation to members of unaffiliated unions whom he met there. At that month's Management Committee meeting Allen Gee reported his abortive attempts to negotiate in the musicians' dispute at Huddersfield. March witnessed continuing disputes in theatres at Huddersfield and Middlesbrough. Pete Curran dealt in that month with a new cop packers' association which had broken away from the spinners and wanted to affiliate independently to the General Federation. They were not permitted to affiliate, but Curran brought together their representative with one from the spinners, who were not allowing the cop packers any say in running the union. Arrandale and Appleton reported on an ironmoulders' dispute in Glasgow and Appleton on a strike by engineers and moulders in Bradford. There were complaints by the National Union of Quarrymen that the gasworkers had been poaching their members and by the Furnishing Trades Association that the United Kingdom Coachmakers had refused to accept the terms of a working agreement which the GFTU had suggested.[86] At the end of March Gee, Richards and Mallalieu were deputed to look into the difficulties between the quarrymen and the gasworkers, and Appleton attended a conference at the Board of Trade on the theatrical employees' dispute at Middlesbrough.

The absence of serious disputes in the first three months of 1909 freed the Management Committee to consider more general matters. Curran's and Appleton's report on state insurance against unemployment was presented to the Management Committee as a sequel to that produced by Gee, Tillett and Appleton in the previous October. They still felt that the Joint Board was the right body to further their policy on unemployment, but a note of impatience at the board's inaction was creeping into the Management Committee minutes. Ben Tillett was 'so pleased with [this] report and its constructive character' that he leaked it to the *Manchester Dispatch*, very much to the disgust of the more diplomatic Pete Curran. At the meeting which considered the report Appleton also presented a memorandum on the subject of soldiers and trade unions. He wanted to draw the Management Committee's attention to the government's policy of teaching soldiers a trade with a view to their future civilian employment. This had far-reaching implications for the membership and apprenticeship policies of craft unions. Appleton apparently drew up the memorandum on the subject on his own initiative, and it is an early example of his way of taking the lead. The question was at least in part a political one and so more suited, in theory, to be considered by the Joint Board.

In April, another relatively quiet month, purely industrial concerns occupied the committee. Appleton visited Cradley Heath near Birmingham, where a group of women chainmakers were resisting a reduction of between 10 and 30 per cent in piece rates, and helped them to reach a settlement. The Management Committee, however, refused to admit their new association into the GFTU on the grounds that no fewer than four other unions already catered for their trade. Although the minutes make no mention of it, these women were very much at the mercy of middlemen. In the following year they suffered a lockout when resisting the middlemen's attempts to stockpile chain which had been paid for at less than the minimum rate. On that occasion, having received less than full satisfaction from the GFTU, they turned to the National Anti-Sweating League and to Mary Macarthur's National Federation of Women Workers, to which they later transferred their growing membership.[87]

During April 1909 Appleton also visited Falkirk with Allen Gee, to look into a dispute involving the Central Ironmoulders of Scotland. Here the Board of Trade was already involved, with Arthur Henderson representing the men, and the GFTU's only concern was to ascertain whether the ironmoulders qualified to receive federation benefit. Appleton and Gee were involved at the same time in talks with the football players' union which had applied to affiliate. They advised the players to make no further requests for better conditions until after they had played in the international Scotland v. England match, so that there would be no excuse for rumours that they planned to disrupt the game in furtherance of their claim. Meanwhile Mallalieu was visiting the paperstainers in Darwen, where he offered suggestions for a careful review of their working conditions. Other business in April included further intervention at Cradley Heath and requests for help from the Congleton weavers who could not get their employers to discuss working conditions. The frost cog and screw makers wrote about sweating conditions in their trade. Gee, Richards and Mallalieu presented a report on the differences between the gas-workers and the quarrymen as a preliminary to further action by the federation. The Management Committee also brought together representatives of the three theatrical trade unions to discuss measures to reduce unemployment in their profession. It was quite a tribute from the Variety Artistes' Federation that they should still seek GFTU help after their haughty behaviour only three months earlier. All in all, April 1909 was a good month, with a low level of disputes and a good record of constructive activity by the Management Committee.

May saw a rise in the amount of benefit claimed, though there was still nothing to compare with the nightmare of the previous autumn. One hundred plasterers were on strike in Swansea for an extra $1d$ a week and later in the month a hundred cardroom workers struck in Rochdale to maintain the universal price list and to enforce the safe-guarding of machinery. Ben Tillett's union had submitted seven resolutions in April for the annual general council meeting and in May a subcommittee spent some time knocking them into shape for presentation to the Joint Board, which it considered to be the more suitable forum. The resolutions called for the appointment of a minister of labour, a national department of industrial arbitration and conciliation, a labour legal department, and various measures, including national insurance and a programme of public works, to deal with unemployment and distress. An eighth resolution called on the Management Committee to prepare a scheme dealing with unemployment which would cover: registration of the unemployed; the co-ordination of trade union with local and national authorities in administering schemes for provision of work, and so on; similar co-ordination in insurance schemes; provision for feeding and main-taining the unemployed and their children including free medical care. In this instance Tillett was not so firmly headed off. The sub-committee decided that part of his proposals had been met by the government's measures dealing with labour exchanges and unemployment insurance; but that the full committee should

> consider the location of labour exchanges, and press for the appointment of experienced officials to watch carefully the effect of the measures on strikes and lock-outs, and to take . . . steps . . . to secure the workman's right to refuse temporary employment which might jeopardise his return to his ordinary occupation.

They also worried about the definition of casual employment. These proposals were to be placed before the Joint Board 'with a view to concerted action', but the Management Committee itself would 'approach the President of the Board of Trade for the purpose of explaining the Trade Union position'. If the increased politicisation of the GFTU, which would later hasten its decline, is to be dated from such interventions in public policy, by no means all the responsibility attaches to William Appleton. Ben Tillett, for one, was certainly using the federation as a platform for industrial politics.

The annual general council meeting of 1909 was to be held in Blackpool at the beginning of July, and the minutes of Management Committee meetings in late May and June reflect the press of other business at that time of year. The secretary was preparing his annual report and making final arrangements for the Blackpool meeting. Plans had to be made also for the international conference of trade unions which had been moved back from 1910 to 1909 because Samuel Gompers, president of the American Federation of Labor, was visiting Europe that year. Gompers was coming first to Britain for both the GFTU and TUC annual meetings, and special plans had to be made for the reception of this important guest. Among more routine business, Alexander Wilkie had been trying to negotiate between some workmen of unspecified trade in Gateshead. The theatrical unions were still attempting to set up a co-operative employment scheme. Richards, O'Grady and Ward were deputed to help settle disputes respectively involving the Midland Counties Trades Federation at Stourbridge, women members of the Chainmakers' and Strikers' Association, and the Lace Pattern Readers at Nottingham. William Mosses of the Patternmakers' Association wrote on behalf of the Federation of Engineering and Shipbuilding Trades to draw attention to the government's proposals to set up labour exchanges, a matter referred to the Joint Board. Benefit had to be paid out for a strike of London tailors involving 354 members and to 162 gas-workers in Cork who were on strike for better wages and working conditions. Pete Curran reported that at last the cop packers had settled their differences with the spinners. And the Management Committee finally decided, after a long delay, to admit the Professional Football Players' Association, with a membership of 1,214. In the event, this colourful addition was short-lived. The football players, having amended their rules to satisfy the GFTU, found all members of their union suspended by the Football Association who objected to the strike benefit system. The players therefore seceded from the General Federation in 1910.

Appleton's annual report wound up the year 1908–9 on a note of relief. The federation had exhausted its bank account that year and had had to call on the Co-operative Wholesale Bank for an overdraft.

The growing strength of the GFTU had attracted some adverse comment from other trade unionists, but this, according to Appleton, 'was never true of the rank and file, and it is the rank and file whose interests are involved'.[88] He recorded the amalgamation of several affiliated societies and the affiliation of fifteen new ones during the year, and asserted that the rank-and-file membership of many other unions wanted to join the federation. The GFTU's work to create closer unity between unions of kindred trades was as always a matter for particular pride. More sombrely, there was this year a long section on unemployment; but the report ended on a cheerful note with a rather rosy account of the amicable relations on the Joint Board and of the state of cordial understanding in international trade unionism.

Notes: Chapter 2

1 GFTU, *Quarterly Report*, March 1907.
2 See above, pp. 22 and 32, n. 77.
3 Clegg, Fox and Thompson, *History of British Trade Unions*, Vol. 1, p. 472. On p. 356, however, the authors note the intervention of the GFTU on the Clyde in 1905–6.
4 Phelps Brown, *Growth of British Industrial Relations*, pp. 250–60. But Phelps Brown, despite the fact that like Roberts he considers the GFTU to have been shunned by large unions (a mistake not made by Clegg *et al.*) and is also unduly hard on its policy of financial caution, gives the best consideration of the GFTU's early history published to date.
5 Roberts, *The TUC*, p. 163. The present work was written before the publication of Ross M. Martin, *TUC: The Growth of a Pressure Group 1868–1976* (Oxford: Clarendon Press, 1980), which does give more serious consideration to the GFTU, although it does not draw on GFTU sources.
6 Allan Flanders, *Trade Unions*, revised edn (London: Hutchinson, 1968), p. 57.
7 Clegg, *The System of Industrial Relations in Great Britain*, p. 397.
8 GFTU MS minute book, meetings of 5 July and 15 August 1900.
9 GFTU, *Annual Report*, 1907. This decision was debated hotly at the 1907 agcm.
10 The view that employers were mounting a deliberate counter-offensive against trade unions was widespread among trade unionists at that time. See F. Bealey and H. Pelling, *Labour and Politics, 1900–1906. A History of the Labour Representation Committee* (London: Macmillan, 1958), p. 75.
11 TUC, *Report*, 1903. The GFTU quarterly report for December 1903 called for the Board of Trade to be empowered to investigate disputes whether the parties wished for it or not.
12 GFTU MS minute book, meeting of 8 September 1900; printed minutes, meeting of 18 September 1900.
13 G. N. Barnes, general secretary of the ASE and later a Labour MP and eventually wartime Cabinet minister, joined the Management Committee at the agcm in 1900.

14   GFTU, *Proceedings and Reports*, 1901–2, report of agcm of August 1901, p. 9.
15   GFTU, *Annual Report*, 1902, also quoted in Clegg, Fox and Thompson, *History of British Trade Unions*, Vol. 1, p. 355.
16   For the federation's defence of responsible trade unionism, published in *The Times* in 1900, see below.
17   Other examples scattered throughout the GFTU *Proceedings and Reports* include the printed minutes of a Management Committee meeting on 30 July 1908, where 634 engineers in Dublin seeking union recognition are listed in six separate entries and 43 ironfounders seeking an advance of 2 shillings in South Wales appear in fourteen separate entries.
18   Phelps Brown, *Growth of British Industrial Relations*, p. 259.
19   GFTU, *Proceedings and Reports*, 1900–1, 1901–2, *passim*; *Quarterly Report*, December 1906.
20   The following account of this dispute is drawn from the report cited and from PRO, LAB 2/CL & SL/1302/1908, Board of Trade file. Mitchell's friendship for Steadman was warmly expressed in GFTU, *Quarterly Report*, September 1905, when Steadman became secretary to the TUC Parliamentary Committee.
21   A colourful description of the dispute and arbitration appears in Lord Askwith, *Industrial Problems and Disputes* (London: John Murray, 1920), pp. 103–8.
22   PRO, LAB 2/CL & SL/1302/1908.
23   'We are business men and you are business men' said Isaac Mitchell to the employers on the Clyde on another occasion (GFTU, *Annual Report*, 1906, p. 27).
24   Quoted in GFTU, *Proceedings and Reports*, 1908–9, minutes of Management Committee meeting, 21 January 1909.
25   See, for example, the report on the Locomotive Combine, GFTU, *Quarterly Report*, September 1906. The following account is taken from GFTU, *Proceedings and Reports*, 1905–6, and *Quarterly Report*, September 1906.
26   Jefferys, *The Story of the Engineers*, p. 143.
27   The unions involved were: the Associated Blacksmiths; Boilermakers; Brassfounders and Coppersmiths; Amalgamated Cabinetmakers; Amalgamated Carpenters and Joiners; Associated Carpenters and Joiners; ASE; Steam Engine Makers; Amalgamated Furnishing Trades; French Polishers; Scottish Ironmoulders; National Amalgamated Union of Labour; Machine Workers; Patternmakers; Plumbers; House and Ship Painters; Smiths and Strikers; Scottish Saw Mill Operatives; Woodcutting Machinists; Associated Shipwrights and Amalgamated Toolmakers.
28   See Curran's addresses to the annual general council meetings of 1902 and 1903, printed in GFTU *Proceedings and Reports*. For the affiliation of the boilermakers, along with the Central Ironmoulders' Association of Scotland which also had cause to be grateful for the federation's help, see printed minutes of meetings of the Management Committee in *Proceedings and Reports*, 1905–6, meeting of 25 January 1906.
29   GFTU, *Quarterly Report*, September 1906. Under federation rules the newly affiliated boilermakers were not yet entitled to benefit, so this display of enthusiasm cost nothing.
30   See GFTU, *Annual Report*, 1909, p. 10, for W. A. Appleton's restrained comment on disunity among unions on the north-east coast. The disputes of 1906–9 are summarised in Clegg, Fox and Thompson, *History of British Trade Unions*, Vol. 1, pp. 435–8. See also Phelps Brown, *Growth of British Industrial Relations*, pp. 258ff., where the role of the GFTU in 1905–6 is mentioned as one of its few successes.
31   See above.
32   For a general consideration of the growth of collective bargaining in this period, see Clegg, Fox and Thompson, *History of British Trade Unions*, Vol. 1, ch. 12.

33 GFTU, *Annual Report*, 1900, pp. 1, 7.
34 GFTU, *Annual Report*, 1901, pp. 15–16.
35 ibid., 1908, p. 8.
36 GFTU MS minute book, meetings of 17 August and 18 September 1900.
37 F. Burchill and R. Ross, *A History of the Potters' Union* (Hanley; CATU, 1977), p. 152.
38 GFTU, *Annual Report*, 1902.
39 GFTU, *Quarterly Report*, March 1907.
40 Burchill and Ross, op. cit., pp. 159–60, briefly describe the formation of the new union. The unions involved were the China, Furniture and Electrical Appliance Makers' Union (which joined a year after the others); the Holloware and Sanitary Pressers' Trade Protection Association; the China Potters' Federation; and the Printers' and Transferrers' Trade Protection Association. See also GFTU annual reports for 1907 and 1908.
41 GFTU, *Annual Report*, 1908, p. 7.
42 Burchill and Ross, *History of the Potters' Union, passim*, especially p. 162.
43 For example, the quarterly report of December 1906 comments on the growing tendency towards federation and amalgamation, and claims credit for always encouraging and sometimes actively assisting this process.
44 GFTU, *Annual Report*, 1908, pp. 7, 20–3. The fortunes of the Glassworkers' Federation can be followed in the reports of the Pressed Glassmakers' Society of Great Britain, 1908–9. The society joined the new federation and affiliated to the GFTU in 1908. It has been affiliated to the GFTU ever since but withdrew from the Glassworkers' Federation, along with the glassblowers, in 1909.
45 For example, in the cases of the boilermakers and the Variety Artistes' Federation. See above.
46 GFTU, *Quarterly Report*, March 1907.
47 The unions forming the council were: the United Order of General Labourers of London; the Workers' Union; the British Labour Amalgamation; the Navvies', Builders' Labourers and General Labourers' Trades Union; the Dock, Wharf, Riverside and General Workers' Union; Amalgamated Union of Machine and General Labourers; Amalgamated Society of Gasworkers, Brickmakers and General Labourers; Amalgamated Association of Tramway and Vehicle Workers; National Amalgamated Union of Labour; National Union of Gasworkers and General Labourers.
48 GFTU, *Quarterly Report*, March 1909.
49 Bell quoted the figure of 100,000 members in an article in the GFTU quarterly report for March 1907. Webb, *History of Trade Unionism*, p. 499, gives 800,000 as the membership in 1919. The Webbs expected great things of the NFGW and accorded praise to the work of its predecessor, the General Labourers' National Council.
50 'The political organisation of Labour', article by Mitchell in GFTU, *Quarterly Report*, December 1904, p. 19.
51 BLPES, Beatrice Webb's diary, typescript version, p. 2291, entry for 2 May 1904.
52 ibid., p. 2176, entry attributed to November or December 1902.
53 PRO, MacDonald papers, Lansbury to MacDonald, 7 May 1907, PRO 30/69/1151.
54 See Bealey and Pelling, *Labour and Politics*, for a discussion of the wider context.
55 This is spelled out in Mitchell's article in GFTU, *Quarterly Report*, December 1904.
56 Article by Curran on 'the Labour representation movement', ibid.
57 For example, in GFTU *Quarterly Report*, March 1906.
58 Beveridge, *Power and Influence*, p. 84, Beveridge acknowledged Mitchell's influence over both himself and other trade unionists. See also José Harris, *William Beveridge. A Biography* (Oxford: Clarendon Press, 1977), pp. 51–2.

59   On Tillett's conversion to the merits of compulsory arbitration (which was further than most of his colleagues would go) see Roberts, *The TUC*, p. 174.

60   The Penrhyn quarrymen's case made a particularly strong impression. See above, pp. 35–6.

61   PRO, Treasury in-letters, H. Llewellyn Smith to Treasury Secretary, 14 August 1908, T1/1086B (paper 14574).

62   PRO, CAB 37/110/62, 63 and 66, papers on the labour unrest presented to the Cabinet in 1912.

63   Askwith, *Industrial Problems and Disputes*, p. 110.

64   Interview with Sir Harold Emmerson, formerly permanent secretary, Ministry of Labour (who entered the ministry in 1920), 6 August 1979.

65   Norman H. Cuthbert, *The Lace Makers' Society. A Study of Trade Unionism in the British Lace Industry* (Nottingham: Amalgamated Society of Operative Lace Makers and Auxiliary Workers, 1960).

66   GFTU, *Annual Report*, 1907, summary of income, expenditure and membership.

67   Cuthbert, *The Lace Makers' Society*, p. 70 and *passim*.

68   Interviews with Mr Horace Moulden and Mr Leslie Hodgson, May 1977.

69   Cuthbert, *The Lace Makers' Society*, pp. 50–1.

70   Cuthbert, op. cit., p. 74, states that Appleton was a member of the Parliamentary Committee but I have found no evidence that this was so.

71   GFTU, *Quarterly Reports*, March 1903 and March 1906.

72   GFTU, *Proceedings and Reports*, 1907–8, special report of the election bound at the back of the volume.

73   GFTU, *Quarterly Report*, September 1907.

74   GFTU, *Proceedings and Reports*, 1907–8 and 1908–9, *passim*. The missing bond was discussed at length at the 1908 agcm.

75   Cuthbert, *The Lace Maker's Society*, pp. 80–3.

76   GFTU, *Annual Report*, 1909, p. 5.

77   These figures are taken from the table of trade union membership in Clegg, Fox and Thompson, *History of British Trade Unions*, Vol. 1, pp. 489–90, and in GFTU, *Annual Report*, 1909, p. 6.

78   GFTU, *Annual Report*, 1909, summary of income, expenditure and membership.

79   This improvement was carried against the opposition of the ASE, which thought a large reserve fund in the GFTU would menace individual unions, and of Will Thorne of the gasworkers, who felt that if the fund increased contributions should also (*Proceedings and Reports*, 1908–9, report of agcm, pp. 25–8).

80   GFTU, *Annual Report*, 1909, p. 5.

81   Minutes of meeting of 1 July 1908. The printed minutes of Management Committee meetings for the whole year are bound with the *Proceedings and Reports*. Unless otherwise stated, details and quotations cited in this section (to p. 65) are taken from these printed minutes.

82   For Tillett's election, see report of the 1908 agcm in *Proceedings and Reports*, 1908–9, pp. 29–30. For his further meddling in politics through the GFTU, see pp. 63, 105, 113, 118. Although this proposal, like others of his, was sent on to the Joint Board, like the others it was not received without sympathy by his fellow committee members. Some of them had spoken on the subject in the House of Commons, and the committee minutes record a continuing interest.

83   Curran, Ward, O'Grady, Richards (of the Boot and Shoe Operatives) and Wilkie (of the Associated Shipwrights).

84   Meeting of 27 August 1908.

85   Meetings of 15 September and 1 October 1908. For the history of Larkin and the union at this period, see Emmet Larkin, *James Larkin, 1876–1947: Irish Labour Leader* (London: Routledge, 1977).

86   This difficulty arose in February. By 10 March a ballot of the coachmakers had

confirmed their union's opposition to the agreement and the GFTU was threatening
to arbitrate compulsorily under federation rule 8.

87   BLPES, Webb Collection A, vol. 47, no. 50.
88   GFTU, *Annual Report*, 1909, pp. 5–6.

3
The General Federation in a Wider World, 1900–10

The Position of Trade Unions at the Turn of the Century

The General Federation of Trade Unions intended to stay out of politics, but political issues were difficult to ignore. The first ten years of the federation's existence saw momentous changes in the position of labour in British society, which brought social and industrial questions right into the centre of government policy and public debate and made it impossible for any national trade union organisation to avoid the political arena altogether. The Labour Representation Committee, founded in 1900, would soon propel leading trade unionists, including several members of the GFTU management committee, into the House of Commons. Two important legal decisions, in the Taff Vale case at the beginning of the decade and the Osborne case at the end, threatened the activities of trade unions as they had not been threatened since the 1870s, necessitated new legislation and gave rise to heated political debate. Furthermore, government was entering into the lives of individual citizens in new ways that profoundly affected trade union members: the Royal Commission on the Poor Laws, legislation on workmen's compensation, free school meals for poor children, old age pensions and unemployment insurance all had implications that could not be written off as merely political.

It was especially difficult for the GFTU Management Committee to hold back when the Parliamentary Committee of the Trades Union Congress itself did not enter into the fray. An early example of this sort of abdication by the TUC arose when Edwin Pratt, industrial correspondent of *The Times*, began a sustained attack on trade unions in 1901. Under the title 'The crisis in British industry' Pratt published a series of articles (later reprinted as a book) accusing the unions of causing a decline in the efficiency and productivity of the nation's industry. He did not object to the existence of trade unions and even singled out the Lancashire cotton spinners for special praise; but aiming his fire at 'new' unions in particular, accused them of following a 'ca'canny' policy which meant encouraging their members to go easy and keep production low, as an alternative to strike action. He also claimed that the unions resisted new technology and insisted on less able men receiving the same wage as their more skilled fellow workers. A leading article in *The Times* of 3 December 1901 suggested that since no trade unionists had yet replied to Pratt's accusations, this must mean that organised labour accepted the truth of what he said. This challenge was too much for the leaders of the GFTU, and they plunged into the debate.

As the Management Committee saw it,[1] the *Times* articles were part of a disturbing picture of mounting opposition to trade unions, which included the rise of free labour and a series of legal decisions culminating in that of Mr Justice Farwell in the Taff Vale case. They pointed to the federation's declared object of promoting industrial peace. The main purpose of trade unions was to obtain decent minimum working conditions, not, as *The Times* would have it, to prevent the able workman from rising above the minimum. They wanted to remove labour from the market place where it was treated like any mere commodity, and give it 'the power to bargain on the plane of reason and justice'. Whereas Pratt and *The Times* accused the unions of standing in the way of new technology, the GFTU retorted that 'in such trades as engineering, shipbuilding, mining etc. labour has by organisation won for itself better conditions in regard to wages and hours, which betterment has led to the stimulation of invention and the introduction of machinery'. *The Times* printed its own riposte on the same page: the individual should be left free to fix his own level of exertion; one man's sweating was another man's normal working; and an intangible, 'healthy natural process' would fix the best minimum wage. The editorialist went on to reveal some even more blatant prejudices. He claimed that 'after ages of competition the world is doing very well upon the whole' and refuted the arguments against unorganised sweated labour thus: 'Polish Jews and other wretched aliens are paid miserable wages in the East-end. Why? Because they have no trade union? Not at all; but because their intelligence and their general standard of decency are deplorably low.'

The General Federation closed the argument as far as it was concerned in the pages of its tenth quarterly report.[2] In a way, its statement summed up what has been a guiding principle throughout its history. *The Times*, claimed the GFTU Management Committee, was completely wrong to assume that trade unionists incited workers to strike and harass employers at every opportunity. 'The exact contrary is the case, trade union officials seldom if ever order a strike, and on very many occasions stand between the men and their employers for peace and conciliation.' It went on to refer to the 'harmonious relationship' between trade unions and the vast majority of employers, and held that the cause of intractable disputes was often the employers' refusal to accept arbitration. The General Federation obviously could not be regarded as impartial in this debate, but its view was supported by two more objective observers of the British industrial scene, the Frenchmen Paul Mantoux and Maurice Alfassa. They quoted the GFTU's defence in their book[3] and commented on the irresponsibility of *The Times* in using some very suspect evidence. They followed George Barnes, one of several trade unionists they had interviewed, in rejecting the fear that capital was mounting an all-out attack on trade unionism. Rather, the *Times* campaign had been prompted by a more general anxiety on the part of industrialists, a few of whom wanted to blame their workmen for a potentially serious trade recession for which they themselves were very much to blame.

In this uneasy climate the case of the *Taff Vale Railway Company* v. *Amalgamated Society of Railway Servants* struck a heavy blow at trade unions. The original judgement had ordered the union to pay damages to the railway company for the effects of a bitter strike in 1900, and in July 1901 the House of Lords upheld this decision. The trade union world had been watching the case closely, for this was only the latest in a series of decisions against unions, including that in *Lyons* v. *Wilkins* which had seriously limited picketing. In the Taff Vale case the unions lost the immunity from actions for tort which they had supposed that they enjoyed under the Trade Union Acts of 1871 and 1875. But the issue was not clear-cut. In the first place, the railwaymen's strike in 1900 had been called against the wishes of Richard Bell, general secretary of the ASRS, and had grown partly out of the personal antagonism between the militant district secretary of the union and the equally militant, anti-union, company manager. Secondly, the Lords' decision, while it bore grievously on the funds of the ASRS, also had the effect of giving corporate status to the unions. This did not protect strike funds from actions for damages, but it offered certain other legal advantages, especially in the eyes of those who wanted legislation for compulsory arbitration. Trade unionists therefore differed among themselves about whether to seek new legislation that would restore the position as it had been interpreted before Taff Vale, or to reform union structure so that they could take advantage of the state of affairs created by the Taff Vale decision. The implications of the Taff Vale case have received exhaustive treatment elsewhere, but some consideration is needed here of the part that the GFTU played in the affair.

The General Federation of Trade Unions did not number the

Amalgamated Society of Railway Servants among its members, but it hoped to do so and its interest in the implications of Taff Vale for other unions could not be doubted.[4] The Management Committee tried without success to contact the TUC Parliamentary Committee for consultations and then published its own report, calling for two Bills, one to safeguard peaceful picketing and one providing that a trade union could not be sued for the actions of its members unless it was proved that they had acted 'with the directly expressed sanction and authority of the Trade Union rules'.[5] The TUC in September 1901 had called in general terms for a change in the law, and the Parliamentary Committee was receiving the advice of three leading Liberal lawyers, Asquith, Haldane and Sir Robert Reid. The barrister Clement Edwards, junior counsel for the ASRS during the Taff Vale hearings and later a Liberal MP, advised the GFTU on the legal status of federations of trade unions.[6] In April 1902 two legal decisions added force to their specific proposals. In *Giblan* v. *Williams* a decision in favour of the National Amalgamated Labourers' Union ruled that union funds could not be held liable for damages for the actions of a member against its rules; but most confusingly the judge in *Thomas* v. *Amalgamated Society of Carpenters and Joiners*, which concerned a similar issue, decided the opposite way in the same month.[7] On 14 May 1902 the TUC and GFTU committees showed a rare and impressive unity by turning up at the House of Commons together in full force to hear the Liberal MP Wentworth Beaumont move 'that legislation is necessary to prevent workmen being placed by judge-made law in a position inferior to that intended by Parliament in 1875'.[8] The GFTU and TUC remained in contact after that and at the end of 1902 formed a joint subcommittee with the LRC to draft legislation.[9] A national labour conference in the following March, presided over by W. B. Hornidge with Pete Curran as vice-president,[10] approved a draft Bill very much along the lines that the GFTU had proposed.[11] It provided protection for pickets (as had a Bill introduced by Richard Bell in May 1902), abolished the doctrine of civil conspiracy as far as trade disputes were concerned and provided that no union should be liable for damages unless it could be proved that its members had acted expressly within the union's rules. This Bill turned out to be unfortunately worded, however, for the all-important third clause was ruled out of order on the grounds that it was not covered by the title 'Trade Disputes Bill'; and the abbreviated version was defeated on 2 May 1902.

The debate on Taff Vale at the GFTU's annual general council meeting in Dublin two months later illustrated the dilemmas then facing the trade union movement. 'The position the committee recommended was they they should accept the liability of the unions, define that liability and limit it as far as possible.'[12] But George Barnes warned the meeting that the TUC had changed its ground and would probably pass a resolution in favour of restoring the legal position as it had been interpreted before Taff Vale.[13] John Ward spoke forcefully against this policy: 'the ante Taff Vale position was individualism typified. . . . He thought that human society was an organism and that rights could only be claimed when duties were accepted.' James Sexton, James O'Grady and Alexander Wilkie all favoured the 'ante-Taff Vale' position. Sexton disliked the possibility of a union's repudiating the actions of its own appointed executive, and Wilkie did not want trade unions to be legal entities because he thought members and officials ought to be responsible for their own actions. There was a call from the floor for a stronger lead from the Management Committee, and in the end its policy was endorsed.

When Congress did, as Barnes had predicted, vote in favour of restoring the 'ante-Taff Vale' position, the GFTU quietly fell into line and helped to draft a new Bill.[14] In April 1904 this Bill was 'talked out' by a Conservative MP, a defeat from which Isaac Mitchell in that year's annual report concluded, like many other trade unionists, that political involvement was inseparable from the industrial and social aims of the working classes. As the German trade union leader Carl Legien had told the GFTU annual meeting in 1903, 'If the British workers wished ultimately to solve [their] problems . . . they would have to pay attention not only to the economic side of their struggle but to the political side as well; they would have to . . . capture all the political power of the country'.[15] In the view of the Webbs, Taff Vale had the direct effect of trebling the number of trade unions affiliated to the TUC and placing the LRC on a sound footing with a membership of nearly a million.[16] There can be no question of the importance of Taff Vale in boosting trade union support for the nascent Labour Party; nor of its place in the annals of labour law, where it has laid the foundation for that resistance to statutory regulation which is still typical of British trade unionism. As for the GFTU, it had played a constructive part. It spoke up for a strong body of opinion[17] but in the end it subordinated its policy, which in any case the Management Committee did not endorse unanimously, to that of the TUC.

The co-operation between the Labour Representation Committee, GFTU and TUC over the Taff Vale crisis foreshadowed the formation of the Joint Board in 1905. Almost from the time of the LRC's foundation, labour leaders had animadverted on the unnecessary division of functions between the three national bodies. J. N. Bell contributed an article on 'The confusion of labour interests' to the GFTU's quarterly report for September 1902 in which he suggested that the different sections of the labour movement should form one central committee, pointing to the disarray in the trade union world after Taff Vale as an example of the need for urgent action: 'Between a Parliamentary Committee with a programme and nothing else, a Labour Representation Committee with little or no programme at all, and a Federation that must not act for fear of touching the functions of somebody else who cannot act, the interests of Labour are in a parlous state'. Some people, according to Bell, had suggested that the TUC should be dissolved, leaving the GFTU and LRC to deal respectively with industrial and political questions affecting labour; but this was manifestly ridiculous, because the TUC represented far more members than either of the other two organisations. In the next quarterly report an article by Ramsay MacDonald chided trade unionists for setting up their own parliamentary candidates without reference to the LRC, and attacked the notion that only working men should become Labour MPs.

Co-operation among the Forces of Labour: the Joint Board and Labour Politics

More and more trade unions were affiliating to the LRC, the most important of all being the United Textile Factory Workers' Association, which joined *en bloc* after the notable victory of David Shackleton, the weavers' secretary, at the Clitheroe by-election in 1903. The annual conference of the LRC that year, chaired by the diplomatic J. N. Bell, passed Pete Curran's resolution in favour of independence from the Liberal and Conservative parties, which had been a vexed question among trade unionists. In 1904 on the motion of W. J. Davis, the TUC decided to support all Labour candidates provided they were not opposed to TUC policy and were also endorsed by either the GFTU or LRC. At a meeting in Caxton Hall, Westminster, in February 1905 the three committees signed a 'concordat' to the effect that the LRC would not oppose any 'Lib-Lab' candidates put up by the unions, and vice versa. In a very changeable climate of opinion this was a sensible and important compromise. The labour political bandwagon was beginning to roll. There was everything to be gained from a close co-operation between the national institutions of labour.[18]

The three bodies had conferred informally before 1905, not only on policy relating to Taff Vale but on such matters as establishing a labour newspaper,[19] and on their opposition to the Royal Commission on Trade Combinations and Trade Disputes, which was set up by Balfour in 1903 without a single trade union representative.[20]

Their co-operation was not always harmonious. Ramsay Mac-Donald as secretary of the LRC was adept at keeping its constituent parts from open rift, but he shared some of the general Independent Labour Party distrust of trade union politics.[21] The General Federation and the TUC meanwhile recognised that their functions overlapped[22] but found it difficult to provide a solution. Unions tended to approach both the Parliamentary Committee and the GFTU Management Committee for help in disputes and this quite often resulted in duplication.[23] Jealousies were easy to arouse. When Edmund Browne, permanent counsel to the TUC, invited both the GFTU and the LRC to help formulate a new trade disputes Bill in January 1904, the Parliamentary Committee declared that he was quite unauthorised and that the other two bodies should simply be invited to render assistance in passing the Bill which the Parliamentary Committee would prepare.[24] The GFTU Management Committee, watchful of its own dignity, passed a resolution that if the Parliamentary Committee drew up a circular on the proposed labour newspaper without consulting the joint subcommittee first it would be guilty of a 'breach of faith'.[25] It did not help matters that when colleagues on the same committee fell out, they preferred to do battle in one of the other two arenas. At Jarrow in 1902, for instance, a quarrel that apparently threatened to break up the LRC took place between Liberal supporters of Alexander Wilkie and ILP supporters of Pete Curran. Eventually Wilkie withdrew, leaving the labour parliamentary candidature to Curran.[26] No murmur of this quarrel disturbs the even tenor of the records of the GFTU, where the two men were well established and apparently amicable colleagues on the Management Committee. The LRC faced a similar problem at Stoke-on-Trent where John Ward, now staunchly anti-socialist despite a militant past, had been adopted as labour candidate. At the TUC in Leicester in 1903 Ward attacked Curran for his motion in favour of a separate Labour Party and Curran, replying to the debate, hit back:

> As for Mr Ward, he was a pathetic example of how politics could demoralise a man. His (Mr Curran's) views were conservative as compared with Mr Ward's a few years ago. But Mr Ward was now a candidate for Stoke, and the gentlemen who lived in Stoke would be delighted to observe the moderation of his views ... . Mr Ward would discover that when they went to their next National Conference [of the LRC] Mr Curran would be there![27]

Again, these bellicose feelings were kept well out of the proceedings of the GFTU Management Committee, which Ward had joined in 1901.

Despite such outbursts both TUC and GFTU recognised the need for joint action and in their respective committees' minutes took credit for summoning each other to conferences on particular issues. It was the Parliamentary Committee that took the initiative leading to the 'Caxton Hall concordat'.[28] The GFTU called together the Parliamentary Committee and Labour MPs (later complemented by the LRC) to discuss unemployment.[29] In the spirit of constructive optimism encouraged by these conferences, and encouraged most of all, no doubt, by the fact that a general election was within sight, the labour movement in 1905 hummed with co-operative activity.

The problem of unemployment had been kept on the agenda of labour politics in the earliest years of the century by the Social Democratic Federation and by demonstrations by the unemployed themselves, rather than by the constituent members of the Labour Representation Committee, from which the SDF seceded in 1901.[30] By mid-1904, however, Britain was in the middle of a serious trade depression and the terrible poverty caused by unemployment was once again a matter of urgent anxiety to everyone involved in the administration of the Poor Law. The president of the Local Government Board, Walter Long, was framing proposals for legislation by October 1904 and the trade union movement had to act decisively and in unison if its views were to be taken into account. At Leeds that September the Trades Union Congress had called for a separate department in the Board of Trade to co-ordinate the relief work of local authorities. The meetings of the three committees in November and December produced more comprehensive proposals which they printed in a joint report and then put personally to the Prime Minister in a deputation on 7 February 1905. They urged the regulation of industry to maintain work at a reasonably even level, especially in public and municipal employment, called for the nationalisation of land and for a programme of public works that could include afforestation schemes, and suggested that central authorities in every town, city or country area might be empowered to acquire land for co-operative cultivation. They pointed out that trade unionists were spending £600,000 a year on insurance against unemployment and claimed that it should be for the unions therefore to recommend appointments to the new central authorities. Balfour received the delegation courteously, praised the eloquence with which they had put their case, agreed that some permanent machinery was needed and rejected the rest.[31]

After the government had introduced its Unemployed Workmen Bill the three committees issued a joint statement (with the Labour MPs) opposing it because it only applied compulsorily in London and the other main conurbations and so would attract the unemployed from elsewhere into London, because it provided no funds from the Exchequer and, most damagingly, because it limited the rates of wages to be paid on relief works.[32] They put their views to the new president of the Local Government Board, the Prime Minister's brother, Gerald Balfour, who only promised to consider amending the Bill to include all large towns. Despite this disappointing response the Labour MPs felt able to support the Bill eventually for the good points that it did make public authorities responsible for providing work and that it abolished the disfranchisement of men who had received poor relief.[33] The Unemployed Workmen Act 1905, unsatisfactory and impermanent though it was, paved the way for the more enduring legislation later introduced by the Liberals.[34] It also had the incidental side-effect of securing a brief period of co-operation between the national organisations of labour.

The Hanley TUC in September 1905 approved a resolution on 'the consolidation of labour forces' which endorsed the previous February's Caxton Hall agreement but they threw out as 'hopelessly impracticable' and 'ten years too late' a resolution calling for an amalgamation of the TUC, GFTU and LRC. Each body, it was generally agreed, had its own separate function. The GFTU for its part had already recorded its firm intention to leave political matters to the other two bodies.[35] So the limits of co-operation, from the General Federation's point of view at least, were already clearly defined. This is not to say that politics did not form an important part of the Joint Board's activities; as the Caxton Hall agreement of February 1905 made clear, the elimination of overlapping in political activity was a primary objective. As far as the GFTU was concerned its participation in the Joint Board would provide an outlet for those political endeavours which could not be divorced from its industrial functions.

Representatives of the three committees of the TUC, GFTU and LRC formally constituted the Joint Board at a meeting at the Parliamentary Committee's offices on 29 November 1905.[36] D. C. Cummings, the boilermakers' secretary, became chairman and it was agreed that the secretaries of the three committees, W. C. Steadman, Ramsay MacDonald and Isaac Mitchell, should be secretaries of the board and would jointly sign all the literature that it put out. Isaac Mitchell was to do the work of convening meetings, preparing agendas and keeping minutes, and all correspondence was to be addressed to the board at the General Federation's offices in Temple Avenue. After these formalities the board considered two main items of business. The LRC was thinking of sending a delegation to the colonies 'with a view to solidifying the International Labour Movement', a reference to the importation of cheap Chinese labour into South Africa which had been agitating the labour world for some time. On this matter the unions left the LRC to take whatever action it saw fit. The GFTU representatives, Curran, Gee, Ward and Mitchell, then raised the question of the Royal Commission on the Poor Laws, which had been set up by Balfour's expiring government without a representative of organised labour. The meeting framed a protest to which all present attached their signatures, and left the General Federation with full powers to take any further action.

This was very shortly before the collapse of the Conservative government and Campbell-Bannerman's formation of a Liberal government in December, with a general election to be held in January. January 1906 was a time of triumph for labour politics. The return of twenty-nine LRC candidates to Parliament along with thirteen miners' representatives and twelve Lib-Lab MPs[37] gave the Labour Party, as the LRC now renamed itself, its breakthrough. With attention focused on Parliament and some real hopes of influencing social reforms, the Joint Board looked forward to an active year. As in 1905 in the days before its formal constitution, much of its business concerned unemployment. Ironically John Burns, who as President of the Local Government Board from December 1905 became the first working man to hold office in the Cabinet and who had actually been present at some of the Joint Board's earlier meetings,[38] soon revealed his extreme reluctance to reform the Unemployed Workmen Act. The Joint Board's role as a pressure group clearly would be as important under the Liberals as under the Conservatives.

The annual report of the GFTU for 1905–6 referred to the work of the Joint Board and then spelled out its own position on unemployment. From the various solutions to the problem offered by the board, Mitchell emphatically gave priority to a reduction in working hours. Although unemployment had fallen during 1905 in such trades as textiles and engineering, in building and the London printing trade it had continued to rise alarmingly; and throughout British industry those trade unions which arranged for unemployment insurance were paying out a crippling average of 35 shillings per year for each of their members. Skilled and semi-skilled men did not want work in other trades and scorned work on farm colonies or the artificial employment created by schemes of public works. As the Joint Board later expressed it, 'working hours and not number of employees should be the elastic part of the industrial machine'.[39]

The Joint Board kept the working of the Unemployed Workmen Act under review throughout the year. Both MacDonald and Steadman had been appointed members of the Central (Unemployed) Body for London, where most of the pioneering work in the field of unemployment relief at that time was going on.[40] In

October 1906 Mitchell was nominated by the London County Council to replace Steadman on the Central Body and took a seat on the employment exchanges committee under Beveridge's chairmanship.[41] The Joint Board was well placed, therefore, to know what was going on. Other concerns included the successful nomination of Francis Chandler, secretary of the Amalgamated Society of Carpenters and Joiners, as a member of the Royal Commission on the Poor Laws [42] and a deputation in August to the Prime Minister and the Postmaster-General, to complain about the reservation of civilian jobs, especially in the post office, for ex-soldiers and sailors.

The great success of 1906 was the passage of the Trade Disputes Act, piloted through long negotiations with the government by David Shackleton. After the Royal Commission on Trade Combinations and Trade Disputes reported in February 1906, it became clear that some Liberal lawyers including Asquith were inclined to go back on their party's pledge to pass a Bill along the lines of the old Trade Disputes Bill drawn up by the trade unionists.[43] The Parliamentary Committee acted quickly to get its own Bill substituted for the government one, drawing in the Joint Board later on. The Bill became the subject of protracted discussion at the board that October and a subcommittee was appointed under Shackleton to arrange the final passage of the Bill with Sir John Walton, for the government. The Trade Disputes Act as it finally passed into law embodied the all-important principle of trade unions' immunity from actions for damages and strengthened the safeguards for peaceful picketing and the conduct of strikes. After more than five years the crippling effects of the Taff Vale decision were finally removed. On the day before the Act received the Royal Assent the organisations represented by the Joint Board gave a complimentary banquet to David Shackleton at the House of Commons. It was an occasion, as Keir Hardie remarked, of 'wonderful harmony and unanimity'. Hardie, proposing the toast to Shackleton, went on to say that the trade union movement 'was an organisation for developing the natural born leaders of the working classes' and congratulated the British labour movement, in contrast to those on the Continent, on being led by working-class men.[44]

At the opening of Parliament in February 1907, for the second year in succession the King's Speech contained no reference to any amendment of the Unemployed Workmen Act. In the labour movement disquiet over its working during 1906 had turned gradually into a campaign of organised opposition. The Joint Board issued a circular to trade unions in May 1906 asking for details about the work of local distress committees under the Act and Mitchell later tabulated these for the use of the board. Except in London, where administration centred in the Central (Unemployed) Body, these committees were empowered to carry out all the provisions of the Unemployed Workmen Act including setting up labour exchanges, starting labour colonies and assisting emigration. What worried the board most of all was the potential use of labour exchanges to supply blackleg labour or to undercut union rates of pay. The trade unionists on the board also strongly objected to the fact that the Act catered equally for organised and unorganised workmen, and wanted to include in their report the objection that the Act 'seeks to organise workmen without cost to himself [*sic*] and without reliance upon association with those not of his class'.[45] In October 1906 the board circularised trade unions with a list of three essential conditions for supporting labour exchanges in their localities:

(1) that the exchanges must not give preference to non-union work-men nor supply workers during disputes or at non-union rates and conditions;
(2) that trade unions agreeing to register their unemployed at labour exchanges should be allowed to supply their own 'vacant books'; and
(3) that any existing system of unemployment registration in a particular trade should be continued by the labour exchanges.

The board asked unions to notify them of any action they took in connection with the circular.

Early in 1907 the GFTU and TUC rejected a proposal by the Social Democratic Federation for a demonstration on unemployment, but between March and May 1907 two subcommittees of the Joint Board drew up reports on the economic and political aspects of unemploy-ment, which Mitchell and MacDonald then used as a basis for drafting their own Bill.[46] In April Curran and Steadman formed a deputation to the Central (Unemployed) Body but failed to persuade them to accept union rates as the standard for payment of the unemployed working on its schemes, and in June MacDonald introduced the 'Right to Work Bill' as it became known, in the House of Commons. This called for the creation of a central unemployment committee including representatives of trade unions, with local unemployment authorities appointed by every county and county borough to carry out schemes of relief financed from both local and national funds. All the unemployed should be registered locally at ratepayers' expense and, most important of all, every unemployment authority must be obliged to provide work for the registered unemployed, or, failing that and very much as a last resort, they must provide maintenance. No provision of blackleg labour should be allowed. 'This clause is a Right to Work clause and not a Right to

Doles clause' wrote MacDonald in the pamphlet that publicised the Bill.[47] He did not succeed in getting it past a first reading, nor did the Liberal MP Philip Whitwell Wilson when he reintroduced it in 1908; but a sufficient number of Liberals supported the Bill to give the Cabinet food for thought.[48] Like the Trades Disputes Bill promoted by the national organisations of labour after Taff Vale, the Right to Work Bill did provide a basis for subsequent legislation by the Liberal government.

This was certainly the most constructive piece of work produced by the Joint Board in 1907, although it is worth noting that despite Mitchell's part in drafting both, the Bill differed in emphasis from the *Report on Unemployment* which the board published in the same month. In this report, addressed to trade unionists rather than to the public at large, the board concentrated on recommending what union strategy should be and insisted that the abolition of overtime and, where necessary, the adoption of short-time working held the answer to the problem of unemployment. There was nothing in this strategy inherently incompatible with the contents of the Right to Work Bill, but some differences of opinion lay behind it. The important feature of the Bill was its assertion of government responsibility for employment. Apart from providing that trade unionists must be represented in the administration of unemployment relief, it contained no recognition of the unions as agencies for the regulation of employment. The Parliamentary Committee and the GFTU naturally were concerned that government intervention should not undermine the unions' own arrangements for the welfare of their members. And behind this lay the deeper division between the sort of socialism which concentrated on increasing the responsibility of the state and that which sought first to secure the place of the working class within society.

Other business of the Joint Board in 1907 showed how the differences between its three constituent bodies could limit their co-operation. The questions of establishing offices in the same building had been discussed often before, both in committee and at conferences. Now a subcommittee set out to explore the possibility further but in April the Parliamentary Committee put a stop to this time-wasting by deciding against the whole idea, although it would have been prepared to countenance a scheme for some central building devoted to the general purposes of labour.[49] Another old chestnut was the plan for a labour newspaper. MacDonald, Arthur Henderson and C. W. Bowerman were asked to prepare a report which the Parliamentary Committee could consider before Congress debated the subject in September; but it was to be another five years before the establishment of the short-lived *Daily Citizen*. The Labour Party representatives on the board, meanwhile, had raised the question of overlapping between their work and that of the Parliamentary Committee. After some hesitation a subcommittee consisting of Gill, Hudson, Henderson, Curran, Ward and Wilkie was set up in May 1907 to consider the problem, but the Parliamentary Committee refused point-blank to delete from the TUC agenda any of the subjects that the Labour Party had asked them to delete.[50] In December a meeting between representatives of the Labour Party and Parliamentary Committee still could not agree on any measures to eliminate overlapping.[51]

It was only in February 1908 that the Joint Board acquired a formal constitution which defined its functions as being principally to decide on the bona fides of unions affiliated or wishing to affiliate to any of the three constituent bodies, and to use its influence to bring about the settlement of trade disputes. To these it added a clause permitting the discussion of any matter of joint concern that might be referred to it by one of the constituent bodies, and one authorising joint political action when agreed by all three bodies. In the spring of 1908 the board was much occupied with events on the north-east coast, where a protracted dispute over a reduction in pay had culminated in a lockout and the employers had rejected the unions' demand for arbitration. After the question had been considered at ten separate meetings of the Joint Board, which negotiated with the employers through the Board of Trade, a ballot of the unions arranged by the Joint Board resulted in a small majority in favour of accepting the employers' terms. The men returned to work at a reduction of 1s 6d per week, their only gain being the promise of a conference with the employers with a view to setting up permanent machinery for the settlement of future disputes. A hangover from this dispute, the refusal of between 5,000 and 6,000 engineers to return to work, was left for the GFTU to settle.[52] Apart from the north-east shipbuilding workers, a trickle of less urgent business occupied the Joint Board at its statutory quarterly meetings until in December 1908 it was called upon to help the Amalgamated Society of Railway Servants raise funds to take the Osborne case to the House of Lords. It would be a full year before the Lords upheld the injunction awarded to Osborne against his union's spending its funds for political purposes, and so created a crisis in trade union law second in its importance only to the Taff Vale decision.

Meanwhile the problem of unemployment continued to demand attention. The Right to Work Bill, twice defeated, needed some redrafting if it was to stand a better chance in future, but the labour MPs were determined to press it and Shackleton as chairman of the Joint Board called a full meeting in December 1908 to consider the amended version. There were signs of movement now from within the Cabinet. Winston Churchill, appointed president of the Board of Trade in the previous March when Asquith became Prime Minister, was considering social reforms which John Burns at the Local Government Board had refused to consider until the Royal Commission on the Poor Laws reported. Furthermore, that commission was about to produce its reports at last. It was clear that some reforming legislation would be introduced in the next session of Parliament.[53] The GFTU had already presented a report on unemployment to the Joint Board[54] in which it retained the old call for the abolition of overtime but went on to propose in addition a programme more comprehensive than anything previously put forward by the national organisations of labour. It outlined a scheme of public works including land reclamation and afforestation, cooperative farming, the provision of improved and more sanitary housing for working people and the nationalisation of all canal and railway systems.[55] In addition to these measures, there should be a ministry of labour presided over by a Cabinet minister, with a permanent 'unemployed board' representing in equal measure both national and local government and the Joint Board. Beneath this body would be local unemployment boards.

Interesting though these proposals were, events were overtaking them. Although they were considered at the Joint Board, Keir Hardie was already urging the principles of the amended Right to Work Bill in the House of Commons,[56] and meanwhile the real initiative lay with the government, whose Labour Exchanges Bill constituted the first part of a new programme of social reform that would be put through during the next three years by Lloyd George and Churchill. This Bill together with the government's proposals for unemployment insurance precipitated a crisis in the Joint Board. Its members probably all recognised the wisdom of co-operating with the government's legislative proposals since they were almost certain to be passed, and of attempting to ensure that these took account of the views of labour. Nevertheless it was a shock to find that the Parliamentary Committee had been acting alone in these matters without reporting back to the Joint Board until they were challenged,[57] even though their meetings with Churchill had helped to produce some useful amendments to the Labour Exchanges Bill.[58] In contrast to the Parliamentary Committee, the Labour Party took care to keep the Joint Board informed of its activities, and in August 1909 MacDonald submitted to it his memorandum on the minority report of the Royal Commission on the Poor Laws, which Shackleton subsequently presented in the board's name to the Prime Minister.[59] It was all the more outraged therefore to find in October that Labour

MPs were expected to support the Unemployment Insurance Bill, on which again the Parliamentary Committee had been acting alone. Shackleton, who presided over the Joint Board in his capacity as president of the Parliamentary Committee, insisted that he had no authority to place any information before the board. This provoked his fellow MP, Hardie, to point out the 'possibility of misunderstanding and friction which might arise if any section of the Joint Board arrogated to itself the exclusive right to present matters to Parliament without consultation with the other bodies represented'.[60] The problem was discussed again inconclusively a month later but, as Shackleton pointed out, about three-quarters of the Parliamentary Committee's work involved some kind of parliamentary action and when it had a clear mandate from Congress, as in the case of unemployment insurance, it could not be expected to act in the first instance through the Joint Board. On this occasion Pete Curran closed an acrimonious meeting by moving to refer the whole question to the subcommittee which had been set up to investigate overlapping between the TUC, GFTU and Labour Party. Tempers might rise but the need for unity remained as clear as ever. Funds for the Liberal government's own proposals were contingent on Lloyd George's budget which the House of Lords had refused to pass. In December 1909, moreover, the Lords upheld the Osborne judgement, thus removing the trade unions' right to support the Labour Party and Labour parliamentary candidates financially. In the constitutional crisis of that winter, with a general election planned for January 1910, there could be no doubt about the need for concerted action by the national organisations of labour.

On the last day of 1909 the Joint Board met to plan a strategy to deal with the Osborne judgement. It called for legislation to alter the definition of a trade union so that unions might legally pursue political activities, and decided to issue a circular to all local labour organisations summarising these political activities and suggesting a list of questions to be put to all candidates at the general election. Finally the board laid plans for a special conference to be held in Newport, Monmouthshire, in February 1910. All organisations entitled to be affiliated to any of the constituent bodies of the Joint Board would be invited.

The Osborne judgement divided opinion in the trade union world, where there were still many voices in favour of the unions' keeping their political neutrality.[61] The Newport conference agreed to uphold the right of unions to engage in politics 'provided that their members agree', and the Joint Board prepared a Bill to restore the pre-Osborne position. The government however, refused to grant time for this to be debated and meanwhile injunctions on the pattern of Osborne's were being taken out against unions all over the country, in particular against the miners. At the GFTU annual general council meeting in July, Allen Gee as chairman deprecated a motion to enable the federation to undertake legal action to determine the rights of trade unions, on the grounds that the TUC already fulfilled this function. Shackleton pointed out that 'until the day comes when you represent all the Trade Unionists of the country', they could not properly undertake at federation expense actions bearing on the rights of all trade unions. His moderation had less influence at the TUC in September, however, when the miners carried a strongly worded resolution in favour of the pre-Osborne position.[62] The controversy ended only with the passage of the Trade Union Act 1913 whereby any union wanting to engage in political activity had to secure the consent of a majority of its members by ballot, and once this consent had been obtained an individual who did not want his contributions to be applied to the union's political fund would have to 'contract out' by a recognised procedure.[63]

The General Federation had been a relatively docile partner in the Joint Board during these upheavals. Its secretary remained responsible for managing all of the board's business and information-gathering, however, and while the Parliamentary Committee and the Labour Party squared up to each other at meetings of the board the GFTU, whose commitment to its success was probably the greatest, continued to present proposals for joint policies. In both 1908 and 1909 the annual general council meeting considered reports on unemployment policy which were subsequently put before the Joint Board; and each successive annual report of the federation contained a rosy-hued account of the board's work, although this attitude was not always allowed to pass unchallenged by members of the general council.[64] Relations on the Joint Board were complicated by the fact that most of the men on it were deeply involved in the affairs of more than one of its constituent bodies. Both David Shackleton and Arthur Henderson were Labour MPs and had been for some time leading figures at the annual meetings of the GFTU and TUC when Henderson on behalf of the Labour Party challenged Shackleton as president of the Parliamentary Committee to account for not having consulted the Joint Board in its negotiations with the government on un-employment policy. The leaders of the General Federation were as much bound up in the web of labour politics as those of the TUC, and the GFTU reports illustrate well how intricate the pattern of that web could be.

The federation's quarterly report for December 1904 published three articles on labour representation contributed respectively by Pete Curran, by J. H. Thomas, the future Cabinet minister, then president of the Amalgamated Society of Railway Servants, and by Isaac Mitchell. Curran, who played a particularly prominent part in forming the Labour Representation Committee and steering it towards independence, described how it was then sandwiched between those who thought its policies too socialist (which he defined as meaning class-conscious) and those who thought it not socialist enough. Given the historic importance of trade unionism in British working-class politics, an importance built up long before the principles of socialism took hold, it could not be expected that all trade unionists 'will at one gulp swallow the entire principle of working-class socialism'. He regarded it therefore as an important first step to have won the great majority of trade unions over to the principle of labour's political independence. Although, as a result of these tactics, not all parliamentary representatives of labour would necessarily be socialist, Curran believed that they would all work in the direction of collectivism. He listed the problems that had to be tackled: land ownership; displacement of artisans by new technology; the mining royalties system; the need to nationalise the railways; the need to reduce hours of labour in the country's staple industries in order to increase employment; housing; and above all the urgent necessity to use public funds to provide useful employment. On all of these questions, he claimed, the labour movement was united. Merely palliative though reforms in these areas would be, they would all lead towards 'our ultimate goal, namely, the inauguration of the cooperative commonwealth'. He pleaded for an end to 'sectional jealousy and personal hatred', 'hairsplitting discussions on the definition of the Marxian theory of surplus value, or as to what constitutes the class war' and concluded with Walter Crane's motto, 'The unity of labour is the hope of the world'.

J. H. Thomas's article consisted of a detailed consideration of the LRC's constitution, which it now required that all Labour parliamentary candidates should sign. He dismissed with contempt the idea that only trade unionists should be allowed to belong to the LRC. On the contentious issue of how Labour policy should be formed, he advocated his union's proposal that the executive committee of the LRC and the Labour MPs should form policy jointly, a procedure which he felt would best help to consolidate the forces of labour.

Isaac Mitchell, as we have seen,[65] was a strong believer in industrial organisation as the model and basis of all activity on behalf of labour. In his article he argued that labour's political and economic organisations should be parallel. Reform of trade union law, unemployment, old age pensions, housing reform, factory legislation – these were great issues for working people, but of what direct interest were they to the doctors, journalists, and so on, who led the socialist movement in Britain and abroad? Working people never chose doctors or journalists to lead their trade unions. There was no place for such dilettanti in the labour movement (an opinion which might have puzzled his friends the Webbs if they knew of it). Mitchell's conclusion, in terms of the forthcoming debates at the annual meeting of the LRC, was that all question of a common programme should be rejected. The LRC was a loose federation for the tactical purpose of getting labour men into Parliament, it had no common basic principles and if it were to publish a programme it would be in serious danger of overlapping with the TUC. Here most clearly laid out was the bedevilling paradox of British labour politics in this era: socialists believed in the class war and worked for the ascendancy of the proletariat; but many of those very working-class leaders whose careers exemplified 'class struggle' rejected socialist leadership because it was not proletarian enough, and embraced instead a political pragmatism that led them towards less radical policies.

Mitchell's anti-socialism got him into real trouble with the LRC and made him privately unpopular with Curran.[66] In 1903 he had to be threatened with expulsion from the LRC and with a complaint to his union, the ASE, before he would sign the LRC constitution which committed it to separate labour representation. He actually offered his resignation as labour parliamentary candidate at Darlington, because the local LRC did not like the idea of an electoral pact with the Liberals which, however, they finally accepted. The records of the Labour Party contain a strongly worded correspondence between Ramsay MacDonald and Pete Curran in which MacDonald referred to Mitchell's 'blind and bigoted antagonism' and 'efforts to damage the movement', and Curran agreed that Mitchell's article in the GFTU quarterly report was 'a spiteful attack on the whole movement'.[67] Another powerful foe of Mitchell was George Lansbury, who credited him with an unhealthy political influence over Beatrice Webb.[68]

In common with several other members of the GFTU Management Committee, however, both Curran and Mitchell fought in the general elections of 1906 as labour candidates. Both successful and unsuccessful candidates published accounts of their battles in the federation's quarterly report for December 1905 (which appeared in February 1906). John Ward and Alexander Wilkie, both anti-socialists, fought and won respectively at Stoke-on-Trent and Dundee. Ward had refused to sign the constitution of the LRC after failing to get his own National Democratic League allowed to affiliate to it, and fought Stoke as a labour candidate without LRC backing but endorsed by the TUC Parliamentary Committee. He considered himself the candidate of all the 'Progressive' forces in the town.

Wilkie, who with W. J. Davis was a leader of anti-socialist opinion within the LRC, won one of Dundee's two seats in a five-cornered contest and became Scotland's first Labour MP. At East Leeds the socialist James O'Grady had a straight fight against the Conservatives, under the terms of a secret pact made between Ramsay MacDonald for LRC and Herbert Gladstone for the Liberals. O'Grady gave thanks for his victory in uplifting terms: he never forgot, he wrote, 'to appeal to that divine sentiment woven in the warp and woof of human nature, and the response came . . . attuned to the nobler and holier side of our movement that aims at the complete industrial and social freedom of the common people'. His fellow socialist T. F. Richards of the National Union of Boot and Shoe Operatives who, however, had declined to draw on the support of his local Independent Labour Party, attributed his own victory at West Wolverhampton to 'sheer hard work'. He too had a straight fight, in his case against a supporter of Joseph Chamberlain and tariff reform.

The reports of Pete Curran and Isaac Mitchell were more subdued. Both had missed victory by a narrow margin. At Jarrow the 84-year-old Sir Charles Palmer fought again rather than resign his seat as he had intended, because of the socialist threat posed by Curran. In the event, Curran got his chance before long, and won Jarrow in a famous victory the following year, after Palmer's death. He was not destined to enjoy this success for long, for at the general election in January 1910, suffering from a painful illness, he was defeated by his former opponent's son and on 14 February 1910 he died after a serious operation. He was a sad loss to the labour movement. For the General Federation of Trades Unions in particular, Curran's loss left an unfillable gap. He had worked very hard on the federation's behalf; his strong personality combined with his high standing in the labour movement as a whole gave his chairmanship an unchallenged authority; and, very importantly, his commitment to a constructive form of socialism had helped to balance the General Federation on the tightrope of labour politics.

Isaac Mitchell's candidature at Darlington in 1906 was his first and last attempt to enter parliamentary politics. He had a straight fight against the sitting Unionist MP, Pike Pease, whose father had held the seat as a Liberal Unionist from 1895 to 1900 and whose family name carried great weight in Darlington. Mitchell's strategy after he became Labour candidate for the constituency in 1903 was to build up a strong LRC organisation and from that base to co-operate with the Liberals during the election. He firmly asserted the independence of labour but the local Liberals' support, which included hailing him as 'virtually a Liberal' because of his record with the Progressives on the London County Council, caused him some embarrassment. No doubt it did not help his reputation with the national leaders of the LRC.[69]

Darlington at that time was one of England's cleaner and more prosperous industrial towns, not a leading centre of trade union organisation, and the election campaign focused more than in many Labour battles in the country on issues that were traditionally Liberal and nonconformist. Mitchell was attacked as a 'paid adventurer' intruding from outside. His support for secular education was used to suggest that he was dangerously irreligious, and was linked with the sinister significance of his home address in Voltaire Road, Clapham, in south London. Religious education, temperance, free trade, and home rule for Ireland were the important questions for Darlington's electors, along with the controversy that was then raging over the importation of cheap Chinese labour into South Africa. The campaign was very fiercely fought. Both sides used motor cars on polling day for the first time in a Darlington election, Mitchell's carrying himself, his wife and that great representative of labour in the town, Arthur Henderson, who had just been re-elected MP for Barnard Castle. A local firm sold 'buttonhole medallions' with a photograph of Mitchell printed on them – another new departure – and all three of Darlington's large assembly halls were packed at nightly meetings. Three of these on one night were addressed on Mitchell's behalf by no less a personage than Lloyd George, then president of the Darlington Liberal Association, and the crowds belted out, to the tune of 'Marching through Georgia':

> The Land, the Land, the ground on which we stand,
> Why should we be beggars with the ballot in our hand,
> God made the land for the people.

Pike Pease won the poll by 4,375 votes to 4,087 and the next morning crowds of supporters saw Mitchell off on the train for London. In March he returned with his wife and little daughter Nancy to receive the thanks and lavish gifts of his supporters at a tea party for some 600 or 700 people, entertained with song and by a local humorist. Arthur Henderson made the presentation, to which Mitchell replied with some emotion. The report of these proceedings carried an unmistakable note of valediction. It rather seemed that Mitchell's heart had gone out of the political fight after one engagement.[70]

Despite their general secretary's withdrawal from politics, other members of the Management Committee of the General Federation of course remained deeply involved in parliamentary affairs. In their capacity as federation officials the chief outlet for political policy-making was the Joint Board, but MPs on the Management Committee made sure that the federation membership kept abreast of events in Parliament through the quarterly and annual reports[71] and in December 1909 the GFTU issued its own manifesto on behalf of Labour candidates in the forthcoming general election.[72] This opened by condemning the House of Lords' challenge to the established constitutional practice of 200 years. It pointed to the Trade Disputes Act, to amendments to the Workmen's Compensation Act, Factory and Workshop Act, Provision of Meals Act, Labour Exchanges Act, Trade Boards Act and to the Unemployed Workmen Act as examples of the Labour MPs' proven parliamentary skill. Labour MPs had striven also to place the burden of taxation where it ought to be. Their practical experience of life taught them what taxes on food and commodities meant to labourers, artisans and clerks 'struggling to keep up that respectable appearance which is their stock-in-trade'. Furthermore, the GFTU manifesto went on, Labour MPs had demonstrated their concern with the wider issues of colonial policy and peace. They now looked forward to working for further social reforms, for the just and humane administration of the colonies and for the maintenance of international peace.

The Management Committee of the General Federation of Trade Unions presses upon all who live by labour to sink all minor differences in one great effort to ensure that those who in the past four years have accomplished so much shall again be sent back to Westminster accompanied by new colleagues and rejoicing in the renewed confidence of their class.

International Trade Unionism

One further responsibility of the GFTU in its first decade must be considered here. That is its role as the representative of British labour in the international trade union movement. The TUC, after a distasteful experience of international relationships at the International Labour Conference in London in 1896, took very little official interest in foreign trade unionism (except for maintaining friendly relations with the American Federation of Labor) for more than fifteen years afterwards. It left the foreign affairs of the British trade union movement quite explicitly to the General Federation, which did not hesitate to take them in hand.[73] When Jensen, president of the Danish federation of trade unions, addressed the GFTU's annual general council meeting in 1900, he conferred with Isaac Mitchell about the need to form an association of national trade union centres, and as a result Denmark played host to an international conference of labour in 1901.[74] Another conference in Stuttgart in 1902 was followed in 1903 by one in Dublin, arranged by the GFTU to take place immediately after its own annual general council meeting in the same city.[75] Here, delegates from Britain, Austria, Italy, Denmark, Holland, France, Germany and Norway agreed to send annual reports on trade unionism in their countries to an 'international secretary of the national centres of trade unions' and to make contributions to costs at an agreed rate.[76] In the case of large-scale strikes and lockouts they would submit requests for help through the international secretary, Carl Legien of Germany. He would circulate the appeal and each national centre would forward funds directly to the national centre that had asked for them. This Dublin conference ended inauspiciously. The continental delegates had been deeply offended by the standard of accommodation and hospitality provided for them by the GFTU, and presented a formal list of complaints to Isaac Mitchell, in which they began with the fact that they had been made to sleep four to a room in dirty lodgings where 'every stick of furniture was broken', and proceeded to complain of the lack of guides and translators, unsystematic arrangements for the conference sessions and the inordinate length of the British speeches.

> All those things have created in our minds the impression that the British organisation's delegates were not particularly pleased at having foreign trade union representatives present among them. . . . . [We] will not again trouble our British fellow-workers more than is absolutely necessary.[77]

Although they may have fallen short of continental standards of hospitality, the members of the Management Committee of the GFTU were probably quite as committed to the principle of internationalism as their comrades in most other countries. This is not to credit them with any great degree of commitment, for international co-operation between trade unions was still in its infancy. The three conferences of 1901, 1902 and 1903, however, proved to have laid the foundations for permanent international links where earlier attempts had failed. The next conference, held in Amsterdam in 1905, was depleted by the absence of the French who had wanted to place discussions of anti-militarism and direct action through general strike on the agenda. Against the votes of Holland, Belgium and Austria, the delegates excluded consideration of such theoretical questions from that conference and any subsequent ones.[78] This decision was reiterated at the Christiania (Oslo) conference in 1907 but despite the French and Dutch threat then to found a rival international centre, Paris played host to a reasonably successful conference in 1909 when for the first time the American Federation of Labor was represented, in the formidable person of Samuel Gompers. None of these conferences passed any very notable resolutions and the record of their discussions is extremely slender. But the International Secretariat of National Trade Union Centres (which changed its name to International Federation of Trade Unions in 1913, at the Americans' behest) laid the basis for a valuable network of international contacts. After the upheavals of 1914–18 its re-formation along prewar lines proved that it had had some worth.

The firm and energetic guidance of Carl Legien as international secretary was chiefly responsible for building up the international secretariat into a workable institution. He bullied the affiliated national centres of trade unions into providing the statistics and other information that made up the annual international reports, which nevertheless usually appeared about two years out of date. German and Austrian trade unionism held a middle ground between the syndicalists led by France, who wanted trade unionism to spearhead an attack on all the institutions of 'bourgeois' government, and the very much more cautious consensus of trade unionists in America and in Britain which, in its international aspect at this period and represented as it was by the avowedly non-political GFTU, confined the role of trade unions to the industrial sphere.[79] In Germany and the Austro-Hungarian empire a system of strong trade unions had grown up, resembling the British craft unions in that they gave large benefits, but strengthened by the fact that they usually covered whole industries, unlike the multitude of highly specialised unions to which Britain's earlier industrialisation had given rise. Not only did this place Legien as secretary of the German General Commission of Trade Unions in a good position to mediate, but industrial circumstances in Germany gave him a claim to be especially interested in the international ramifications of labour. The German empire acted like a magnet for workers from other parts of Europe, and German trade unions had been obliged to devise systems for dealing with both organised and unorganised working men from abroad.

Only in Britain among the European nations were there as many members of trade unions as in Germany[80] and even though emigration and immigration both played an important part in the national employment scene, British unions could still justly be reproached, as they were at Christiania in 1907, with far greater insularity than the German unions displayed.[81] This criticism was strengthened by the fact that in Britain the GFTU represented only between a fifth and a quarter of all trade union members whereas by 1905 the vast majority of German trade unionists were affiliated to the Generalkommission.[82] Of the twenty-seven international labour federations and secretariats for particular industries that existed by 1914, almost all were based in Germany, although the international federations of miners and textile workers both had their headquarters in London.[83] The predominance of Germany in international trade unionism was emphasised by its immensely superior contributions to the appeals of workers in other countries. In this league table Britain trailed badly, very much to the chagrin of the General Federation. According to the international report for 1905, for example, Britain came behind Austria, Hungary, Denmark, Sweden and Norway in contributions for the German miners. For the locked-out Swedish metal workers only Holland and Switzerland gave less than Britain. Appleton was particularly mortified by the poor British support for the Swedish general strike in 1909, and estimated that for every shilling contributed by British workers the Germans had given £33 10s.[84]

The General Federation discharged its international duties faithfully in spite of these limitations. It always sent two delegates to the biennial conference[85] and published the international reports in full in its own annual reports. It also fostered interest in the trade union movement abroad by publishing articles by foreign trade unionists and others.[86] In addition to the visit by Jensen in 1900, Legien addressed the federation's annual general council meeting in 1903, and Samuel Gompers addressed it in 1909.[87] Gompers became a firm friend and admirer both of the GFTU and of Appleton, whom he regarded as a 'safe' trade unionist in a world threatened by socialism.[88] Other personal contacts between GFTU and foreign officials included occasional fact-finding visits, as, for instance, when a group of French trade unionists came to investigate conditions of municipal employment in Britain under the General Federation's auspices.[89] The international policy of pressuring governments to prohibit the importation and exportation of blacklegs was duly placed before the Joint Board, reinforced by a plea from the National Council of General Labourers, a reminder that although the GFTU might be less representative than the Generalkommission of its country's trade unionism, it was not without a voice in national affairs.[90]

The first decade of the General Federation's existence had established it as a leading presence in the trade union world both at home and internationally. It had proved itself as an influence for unity between trade unions. Its commitment to conciliation had helped to settle many disputes between unions and employers. This aspect of its work, as the Management Committee often complained, was doomed not to be recognised as it deserved, since it was usually important to the success of any efforts at conciliation that the unions' own officials should be allowed to take public credit for the outcome.[91] Its function as an insurance against the crippling financial costs of strikes had proved worthwhile, as the frequent and time-consuming appeals against the Management Committee's decisions on paying benefits showed.[92] Its published quarterly and annual reports provided a useful vehicle for information of interest to the labour world. But it had not become the great central authority for British trade unions that its founders had hoped. It was becoming clear that further affiliations by the larger trade unions were unlikely, and that the General Federation could not expect much more financial support from its existing membership than the inadequate level of contributions with which it had managed so far. While its emphasis on purely industrial questions enabled it to stand a little apart from damaging frictions between the Labour Party and TUC Parliamentary Committee, the establishment of Labour as a permanent force in national politics also had the effect of enhancing the influence of the Parliamentary Committee. Thus the TUC in 1910 was a very much more important institution than it had been during the doldrums of the 1890s when it had seemed rather as though the best it could do was to hive off the vital functions of labour organisation in order to protect them from its own dissensions. It remained *the* trade union forum, the only form of authority that most unions were likely to accept.

The GFTU, with less than a quarter of the TUC's membership and hampered by the discipline involved in reporting disputes and by the financial obligations it imposed, could not really contest the TUC's leadership. Furthermore, events in the law courts and in Parliament in the latter years of the decade placed the federation in a vulnerable position, not only by increasing the power and influence of the TUC but by making industrial affairs ever more prominent in the political arena. The right to picket, protection for union funds, workmen's compensation, labour exchanges and unemployment insurance were all the legitimate concern of the General Federation of Trade Unions, for they affected the industrial and financial transactions, however narrowly defined, of its affiliated unions. It was no longer possible, if it ever had been, to draw a dividing line between the political and industrial affairs of the labour movement. From this position of incipient weakness the GFTU in its second decade faced the challenging opportunities presented first of all by the government's national insurance legislation and then by the demands of national unity in wartime. Simultaneously it had to deal with the very different challenges of an outburst of industrial militancy that was more sustained and had a greater impact than any since the birth of the 'new' unions in 1888–90. Once again labour leaders and rank and file alike were to pose the questions: what did 'closer unity' in the trade union movement really mean, what should it mean, and what was federation all about?

Notes: Chapter 3

1   *The Times*, 20 December 1901, p. 9, cols *c* and *d*, letter signed by the full GFTU Management Committee.
2   GFTU, *Quarterly Report*, December 1901.
3   *La Crise du Trade-Unionisme* (Paris: Bibliothèque du Musée Social, 1903), *passim*, esp. p. 177. Mantoux's and Alfassa's investigation was prompted by Pratt's articles in *The Times* and they devoted much of their book to considering his charges in detail.
4   GFTU, *Quarterly Report*, September 1901, records that the ASRS annual conference decided to affiliate, but their executive never acted on the decision. The GFTU was offered no explanation and there is no allusion to it in *Railway Review*, the ASRS newspaper.
5   GFTU, *Quarterly Report*, March 1902; *Annual Report*, 1902.
6   *Quarterly Report*, September 1901. Edwards advised that small unions were the most vulnerable of all because it would be easier to prove that a particular officer acted on the authority of a union as a whole. Federations were less vulnerable than any individual union, but should guard against involvement in sympathetic strikes, and against issuing potentially libellous circulars.
7   Bealey and Pelling, *Labour and Politics*, p. 91. The National Amalgamated Labourers' Union based in Swansea is not to be confused with J. N. Bell's National Amalgamated Union of Labour, based on Tyneside.
8   Quoted in Bealey and Pelling, *Labour and Politics*, p. 91.
9   GFTU, *Quarterly Report*, December 1902; TUC Parliamentary Committee minutes, 18 December [November?] 1902.
10   GFTU, *Quarterly Report*, December 1902.
11   The remainder of this paragraph follows the account given in Clegg, Fox and Thompson, *History of British Trade Unions*, p. 322.
12   GFTU, *Proceedings and Reports*, 1903–4, report of 1903 agcm.
13   Barnes himself held no brief for the TUC, since his own union was not affiliated to it. He criticised them sharply in early 1902 for their failure to act quickly over Taff Vale (ASE, *Monthly Journal*, March 1902).
14   GFTU, *Annual Report*, 1904, pp. 6–7.
15   GFTU, *Proceedings and Reports*, 1903–4, report of agcm; *Annual Report*, 1904.
16   Webb, *History of Trade Unionism*, p. 604.
17   As may be seen from the debate at the 1903 agcm.
18   For a detailed analysis of the 'Caxton Hall concordat' see Bealey and Pelling, *Labour and Politics*, especially pp. 209–10, 263. An important influence for closer unity was the *Labour Leader* (especially an article of 16 September 1904).
19   GFTU, *Annual Report*, 1904, p. 10; TUC Parliamentary Committee minutes, 10 and 11 November 1903; 20 January and 3 February 1904, and *passim*.
19   GFTU, *Proceedings and Reports*, 1903–4, report of 1903 agcm.

21 David Marquand, *Ramsay MacDonald* (London: Cape, 1977), pp. 71–2; Bealey and Pelling, *Labour and Politics, passim*.

22 GFTU, *Proceedings and Reports*, 1902–3, report of 1902 agcm, speech by Hodson as fraternal delegate from the TUC.

23 For example, both bodies were involved in the Penrhyn Quarrymen's dispute (see TUC Parliamentary Committee minutes, 10 October 1902) and the Parliamentary Committee minutes frequently record cases of arbitration between unions, with the unions concerned generally being expected to meet the expenses. Standing order 20, which empowered the Parliamentary Committee to intervene in disputes involving blacklegging, is considered briefly in Roberts, *The TUC*, pp. 228–9.

24 TUC Parliamentary Committee minutes, 20 January 1904.

25 ibid., 3 February 1904.

26 Bealey and Pelling, *Labour and Politics*, p. 137.

27 TUC *Report*, 1903, p. 65.

28 TUC Parliamentary Committee minutes, 16 February 1905.

29 ibid., 16 November 1904, 18 January and 21 June 1905; GFTU, *Quarterly Report*, December 1904.

30 For the political divisions within the labour movement in the context of unemployment, see especially Kenneth D. Brown, *Labour and Unemployment 1900–1914* (Newton Abbot: David & Charles, 1971). The history of unemployment relief from 1886 is given in José Harris, *Unemployment and Politics. A Study in English Social Policy 1886–1914* (Oxford: Clarendon Press, 1972).

31 GFTU, *Quarterly Report*, December 1904; *Proceedings and Reports*, 1904–5, special report dated 28 December 1904; report of deputation of 7 February 1905; TUC Parliamentary Committee minutes, 16 November 1904, 18 January 1905.

32 Standard hourly rates were to be paid to the unemployed who were given work in public schemes, but they would work less than a full day, as a disincentive to deliberate unemployment.

33 GFTU, *Proceedings and Reports*, 1904–5, 'Minutes of Conference held at the London Society of Compositors, May 19th 1905, on the unemployed Question'; report of deputation to Mr Balfour, 25 May 1905; TUC *Report*, 1905, pp. 65–6; *Hansard* (20 June 1905), cols 1170–4, 1175–80.

34 While it might seem more accurate to say that the majority and minority reports of the Royal Commission on the Poor Laws (1909) did this, the 1905 Act facilitated practical experience of different forms of unemployment relief under government regulation.

35 GFTU, *Annual Report*, 1905.

36 Minutes of the Joint Board were printed and copies usually bound with the GFTU *Proceedings and Reports.*

37 This analysis is the one given in the GFTU's *Quarterly Report*, March 1906. The results in constituencies contested by working men are tabulated in Bealey and Pelling, *Labour and Politics*, pp. 291–2.

38 GFTU, *Proceedings and Reports*, 1904–5, minutes of conference of 19 May 1905; TUC Parliamentary Committee minutes, 21 June 1905.

39 Joint Board, *Report on Unemployment*, 4 June 1907.

40 Harris, *Unemployment and Politics*, p. 169.

41 BLPES, Beveridge Collection, Coll. B. xi, CUB minutes for 23 November 1905–16 November 1906, pp. 327, 342.

42 TUC Parliamentary Committee minutes, 20 December 1905; 15 February 1906. Despite having delegated a watching brief on the commission to the GFTU, the Parliamentary Committee seems to have acted on its own in this.

43 Campbell-Bannerman had agreed to this before the election and about 60 per cent of Liberal candidates gave pledges, although not all specifically in favour of the

original Trade Disputes Bill. For a more detailed summary of its passage, see Clegg, Fox and Thompson, *History of British Trade Unions*, pp. 393–5.

44   Banquet of 19 December 1906 reported in GFTU, *Quarterly Report*, December 1906. Strictly, the banquet was given by the Parliamentary Committee, GFTU and Labour MPs, and not by the Joint Board as such.

45   A typescript draft report with amendments is included with the Joint Board minutes for July 1906. The sentence quoted could not be agreed upon, and reading between the lines we can assume that objections were raised by Labour Party members.

46   Accounts of the events surrounding the 'Right to Work Bill' are given in K. Brown, *Labour and Unemployment*, pp. 68–84 and in Harris, *Unemployment and Politics*, pp. 241–4.

47   *The New Unemployed Bill of the Labour Party*, 1907. MacDonald's own copy is in the MacDonald papers, PRO, PRO 30/69/1027.

48   Harris, *Unemployment and Politics*, pp. 244–5.

49   TUC Parliamentary Committee minutes, 18 April 1907.

50   ibid., 16 May 1907.

51   ibid., 19 December 1907.

52   Joint Board minutes, 29 April–29 July 1908; GFTU Management Committee minutes, 30 July and 27 August 1908.

53   See Harris, *Unemployment and Politics*, esp. pp. 264–72.

54   Joint Board minutes, 4 November 1908.

55   W. A. Appleton had been associated with reforms of this type when president of Nottingham Trades Council (Cuthbert, *The Lace Makers' Society*, p. 74), and the detail and comprehensiveness of the programme suggested by the GFTU should almost certainly be attributed to him.

56   For example, *Hansard*, (17 February 1909), cols 179–86.

57   TUC Parliamentary Committee minutes, 11 July 1909.

58   Churchill inserted a clause at the committee stage which provided that no registered unemployed workman should be penalised for refusing a vacancy that was caused by a dispute or for turning down work at less than recognised rates. He also agreed that unions should be permitted to display notices of recognised rates and to publicise disputes at labour exchanges. See Harris, *Unemployment and Politics*, pp. 290–2.

59   Joint Board minutes, 18 and 26 August; 4 November 1909.

60   Joint Board minutes, 6 October 1909.

61   The controversy is considered in Clegg, Fox and Thompson, *History of British Trade Unions*, pp. 413–20.

62   The issue was the degree of militancy with which to pursue a change in the law, rather than whether the law should be amended or not.

63   See R. Y. Hedges and A. Winterbottom, *Legal History of Trade Unionism* (London: Longman, 1930), *passim* and esp. pp. 98–107. The Trade Disputes and Trade Unions Act 1927 undid much of the work of the 1913 Act by replacing the requirement to 'contract out' by one to 'contract in'.

64   For example, at the 1909 agcm where Anderson of the stevedores' union objected to the joint policy on labour exchanges which he thought threatened casual labour in particular, and where two members of unions affiliated to the London Trades Council challenged the board's right to adjudicate the bona fides of trade unions.

65   Above, pp. 45–7.

66   On this, see Bill Purdue, 'Isaac Mitchell and the "Progressive" Alliance', in North East Group for the Study of Labour History, *Bulletin*, no. 11 (1977), pp. 1–12. Purdue incorrectly calls Mitchell 'president' of the GFTU and exaggerates his public alienation from the LRC. But the article sheds much light on Mitchell's relations with the labour movement, seen from the LRC perspective.

67 Letters of January 1905, quoted ibid.
68 See above, pp. 88–9.
69 See for example *Mr J. B. Hodgkin versus Mr Pike Pease*, 1906, pamphlet in Darlington Public Library. (Hodgkin was a prominent local Liberal who had taken up Mitchell's cause.) Mitchell's article on the campaign in GFTU, *Quarterly Report,* December 1905, refers also to the criticisms he received for co-operating with the Liberals. The criticism he endured for his publicly made pact, compared with the position of O'Grady and other candidates who benefited from the secretly made national pact between MacDonald and Gladstone, shows up the extremely confused state of labour politics in 1906.
70 GFTU, *Quarterly Reports*, December 1905 and March 1906; *Darlington and Stockton Times*, 13 and 20 January 1906; 26 September 1964; *Northern Echo,* 12 March 1906; pamphlet issued by Darlington LRC (1903) reporting Mitchell's adoption as Labour candidate on 8 April 1903.
71 For example GFTU, *Quarterly Report*, December 1906, where Ward, O'Grady and Richards each summed up their impressions of their first parliamentary session.
72 Minutes of Management Committee meeting, 22 December 1909.
73 Phelps Brown, *Growth of British Industrial Relations*, pp. 261–2; GFTU, *Proceedings and Reports*, 1902–3, report of third agcm, fraternal greetings from Hudson on behalf of the TUC Parliamentary Committee.
74 J. Sassenbach, *Twenty-Five Years of International Trade Unionism* (Amsterdam: International Federation of Trade Unions, 1926), p. 7. A summary of the early history of international trade unionism is given in Lewis L. Lorwin, *The International Labor Movement. History. Policies. Outlook* (New York: Harper, 1953).
75 Report of the third international conference of trade union federations, in GFTU, *Proceedings and Reports*, 1903–4.
76 The rate agreed in 1903 was 6*d* per year per 1,000 members. This was doubled in 1905 and raised to 1*s* 6*d* in 1907.
77 Sassenbach, *Twenty-Five Years of International Trade Unionism,* pp. 10–12.
78 op. cit., pp. 13–17.
79 This analysis is based on Lorwin, *International Labor Movement*, pp. 32–3.
80 GFTU, *Annual Report*, 1907, third international report of the trade union movement, 1905, table II, gives figures of 1,866,755 for 'England' and 1,822,343 for Germany. The next highest number was for Austria with a total of 322,049 trade union members. By 1906 Germany and England had both reached over 2 million, with Germany ahead of England.
81 This conference considered complaints against British trade unions' refusal to accept immigrants who had been members of equivalent unions in their country of origin, and recommended that all countries should adopt the continental practice of honouring such membership.
82 Third international report, table VI.
83 Lorwin, *International Labor Movement*, p. 31. His figures almost certainly do not include Appleton's international federation of laceworkers, which had collapsed by 1914 and which in any case covered only Scotland, England and northern France. There are probably other omissions.
84 GFTU, *Proceedings and Reports*, 1905; *Quarterly Report,* September 1909.
85 Except for the first in 1901, when only Mitchell attended, and the third in Dublin in 1903, when all the members of the Management Committee appeared to regard themselves as delegates (Sassenbach, *Twenty-Five Years of International Trade Unionism,* pp. 80–1).
86 For example, articles on French trade unionism by Jean Longuet the labour leader (GFTU, *Quarterly Report*, December 1906) and by Metin, head of the French Ministry of Labour (*Annual Report*, 1908); and one by Edward Bernstein, member

of the Reichstag, on social democracy and trade unions in Germany (*Quarterly Report*, September 1906).

87   For Legien's remarks at the GFTU meeting, see above.

88   Rowland Hill Harvey, *Samuel Gompers, Champion of the Toiling Masses* (Stanford, Calif.: Stanford University Press, 1935), p. 236; Samuel Gompers, *Seventy Years of Life and Labor*, 2 vols (New York: E. P. Dutton Co., 1925), Vol. 2, *passim*, esp. p. 508.

89   GFTU, *Annual Report*, 1909.

90   Joint Board minutes, 26 November 1907 and 25 February 1908.

91   This point is made often in the GFTU's annual reports and elsewhere (for example, *Annual Report*, 1911, pp. 29–31, article by Appleton). Its importance has not diminished, for it was an article of faith with the late Leslie Hodgson, general secretary to the end of 1977, that any intervention by the GFTU should be as inconspicuous as possible in order to preserve the unions' standing with their own members.

92   Examples of these occurred at almost every agcm and are scattered throughout the minutes of Management Committee meetings.

4
A Turbulent Decade. The Challenges of Syndicalism and War, 1910–20

The General Federation in the Period of 'Industrial Unrest'

In the middle of 1910 a new influence burst upon British labour. Tom Mann returned from Australia. Mann had become prominent as a labour leader during the great London dock strike in 1889. Among many other enterprises, he had been involved in founding the Workers' Union in 1898 and the National Democratic League in 1900, but left England in 1901, attracted by the vigour of the labour movement in New Zealand and Australia. During his stay of nearly nine years there the Australian Labour Party led by John Christian Watson became the first labour party in the world to form a government in its own right and later participated in a Lib-Lab coalition. Its modest achievements in office disappointed many supporters, and Mann became convinced that participation in the existing institutions of the state was not the way for labour to win control of its own destiny. He abandoned the faith in compulsory conciliation and arbitration which he had shared with Ben Tillett, his old friend from dock strike days. By 1905 he could write that 'the battle of the working-class against Capitalist exploitation is necessarily a political battle'.[1] By this he meant that the working class must pit its own institutions, notably the trade unions and trades councils, against the institutions of capital, which included corporations and trusts as well as the existing apparatus of the state. After the failure of the Broken Hill miners' strike which he had organised, Mann returned to Britain fired with enthusiasm to put into practice there the syndicalist ideas which he had developed in Australia. He drew much of his inspiration from the American and French examples of the Industrial Workers of the World (IWW) and Confédération Générale de Travail (CGT) and from the ideas of such leaders as Daniel de Leon and Léon

Jouhaux. Nevertheless, his plans for industrial unionism and 'direct action' in Britain were very much the product of his own dynamic intellect. In Britain a native tradition of syndicalist thought and an industrial milieu very different from that of France or the USA provided the origins for the prolonged period of 'labour unrest', and Mann's leadership was the catalyst.[2]

Mann saw that 'dual unionism', the policy of recruiting workers into new trade unions with explicitly revolutionary objectives, was not appropriate in Britain where so many more workers than in France and the USA were already organised, including many unskilled.[3] He intended to spread his propaganda through existing institutions and was confident that many thousands of unions in Britain 'under[stood] the class war and wish[ed] to take their rightful share in the fighting'. It followed that

> The only existing organisation in this country which is, as it were, marked out to undertake the all-important task, is *The General Federation of Trade Unions* of which Mr Appleton is the able Secretary, and there is no reason why it should not become the responsible, re-constructive agency, and supervise, control and direct the entire Unionist movement.[4]

Mann was not blind to the limitations of the General Federation as an instrument of revolution. When it was founded, in his view, the soul had gone out of the industrial unionism which brought the federation into being. But now it had its chance, if it possessed 'the spirit, the will and the vim to take the responsibility'.[5] It must unite the unions in the equivalent of a real amalgamation, pooling their strike funds although their benefit funds could remain separate and independent. The resulting movement must be avowedly revolutionary, it must set out to destroy the existing system of wages and must refuse to enter into any long-term agreements with the employers.[6] Some other features of Mann's policy included an emphasis on educating the masses in the spirit of revolt through journals and lectures and by establishing a central information bureau. An important element in the doctrines of syndicalism in general, and also in Mann's theories, was the primacy given to the union rank and file, with a corresponding distrust of officials and their established negotiating procedures. French and American syndicalism went further and rejected all forms of political action except for 'direct action' through strikes and eventually through the general strike. But although Mann soon moved closer to this position, when he first returned to Britain he still accepted parliamentary politics as a subordinate but valid part of working-class tactics.[7] It was in this non-exclusive context that he made his call to the GFTU to take up the fight. He repeated his challenge in an article in the GFTU quarterly report for June 1910, where he addressed his remarks especially to skilled workers, whom he blamed for the sectionalism of the British working-class movement.[8]

The wave of strikes, lockouts and riots that surged over Britain between 1910 and 1914 can be attributed to many causes. Syndicalist leaders encouraged the rank-and-file members of trade unions to repudiate the caution and moderation of most of their officials; but at the same time their agitation contributed enormously to the great rise in trade union membership and this strengthened unions that were not necessarily influenced by syndicalism. The example of men like Mann, who intervened in most of the important strikes of the period starting with the South Wales miners' strike in 1910, and the work of the unions' own leaders like Tillett in the English docks and James Larkin and James Connolly, who organised the transport workers' resistance in the bitterly fought Dublin lockout (August 1913–January 1914) had the effect of strengthening union organisation and taught valuable lessons in the conduct of strikes on a mass scale. Their words and their methods worked upon a well-prepared soil. Only a very small minority of workers may have been consciously revolutionary, but infinitely more of them were fed up with the rising cost of living, disenchanted with the performance of the Labour Party in Parliament, disoriented by the pace of technical change in their jobs, discouraged by persistent high unemployment and disgusted by the showy opulence in the higher echelons of Edwardian society.[9]

Whatever the precise causes, between the autumn of 1910 and the outbreak of war in August 1914 Britain was convulsed by several large-scale strikes more violent and more 'revolutionary' in character than any working-class campaign that the country had seen before. The upheavals began with the lockout of 800 miners at the Ely pit of the Cambrian Combine in September 1910 over a dispute about the price list for a new seam, and with the miners' retaliatory strike throughout the Cambrian Combine's pits, which began that November. At Tonypandy the miners put up their fiercest resistance to the introduction of blackleg labour, and brutal police tactics were reinforced by troops under General Macready. The name Tonypandy became a symbol of the new style of struggle.[10] For the next eighteen months, until the conclusion of their first ever national strike and the enactment of the Coal Mines (Minimum Wage) Act 1912, the Miners' Federation of Great Britain was seldom far from the centre of the industrial stage. The other leading contributors to the 'labour unrest' were the transport workers, seamen and dockers.

Their violent and dramatic strikes in Dublin, Liverpool, London and elsewhere from 1911 to 1914, the railwaymen's strikes and mass demonstrations in 1911 and 1913 and the London building trades' lockouts in 1914 took place against a background of widespread strikes in other industries. Alongside these dramatic demonstrations of the workers' new mood, the agitation and political activities of Tom Mann, Guy Bowman and other British syndicalists and industrial unionists appeared extremely significant. The Industrial Syndicalist Education League (formed in November 1910), the National Transport Workers' Federation (November 1910), the formation of the National Union of Railwaymen (1913) and of the Building Workers' Industrial Union (1914) and the tentative agreement to form the Triple Alliance between miners, railwaymen and transport workers (June 1914) could all be seen as part of the same phenomenon. That most reliable observer of and participant in the industrial scene, Sir George (later Lord) Askwith, certainly believed that an important change was taking place in the nature of British trade unionism, and that the unrest would continue.[11] The government agreed, as it showed by its readiness to supply troops to keep the peace and by its use of the Mutiny Act 1797 to imprison Mann and Bowman and others after the publication of the *Don't Shoot* leaflet in 1912, in which the syndicalist stonemason Fred Bower appealed to the troops to join the workers' cause.[12]

This was the background against which the General Federation of Trade Unions had to function. The challenge thrown down by Tom Mann in 1910 in the first issue of *The Industrial Syndicalist* and in the pages of the federation's own reports was by no means so inappropriate to the GFTU as in retrospect it might seem. Manifestly the federation was no hotbed of revolution, but the organisational changes that Mann called for and the development of the federation into a real fighting force had always been part of Management Committee policy. There was much in the detail of his and other thinkers' proposals that also accorded well with the General Federation's work. It would take a book in itself to place the federation, its officials and general council precisely in the extremely confused picture of ideas about trade unionism that contributed to the ferment of 1910–14. Nor is this the place to add one more item to the literature on what exactly syndicalism amounted to in this country. What is interesting from the standpoint of the GFTU is to inquire why the events and ideas which might have established it at the centre of a rapidly growing national trade union movement instead contributed to its decline.

Four proposals, all of which were defeated at the annual general council meeting in 1910, suggest the direction that the General

Federation might have followed. James Anderson of the stevedores moved to allow the GFTU to form a fighting fund to take legal cases to the House of Lords. He deplored the way in which the TUC exercised its power to levy the unions for such expenses: in the important case of *Conway* v. *Wade*[13] the National Amalgamated Union of Labour had had to bear all the costs itself and then wait to be reimbursed until the TUC had raised the appropriate sum. Such a procedure only encouraged employers to engage small unions in legal battles, but if they were confronted by a fighting fund that was ready and waiting to incur legal expenses on the unions' behalf, they would think twice. A note of truculence came into Anderson's speech as he declared that some leading officials of the GFTU seemed to think it was becoming too strong, but he thought it should take a *more* prominent part in the trade union movement, 'whether the big heads desire it or not'. 'In my opinion the Federation is the best organisation we have got to help in the work of the labour movement.'

Some of the 'big heads' undoubtedly sympathised with him. Will Thorne (who was never a member of the Management Committee but often took a prominent part at the annual meetings) strongly supported proposals to extend the payment of dispute benefit to workers who were affected by other people's strikes. This back door to an endorsement of the sympathetic strike had been tried at previous annual meetings but always failed. Not for the first time, Thorne disgustedly chided his fellow trade unionists for their timidity. Then Tillett moved, with equally negative results, that the Management Committee should present systematic periodic reports on unemployment. He claimed that the Board of Trade figures did not represent the true picture, especially in respect of the shift from skilled or at any rate settled employment towards casual labour, a phenomenon which worried Tillett particularly. Using a phrase beloved of his friend Tom Mann, he told the meeting that this sort of information-gathering would greatly assist 'the oneness of the movement'.

Nothing would have done more for the 'oneness of the movement' than the motion of J. E. Smith on behalf of the gasworkers: 'That the Management Committee be instructed to set aside annually a sum of £3,000 for organising purposes, and that a scheme be drawn up for the appointment of six organisers to work in the interest of all societies, connected with the Federation.' Will Thorne, seconding, pointed out that the proposal would help promote solidarity between skilled and unskilled workers, and predicted that the federation would get its money back within six months as a result of the increased membership that organisers would bring. 'Talk about stick-in-the-muds,' he exploded, knowing that the proposal would fail, 'I think you are making a huge mistake.' His fellow MP Arthur Henderson, also a familiar figure at the GFTU's annual meetings as a delegate from the ironfounders, spoke against the motion. He probably expressed the more common Labour Party view of the General Federation when he referred to the many labour organisations that already existed and said that the Management Committee and secretary could cope with all the work necessary to bring in new affiliations to the federation and that any organising work on behalf of the unions themselves ought to be done by their own organisers. The general council's failure to adopt the gasworkers' proposals on organisation turned out to be, in the Management Committee's view, one of its most disastrous mistakes.[14] It is scarcely surprising that the Gasworkers' and General Labourers' Union, which had provided some of the GFTU's best leadership, notably in the person of Pete Curran, should have been among the first crop of damaging secessions, less than three years later.

All of these proposals to extend the powers of the federation in various ways failed because the general council was not prepared to allocate funds. The Management Committee could not be charged with undue meanness or unadventurousness when year after year its proposals to raise contributions met with a flat negative from the general council and this refusal inhibited them from using their power to raise the contributions without the general council's consent. The majority of the federation's member unions unmistakably lacked the will to build it into something more worthy of its name. Given the card voting system which it had inherited along with much of the rest of its procedure from the TUC, and hence the built-in strength of the larger unions, the smaller craft unions cannot take the blame for blocking the federation's progress in this way; the need for closer unity among trade unions seems to have impressed the larger unions no more than the smaller. But despite this depressingly widespread apathy, it was possible for the officials of the General Federation to take the initiative on many questions. During the period of the labour unrest and afterwards, during the First World War, both Appleton and the Management Committee as a whole produced a quantity of publications and proposals to meet the challenge of the rapid changes that were taking place in the labour world.

The next quarterly report after that in which Tom Mann had published his call to the GFTU captured something of the new spirit and showed that the Management Committee was ready to respond.[15] In it Appleton fiercely rebutted the intemperate attacks on trade unions that had been appearing in the press and called on the unions to make these misrepresentations the occasion for new efforts at consolidation and reform. 'The question of consolidation is of profound importance. At present there are too many Trade Unions in some industries and not enough Trade Unionists.' The GFTU intended to renew its efforts to bring about amalgamations. In the meantime it had already made contact with local trades councils all over the country, and hoped to arrange a large number of meetings with them during the winter in order to discuss mutual difficulties. Trades councils had been excluded from membership of the TUC in 1895, mainly because their more socialist leanings were unpopular.[16] Mann and others had advocated their use then as centres for educating trade unionists in the ideas and practice of socialism, and he was doing so again now. So the GFTU's overtures to trades councils at this moment must be seen as a positive response to Mann's appeal. In a second new venture in the syndicalist spirit, the chairman (then Allen Gee) and secretary had taken up an invitation from the Confédération Générale de Travail to its annual conference at Toulouse and were to take that opportunity of studying French trade unionism at first hand.

> The international organisation of the workers has been accounted the wildest of dreams, but present indications suggest that the dreamers but anticipated actualities, for the machinery of organisation has already been erected, the educative influences are at work, and the possibility of an understanding and common effort becomes daily more apparent. (GFTU, quarterly report, September 1910)

During the next two years the General Federation grappled with the problems caused by the labour unrest as well as attempting to rise to the new demands of labour activists. For two years in succession it paid out more in benefits than its total annual income, until by the end of 1911 it had only enough in reserve to pay benefit to 4 per cent of its members for one week.[17] The boilermakers' lockout alone cost the federation £53,000 in dispute benefit and in the end it resorted to a special levy.[18] This method of raising funds was one that the general council in 1911 instructed the Management Committee to consider carefully before presenting another request for increased contributions, but as the committee pointed out in a special report, it was highly unsatisfactory, becoming necessary always during an emergency when at least some of the affiliated unions (those involved in the dispute) could not be levied, and always evoking a reluctant and partial response from the others.[19] It was right to dislike special levies, for before long the National Union of Dock Labourers (James Sexton's Liverpool dockers) used its objection to the levy on behalf of the textile workers as a pretext for secession;[20] and it was the federation's attempts on behalf of the Joint Board to make the Amalgamated Society of Engineers pay its share of the Osborne case expenses that led, in part, to that union's secession in 1915.[21] As the Management Committee summed it up,

> One of the fundamental theories of Federationists was that the many could help the few, because only the few would need help at one and the same time. The adoption of the principle of the general strike and the general lock-out has changed all this. It is the many who now need help, and the few only who can give it. Labour must, therefore, of necessity make more adequate provision or risk serious defeats.[22]

Eventually, at a special general council meeting in January 1912, contributions were doubled for a twelve-month period[23] and the annual meeting in July regularised the level of contributions at the old rate of 6*d* per member per quarter on the higher scale and 3*d* on the lower.[24] The annual report for 1912 reflected the severe strain under which the Management Committee had worked for the previous two years. Although expenditure on dispute benefit in 1911–12 was very slightly less than in 1910–11, it still exceeded income, and the pressure of business connected with disputes had obliged the Management Committee to meet twenty-six times as opposed to seventeen in the previous year, with twenty-seven sub-committee meetings. Hardly a week had passed without a member or members of the Management Committee giving personal assistance in a dispute. The committee had issued more than a million copies of pamphlets, leaflets and circulars in the year 1911–12 alone, including one it considered especially important, on the campaign by chambers of commerce and other business organisations to place renewed legal restrictions on trade unions. Meetings and conferences of trade unionists and trades councils had been held under the federation's auspices in many parts of the country, and liaison with trades councils, on which it had embarked in 1910, was now a flourishing part of its activities. The 1911 annual general council meeting had passed a resolution in favour of the federation's setting up an international information bureau, a task that the committee could not perform while it lacked the accommodation, although it had tried to meet the many requests for information that came in from different parts of the world. Invitations to attend trade union congresses in several European countries had had to be turned down because of the pressure of other business. Most time-consuming of all had been the establishment of the General Federation's insurance section under the terms of the National Insurance Act, a new departure with far-reaching consequences for the GFTU, which will be discussed below.

The year that ended with the annual general council meeting of 1912 may have been one of strains and difficulties for the Management Committee, but it witnessed the greatest rise in aggregate membership since the General Federation was founded, and this not simply from the increased membership of unions already affiliated but from several new affiliations. The total membership rose by over 172,000 and new recruits included the large and vigorous National Federation of Blastfurnacemen. In the following year the position altered sharply. Membership actually declined from its peak of 884,000 to 874,000. The only previous year in which it had declined was 1905, when unemployment and the recession in general had cut into the membership of the affiliated unions; but this time nine secessions, almost all by major unions, dealt a severe blow to the federation which seventeen new affiliations by small craft unions could not repair.* These losses, which even included the blast-furnacemen who had only just joined, weakened the federation not only in numbers. They deprived it of some of its most influential voices and shifted the balance of membership from large unions to the smaller and on the whole, more sectional, craft unions.[25] Although membership began to rise again in 1913, the loss of these societies was a turning point in the federation's history. It is interesting that such a large influx should have been followed immediately by decline, just in the middle of a period of growth in trade union militancy in the country as a whole.[26] One immediate cause was the doubled contributions payable in 1912.[27] If there were any more profound reasons for this reverse than the rather superficial excuses offered by most of the seceding unions, we must search for them in events in the wider labour movement between 1910 and 1912.

The TUC and the Labour Party at their respective conferences in September 1910 and March 1911 both debated motions calling for fusion of the three national organisations and the provision of a large central building in London for the use of the labour movement. The TUC rejected the proposal by a small majority, but the Labour Party conference passed a motion in favour of fusion which had originally included only the Labour Party and the TUC but was broadened during the debate to include the GFTU.[28] The question was referred to the Joint Board and in April 1911 the three full committees met twice

---

*The unions that left were: the blastfurnacemen, brassworkers, Liverpool dockers, enginemen and cranemen, gasworkers and brickmakers, gasworkers and general labourers, Scottish painters, patternmakers and the shopworkers (*Annual Report*, 1913).

at the House of Commons to consider it.[29] At that stage the Management Committee of the GFTU was cautiously in favour of the proposal, even if a little injured that it should have been left out at first.[30] For the Labour Party, Arthur Henderson who chaired the meeting was the most enthusiastic for unity. Ramsay MacDonald thought that all three organisations should share the same roof and do common business in common, but that complete fusion was impracticable because each body had areas of work that were peculiarly its own. C. W. Bowerman, for the TUC, wanted all three offices to be under one roof, with a proper labour club which could provide accommodation for delegates in the provinces, on the same lines as clubs that already existed in Germany and elsewhere. Keir Hardie warmly supported this idea and sounded a warning note about secessions from the TUC, which had suffered a fall in membership in 1910. Some action should be taken, in his opinion, to prevent Congress from 'fizzling out'. The problem of relations with trades councils was raised by James Sexton, for the GFTU. Alexander Wilkie, also representing the GFTU, expressed the general lukewarmness. Any critic of British trade unionism might choose Wilkie's words to exemplify its besetting sin of sectionalism. He thought 'that the three [separate] Committees were necessary in the face of the many committees which Capital possesses'. His colleague Ben Tillett, who was present, did not protest, but he had recently contributed an article to the federation's reports in which he pointed out that the separation of labour interests into small units was exactly what capitalists wanted, while they themselves were aggregating their resources into ever larger and more powerful corporations, trusts and federations.[31]

The three committees separated to consider what their respective official views should be on fusion and, when they met again, agreed on the formation of a Joint Board subcommittee to prepare a report for submission to each of the three national conferences. Both the TUC and GFTU committees contented themselves with only very vague allusions to co-operation between the three bodies. The Labour Party, however, adopted Henderson's approach and called for 'the amalgamation of the national bodies without delay', and for a scheme to build a central labour building.[32] Its proposals to look into the possibilities of achieving these two aims were approved by both TUC and GFTU conferences in 1911, and the Newcastle TUC that year resolved in favour of a scheme put forward by the boilermakers, whose secretary John Hill was a leading advocate of fusion, just as his predecessor Robert Knight had always been a staunch supporter of trade union federation. They proposed that there should be one 'Labour Congress' which would be a 'federation of trade unions, trade and socialist societies' to '(i) watch over all legislation affecting

Labour, (ii) establish a fund for mutual assistance and support'. An annual congress meeting every September would elect a Grand Congress Committee of twenty-four members and this would appoint three subcommittees to deal respectively with legislation and parliamentary affairs, 'labour representation' and insurance. This interesting proposal was the nearest that the British labour movement ever came to an amalgamation of its industrial and political wings. The GFTU Management Committee finally decided against it and although the issue was discussed again at the national conferences of 1912, the peak of enthusiasm for closer unity had passed.

Arthur Henderson appealed to the delegates to the GFTU annual general council meeting in 1912 over the heads of the Management Committee, pointing out among other things that the federation 'had been meddling with political work' and if they wanted to do so properly, 'they ought to do it in the closest cooperation with those who were in a better position to do it than they were'.[33] Appleton replied provocatively that the federation had never made 'political pronouncements which it had not been possible for the others to follow'. In any case, he said, the main reason for the Management Committee's decision to remain outside any possible amalgamation was its new involvement in national insurance. This was an additional industrial function which made it inappropriate, in its view, for the federation to amalgamate with the political wing of the labour movement. John Ward spoke later in support of Appleton, reviving the old Lib-Lab charge that some elements in the Labour Party were hostile to trade unions. He referred in particular to the Joint Board's failure to treat as a serious threat the campaign for anti-trade union legislation which the GFTU had brought to its attention. This was not good enough for many of the delegates, but on a show of hands Henderson's motion in favour of fusion was lost by 21 votes to 46. Henderson, in fact, was probably the only member of the Joint Board who favoured a complete amalgamation of all three bodies. The apathy of the General Federation was used by the board to drop the whole idea.[34]

All that remained of it was a grand scheme for a Labour Congress Hall to be built somewhere in London. The architect G. P. Catchpole described this in glowing colours in the GFTU quarterly report for December 1912. Presumably he intended no irony when he wrote:

> The great building scheme, which will cost Labour about £125,000, will prove of illimitable value in its effect upon the power with which the great force pulsates and its inculcation of a greater spirit of self-esteem in the movement.

Catchpole's design incorporated separate offices for a labour and co-operative bank and an insurance society, with suites of offices for trade unions, 'political parties, approved societies, Wholesale Co-operative Society' and others. Conference and committee rooms of various sizes included the circular, galleried 'great Congress Hall' with seating for 4,000 people. It was to be 'treated in the French Renaissance style', with a 'domed and richly panelled roof'. Plans were afoot to appeal to all labour supporters in the country to make contributions of $\frac{1}{2}d$ a month for two years and, should this fail, for trade unions to invest funds in the project. W. A. Appleton and James O'Grady (who became chairman of the GFTU in 1912) were the two sponsors of the scheme, which suggests that they may have exceeded their exploratory brief from the Joint Board. The Labour Congress Hall, had it been built, would have symbolised in bricks and mortar a unity of purpose and method which no democratic labour movement has achieved, but perhaps at the expense of a diversity which few would wish to give up. At all events, in the context of Britain in 1912 the scheme was as visionary as its French renaissance architecture would have been unsuitable.

The overall impression given by the General Federation, notwithstanding its efforts to the contrary, was one of only a lukewarm commitment to the greater unity of the labour movement. This impression was not quite fair, as Appleton's and O'Grady's sponsorship of the Labour Congress Hall alone would suggest. In addition to this, the federation's officials put a great deal of work into the practical tasks of conciliation and forging closer unity between particular unions, as even a glance at the annual reports or minutes of their meetings shows. Their co-operation with local trades councils won them praise from the councils[35] but seems to have been little regarded by the affiliated unions. Individual members of the Management Committee went out of their way to affirm their commitment to the new spirit of industrial solidarity. Ben Tillett, as leader of one of the most famous strikes of the period, needed no other credentials in this respect, and he kept the federation aware of his point of view with his motions to found information centres at the annual general council meetings of 1910 and 1911, and his article preaching against sectionalism in the federation's quarterly report for December 1910. J. N. Bell was another champion of a strengthened federation which would both act as a central authority and assist its member unions with recruitment. He moved resolutions on these subjects at the annual meeting in 1911, including one for a new scheme of district committees. Allen Gee, addressing the general council as outgoing chairman in 1912, delivered a fighting speech in favour of continued industrial militancy and asked the delegates to improve the federation's financial position so that it could establish 'a large national industrial reserve'. W. A. Appleton continually spelled out the message that the federation was very much more than a mere trade union benefit society[36] and John Hill, who was one of the auditors, was well known for his advocacy of labour unity. Perhaps the best known of them all in this respect was James O'Grady. For three years running he introduced a Bill into the House of Commons which would have released unions wishing to amalgamate from the legal requirement to obtain a vote of two-thirds of their total membership in favour. This requirement was a major obstacle to the closer unity of unions which could hardly ever expect two-thirds of their membership to vote on anything, and the failure of the Labour Party to back up O'Grady's efforts to get it removed was a bone of contention.[37]

But there were other voices on the Management Committee, and those who did want to turn the federation into some kind of central force in the movement did not always agree among themselves. It must have been generally known or assumed, for instance, that Appleton had a personal preference for craft unionism, as he later avowed in print.[38] In 1912, also, the question of his personal straightforwardness, which had been raised earlier by the laceworkers, was renewed for the edification of the general council when John Hill queried part of the previous year's accounts. Hill did not question Appleton's honesty but he threw doubt on the efficiency of his accounting methods. Appleton chose to take this as an aspersion on his honesty, saying that 'he would sacrifice everything rather than endure the suspicions created by the auditors'. His defensiveness, revealed on other occasions at annual meetings and often in the rather personal tone of his writing, cannot have helped to make him a unifying force in the federation. Moreover there clearly was a certain amount of distrust in the air, and this was probably not confined to financial matters. The federation was not getting the assured and confident leadership that it needed. A further weakness in the leadership was the division not only over how the federation might be made into a more effective central body but over whether this was the really important issue. At the 1912 annual general council meeting Ben Tillett's motion that the GFTU should help affiliated unions to organise was rejected decisively after Arthur Henderson had spoken strongly against it. Henderson himself, as we have seen, failed at the same meeting to get support for his motion in favour of the amalgamation of the Labour Party, TUC and GFTU. Although strictly speaking he was not a leader of the GFTU as he was not then on the Management Committee, his voice as a leading Labour MP must have been heard with great respect; and in 1911 and 1912 it undoubtedly contributed to the picture of confusion and disunity that the other delegates to the general council reported back to their unions.

As the roll-call of important secessions from the federation grew, the Management Committee heard three different sorts of reasons for the unions' decision. Some, like the gasworkers, argued that they did not get a reasonable financial return on their contributions. Appleton might criticise such unions for being selfish and short-sighted[39] but a more serious problem lay behind secessions of this kind. More than once at annual general council meetings, officials of the gasworkers had tried to get the payment of dispute benefit extended to labourers who were affected by strikes not of their making. General unions like the gasworkers were particularly vulnerable to strikes caused by other groups of workers, and they could argue quite fairly that a system of benefits that did not cover these cases was of little real use to them. After Will Thorne's plea in 1910, repeated by J. R. Clynes in 1911, there was in practice some recognition of these and even of some purely 'sympathetic' strikes. Indeed, in the industrial ferment of 1910–12 it was often difficult to distinguish which unions were genuinely directly involved in a particular dispute and which might be deemed to have come out in sympathy. By mid-1912 the Management Committee believed that this *de facto* recognition of the sympathetic strike was to blame for the federation's financial difficulties;[40] but its support for sympathetic strikes, unendorsed by the general council, was not dependable enough to prevent the gasworkers from seceding. Other unions, like the Liverpool dockers, objected to paying levies. In their case, under the leadership of James Sexton they were resisting the spread of syndicalism and other militant tactics in the dock and transport industries and a refusal to meet levies on behalf of other unions should be seen partly as resistance to a trend. Sexton also believed that national insurance had little to offer the casual labourer, and this must have been an important source of disagreement with the GFTU's new policies.[41] A third category of secession came from unions which, like the Society of Enginemen, Cranemen and Boilermen, wanted the General Federation to be much more of a central authority than it was.[42]

None of these problems could have been solved without very much higher contributions than the general council would grant. The financial basis of the General Federation, which was supposed to have been its great strength, proved in fact to be a serious weakness. It was all the more so in that the unions clearly expected more from an institution to which they made significant contributions and had to report on any disputes for which they claimed benefit than they expected from their much looser affiliation to the TUC. For this reason the confusion and disunity among the General Federation leadership over questions that were shaking the labour movement were much

W. A. Appleton, GFTU General Secretary,
1907-1938

George Bell, GFTU General Secretary,
1938—1953

Isaac Mitchell, Amalgamated Society
of Engineers, GFTU Secretary
1899-1907

Peter Potts, GFTU General
Secretary, 1978-

Leslie Hodgson, GFTU
General Secretary, 1953-1978

more damaging to the GFTU than the similar confusion in the Parliamentary Committee were to the TUC. Congress was every bit as divided as the General Federation; it witnessed scenes more violent than any offered at the annual general council meetings of the federation, and when Ben Tillett punched a fellow trade unionist on the jaw he did it at the TUC, not in the calmer atmosphere of the GFTU.[43] But episodes like this did not threaten to affect the pockets of trade unions in the same way as decisions or the lack of decisions at the GFTU. As delegates pointed out when the question of raising contributions to the federation was discussed, some unions collected the money for their GFTU dues by a specific levy on their members.[44] For these in particular, the activities of the General Federation came far closer to home than did those of the TUC, which could still seem comfortably remote from the rank and file of trade union membership.

The General Federation's part in the prewar labour unrest should not be left on a negative note, however. Despite all the inherent weaknesses of the GFTU and however understandable its failures may seem in retrospect, they did not seem irreversible at the time. The quarterly report for March 1912, pleading for unions to consult the federation before embarking on strikes, noted that it had 'passed entirely beyond the purely benefit paying stage of its existence and it is now expected to assist, by exercising its public influence and by direct negotiation with employers, in the settlement of disputes and in general Trade Union work and organisation'. In 1913 the guild socialists G. D. H. Cole and William Mellor published a pamphlet entitled *The Greater Unionism* in which they outlined a scheme for bringing about true industrial unionism in Britain, and insisted that the General Federation of Trade Unions was the only suitable body to organise the necessary centralisation. The guild socialists, like the syndicalists, pinned their hopes for the future on industrial unionism and scorned the Fabian policy of 'permeating' the existing institutions of the state with socialism. They differed from the syndicalists over 'dual unionism' and were in some other ways less revolutionary. 'What the unions really need is "business government" with a revolutionary aim' wrote Cole and Mellor. The role they assigned to the General Federation was that of arranging for overall trade union propaganda and, on the German model, inspiring a consistent policy and a unified aim for the whole trade union movement.[45] They wanted to see the federation reformed and given more funds to carry out these aims. As Cole and Mellor saw it,

The Trade Union Congress is a highly academic body – a debating society rather than a legislative assembly. Its Parliamentary Committee, formed mainly to carry on the work that is now done by the

Labour Party, has of late shown a desire to launch out on the industrial side, and to encroach upon the sphere of the General Federation. The existence of such an ill-defined body is a source of weakness to the Labour movement, and the Parliamentary Committee must hand over its work and powers to other bodies more fitted for the task. All the unions must come into the General Federation. These are the only lines upon which fusion of the two bodies can produce satisfactory results.[46]

The guild socialists' hopes were ill-founded and their revolutionary aim was out of tune with the conciliatory principles of the General Federation. The GFTU Management Committee wanted to co-ordinate trade unionism in order to avoid unnecessary industrial disputes.[47] Cole and Mellor wanted to centralise union power in order to turn the strike weapon into an effective instrument of revolutionary change. But if Appleton favoured gradual change where the guild socialists wanted revolution, their long-term aims were not altogether different from each other.[48] And on a strategy for strengthening British trade unionism, to whatever end, they were agreed. *The Greater Unionism* leaves us with a glimpse of what the General Federation of Trade Unions could mean to idealists in the labour movement before the First World War.

National Insurance and the General Federation of Trade Unions

The GFTU's most successful work in the years immediately before the First World War was in health and unemployment insurance. The Liberal government had been preparing a scheme for limited national insurance since 1908; but like much of its legislation this was delayed by Lloyd George's Parliament Act which curbed the powers of the House of Lords after they threw out his budget in 1909. Only after the passage of the Parliament Act in 1911 did the National Insurance Act, which has been described as the kingpin of Liberal social legislation, become law.[49] Part I of the Act provided for compulsory contributory health insurance for the whole working population. Commercial insurance companies, friendly societies and trade unions were given the option to register as Approved Societies to administer health insurance.

Part II of the National Insurance Act set up machinery for

compulsory unemployment insurance in certain industries* and provided for voluntary insurance for some other workers who wished to participate. Governed by elaborate rules and procedures, the insurance bodies including trade unions were to carry out a system whereby the employer and employee each contributed 2½d a week and the state supplied one-third of the total made up by these contributions. Benefits of 7 shillings a week were payable for up to a maximum of fifteen weeks and, in theory at least, all calculations excluded the old notions that there were 'deserving' unemployed and the 'undeserving' who had brought their unemployment on themselves.[50] Unions providing their own unemployment insurance were to be reimbursed for a proportion of whatever benefit they paid above a minimum of 7 shillings, and in practice this encouraged them to pay more.

The Act marked a further step by the state into the area of social policy. Although it was modelled closely on continental, especially German, examples which operated at a local level, it introduced the first national scheme of unemployment insurance in the world. It established the essentially unconditional, morally neutral, nature of welfare benefits in Britain. And it gave the unions a great opportunity to organise with the blessing of the state. And yet it received only half-hearted support from the Labour Party and trade unions. Most sections of the labour movement would have preferred a non-contributory scheme, and continued to press for the Act to be amended on these lines. The partial nature of the provisions troubled many, and there was especially strong pressure on the government to include all general labourers in the compulsory provisions of the Act. Nevertheless most Labour MPs voted for it and trade unionists supported it after it became law, including James O'Grady who had opposed it in Parliament but then 'threw in his lot with the workers to make the best of the Act' and became chairman of the GFTU insurance section.[51]

The General Federation, and in particular Appleton on its behalf, had played a part in advising the government on the detail of the Act. In March 1909 Appleton presented a report to the Management Committee in which he recommended the state provision of unemployment insurance based on equal contributions from the workmen, employers and the state, and administered by trade unions and the Post Office Savings Bank; but the Joint Board turned down the Management Committee's request for a full meeting of the three national committees to discuss it.[52] Appleton kept a close watch on the government's plans nevertheless, and when he told his committee that the Chancellor of the Exchequer was discussing unemployment insurance with the friendly societies, they arranged to meet Lloyd

---

*These were: building and construction, shipbuilding, mechanical engineering, ironfounding, vehicle construction and sawmilling.

George themselves in March 1911. As a result of this meeting the chancellor asked for someone who could 'confidentially present the Trade Union position' and the Management Committee put Appleton forward for the job.[53] But the Parliamentary Committee of the TUC objected strongly to his being appointed a member of the advisory committee on state insurance, on the rather surprising grounds that since the Chancellor of the Exchequer did not want an MP on the committee he should not have Appleton either.[54] This attitude should probably be attributed to internecine jealousies rather than to any objections of principle. It is reasonable to suppose that in that period of labour unrest, less than a year after Tom Mann had called for the GFTU to become the centre of labour's attack on capital and with every sign that the federation wished to take advantage of the new mood, the TUC Parliamentary Committee felt threatened.

Despite obstruction by the TUC, Tillett encouraged Appleton to attend the meetings of the advisory committee where the insurance companies and friendly societies were represented, and the chancellor and his officials gave him all the information he wanted.[55] Appleton gave an account later which strongly implied that but for his vigilance Lloyd George would have gone ahead with a scheme that excluded the unions. Although he may have believed this, there seems no justification for his suspicions.[56] Similarly, at about this time he warned of a danger that the government would enact legislation to compel unions to go to arbitration before going on strike;[57] but the Cabinet committee papers show that this proposal was barely even considered.[58] It seems likely that Appleton, who personally esteemed Lloyd George very highly, was being deliberately alarmist in order to persuade trade unionists of the need for greater unity in the movement.[59]

As Appleton had foreseen, national insurance opened up great opportunities for recruitment to the unions, and the GFTU Management Committee concentrated in the early months of 1912 on opening its fellow trade unionists' eyes to these possibilities. Between September 1910 and March 1911 it had issued at least 400,000 copies of pamphlets on unemployment and health insurance. During the same period it drew up plans to create its own insurance section which would both administer unemployment insurance and act as an Approved Society for health insurance purposes under the terms of part I of the National Insurance Act 1911. Societies with fewer than 5,000 members were too small to be recognised as full Approved Societies in their own right under the Act, and were to be required to pay any surpluses from their funds into the pool of the county or of a larger society with which they had federated. The GFTU scheme, which involved setting up a separate organisation managed by an executive board, was particularly enticing to small unions because it enabled them to provide health insurance for their members without giving up control to any non-union organisation. As a bonus, membership of the GFTU insurance section lifted from their shoulders the complex and onerous administration of unemployment insurance, a benefit which many of them had provided for a long time, but which became much more complicated under the requirements of the new Act.

The administrative details involved in national insurance were enormously complicated. Appleton gave up his spare time to hammer out with the insurance commissioners suitable rules for the General Federation's insurance section.[60] The federation appointed a new organiser, T. Wilson Coates, who had represented Weardale (County Durham) and Tow Law District Trades Council at Tom Mann's industrial syndicalist conference at Manchester in November 1910.[61] With his help it had recruited 160 unions, almost all small craft unions with an average membership of less than 1,500, into the insurance section by July 1912, and had issued nearly half a million insurance cards. The affiliation of the Scottish dockers had encouraged it to open an office in Glasgow.[62] Both for the unions and for the General Federation, there were indeed great opportunities. The unions, acting as branches of the GFTU insurance section, could accept members for insurance purposes who were not necessarily trade union members, but would of course hope to recruit them for the union as well. The General Federation insurance section could accept affiliation by unions which were not affiliated to its industrial branch, but hoped to persuade them to join that too; and in the event a very large proportion of new affiliations in 1911–12 seems to have come through the insurance section. As Appleton told its first annual meeting, the Management Committee was 'hoping that they would be so successful that they would be able to do what the General Federation had never yet been able to do, get Organisers and advisers in different parts of the country'.[63] Insurance, in other words, could be the General Federation's route to pre-eminence in British trade unionism.

By the autumn of 1912, however, it was already clear that trade unions in general did not see the advantages of national insurance in the same light. Many of them preferred to leave it alone altogether. Unemployment insurance in particular not only presented heavy administrative difficulties but conflicted with the practice built up by the trade unions themselves; for example, the state scheme did not permit payment of insurance to men on strike.[64] The government added to the expense and complexity of their scheme by establishing four separate health insurance commissions for different parts of the country.[65] Commercial insurance companies mounted successful advertising campaigns offering favourable rates, and it was of little use for the unions to point out that they could undercut commercial rates because they did not have to offer dividends to shareholders. The GFTU carried out clerical work on behalf of its affiliated societies for 1s 10d per head per year, as compared with the 2s 6d of which the commercial companies boasted.[66] But the vast resources and prestige of companies like the Prudential tended to undermine that argument in the eyes of the bemused worker who had to choose his own insurance policy.

In a rather incautious article in *National [Insurance] Weekly* in September 1912, Appleton revealed the high hopes that the federation pinned on its venture into national insurance, and incidentally shed light also on its reasons for withdrawing from the discussions of fusion with the TUC and Labour Party.[67] He berated both organisations for their inaction, and the Parliamentary Labour Party in particular for failing to oppose the inclusion of commercial companies in the 1911 Act. 'By this action it deliberately sacrificed the interests of the trade unions and the friendly societies to the personal interests of a few insurance agents, and it did this apparently without consulting any representative body of trade unionists.' Many union officials had been deluded by 'rosy visions of running their trade union side at the expense of the State', without understanding how difficult the administrative requirements of the Act would be. But even now it was not too late. The General Federation stood ready to welcome unions which had seen the folly of their ways; it offered supplementary benefits for sickness and death and was preparing other plans. Appleton concluded his article on an exalted note: 'Men of the trade union movement, you who work at bench and lathe, at wheel or loom, at making commodities or in distributing them, make your will felt. I know you are waiting for a higher and fuller form of industrial organisation than has yet been achieved.'

If this clarion call received no answering cry from the unions, it did not mean that the General Federation's insurance scheme was useless. It merely failed to achieve the high ambitions of its creator. During the short period of peace time when the National Insurance Act was in operation unamended (and payment of benefit did not begin until 1 January 1913) the GFTU insurance section performed a great service for its affiliated societies, taking on most of the very considerable administrative burden and offering abundant practical advice. The federation's experience of national insurance also lent weight to the advice it gave the government and when Appleton along with other trade union leaders pressed Lloyd George to create a comprehensive national medical service, he was heard with respect.[68] The General Federation was continually urging reform of the National Insurance Act, a cause that they would take up again in the 1920s. Insurance was *par excellence* the province of the GFTU, and leading figures in the federation who criticised much of the rest of its work would have liked to see it succeed as a large trade union insurance service.[69]

The context in which the GFTU took up national insurance was unfortunate. The TUC, as we have seen, was already uneasy about the respective roles of the GFTU and itself in British trade unionism. On 8 October 1912 the Parliamentary Committee considered a letter from John Hill complaining that Appleton had called the committee 'futile' in his article in *National Weekly*, and Appleton was asked to explain.[70] In the next few months relations between the TUC and GFTU deteriorated into open feud. In January 1913 Appleton resigned as secretary of the Joint Board, partly because of the pressure of other work but chiefly because he knew that he was unpopular and C. W. Bowerman, secretary of the Parliamentary Committee, wished to take over.[71] The next week Ben Tillett published an article criticising the Joint Board in the *Daily Herald*, and the board summoned him to account before a special meeting.[72] In February the Jewish bakers, who were already aggrieved at the TUC's delay over their request to affiliate, were involved in a dispute over the presence of blackleg English bakers in one particular shop. At the Joint Board Appleton virtually accused the Parliamentary Committee of planting the blacklegs and Bowerman angrily repudiated the slur.[73] The GFTU meanwhile was in turmoil on its own account. A series of very damaging secessions had impelled it to set up an investigating committee and, more significantly, to break its founding rule that no branches of unions should be allowed to affiliate separately. The principle was conceded in January 1913 when the National Federation of Blastfurnacemen seceded and the Cleveland and Durham Blastfurnacemen's Association was allowed to remain affiliated; and by the end of the month the Management Committee had repeated the concession for the Aberdeen branch of the seceding Scottish painters.[74]

Such was the position when the Miners' Federation embarked on a campaign to squeeze the General Federation out of the national trade union movement.[75] At the end of January 1913, the National Amalgamated Union of Labour (NAUL) asked the GFTU to intercede with the miners in a dispute at Moss Bay, where Cumberland miners were blacklegging during a strike by members of the smaller union. The GFTU Management Committee invited representatives of the Miners' Federation to a meeting with representatives of the NAUL, but the miners refused point-blank. The federation referred the problem to the Joint Board, as they had done before with disputes they were uanble to solve; but on this occasion the board's subcommittee had no better luck than the General Federation.[76] On 22 May 1913 the TUC Parliamentary Committee received a letter from the Miners' Federation of Great Britain asking why the GFTU had any more right to be represented on the Joint Board than they, the miners, had themselves.[77] The printed minutes of the Joint Board proceedings appeared in the annual report of the TUC for 1913, and at Congress that September Robert Smillie, president of the Miners' Federation, moved the deletion of these references and claimed, absolutely without foundation, that the Joint Board had never been approved by the TUC.[78] The miners were criticised severely for their bullying tactics, but the truth was that they were by far too powerful in the trade union movement to be withstood. Although they lost their motion to delete the Joint Board reports, from then onwards they refused to have anything to do with the board while the GFTU remained a member.

The miners' campaign continued throughout 1914 and on into the radically changed circumstances of wartime, when they refused to contribute to the levy for the War Emergency: Workers' National Committee on which the GFTU was represented.[79] By this time the Parliamentary Committee had come round to the view that such levies should be made only through the TUC, and the Labour Party also favoured excluding the GFTU.[80] A series of meetings considered reconstituting the Joint Board and in September 1916 Congress passed the miners' resolution that the TUC and Labour Party were fully representative of the industrial and political sides of the labour movement and that therefore the Joint Board ought to be dissolved and re-established to include only those two organisations.[81] At the end of 1916 that is what happened.[82]

The miners' vendetta against the General Federation of Trade Unions has to be understood in the context of their own dynamic brand of trade unionism at that period. Their annual meeting in 1913 called for closer co-operation with other large unions, and by the spring of 1914 they had laid the foundations of the Triple Alliance with the National Union of Railwaymen and the Transport Workers' Federation. The Miners' Federation itself was fighting to be recognised by the mine owners as the organ of national collective bargaining in the industry, replacing the district bargaining system to which the employers clung. Robert Smillie and his other militant colleagues fought single-mindedly to better the living and working conditions of an exceptionally deprived group of workers against a collection of employers who were, on the whole, exceptionally obdurate. 'No other trade union leaders can speak on behalf of the miners' Smillie told Lloyd George, and he proved it by successfully resisting all attempts to force the miners to comply with the terms of the Munitions of War Act 1915 as almost all the other unions did.[83] Smaller unions on the fringes of the mining industry were an irrelevance,[84] and Smillie would have seen no contradiction between his own belief in trade unionism and crushing the membership of the NAUL at Moss Bay. At the time of this strike the GFTU was visibly turning into the patron of the smaller unions. Its best known work in 1912–13 was as an insurance organisation for unions too small to fend for themselves. The gasworkers and other big fish were being replaced by shoals of minnows. None of this excuses the miners' over-bearing behaviour. But it helps to explain how such tactics could still be compatible with a heartfelt commitment to trade unionism; and it shows, too, that the new spirit behind industrial unionism was not necessarily a force for unity.

The members of the Parliamentary Committee probably shared some of Smillie's reasons for wanting the General Federation off the Joint Board. More important, they were worried about rivalry between the TUC and GFTU, and overlapping between the two institutions undoubtedly had increased. Institutional jealousies ought not to be over-emphasised, for several individuals had served on both committees, though not on both at the same time. Personal dislikes, however, could be strong and there seems to have been no love lost between Appleton and the secretary of the Parliamentary Committee, Bowerman, even though both men's politics belonged to the non-socialist wing of trade unionism. Appleton's pronouncements on politics had increased when he became involved in national insurance and were annoying the Parliamentary Committee even before he was unwise enough to call it 'futile' in the pages of *National Weekly*. As for the Labour Party, an opportunity to reduce trade union representation on the Joint Board could only be welcome to most of its leaders. This was especially true because two of the regular GFTU representatives on the board were Alexander Wilkie, the archetype of an old-fashioned non-socialist trade union MP, and John Ward who was really a Liberal MP by this time, while William Appleton, though still careful about his public stance on specifically party politics, was probably known to be a Liberal supporter.[85]

The First World War

In August 1914 war broke out in Europe, German armies invaded Belgium and the British government declared war against Germany and Austria, the 'Central Powers', on the side of Belgium and France, the 'Allies'. It was to become the most horrible war ever fought on European soil, more costly in the lives of fighting men than any war in the history of the world, more disruptive to the lives of civilian populations than any previous upheaval. The national labour movements of Europe were, for the most part, aghast and, for the most part, threw their separate endeavours behind the war policies of their countries' governments.[86] In Britain some members of the Independent Labour Party and a few others, the most prominent individual being Ramsay MacDonald, refused to support the war.[87] The great majority of the labour movement, though with greatly differing emphases, broadly supported the view that until German militarism had been defeated, democracy would not be safe. It was, however, an important task of the British labour movement to ensure that the government and capitalist interests did not take unfair advantage of the sacrifices that were to be made by millions of working people.

The separate organisations of British labour declared their positions in August and September 1914. Among trade unionists, the GFTU was first off the mark with its 'Manifesto to its members and to its affiliations in Europe and America', in which it dwelt at some length on Germany's responsibility for the war and (with a superfluous show of learning that was typical of Appleton's style) quoted passages by Bernhardi and Treitschke to show that militarism was deeply rooted in German culture and society. It proceeded, more practically, to outline the policy that British trade unions ought to press on the government during the war, a programme followed fairly closely by the War Emergency: Workers' National Committee, on which it was represented. Proper assistance must be given to soldiers and sailors, with a minimum of £1 per week for all disabled servicemen and dependents of the dead. The unions must also learn from the measures taken by government during the emergency – for instance, its takeover of control of the railways – to ensure that after the war such advances in social policy would be maintained.[88]

Soon afterwards the TUC issued its own 'Manifesto to the trade unionists of the country' in which it endorsed the decision announced by the Labour Party to support the national recruiting campaign and called on 'the manhood of the nation' to volunteer for service in order to avoid the need for conscription. A further manifesto appeared, signed by most Labour MPs and many individual socialists and trade unionists as well as the committees of the GFTU and TUC. This and the General Federation's and TUC's own manifestos were issued together in a leaflet in French, designed to reassure the Allies that British labour stood solidly behind them.[89] The next chapter will consider the international policies of British trade unions during and after the war, with their differences over apportioning blame for the war and their different approaches to peace-making. In the international sphere as in the domestic, the Parliamentary Committee of the TUC was becoming intolerant of the General Federation's prominent role and set out, successfully, to diminish it. Far from disappearing during the war, moreover, the rivalries between the two organisations in home affairs also tended to grow. But there was much important work for trade unionists to do in spite of their disagreements, and the General Federation built up an impressive record of activity undertaken both on its own account and in collaboration with the rest of the labour movement.

On 6 August 1914 a labour and socialist emergency conference called by Arthur Henderson formed the War Emergency: Workers' National Committee (WEWNC) representing not only the TUC, GFTU and the Labour Party but also the Co-operative Movement, organisations of women's labour and others. This committee, 'at once the most, and the least, representative ever established in the British labour movement',[90] formed a basis for practical, united action far superior to the divided and faltering Joint Board. The GFTU representatives were Appleton (who was treasurer, but very seldom attended the full committee meetings), Ben Cooper and Ben Tillett. In June 1915, after the resignation of Henderson and W. A. Brace to join the coalition government, J. A. Seddon of the TUC became chairman (succeeded three months later by Robert Smillie) and James O'Grady vice-chairman.[91] The secretary, and kingpin of the organisation, was J. S. Middleton, assistant secretary to the Labour Party. Apart from him, Sidney Webb was probably the committee's most active member, and has been credited with most of the diplomatic compromises that helped to make it more united and effective than other labour organisations during the war.[92] The WEWNC was as its best during the first eighteen months, before differences of opinion about labour policy after the war bedevilled its proceedings. Through a few local committees and a simple central organisation, it maintained close links with the rank and file of workers and with local trades councils and co-operative associations.[93]

At first the WEWNC concentrated much energy on a campaign against the unemployment that was widely expected to result from the war. It opposed the scale of relief set up by the government and fought unsuccessfully for a minimum relief grant of £1 per week per family. It also turned its attention to rising food prices, and organised a series of simultaneous local demonstrations early in 1915. Neither of these campaigns met with much success, in the first case because it turned out that an economy geared to war generated more, not less, employment and in the case of food prices because family incomes in general were actually rising, with more and more women at work in the absence of men at the front, and many people earning war bonuses.[94] (Beatrice Webb, attending the TUC in 1915, was astonished to overhear two delegates complaining to each other of the scandalously *high* wages then being earned.[95]) The subcommittee on government contracts, of which Appleton was a member, had at first a more promising field for constructive work, and earned the praise of G. D. H. Cole for its revelations of sweating in hut-building and clothing projects sponsored by the War Office. They pressed in vain for a full-scale inquiry into the granting and administration of government contracts,[96] but probably helped to curb the abuses by drawing attention to them. In April 1915 Mary Macarthur, the remarkable founder of the Women's Trade Union League which she represented on the WEWNC, chaired a national conference on war service for women.[97] The committee did much to draw the public's attention to the exploitation of child and female labour and through its publications spread information about cases where women were being employed at lower rates than men and about the need to guard against any continuance of such 'dilution' after the war. On food prices, despite the initially tepid public response to their campaign, the WEWNC also succeeded in persuading the government to adopt most of its suggestions for effective control, and published regular statistics showing the rise in prices of basic foodstuffs. Another successful campaign was waged against rising rents, which the government curbed in December 1915 by an Act prohibiting any rise in the rent of small dwellings during the war. In 1916 Middleton pushed the TUC into holding a special conference on conscription, both military and industrial, and on food prices, old age pensions and other policies. This conference, publicised by the WEWNC, adopted the demand for 'conscription of riches' by means of a form of wealth tax.[98]

Difficulties arose in the War Emergency: Workers' National Committee when it dealt with more contentious issues. It divided, for instance, over opposition to Lloyd George's Treasury Agreement and the Munitions of War Act, which imposed a compulsory agreement and arbitration procedure on most workers in essential industries except for the miners.[99] In 1915 the TUC Parliamentary Committee took over administration of the Royal Patriotic Fund to supplement military pensions without first consulting or informing the WEWNC,[100] and in the spring of 1916 there were protracted difficulties over a policy for labour after the war. Most trade union members of the committee were involved in frequent discussions with the government and (with the notable exception of Smillie) tended to endorse its wartime policies. This was true of the Parliamentary Committee, which even invited Lloyd George to the 1915 Congress at a moment's notice, without seeking the permission of delegates, to counteract the militant opposition of Smillie and a large group of others to his munitions Act.[101] The same attitude characterised most members of the GFTU Management Committee. Appleton therefore objected strongly to the anti-government tone of the WEWNC report on *Labour After the War*, published in the spring of 1916. This prefaced a 9-point programme for reconstruction with some fairly strong criticism of the coalition's failure to make adequate plans to prevent the recession and unemployment that were all too likely to follow the war.[102] Appleton protested to Middleton that the report was ill-written, stupid and unfair to the government.[103] The GFTU, Labour Party and TUC all had subcommittees dealing with the problems of labour after the war, and to complicate matters still further the Joint Board had also set up a subcommittee on demobilisation and the employment of the disabled.[104]

The conflict was resolved at Sidney Webb's suggestion by the setting up of a Joint Committee on Labour Problems After the War, on which O'Grady, Cooper and Tillett represented the GFTU.[105] The federation, however, only reluctantly agreed to participate.[106] Although the joint committee did some useful work on plans for the restoration of trade union customs and conditions in peace time, it did not succeed in preventing its constituents from undertaking their own separate activities.[107] As the problems of postwar reconstruction came to occupy an increasingly important place in labour's discussions, the unifying influence of the WEWNC diminished. It is noteworthy that, although others were also approaching the government independently,[108] it was Appleton who chose to make an issue of the WEWNC's anti-government stand. The General Federation of Trade Unions was becoming rather closely identified with a policy of co-operating with the government. It was not easy for any section of the labour movement in wartime to find a separate policy that was consistent with responsible patriotism, especially after Asquith had brought Labour ministers into his coalition. The GFTU seemed to many observers scarcely interested in making the attempt.

The truth was not that the General Federation or its officials were hand-in-glove with the government, but that they found it increasingly difficult to work in harmony with their colleagues in the labour movement. The exclusion of the federation from the Joint Board, continuing secessions by large unions and the challenge to its position in international affairs (which will be considered in the next chapter) all encouraged the Management Committee to assert the federation's own identity rather than merge it with that of other sections of the movement. The policies with which the members identified themselves were not by any means all pro-government, and in some cases the General Federation was among the first to put forward ideas later adopted by the supposedly more militant wings of the movement. As Cole noted, most of the GFTU policies at the outset of the war became part of the WEWNC programme in practice.[109] It was therefore understandable that when the WEWNC was embarking early in 1915 on its campaign to keep food prices down, the GFTU also published propaganda on the same subject.[110] In May 1915 the Management Committee repeated these in a more wide-ranging statement of its position, in which it also repeated the suggestion it had first made when war broke out, that the government should appropriate any 'abnormal profits' made by armaments firms and others as a result of the war.[111] This was very close to the 'conscription of riches' policy adopted by the TUC at its special Congress in June 1916. The Management Committee, in making this call, criticised the government for inactivity on behalf of the working people and for its failure to take the people into its confidence. In its view, this and other 'signs of vacillation and disagreement in high places' discouraged the war effort and were responsible for much of the mounting industrial unrest. Even so, the committee encouraged trade unionists to avoid industrial disputes as far as possible, and (with the exception of T. F. Richards) showed little hesitation in supporting the government's plans for conscription.[112]

One question to which the General Federation paid particular attention was soldiers' and sailors' pay. This had not been taken up with noticeable vigour by other bodies and the General Federation saw the need to correct a great injustice. At the beginning of the war the basic minimum rate of pay for servicemen was 6*d* per day, with small additional proficiency payments available on the recommendation of non-commissioned officers after two years' service. Allotments for dependants' allowances were in part deducted from the men's pay, and wounded men were paid nothing while they were in hospital. The conscript French and Italian armies received even less than the British, which even after the introduction of conscription remained mainly an army of volunteers, but the Australian, New Zealander and Canadian troops with whom the British fought side by side were getting four or five times as much. When the Americans entered the war in 1917, they too received five times as much as the British, with double the size of dependants' allowances. By contrast with the troops, workers at home were gaining pay *rises* of the order of 16 shillings per week or more in some cases. Even taking into account the steep rise in food prices during the war and the fact that most soldiers and sailors received their board, lodging and clothing free of charge, there was an astonishing discrepancy. Many men home on leave were attending union meetings and expected their unions to do something for them.[113]

The GFTU Management Committee had demanded an improved rate of pay for soldiers and sailors in its manifesto at the beginning of the war. It continued to press the question, along with several other unions, notably the dockers, with the energetic involvement of both Ben Tillett and their brilliant young organiser Ernest Bevin. Eventually, on the instructions of the annual general council meeting of 1917, the Management Committee sent out a circular letter on service pay to peers, bishops, trade unionists, MPs and others. They received over a hundred replies of which only three (two from bishops and one from a trade unionist) were unfavourable. They then took the unusual step of summoning a conference at the House of Commons which O'Grady, as chairman, explained on the grounds that since the GFTU was a non-political organisation its invitation might be acceptable to people of all parties, a hope justified by the wide cross-section of MPs who had given their support.[114] A committee was formed,[115] the Prime Minister (since December 1916 this was Lloyd George) was approached. Appleton spent one Sunday morning at Downing Street urging him to take action,[116] and at last the War Cabinet made some concessions. The government undertook to pay the allotments towards dependants' allowances, they increased proficiency pay and reduced the qualifying period for it from two years to six months; and they decided to pay servicemen while they were in hospital except for 'self-inflicted' illness, which included venereal disease. Rather more niggardly concessions were made for the navy and pay for both services, though with large exceptions, was raised to 1 shilling per day. O'Grady and Appleton reported on these 'pettifogging' gains and on the special committee's continuing activity to a special general council meeting in Birmingham on 11 October 1917. They had held another meeting with the Prime Minister on 9 October and pressed for more, especially for the large categories of men who had been excluded from the first increases.[117] Lloyd George, however, had not promised anything, though he agreed to refer the question back to the subcommittee of the War Cabinet that had considered it before.

The GFTU general council meeting that heard this report unanimously condemned the government's measures as inadequate and carried a resolution in favour of 3 shillings per day minimum for all servicemen. The speakers were all careful to avoid open threats of mutiny but Tillett reported that 'plenty of our dockers are quite as ready to take action at the front as they are at home, because they feel they are not being treated fairly'. He repeated the cry that 'if human bodies can be conscripted wealth also must be conscripted and made to bear the cost of the war'.[118] Two other speakers added force to the resolution by suggesting that all affiliated unions should send copies of it to the government, so demonstrating that the campaign was far from being the 'movement only of an executive'.

In the last year of the war, financially hard-pressed and increasingly conservative in outlook (or so many former supporters believed), Lloyd George's government was slow to act for the welfare of the armed forces. Nevertheless it paid serious attention to the campaign of the GFTU. The minutes of the War Cabinet committee on soldiers' and sailors' pay record several meetings in the autumn of 1917 devoted almost entirely to considering the federation's proposals.[119] It was clear that the practical suggestions for implementing higher pay put forward by Appleton and O'Grady in particular won the respect of the committee members. Only the future Conservative Prime Minister, Stanley Baldwin, voiced the fear that if the government conceded anything, the unions would simply come back with new demands. The weight of the GFTU and its special council meeting was quite enough to convince the rest of the committee that trade union opinion must be appeased, and Baldwin was overridden. By the summer of 1919, following a trickle of smaller concessions, Appleton was able to report that at last soldiers were getting their 3 shillings a day.[120] The General Federation's campaign had won it credit among its affiliated unions. No doubt this impression was reinforced when Appleton visited the troops in France in December 1917 and published an emotionally patriotic article under the title 'A visit to France. "Carry on" '.[121]

'Carry on' must have been Appleton's watchword for more reasons than one during the war years. The General Federation itself was embattled from outside and from within. Before the war the number of secessions had been serious enough to cause dismay; but with a renewed, slight rise in membership during 1913–14 it was possible to believe that the rot had stopped. In December 1913 the GFTU began publication of a monthly newspaper, *The Federationist*, 'because the time has arrived when the work and activities of the General Federation of Trade Unions should be better known, and the animadversions of interested opponents more fully dealt with'. The tone of the first issue was internationalist and optimistic. It called upon affiliated unions to forward copies of their reports and journals to the GFTU because the federation wished to become 'the head centre for the spread of actual facts and information concerning Trade Unionism'. The influence of the ideas put forward in Cole's and

Mellor's pamphlet *The Greater Unionism* earlier in the year was strikingly apparent.

Not only did *The Federationist* emphasise its role and that of the federation itself as a centre for trade union information, which was an important part of the new equipment of British trade unionism that Cole and Mellor proposed, it also devoted much space to the re-organisation of trade unions along guild socialist lines.[122] The first issue reprinted from the *New Statesman* an article by W. S. Sanders which it headed 'The splendid story of German trade unionism. Why not visit Germany?' and in its leading editorial declared: 'In Germany the closest relationship exists between the Trade Union, Co-operative and Political sections of the working class. We desire to bring about the same state of things in the United Kingdom.' There was a report on the conference arranged by the Joint Board in Dublin on 9 December 1913 to rally support for the Irish transport workers' strike. An article on the 'wonderful growth of the American Federation of Labour' appeared along with a potpourri of other international news: a unity congress in New Zealand, unemployment in Australia, tariff agreements in Denmark, the development of Bohemian trade unions in 1912, accidents in Rotterdam harbour, the growth of unemployment insurance in European countries. A column of quotations designed to inspire included one from William Morris's *Communism*. On the back page appeared an article on trade union insurance together with names and addresses of agents for the GFTU friendly and collecting society (its insurance branch) and the rules for the conduct of the Joint Committee of Trade Unionists and Co-operators.[123]

The Federationist continued, at ½d an issue, until April 1919, when it gave way to the weekly *Democrat*. From the beginning it was unashamedly political, pronouncing on national and international affairs and only superficially avoiding involvement in party politics. As a potential instrument of trade union unity it could have been far worse. Its contents were lively, readable and varied, and its inter-national reports in particular conveyed news that few of the 50,000 readers it claimed to reach would have found elsewhere. Nor did it devote an undue amount of space to the exclusive affairs of the General Federation.

One crisis in the GFTU's affairs, however, was too momentous to pass without debate in the pages of *The Federationist*. This was the secession of the Amalgamated Society of Engineers. The ASE had never been an easy partner with other unions. Except briefly in 1905–7, it had not been affiliated to the TUC since 1899. It joined the Federation of Engineering and Shipbuilding Trades, late and grudgingly, in 1905.[124] Its delegates to GFTU annual meetings had tended to report back unfavourably: 'One sees the same old ample waistcoats and gold watch-chains, accompanied by fat cigars and the business is not taken as seriously as it might be.'[125] By 1907 the federation was being represented in the engineers' *Monthly Journal* as a 'white elephant'[126] and, although a succession of ASE officials held places on the Management Committee, the commitment of the executive to the GFTU was never strong. In 1913 the Joint Board levied all unions affiliated to the TUC or GFTU for contributions to the costs of the Osborne case. The ASE refused to pay and since it was not affiliated to the TUC, the GFTU was asked to press for payment.[127] This became a grievance, although since the executive finally decided to pay up immediately after leaving the federation, it was obviously rather a phoney one.[128] Another grievance in 1915 was that the ASE had no representative on the Management Committee since the death of T. H. Wilkins two years before.[129] In August 1915 J. Brownlie, president of the union, put the case for secession very briefly in the *Monthly Journal*, using figures up to 1913 to show that the ASE had paid far more into the General Federation than it got out of it. He ignored the rather more favourable figures for 1913–14 and made no mention of the wider benefits connected with membership of the General Federation. The general secretary and editor of the *Monthly Journal*, Robert Young, deplored this policy but in October 1915 he had to report that a vote by the membership had produced 16,075 votes in favour of secession and 14,259 against, a majority of 1,816. The ASE, with a membership of 154,350, seceded from the General Federation of Trade Unions on the vote of fewer than 2,000 members.[130]

In September 1915, W. F. Watson, secretary of the Metal, Engineering and Shipbuilding Amalgamation Committee, contributed to *The Federationist* a plea for the ASE not to secede from the General Federation. He believed that the GFTU would eventually become a federation of industrial unions and that it could help the engineering unions there and then in their movement towards amalgamation. Watson's plea is of more than passing interest, even though it failed to prevent the ASE from seceding. For with Tom Mann he formed part of the inner core of syndicalist leaders in Britain between 1910 and 1914. During the First World War he was a leading figure in the shop stewards' movement in the engineering industry, an extreme industrial militant and agitator, a believer in the policy of 'dual unionism' which would have created separate revolutionary unions.[131] What was he doing supporting an institution whose policies were so non-revolutionary as those of the General Federation?

The answer lies partly in the internal affairs of the ASE. Watson was conducting a campaign against the executive's modified co-operation in the dilution of labour and compulsory enforcement of agreements in war work, through the Treasury Agreement and Munitions of War Act. Brownlie, who as president was the main proponent in the ASE of secession from the General Federation, had contributed a short article on the evils of syndicalism to the first issue of *The Federationist* and, though he may have been influenced by guild socialism,[132] clearly was not interested in the much more revolutionary implications of syndicalism and the 'direct action' tactics employed by Watson. In February 1915, when engineers on the Clyde struck over a demand for an extra $2d$ hour, the ASE executive responded to the government's plea for industrial peace by suspending strike benefits and threw its energies into trying to stop the strike.[133] Opposition to Watson and the Clydeside militants, however, did not necessarily mean opposition to the General Federation. Robert Young, the general secretary, agreed with Watson's view on this and argued strongly in his *Monthly Journal* that:[134]

all trade unions should be one federation. . . . What is needed is a national federation of all Trade Unions, with sub-federations or committees representing and looking after the interests of the separate industries within the federation. Such a federation would increase the evolutionary progress of Trade Unionism towards amalgamation along industrial lines.

The General Federation therefore, in Young's view as well as in that of the syndicalist Watson, was still in 1915 a potential force for the organisation of the trade union movement along industrial, and militant, lines. It seems quite likely that Brownlie saw it in rather the same light, or at least may have feared what his more militant colleagues might make of it if given the chance. At this period the GFTU represented to some observers rather more of whatever activity and forcefulness there was at the centre of the trade union movement than did the Parliamentary Committee of the TUC. From this point of view some union leaders, like the miners and like Brownlie of the engineers, regarded it as a threat while others of an equally or even more militant stripe may have hoped to forge it into a truly effective weapon in the working-class war against capitalism. Some well-informed observers as well as many trade unionists believed that they were witnessing the beginning of a class war 'more bitter than anything we have yet experienced'.[135] If this was so, then the objects and constitution of the GFTU, even if not the personalities who led it, provided a more solid base for operations than the looser affiliations of the TUC.[136]

Events decreed otherwise. The GFTU might deplore the way in which the ASE seceded but it was powerless to reverse the union's decision; and this loss was a real body-blow.[137] By the autumn of 1917 the federation's weakness was serious enough to form one of the topics of debate at the special council meeting which also discussed servicemen's pay.[138] The Management Committee presented a report in which the list of considerable unions that had seceded since 1910, with their 1917 membership, made depressing reading:

Beamers and Twisters (5,000)
Brassworkers (18,000)
National Union of Dock Labourers (47,000)
ASE (230,221)
Gasworkers (164,681)
Gasworkers and Brickmakers (22,124)
Gold, Silver and kindred trades (6,000)
British Labour Amalgamation (3,000)
Musicians (10,000)
Machine workers (20,000)
National House and Ship Painters (29,000)
Scottish Painters (6,000)
Patternmakers (9,665)
Printers' Assistants (8,000)
Smiths and Strikers (10,622)
Steelworkers (3,000)
Amalgamated Society of Tailors (21,000)

It called on the meeting to authorise it to appoint organisers as the gasworkers had suggested before their secession. The federation might be organised on the American model, where the AFofL had scores of organisers working among the existing unions to increase their membership. Or it could become a federation of amalgamations. The strong movement towards amalgamation amongst the unions, which had been gathering momentum since the formation of the National Transport Workers' Federation, the National Union of Railwaymen and the Triple Alliance before the war, received in 1917 its final impetus with the lifting of onerous legal restrictions on the procedure by which amalgamations could be agreed.[139] The proposal to make the GFTU into a federation of such newly formed unions (which had been suggested, in principle, as far back as the 1890s) was therefore timely, even if over-optimistic. A further suggestion was to provide associate membership, whereby unions might pay nominal contributions in return for the services of advice and information which the General Federation was planning to increase, but would have no right to dispute benefits.

During the debate on these proposals Tillett made a strong pitch for strengthening the federation into a central body which would deal with big national questions on behalf of affiliated industrial federations. Tom Shaw of the cotton weavers pleaded for the GFTU to stick to the type of work that it was formed for, although he supported the appointment of organisers. Thomas Mallalieu attempted to justify the federation's incursions into politics on the grounds that it had to defend itself against the Miners' Federation. Opinion seemed to be fairly evenly divided between his and Tillett's school of thought and those who preferred to limit the federation to exclusively financial functions. Eventually the Management Committee's report was referred to the executives of the affiliated unions, and yet again the appointment of organisers was put off indefinitely.

At this time the Management Committee was also engaged in a public slanging match with the Parliamentary Committee of the TUC. Each organisation issued to its affiliated unions leaflets setting out a comparison of facts, figures and dates to show that it was in the right and the other body was the usurper.[140] At Blackpool in September 1917 Congress had voted to extend and strengthen the work of the Parliamentary Committee very comprehensively, in the first step on the long road to reform that would culminate in the formation of the TUC General Council in 1921.[141] The General Federation protested that its own work in no way deviated from its original objectives. It showed with perfect truth that on the matters of organisation, international relations and the establishment of a labour bureau of information its own general council resolutions and the subsequent work of the Management Committee had predated the decisions of the Blackpool congress in every particular.

But it was not enough to be in the right. With the departure of so many of its larger and more influential unions the General Federation had become ever less representative. New amalgamations within different sectors of the workforce were taking up the energies of the most enterprising trade union leaders just when the General Federation appealed to them to build a strong central organisation. Even if they had had the time to give to such an undertaking, few saw it as being in their interests; and in any case developments within the TUC held out the hope that that body could become at last the purposeful pilot of the nation's trade unionism that some leaders had been trying to make it for years. James O'Grady commented to the GFTU's annual meeting in 1917, a year before he himself relinquished the chairmanship to become secretary of the National Federation of General Workers, that unions affiliated to the TUC were leaving when they became amalgamated with other unions.[142] He hoped to see this process reversed but in fact it continued with greater vigour. The formation of the British Iron, Steel and Kindred Trades Association in 1917, and of several smaller amalgamations, foreshadowed the epoch-making creations of the Amalgamated Engineering Union (1921), Transport and General Workers' Union (1922) and National Union of General and Municipal Workers (1924).[143] All of these sapped the strength of the General Federation of Trade Unions whose Management Committee still hoped that it too might step triumphantly across the new threshold of British trade unionism.

Notes: Chapter 4

1   Tom Mann, *Socialism* (1905), quoted in Geoff Brown's introduction to *The Industrial Syndicalist* (1910–11), repr. (Nottingham: Spokesman Books, 1974).
2   See Bob Holton, *British Syndicalism 1900–1914: Myths and Realities* (London: Pluto Press, 1976), pt 1, pp. 27–69.
3   *Industrial Syndicalist*, vol. I, no.1 (July 1910), pp. 16–18.
4   ibid., pp. 18–19. His emphasis.
5   ibid., p. 21.
6   ibid., pp. 19–22.
7   A useful brief summary of Mann's theoretical progression is given in Brown's introduction to *Industrial Syndicalist*.
8   Mann's article in the GFTU *Quarterly Report*, June 1910, entitled 'Industrialism and Parliamentary action' carefully included parliamentary and municipal politics among the desirable ways of advancing the cause.
9   All of these factors were cited by W. A. Appleton in his paper on 'The causes of the labour unrest' (GFTU, *Quarterly Report*, December 1910). Holton, *British Syndicalism*, ch. 4, pp. 73–7, summarises views of the causes of the labour unrest. See also H. Pelling, 'The labour unrest 1911–14', in *Popular Politics and Society in Late Victorian Britain. Essays* (London: Macmillan, 1968).
10 For the events in South Wales see R. Page Arnot, *The Miners,* Vol. 2, *Years of Struggle*, pp. 57–77.
11 Askwith, *Industrial Problems and Disputes*, p. 349.
12 Holton, *British Syndicalism*, pp. 114–15.
13 See M. A. Hickling (ed.), *Citrine's Trade Union Law*, 3rd edn (London: Stevens, 1967), pp. 56, 602; Hedges and Winterbottom, *Legal History of Trade Unionism*, pp. 146–7 and *passim*.
14 GFTU, *Proceedings and Reports*, 1917–18, report of the special general council meeting, Birmingham, 11 October 1917, pp. 20–3, Management Committee statement on organisation.
15 GFTU, *Quarterly Report*, September 1910.
16 Roberts, *The TUC*, pp. 144–5.
17 Financial report, 24 April 1912, prepared at the request of the 1911 agcm, in GFTU, *Proceedings and Reports*, 1911–12. In 1913 it had to report its third

successive year when expenditure exceeded income, but during the war its finances recovered.

18 GFTU, *Annual Report*, 1911.
19 Financial report, 24 April 1912, in GFTU, *Proceedings and Reports*, 1911–12.
20 Management Committee minutes, 28 November 1912.
21 See below, pp. 132.
22 Financial report, 24 April 1912.
23 GFTU, *Annual Report*, 1912.
24 GFTU, *Proceedings and Reports*, 1912–13, report of 1912 agcm.
25 This generalisation ought not to obscure wide variations in the nature of the seceding unions.
26 Total membership of trade unions in Great Britain and Northern Ireland rose from just over 2½ million in 1910 to nearly 3½ million in 1912, and over 4 million by the end of 1913. See B. R. Mitchell and Phyllis Deane (eds), *Second Abstract of British Historical Statistics* (Cambridge: Cambridge University Press, 1971), p. 68.
27 GFTU, *Annual Report*, 1913.
28 Roberts, *The TUC*, pp. 244–5, summarises the general debate from the TUC point of view.
29 Joint Board minutes, 25 and 26 April 1911.
30 Joint Board minutes, 26 April 1911. Appleton's reply to a motion in favour of fusion at the 1912 agcm (GFTU, *Proceedings and Reports*, 1912–13) summarises the Management Committee's thinking on the matter since 1910.
31 GFTU, *Quarterly Report*, December 1910.
32 Joint Board minutes, 26 April 1911; TUC Parliamentary Committee minutes, 26 April 1911.
33 GFTU, *Proceedings and Reports*, 1912–13, report of 1912 agcm.
34 Roberts, *The TUC*, p. 244. Joint Board minutes, 19 June 1912.
35 For example, in GFTU, *Annual Report*, 1912.
36 For example, in a signed article in GFTU, *Annual Report*, 1911; *Quarterly Report*, December 1912.
37 See G. D. H. Cole and W. Mellor, *The Greater Unionism*, pamphlet published by the National Labour Press, London and Manchester [1913], p. 20.
38 W. A. Appleton, *Trade Union Organisation: How to Make the Movement More Effective*, GFTU pamphlet (London: GFTU, 1916).
39 For example, in GFTU, *Quarterly Report*, September 1912, which recorded the departure of the gasworkers, patternmakers and brassworkers.
40 Management Committee minutes, 4 July 1912. For Thorne's speech at the 1910 agcm, see below, p. 105.
41 J. Sexton, *Sir James Sexton, Agitator The Life of the Dockers' MP. An Autobiography* (London: Faber, 1936), *passim*, esp. ch. 33.
42 GFTU, *Proceedings and Reports*, 1912–13, report of 1912 agcm, reply by Appleton to an inquiry about the enginemen's and cranemen's secession.
43 Roberts, *The TUC*, ch. VII, pp. 232–69, esp. pp. 245–6n.
44 GFTU, *Proceedings and Reports*, 1911–12, 1912–13, reports of 1911 and 1912 agcms.
45 Cole and Mellor, *The Greater Unionism*, p. 20.
46 ibid., p. 18.
47 GFTU, *Quarterly Report*, March 1912.
48 For Appleton's political views in greater detail, see below, pp. 158–63.
49 See Derek Fraser, *The Evolution of the British Welfare State: A History of Social Policy since the Industrial Revolution* (London: Macmillan, 1973), p. 161.
50 Fraser, op. cit., pp. 157–63, summarises the thinking behind the Act. So do Bentley B. Gilbert, *The Evolution of National Insurance in Great Britain. The*

Origins of the Welfare State (London: Michael Joseph, 1966); Brown, *Labour and Unemployment*, and Harris, *Unemployment and Politics.*

51   GFTU, *Proceedings and Reports*, 1912–13, report of first annual meeting of GFTU insurance section; speech by O'Grady.

52   Management Committee minutes, 10 and 18 March 1909. This was the report that Tillett leaked to the press. See above, p. 113.

53   GFTU, *Proceedings and Reports*, 1911–12, report of special council meeting, 14 March 1912, statement by Appleton.

54   TUC Parliamentary Committee minutes, 26 April 1911.

55   Report of special council meeting, 14 March 1912, statement by Appleton.

56   Harris, *Unemployment and Politics*, pp. 295–334, gives a detailed analysis of how the government arrived at its eventual policy.

57   GFTU, leaflet dated 5 October 1911 on 'Threatened Trade Unions' (bound with *Proceedings and Reports*, 1911–12).

58   PRO, CAB 37/110/62, 63 and 66.

59   For Appleton's regard for Lloyd George, see his article in *National [Insurance] Weekly*, 28 September 1912, pp. 477–8, and GFTU, *Rheolau a threfiadau ...* (Caernarfon: GFTU, 1913), British Library copy inscribed by Appleton to Lloyd George 'as a souvenir of ideals attempted and work done'.

60   GFTU, *Proceedings and Reports*, 1912–13, report of first annual meeting of insurance section, p. 8.

61   ibid., p. 4; Mann, *Industrial Syndicalist*, reissued with introduction by Geoff Brown (Nottingham: Spokesman Books, 1974), p. 166.

62   Report of first annual meeting of GFTU insurance section, pp. 2–4.

63   ibid., p. 4.

64   The opposition of unions to the National Insurance Act 1911 and its operation is discussed by Noelle Whiteside, 'Welfare legislation and the unions during World War I', *Historical Journal*, vol. 23, no. 4 (1980), pp. 857–74.

65   GFTU, *Quarterly Report*, September 1912.

66   *National [Insurance] Weekly*, 28 September 1912, pp. 477–8.

67   ibid.

68   PRO, T172/105 (Treasury private office papers), meeting of 1 January 1913 between trade union representatives and C. F. G. Masterman, acting for Lloyd George. Here Masterman referred to an earlier meeting where Ben Turner and Appleton had strongly impressed Lloyd George with the need to replace the 'panel' system with a national health service.

69   For example, Ben Turner, *About Myself 1863–1930* (London: Cayme Press, 1930), p. 143; Horace Moulden, in an interview at Edinburgh agcm, 1977.

70   TUC Parliamentary Committee minutes, 8 October 1912.

71   GFTU Management Committee minutes, 2 January 1913.

72   Joint Board minutes, 8 January 1913.

73   ibid., 19 February 1913.

74   Management Committee minutes, 2 and 30 January 1913.

75   Much of the following account is taken from a leaflet circulated by the Management Committee to affiliated unions in 1915. It is bound with *Proceedings and Reports*, 1914–15. Roberts, *The TUC*, pp. 263–5, gives a brief outline of the quarrel.

76   Joint Board minutes, 18 June 1913.

77   TUC Parliamentary Committee minutes, 22 May 1913.

78   TUC, *Report*, 1913.

79   TUC Parliamentary Committee minutes, 3 September, 8 October and 12 November 1914. Robert Smillie did, however, become chairman of the committee. The miners' objection was to paying their levy through the Joint Board. They preferred to pay through the TUC.

80 ibid., 12 November, 8 and 9 December 1914.

81 TUC, *Report*, 1916, p. 310–20.

82 TUC Parliamentary Committee minutes, 14 November 1916.

83 For the history of this struggle and the formation of the Triple Alliance, see Arnot, *The Miners*, Vol. 2, *Years of Struggle*, ch. VI, pp. 153–81. For Smillie's confrontation with Lloyd George, see R. Smillie, *My Life for Labour* (London: Mills & Boon, 1924), pp. 156–65.

84 So irrelevant that neither Smillie nor Arnot refers to this episode.

85 At the 'coupon election' of 1918, Ward stood as a coalition Liberal.

86 Appleton and Tillett, attending a conference in Germany in June 1914, gained the impression that the German people as a whole 'were full of desire for German world-politics and domination' (see the speech by Appleton at the 1915 agcm, in GFTU, *Proceedings and Reports*, 1915–16). This charge could never have been levelled at Carl Legien, however. Lorwin, *International Labor Movement*, surveys the positions taken by the different national trade union and labour movements during the First World War.

87 MacDonald's attitude to the war was not clear-cut. He did not lack patriotism as the jingoists asserted; but his internationalist and pacifist principles forbade him to lend active support, and he resigned the leadership of the Labour Party to Arthur Henderson. See Marquand, *Ramsay MacDonald*.

88 G. D. H. Cole, *Labour in War Time* (London: Bell, 1915), pp. 37–8, gives an outline of the GFTU manifesto and implies that it took the initiative on behalf of the trade unions.

89 *Le Mouvement Travailliste Anglais et la Guerre* (September 1914). This is bound in a volume of GFTU pamphlets at the British Library (WP 4743). For some consideration of the Labour Party during the First World War, see Ross McKibbin, *The Evolution of the Labour Party 1910–1924* (London: Oxford University Press, 1974), ch. V.

90 Royden Harrison, 'The War Emergency Workers' National Committee 1914–1920', in A. Briggs and J. Saville (eds), *Essays in Labour History 1886–1923* (London: Macmillan, 1971), p. 212.

91 WEWNC printed minutes, 15 June and 23 September 1915.

92 Harrison, 'The WEWNC'.

93 Cole, *Labour in War Time*, pp. 97–107, gave great praise to the WEWNC which he hoped to see continue after the war with a proper democratic constitution.

94 Harrison, 'The WEWNC'.

95 BLPES, diary of Beatrice Webb, p. 3369, September 1915.

96 Cole, *Labour in War Time*, pp. 97–107.

97 WEWNC minutes, April 1915.

98 ibid., *passim* and Harrison, 'The WEWNC'. The TUC Parliamentary Committee minutes for 1915–16 suggest that Harrison does rather less than justice to their activity on the question of conscription. But what presumably worried Middleton was that they were not being seen to be active, and were not involving the wider trade union movement in their deals with the government.

99 Harrison, 'The WEWNC'.

100 ibid.

101 This episode is described in Beatrice Webb's diary, p. 3370, September 1915. Roberts, *The TUC*, p. 279, paints a picture of rather greater resistance to the straight government line than Mrs Webb gave the Parliamentary Committee credit for, but does not mention the exact circumstances of the invitation to Lloyd George.

102 WEWNC, *Labour After the War. First Report* (London: WEWNC, 1916).

103 Harrison, 'The WEWNC'.

104 WEWNC minutes, 13 January 1916.

105   ibid., 27 April and 25 May 1916; Harrison, 'The WEWNC'.
106   Harrison, 'The WEWNC'.
107   Harrison, op. cit., states that the WEWNC did not proceed with its decision to appoint a joint subcommittee, but the printed minutes suggest that it did come into being. At least three pamphlets appeared under its imprint in 1916–17, all on trade union customs and conditions. It appears not to have taken over any deputations to the government, however.
108   One among many examples of such independent dealings is the discussion that took place on conscription between representatives of the Joint Board (including the GFTU) and the Prime Minister and Lord Kitchener, on 28 September 1915. This resulted in a scheme of labour recruiting committees and was followed on at least one occasion by further consultations on recruitment with the government (TUC Parliamentary Committee minutes, 28 and 30 September 1915; 26 April 1916). Another body through which labour representatives regularly had dealings with the government was the National Labour Advisory Council, presided over by Arthur Henderson (see Roberts, *The TUC*, pp. 277–8).
109   See above, p. 139, n. 88.
110   GFTU, *High Prices of Food*, manifesto by the Management Committee (27 January 1915).
111   GFTU, *The Management Committee and the General Situation*, (27 May 1915).
112   Management Committee minutes, 12, 19 and 26 April 1916. Interview with O'Grady on industrial conscription, *The Times*, 23 April 1915.
113   The details in this paragraph are taken from GFTU, *Report of the Special General Council Meeting Held in the Queen's College, Birmingham, on Thursday, October 11th, 1917, to Consider Sailors' and Soldiers' Pay, National Reconstruction and Organisation, Organisation of the Federation* (11 October 1917).
114   GFTU, *Soldiers' and Sailors' Pay. Report of a Conference at the House of Commons* (1 August 1917).
115   ibid. The members of the committee were: Sir Charles Nicholson, Colonel Wilson, Colonel Burn, Major Bowden, Harold Smith, Tom Wing, Colonel Penry Williams, Bartley Dennis, C. B. Stanton, A. W. Yeo, J. O'Grady, A. Wilkie, Lords Peel, Ancaster, Russell, Sydenham, Charnwood and Beresford, and W. A. Appleton, secretary.
116   GFTU, *Report of the Special General Council Meeting....*
117   Unless they were married men, able seamen, stokers and privates in the marines and army stood to gain nothing from the government's concession.
118   GFTU, *Report of the Special General Council Meeting....*
119   PRO, CAB 27/21, especially meetings of 17, 25 and 29 October 1917.
120   GFTU, *Annual Report*, 1919.
121   In *The Federationist* and *The Sheffield Daily Independent*, December 1917, reprinted as a pamphlet.
122   The guild socialism of G. D. H. Cole is described, *inter alia*, in S. T. Glass, *The Responsible Society: The Ideas of the English Guild Socialists* (London: Longman, 1966); Dame Margaret Cole, *The Life of G. D. H. Cole* (London: Macmillan, 1971), and J. M. Winter, *Socialism and the Challenge of War* (London: Routledge, 1974).
123   This committee failed initially because of the Co-operative Movement's suspicions of trade unionism. But during the war, beginning with the WEWNC, the basis was laid for much closer links between the two movements. See Roberts, *The TUC*, pp. 307–8; Harrison, 'The WEWNC'; McKibbin, *Evolution of the Labour Party*, pp. 178–91.
124   Jefferys, *The Story of the Engineers*, p. 163.
125   ASE, *Monthly Journal*, August 1905, quoted in Jefferys, *The Story of the Engineers*, pp. 162–3.

126 ibid., p. 163.
127 Joint Board minutes, 14 November 1912.
128 GFTU, *Proceedings and Reports*, 1915–16, report on secession of the ASE, ASE, *Monthly Journal*, October 1915.
129 GFU report on secession of ASE; ASE, *Monthly Journal*, August 1915.
130 GFTU report on secession of ASE.
131 The outlines of Watson's career during this period can be found in James Hinton, *The First Shop Stewards' Movement* (London: Allen & Unwin, 1973).
132 ibid., pp. 50–1, where, however, Brownlie's and Young's respective offices in the union are incorrectly cited.
133 ibid., pp. 50, 103–9.
134 October 1917.
135 BLPES, Passfield Papers, Beatrice Webb to Betty Balfour, 28 October 1915.
136 This observation was made many times by GFTU officials, for example, by O'Grady in his last speech to the agcm as chairman, in 1918.
137 GFTU, *Proceedings and Reports*, 1915–16, report on the secession of ASE.
138 ibid., 1917–18, report on special general council meeting, Birmingham, 11 October 1917.
139 The Trade Union (Amalgamation) Act 1917.
140 TUC, *Report*, 1918, pp. 108–9; GFTU, *Proceedings and Reports*, 1917–18, pamphlet signed by the Management Committee (undated, but autumn 1917).
141 Roberts, *The TUC*, pp. 295–6.
142 GFTU, *Proceedings and Reports*, 1917–18, report of 1917 agcm.
143 On the trend towards amalgamation before 1920 see Webb, *History of Trade Unionism*, pp. 546–54. See also H. Pelling, *A History of British Trade Unionism* (Harmondsworth: Penguin, 1963), pp. 167–8.

5
International Affairs and the Exclusion of the General Federation from British Representation, 1913–22

International Trade Unionism during the First World War

In the last year of the decade the General Federation had much useful work to do. The government in making its plans for postwar reconstruction called for a stream of advice from labour representatives. The GFTU played its part, even though it had been clear since before the war that ministers were prone to regard the TUC as the proper body to consult first when it wanted the advice or co-operation of trade unionists.[1] Appleton spent much time visiting ministries and gave evidence on behalf of the Management Committee to ministerial committees on postwar finance, on women in industry and on emigration (which he thought should be encouraged).[2] Much effort was spent on plans for re-employing disabled servicemen.[3] The Management Committee held a special conference in January 1919 in the presence of a Ministry of Labour official to consider the problems of soldiers returning from war service to interrupted apprenticeships. The same conference reaffirmed the General Federation's opposition to compulsory unemployment insurance, and this heralded the renewal of its involvement in the debate over insurance policy.[4]

None of this useful activity could save the GFTU from the bitter blow of exclusion from international trade unionism. This turning point in the federation's existence came in 1920 but the first steps towards it were taken before the war. In this as in the GFTU's exclusion from the Joint Board, the miners played a part, for it was they who pushed the TUC into being more active in international affairs. The Miners' Federation of Great Britain had been an active member of the International Miners' Federation since its formation in London in 1890, and in 1912 during its fight for a minimum wage it had drawn strength from the continental miners' agreement not to allow their coal to be sent to Britain during the British strike.[5] In 1913, at its suggestion, the TUC Parliamentary Committee sent Bowerman as a non-voting fraternal delegate to the international conference in Zürich.[6] That year there were fraternal delegates at Congress from Canada, France and Germany in addition to the usual delegation from the American Federation of Labor, and the TUC sent fraternal delegates to their national conference in return.[7] With the mounting threat of war an emergency conference of international labour met in the summer of 1914, but to the intense disappointment of those who placed their hopes for world peace on the international solidarity of labour, they failed to agree on a common policy of resistance to their national governments' preparations for war. It was in this atmosphere that both Appleton and W. J. Davis attended the German national trade union conference at the end of June 1914. Appleton represented the GFTU. Davis, whose Amalgamated Brassworkers' Society had left the General Federation in the previous autumn, represented the TUC as chairman of the Parliamentary Committee. He reported back with great chagrin that when he arrived in Germany he was directed to the wrong hotel and took two days to find the German leaders. Moreover, he was not permitted to deliver the address he had prepared because Appleton spoke on behalf of the British trade unions and the Germans had a rule that not more than one delegate might speak for each foreign nation. After the special invitation he had received at the Manchester TUC in 1913, 'this was certainly a strange manner of welcoming the accredited representative of the British Trade Unions'. He rejected the Germans' efforts to placate him, and Bowerman wrote to Carl Legien to ask for 'an explanation of the manner in which the British representative had been treated'.[8]

The General Federation did not lose its position in the international movement, however, until the end of the First World War. It had several active years ahead on the international scene. The International Federation of Trade Unions had become quite a flourishing organisation before the outbreak of war, with affiliations from nineteen countries, including the American Federation of Labor, which had affiliated in 1911 after a long quarrel over international representation with the Industrial Workers of the World.[9] The Budapest conference in 1911 carried resolutions to suspend emigration at times of major national strikes and to prevent the export of strike-breakers. In 1913 the International Federation of Trade Unions began publishing a bi-monthly newsletter in German, French and English and it reported to the Zürich conference that the equivalent of more than $700,000 had been collected to help workers on strike or locked out in various countries. It was also able to report that trade union information bureaux had been set up in various countries, which no doubt inspired the GFTU Management Committee to carry out part of the general council's instructions in this respect by starting *The Federationist* in December 1913.[10] The international reports of this paper remained its strong point throughout its existence, and were almost all supplied by the International Federation of Trade Unions until the outbreak of war. Among other activities to the credit of the international federation were investigations into the use of industrial poisons and the regulation of night and home work. It was at the very least a promising foundation for international co-operation, and one worth preserving if possible from the obliterating forces of war.

Carl Legien, who had done more than anyone to build up the International Federation of Trade Unions, tried very hard to keep it going after the outbreak of war. At first Gompers of the American Federation of Labor and Appleton were reasonably friendly to Legien's advances, but Jouhaux of France and Mertens of Belgium were not. Legien suggested that the Dutch trade union centre under Jan Oudegeest might become a branch office of the international federation, responsible for conducting all business with allied and neutral countries' trade unions while hostilities continued, but the French found this unacceptable and Appleton soon adopted their position. Jouhaux set up an international correspondence centre for Allied trade unions in Paris; and in effect the international trade union movement was broken up into three parts, more or less for the duration of the war, with centres in Berlin, Amsterdam and Paris.

Appleton and the Management Committee of the GFTU remained very much aware of their international obligations throughout the war. *The Federationist*'s first issue had proclaimed that they wished to make the General Federation 'the head centre for the spread of actual facts and information concerning Trade Unionism', and devoted much of its space to international items, including a paean of praise to German trade unionism. It maintained its international flavour during the war in spite of a sorrowful change of mind about the Germans. Behind this public stance lay an assiduous attention to contacts with American and Allied trade union leaders.[11] Appleton and Jouhaux arranged a conference in Leeds in July 1916 to which delegates were invited from Britain, Belgium, France, Italy, Portugal and Russia and were sent from all but Portugal and Russia. The main topic of discussion was the joint American and French proposal that an international conference of labour should be held at the same time as the peace conference between the belligerent governments. They wanted to ensure that the peace treaty would include clauses on labour, for

> it is with a working class at higher wages, with better conditions of life, enjoying more liberty, that a home market is developed to its highest point and that a larger consumption is further developed.[12]

The French prepared an historical survey of international labour legislation for the conference. They wanted to 'pave the way to the federation of the united states of the world' and hoped that the peace conference that ended the war would confer on European nations the blessings of political and economic independence, disarmament and obligatory international arbitration. Their detailed proposals for the labour clauses of a future peace treaty formed the basis of the 'International Labour Charter' agreed by the conference, which the GFTU Management Committee proposed to Asquith in August 1916 and sent out in a circular to Labour organisations.[13] In this document the General Federation asked the Prime Minister to consider the international regulation of: the labour of women and children, night work, weekly rest days, and the maximum length of the working day. They also wanted an international commission on the laws of safety and hygiene and proposed the establishment of an international labour office to collect statistics. Appleton avoided the visionary flights of the document prepared by the Confédération Générale de Travail but he put in a strong plea that the sacrifices made by working people during the war entitled them to be considered in the peace.

> The poor people have had no part in the making of war or peace; they have suffered, they have endured contumely and they have died, but never yet has monarch or statesman made their situation a determining factor in a treaty of peace.[14]

Hopes for peace in 1916 were delusory, but when at last the armistice had been concluded and a peace treaty was hammered out at Versailles, the inclusion in it of a Labour Convention was a new and very important departure in the history of international relations.[15] The small conference held under the GFTU's auspices in Leeds in 1916 was the first of several to call for some kind of international labour charter. It was followed by a succession of abortive attempts at conferences that were supposed to include trade unionists from both Allied and Central Power countries, and in Britain the conflict between GFTU and TUC bred rivalry over who should take credit for calling the international conferences. Early in 1917 the

Swiss tried to arrange a conference in Berne and Carl Legien called a meeting of Central Power trade unionists in Stockholm. Neither proposal met with much support from Allied trade unions.

For much of 1917 the most absorbing topic in labour circles was provided by Russia. The March revolution was hailed with joy in Britain, where expressions of sympathy with the oppressed Russian workers had formed a regular part of TUC and GFTU conference proceedings for years. Lloyd George, who became Prime Minister in December 1916, sent his Labour Cabinet minister Arthur Henderson to Russia to attempt to keep them in the war. But Henderson returned believing that the best way to keep the Russians as allies of Britain was to explore the possibilities of a negotiated peace which Russia, her people starving and exhausted, desperately needed. The Russians were backing an international socialist conference in Stockholm, which the German socialists were expected to attend, and the Labour Party supported Henderson's proposal that Britain should also send a delegation to Stockholm. Henderson was rebuked by the War Cabinet for this policy and resigned in indignation. He and the other British delegates were subsequently refused passports to go to Stockholm. His departure from the Cabinet, even though the Prime Minister placated Labour by replacing him with George Barnes, is generally seen to have marked the point where the Labour Party really severed its links with the Liberals and began on the strategy that would lead to power in its own right.[16]

While British labour's political wing was preparing a new constitution and a new strategy under the impact of events in Russia and at home, trade unionists, deeply involved though they were in these changes, also continued their attempts to draw up a formula for agreement on the clauses that international labour would wish to see in an eventual peace treaty. The General Federation, adamantly opposed to any conference with the Germans while the war continued, held its second conference of Allied trade unionists at its own offices in September 1917, immediately after that year's Trades Union Congress.[17] Delegates from France, Serbia, Canada and the USA as well as from several British organisations[18] heard James O'Grady declare that German trade unionists had lost the confidence of the British trade union movement and that free nations would only be able 'to breathe the atmosphere of liberty' again when 'the German military machine is smashed beyond all possibility of repair'. This was meant as a counterblast to the TUC which decided in July to establish itself as the British centre for dealing with international trade union matters and had just given strong support to Arthur Henderson's view that it was better to 'consult with the German minority before peace than ... with the representatives of a

Central House following the addition of
an extra floor in 1971

PROPOSED
LABOUR HALL
LONDON

W. A. Appleton
VERNON HOUSE
BLOOMSBURY SQ.,
LONDON W.C.

Proposal for a Central Labour Congress Hall in London, first mooted by W. A. Appleton in 1912

discredited autocratic government when a military victory has been secured'.[19] Following its own conference, the GFTU issued a report of the proceedings, which had confirmed the policies agreed at Leeds in 1916. It circulated its report to foreign trade unionists in order to reaffirm its own position as the legitimate representative of British labour abroad. This was all part of the open warfare now being conducted between the General Federation and the TUC. The GFTU Management Committee had even gone so far as to send a telegram urging the American Federation of Labor not to support the proposed conferences in Stockholm and (the second attempt that year by the Swiss) in Berne; and Samuel Gompers complied.

After the USA entered the war in the spring of 1917, Gompers twice asked the British government to send Appleton over to America as one of a delegation to help persuade American trade unionists of the justice of the Allied war aims.[20] On the second occasion, early in 1918, Appleton headed the delegation and had an opportunity to tell Gompers in person about the TUC's takeover of international affairs in British trade unionism. At that time Gompers still regarded the General Federation as the true representative of British trade unions. It was a justifiable misapprehension, for although the Trades Union Congress had three or four times the membership of the federation[21] it had only just begun to cultivate international relationships. Even in 1918 most continental trade unionists would have agreed with the Americans in regarding the General Federation, and above all its general secretary, as the official voice of organised British labour in international affairs. The developing interest of the TUC, however, caused great confusion, especially when it was seen to be following a more conciliatory line towards German trade unionists than that adopted by the GFTU.[22] Sooner or later one of the two organisations would have to give way, not least because any reconstituted postwar international trade union organisation was likely to adopt the prewar rule that only one trade union centre could represent each country.

The ousting of the General Federation took place between 1918 and 1920 in the context of almost continuous international negotiations and conferences. Arthur Henderson was the leading figure in formulating British labour's war aims in the last year of the war. After his resignation from Lloyd George's War Cabinet and his championship of the Stockholm international conference, he both enjoyed heightened prestige as the untramelled leader of the Labour Party and had more time to bring to the task. As we have seen,[23] he had taken up the cause of labour unity before the war but somewhat at the expense of the General Federation, whose attempts to strengthen its own separate organisation he vehemently opposed. Now that he favoured a negotiated peace, the GFTU's opposition to this policy ensured that

Henderson would not be anxious to involve the federation in discussions either at home or internationally. In December 1917 a joint committee of the Labour Party and TUC, chaired by Henderson, agreed on a statement of the war aims of the labour movement and an Allied labour and socialist conference in the following February endorsed this document with only minor modifications. It called for very much the same terms of peace as those put forward by President Wilson in his 'Fourteen Points' which became the basis for the Treaty of Versailles.[24] Prominent among these were the call for 'open covenants, openly arrived at' (secret diplomacy had been denounced frequently at Labour Party and trade union conferences since the outbreak of the war and before), for a recognition of national rights to self-determination, including those of colonial peoples, for the removal of fiscal barriers to international trade and for the establishment of a League of Nations.

The GFTU played no direct part in this formulation, but its own peace policy was broadly in line with it. Many of the schisms in the British labour movement during the First World War arose from differences in attitudes towards Germany and the apportionment of blame for the war, and not from fundamental differences of opinion about industrial and social policy. This was the time when British labour first began to make itself felt in foreign policy, as the Webbs noted with almost starry-eyed satisfaction.[25] In this important development the General Federation of Trade Unions had played no negligible part. Before the war it was the only British national trade union organisation to take part systematically and regularly in international relations. In 1915 Ernest Bevin, the future Foreign Secretary, then a rising star in the Dock, Wharf, Riverside and General Workers' Trade Union, chose the General Federation's annual general council meeting as the forum in which to recommended the establishment of an advisory diplomatic committee in the labour movement.[26] Much more important, the proposals in the 'labour charter' drawn up at the Leeds conference held by the GFTU in 1916 were adopted in the following year by delegates from the Central Powers and neutral countries, meeting under the auspices of the Swiss Federation of Labour in Berne.[27] Much of the credit for these proposals is due to the French, but the GFTU collaborated closely with Jouhaux and the CGT in drawing them up, and took on the work of organising the Leeds conference and then of publicising its labour charter. The importance of these and all the other proposals for international labour agreements after the war did not lie in their originality, since few trade unionists would have disagreed with their generalised calls for labour to be more represented in future policy-making, or for international agreements on emigration, unemployment insurance and standards of health and safety. What mattered more than the substance of such proposals was that they were formulated at all, and kept before the notice both of governments and of the national labour movements themselves. The existence of a standard upon which labour in all the countries involved in the war could agree was absolutely necessary if the eventual peace treaty was to include clauses dealing with international labour. And this innovation of principle was in itself as important as the substance of the labour clauses in the treaty.

The British contribution to labour's peace-making remained for most of 1918 fraught with enmities. The General Federation continued to assert its interests, and the Parliamentary Committee firmly intended to squash them. In August 1918 Samuel Gompers, whose contacts with Appleton and the GFTU had been close and frequent throughout the war, arrived in England to see for himself what lay behind the divisions in British labour. It was less than a year since the Bolsheviks had seized power in Russia and Gompers, in his biographer's words, saw 'bolshevism, a whiskered terror darting ruffian-like through the paths and lanes of trade unionism'.[28] He made this attitude plain, both at the Trades Union Congress in September and at the international conference which followed. This squat, dynamic little man who had been born in the East End of London, started work as a child in the tobacco industry and then emigrated with his parents to New York, loved his adopted country with all the passion and idealism of a first-generation immigrant. In a lifetime devoted to building up the American Federation of Labor, much of his achievement was due to sheer force of character. His attempt to impose his distinctively American view and his own will on the Allied trade unionists in 1918 was met with polite dislike.[29] Nevertheless, as he soon discovered, he had no cause to fear Bolshevism among the majority of British trade union leaders.[30] Henderson, who was by this time by far the most respected spokesman for British labour on the coming peace, deftly steered his course between Gompers and the jingoistic Havelock Wilson, the seamen's leader, both of whom wanted no negotiations with German labour until its leaders had repudiated German war policies, and the left wing led by James Maxton of the ILP and the French grandson of Karl Marx, Jean Longuet, who wanted unconditional negotiations with German labour to bring about an end to the war.[31]

By this time the TUC and GFTU were patching up a sort of truce. The Parliamentary Committee was proceeding with plans to set up its own international department, but it did arrange a meeting with the GFTU Management Committee before Congress assembled, and so avoided a showdown during the debate.[32] Even so, Congress referred back the part of the Parliamentary Committee's report that dealt with relations with the GFTU.[33] There was a strong feeling among delegates to the TUC that the federation was being treated shabbily and that the Parliamentary Committee's wanton neglect of international affairs for many years should be blamed for the conflict that they now witnessed. As Ben Cooper, the cigar-makers' leader and a long-standing member of the GFTU Management Committee, pointed out, what the Parliamentary Committee was really trying to do was to reduce the GFTU to a mere benefit-paying organisation. Arthur Pugh, secretary of the Iron and Steel Trades Confederation, moving a resolution in favour of closer unity and industrial unionism, drew a parallel between the supine behaviour of the Parliamentary Committee in international affairs and its failure to take the initiative on the home front. 'There is a stirring of the dry bones,' he warned Congress.[34] While reform of the TUC itself was in the air, the Parliamentary Committee clearly had to tread carefully in dealing with the General Federation.

By this time, however, the GFTU was seriously weakened by the long series of secessions that had begun before the war. Furthermore its old allies the French brought with them for the international conference that was to follow Congress a left-wing detachment headed by Jean Longuet. He insisted that since the Socialist Party of America had not been invited to accompany AFofL representatives to the conference, the GFTU ought to be excluded, too. This claim had some foundation in the old principle that only one organisation should represent each country, and despite Gompers's protests the GFTU was excluded.[35] It was in no position to resist the TUC, and so the Management Committee proposed a compromise.[36] It would not give up its international role altogether but it was prepared to co-operate with the Parliamentary Committee in developing an international trade union bureau, to be controlled by Congress. It would sponsor a joint application for affiliation by both the TUC and GFTU to the International Federation of Trade Unions. The General Federation was giving up a great deal in going so far to meet the usurper; but at first the Parliamentary Committee was unwilling to consider even these proposals.[37]

The Reconstruction of the International Federation of Trade Unions

The General Federation therefore went ahead with plans for reconstituting the old International Federation of Trade Unions. In January 1919 the president and secretary of the Dutch trade union federation, Jan Oudegeest and Edo Fimmen, visited London to discuss the arrangements for a conference where this could be done.[38] The Dutchmen tried but failed to bring together the GFTU and TUC committees to patch up their differences. At Berne in the following February, therefore, the first international conference since 1914 which brought together trade unionists from the Allied and Central Powers met in the absence of the GFTU. The TUC Parliamentary Committee insisted on sending a delegation even though the team it first appointed all dropped out and it was rather obviously a second team that went in the end.[39] The General Federation declined to appoint delegates in protest against the fact that the Berne conference was being held at the same time as the Socialist International. It wanted to keep international trade unionism out of the political arena as it had been, in theory at least, before the war.[40] No doubt its position was also influenced by pique because the British government had invited only TUC representatives to advise it on the labour clauses of the peace treaty which was being hammered out in Paris.[41]

It was at Berne and without the participation of the GFTU that the objectives of international labour in peace time were finally agreed. Drawing on documents prepared by the many previous sectional conferences, the Berne delegates drew up an International Labour Charter. It called for:

  (i)   compulsory free primary and higher education
  (ii)   an eight-hour working day
  (iii)   a minimum weekly rest period of thirty-six hours
  (iv)   the abolition of night work for women
  (v)   'social insurance'
  (vi)   labour exchanges
  (vii)   an international code of labour for seamen.[42]

This charter was presented to the peace conference in Paris where Samuel Gompers, closely identified with President Wilson's peace initiatives, became the leading negotiator on behalf of international labour and fought hard for the adoption of the charter. Eventually the Labour Convention in the Versailles Peace Treaty included most of the trade unionists' clauses. It omitted, however, numbers (iv) and (vii) on the abolition of night work for women and the establishment of an international code for seamen; and it cut the agreed weekly rest period from 36 to 24 hours.[43]

Meanwhile Jan Oudegeest had at last persuaded the Parliamentary Committee to agree on joint representation with the GFTU.[44] Perhaps the TUC leaders were afraid of looking bad in the eyes of their foreign colleagues. They may also have borne in mind the strictures of speakers at Congress in 1918, and possibly they were beginning to realise, too, that international trade unionism could be hard work. At all events, they now formed a joint international committee with the General Federation, agreeing to be represented with them as one national organisation at all international conferences and other meetings, but pressing for a proportional representation.[45] Both the TUC and GFTU therefore sent delegates to the conference in Amsterdam which reconstituted the International Federation of Trade Unions.[46]

The aftermath of war was as messy in international labour politics as it was in the dealings between the nations at Paris. Just as the national labour movements of Europe had chosen patriotism rather than the vague impracticalities of international solidarity when their governments went to war in 1914, so in 1919 they too talked about guilt and reparations and 'making Germany pay'.[47] At Amsterdam it was the Belgians who, not surprisingly, first demanded an admission of guilt for the war from the German and Austrian delegates. Their specific complaint was that German trade unionists had done nothing to prevent atrocities perpetrated in Belgium or the deportation of Belgian workers. The American delegates backed them up forcefully, with some support from Appleton. Carl Legien, the tragic figure of this conference, could not endure the humiliation. He refused to make any admission of guilt and in a confused speech tried to justify what had happened in Belgium by reference to subsequent events. But his fellow German Johannes Sassenbach and the Austrian Anton Hueber produced a statement that was accepable to the Allied delegates, which also pointed out that German labourers had been misled into believing that they were fighting a defensive war. Even though the rest of the German delegation later insisted on a weaker version, this compromise provided a sufficient foundation for the rebirth of the International Federation of Trade Unions. The headquarters were moved to Amsterdam, Fimmen became secretary, and against the candidature of Oudegeest and the opposition of Legien, Appleton was elected president. The conference appears to have divided at one stage into a pro-Appleton and a pro-Legien camp, with the Scandinavian, German and Dutch delegates enthusiastically fêting Legien one evening and the Scandinavians presenting him with a bronze vase full of red roses three feet high.

Appleton's own account of the conference was couched in moderate and conciliatory tones. He had known and admired Legien for years before the war and sincerely regretted his exclusion from the international federation. He had never indulged in the excesses of jingoism exhibited, for instance, by Havelock Wilson, the seamen's leader, and had been careful to say that when the GFTU refused to negotiate with German trade unionists during the war it did so not from hatred of 'the Hun' but from the practical consideration that animosities at any such conference would be too heated for any real good to be done.[48] His own position as president, a source of great pride, was not going to be easy. As he himself remarked,[49] there were great differences between the procedures adopted by continental and British trade unionists:

> In Britain the president of a meeting or organisation must himself govern according to standing orders. On the Continent he is an autocrat who governs as he chooses. Here he must deal out impartial justice to all. There he considers mainly the needs of his committee or his party. Here he guides, but does not initiate. There he may suspend a discussion and himself introduce any motion. . . . Here a speaker must catch the president's eye. There he must send up his name or he has only a disorderly chance of speaking. It is very difficult for an Englishman to divest himself suddenly of generations of tradition and training and pass from the judicial to the partisan control of a conference.

Furthermore, Appleton's election was obviously a compromise. It was well known that he lacked the support of the majority of trade unionists in his own country, even though the British delegation nominated him unanimously for the job; and he was patently out of sympathy with the political stance of most European trade union leaders.

The Amsterdam conference was divided and disorganised, but before the delegates departed they did succeed in drawing up rules and defining an international labour policy. The rules were substantially those suggested by the British but on the initiative of the Swiss they gave more votes proportionately to the smaller nations than was at first intended. At international conferences before the war it had always been possible for trade unionists from the smaller countries to band together to outvote the larger ones. The new rules perpetuated this by giving 3 votes for the first 1 million members of each national trade union centre, with 1 vote for each additional 500,000 or fraction thereof. Other rules provided for a bureau meeting once a month and management committee meeting twice a year, both bodies to be appointed by a biennial conference, with due regard to the representation of each nationality. Different tasks were allotted to separate vice-presidents, to a treasurer and to a secretary-editor who was to produce a journal as well as occasional publications. Contributions were fixed at £1 per 1,000 members per year (reduced by the Americans and British from the £2 proposed by Sweden)[50] and considerable emphasis attached to the rule that only one trade union centre might represent each country. The programme set out in the rules of the international federation consisted of ten points which defined it as a forum, an information bureau, a centre for encouraging social and economic legislation in all countries and a kind of mutual aid organisation which would promote freedom of movement for international labour and organise appeals for financial help. Unlike the British General Federation, it involved no contributory insurance scheme against the costs of industrial action.

In addition to these rules, the Amsterdam conference published three special declarations. The first dealt with the League of Nations, which was then being brought into existence by the Treaty of Versailles. The trade unionists wanted the League to have legislative as well as judicial functions and to operate in the economic sphere to regulate the conditions of labour. The International Federation of Trade Unions ought to be, according to their declaration, 'an effective controlling organ of the League of Nations'. A second declaration called for the federation actively to promote 'the socialisation of the means of production'. The third was a message of support to Hungarian and Russian trade unionists, condemning the Allied blockade of those countries. It was these declarations, particularly the first two, that marked the newly constituted international federation most clearly as the child of its times. In the course of the upheavals of 1914–18, and most especially under the impact of the Bolshevik revolution in Russia in November 1917, European labour in general had become more committed to socialism. In Britain this was manifest in the 1918 constitution of the Labour Party, whose clause IV called for the common ownership of the means of production, supported by a series of resolutions in favour of nationalisation and other forms of collectivism.[51]

The Amsterdam delegates also passed a resolution not to attend the special labour conference that was to be held in Washington in the autumn unless German and Austrian trade unionists were invited. This created serious difficulties, since the AFofL under the tutelage of Gompers continued to oppose full participation by the Germans in the peace-making. Appleton found himself in the centre of a flurry of diplomacy.[52] He persuaded his old Management Committee colleague George Barnes, who was one of the British ministers negotiating in Paris, to intercede. Meanwhile Jouhaux had seen the French Prime Minister, Clemenceau, and together Barnes and Clemenceau secured large concessions which resulted in the issue of invitations to the Austrian and German trade union leaders to participate in the discussions at Washington. Appleton pressed them in vain to accept and offered help with transport, which was a problem that had already persuaded the Swiss to stay away. The Washington conference laid the foundations for the International Labour Office and finalised the terms of the Labour Convention in the Treaty of Versailles, but European labour leaders in general did not consider it a success. Trade union representatives only formed about 25 per cent of all delegates, and Gompers's failure to secure more of the points of the International Labour Charter earlier in the year, during negotiations in Paris, was condemned. Appleton himself, going to Washington at the wish of the international federation, was dissatisfied with the small gains made by international labour, compared with all their endeavours and high hopes during and immediately after the war.[53]

Appleton's commitment to international trade unionism was not matched within the ranks of the TUC, as the Parliamentary Committee's conduct of international affairs made plain. Despite having agreed with him that they would present a joint report on the Amsterdam conference, Stuart-Bunning inserted his own version in the Parliamentary Committee's report to Congress, and no discussion of international affairs took place at Congress in 1919 at all.[54] The committee also delayed paying contributions to the international federation on the grounds that it was difficult to sort out the overlap between GFTU and TUC membership, although the proportional payment with which they eventually solved the problem could have been worked out at the beginning.[55] When asked by the international federation to appoint a correspondent to send regular contributions to the proposed international journal, their only response was to forward copies of the *Trade Union Review*.

In May 1920 Appleton accompanied Oudegeest, Fimmen and the Belgian Cornelius Mertens to a meeting with the Parliamentary Committee to press for closer unity between the TUC and GFTU in international relations.[56] They upbraided the Parliamentary Committee for taking international action without consulting or even informing the bureau in Amsterdam: for instance, the Parliamentary Committee and the international federation were both sending delegations to Russia, which seemed a needless duplication of effort. It was also suggested that trade unions should take no part in the forthcoming international labour congress in Geneva (where in fact European labour split decisively between adherence to the old, socialist, Second International and to the Communist Third International); but the TUC had already appointed delegates. The exasperation was mutual. The international federation bureau, in keeping with the tone of the Amsterdam declarations, was beginning to issue telegrams and letters urging some highly impractical policies on its affiliated national trade union centres and both GFTU and TUC representatives agreed in condemning it for 'unwise exuberance and equally unwise attempts to threaten government or peoples, and . . . talk of exercising powers we do not possess'.[57] The Americans were deciding against affiliation to the international federation, and Appleton warned that the TUC might do the same.[58]

Some Explanations for the Decline of the General Federation Abroad and at Home

Lukewarm though it was about its own international role, the Parliamentary Committee was now quite determined to push the GFTU out. The Portsmouth Congress in 1920 passed a resolution to make the TUC the only body representing British trade unionism abroad. In November, preparing for an international conference which it had rather reluctantly agreed to hold in London that month, the Parliamentary Committee wrote to Appleton reminding him of the decision of Congress, and proposed that 'in the event of the resignation of Mr Appleton' J. H. Thomas should take his place as president of the international federation.[59] The short London conference, therefore, saw Appleton's last appearance at the centre of the international labour stage. He wrote mournfully to Gompers at about this time,

> I stood for office [in the IFTU] as a trade unionist, not as a politician, and by a trade unionist I mean one who has asserted and practised his right to combine with his fellows for the purpose of selling his labour at the best possible price.[60]

By 1920, so limited a view of trade unionism was quite out of date. Never a man to take defeat lying down, Appleton attempted straight away to arrange an English-speaking international conference, and made plans for the GFTU to set up a statistical department to collect information and statistics on international labour matters. But, as the Parliamentary Committee realised,[61] he could no longer hope to challenge its position.

The International Federation of Trade Unions had a useful existence ahead of it. It enhanced its standing by taking on relief work for the workers of the most war-torn parts of Europe and by embarking on educational links between trade unionists,[62] even though, as we have seen, it laid itself open to criticism, in Britain at least, for some of its political initiatives. The cleavage in international socialism found its counterpart in the trade union world in a schism between the IFTU and a new Red International of Labour Unions based in Moscow; but this did not prevent the IFTU from gaining strength as an international forum in the rest of Europe. The British contributed a larger affiliated membership than any other country except Germany.[63] Their participation, however, remained at best half-hearted. As for the General Federation of Trade Unions, it would be difficult to argue that, as it was after the events of 1918–20, it could have offered any more dynamic representation of British trade unionism than the Trades Union Congress. More enthusiastic and conscientious in its international duties it probably would have been, but representative it could no longer be.

This state of affairs can be explained partly by straightforward rivalry between the two institutions and by the use of unfair or, at best, overbearing tactics by the Parliamentary Committee of the TUC (which is not to acquit the GFTU of acting similarly but simply to say that it was outplayed). But the causes of the GFTU's relative decline cannot all be laid at the door of the TUC or of one or two powerful unions like the Miners' Federation. Several causes have been considered in the previous chapter. The domestic trade union and labour scene in Britain was confused and divided, but during the war there was a clear tendency to put socialism at the centre of labour policy while at the same time the mainstream of the labour movement remained in the hands of moderate men.[64] This helped trade union leaders, many of whom were now in any case far less conservative than their predecessors, to adopt a more wholehearted support for the Labour Party than the trade union movement had shown before the First World War. In this process the GFTU was out on a limb. Although several members of the Management Committee were Labour MPs, including James O'Grady who as chairman throughout the war played a very active part in the federation's affairs, it did not fit easily into the development of labour politics either domestic or foreign. Sidney and Beatrice Webb, those seasoned experts on the trade union world, attributed this fact very largely to the views and activities of William Appleton.[65] It may be objected that no representative organisation should be seen as the expression of its general secretary's opinions, indeed quite the reverse; but any general secretary tends to be a strong influence within his committee, and Appleton was a particularly forceful figure. The Management Committee minutes show that his drafts of pronouncements on its behalf were seldom amended in substance. On at least one occasion, giving evidence before a government committee, he was told by the GFTU Management Committe to 'do what you think is right' and felt that without further instructions he could express its views, with which he broadly agreed.[66] Without some further consideration of

Appleton's role, therefore, our understanding of the GFTU's decline would be incomplete.

Appleton was not an easy man to get on with. Examples of his defensive reactions to criticisms abound in the printed minutes and reports of the GFTU. And if he could not take criticism he was quite ready, all the same, to dole it out. A man of strong convictions, self-educated to a very high standard and brought up in the rather elitist world of Nottingham lacemaking, his many published articles tended to lay down the law for his fellow trade unionists. Why could they not see and grasp the great opportunities offered by unemployment insurance, he asked. What, other than purblind selfishness, kept them from joining the General Federation? In 1902, when still secretary of the lacemakers, he presented to the TUC the longest resolution Congress had yet heard, part of it in the form of a complete education bill.[67] Education and self-improvement were the cornerstones of his own career and he genuinely sought to extend their blessings to the rest of the working class, to whom after all, he had dedicated his life.[68] But when he invoked Erasmus in support of peace,[69] or German writers to prove his point about German militarism,[70] and perhaps even when he presented to the annual general council meeting in 1912 his own fluent English translation of Léon Jouhaux's speech in French, trade unionists who did not possess these refinements may well have thought him snobbish.

In a later generation, William Appleton would have been more likely to win a scholarship to grammar school, another to university and from there, perhaps, to enter the law or the administrative ranks of the civil service. Such opportunities were not open to a working-class child of the 1860s[71] and when as an adult Appleton spent his leisure at St Luke's Evening School in Nottingham,[72] he did so not in order to remove himself from his own people but so that he could offer higher talents in their service. Nothing that he wrote betrays a sense of humour; the photographs published in the GFTU reports show a tense, unsmiling figure. He never married, and the recreations he listed in *Who's Who* were solitary ones: music and growing flowers (only he called it floriculture). What he had undoubtedly, and in large measure, was a sense of dedication to his calling. He turned down at least one offer of a job, probably in government service, during the war in order to remain with the General Federation.[73] He once told a general council meeting that the federation 'was his life'.[74] During the war he took only one brief holiday and in 1919, complaining of exhaustion and insomnia, proffered his resignation to the Management Committee on the grounds of ill-health. Then aged nearly 60, he wrote 'I need relief from responsibilities I have perhaps taken too seriously ... if I am to avoid breakdown'. The Management

Committee ought probably to have taken that opportunity to provide Appleton with a pension (then a rare privilege for trade union officials) and to seek a new general secretary. It was a difficult time, however, and for reasons which the minutes do not explain they gave him a long holiday and persuaded him to remain in office, which he did for the next nineteen years.[75]

It would be wrong to accept without qualification that 'Appleton was very right-wing in his views'.[76] He was much more complicated than that. But his opinions were frequently and trenchantly expressed, and the Webbs were probably right to suggest that it was his claim to speak for right-thinking trade unionists as a whole that particularly annoyed the TUC Parliamentary Committee and others.[77] Many of his views were in tune with those of a broad cross-section of trade unionists. Thus, for example, during the war, his work for servicemen's pay and, with Ben Tillett, to keep down food prices and get rid of congestion at the ports[78] were uncontroversial endeavours. Appleton also spent a great deal of time dealing with the government, work that he obviously relished. He not only gave evidence before committees on reconstruction but also sat on one.[79] In 1917 he accepted a CBE for his services earlier in the war.[80] None of this conflicted with accepted trade union practice. Beatrice Webb, whose private opinion of the trade union leaders of the First World War and after was caustic, thought that most of them were far too interested in dealing with the government:

> The Trade Union movement has become, like the hereditary peerage, an avenue to political power through which stupid untrained persons may pass up to the highest office if only they have secured the suffrages of the members of a large union.[81]

Her view was exaggerated and unfair. But at a time when the government was entering into people's everyday lives on a scale unknown before the war, one way for responsible trade union leaders who were neither 'stupid' nor 'untrained' to deal with the situation was by limited co-operation with the ministers concerned. In this, Appleton was not particularly out of step. Other examples of policies wherein he was no right-winger include his and the Management Committee's advocacy of railway nationalisation during and after the war and his very fully thought-out schemes for public works to relieve unemployment.[82]

In one respect it is particularly difficult to pin a label on to Appleton's views: as an advocate of trade union unity he could appear to be sometimes more militant and sometimes more conservative than the leaders of the TUC and the large unions.

Syndicalism and guild socialism both had some appeal for him, understandably, since the advocates of both in Britain had suggested that the General Federation might form a centre for their organisation.[83] He was quick to stand up for the hard work and good intentions of trade union officials, in contrast to the syndicalists' campaign against officialdom,[84] but several utterances in the GFTU reports, especially after some large unions had begun to secede, claimed that the rank-and-file membership was being misled or not properly consulted by its national officials.[85] In common with the rest of the Management Committee Appleton repudiated any revolutionary intention but, on the other hand, he certainly believed in the policy, espoused by both syndicalists and guild socialists, of strengthening trade unionism by educating and informing the rank and file. This was the idea behind *The Federationist* and all the many leaflets published by the federation, a source of pride and a matter of policy.[86] Such a policy also, of course, formed part of the propaganda war against the GFTU's assailants.

As to the structure of trade unionism, Appleton claimed to support craft unions and approved of the decision by Congress in 1915 to do the same, a decision seen at the time as a slap in the face for industrial unionism and the guild socialists.[87] So it may have been, and craft unions were undoubtedly havens of conservatism. As a recent historian of the engineers has noticed, however, more radical possibilities were also inherent in the craft ideal.[88] In a pamphlet on *Trade Union Organisation* published in 1916, Appleton pointed out that 'the Trade Union movement originated in craft consciousness' and attached great importance to the craftsman's loyalty to his union. He went on to propose a financial arrangement whereby, when craftsmen moved temporarily into other industries, their union should pay a fixed and agreed basic contribution to the union catering for workers in the other industry concerned. Thus when it became possible for an individual craftsman to return to his own trade, he would automatically return to membership of his original union and not be tempted to forget altogether about his union allegiances.

Had he left it there, Appleton's proposals for trade union reform would have been unadventurous. But in fact, despite his respect for the craft unions, he wanted to make these organisations ultimately part of 'amalgamations covering each organic occupation and industry, and focussed into one intelligently organised federation'.[89] The gap between craft and industrial unionism did not seem to him to be unbridgeable. The friendly benefits paid by the old craft unions were no longer so important as they had been before the introduction of insurance by the state. Demarcations did count 'and when these are reinforced by the inherent individualism of the Britisher they become very formidable indeed. It is no use ignoring the fact that our people are individualists'. Nevertheless, a strong and businesslike organisation of all trade unions, based on amalgamations and united in one central federation, could modify these differences. In conclusion, Appleton characteristically combined his own peculiarly romantic view of the trade union movement with some hard-headed practical proposals. He wanted to see a movement 'which has spiritualised its ideals, which includes all workers, which prepares for all contingencies,' and in order to attain this utopia:

> It is desirable that there should be fewer unions and fewer federations; that the movement must discover and build upon a better financial basis than the one which at present satisfies it; that it must develop a system of transfer; a common risks fund; a central directorate; and an international understanding.[90]

In November 1916, in the knowledge that the new Minister of Labour, John Hodge of the steel smelters, was planning to change the law on amalgamations of trade unions, the Management Committee of the General Federation passed a resolution in favour of industrial unionism and sent it to the affiliated unions for endorsement by their executives. Of the fifty-one (almost all craft) unions that replied, only two voted against.[91] This decision would seem to be quite in line with Appleton's own rather complex ideas on trade union organisation. He repeated these in another pamphlet in 1918 where he specifically used the classic argument of industrial unionists that since capital was organised on a worldwide scale, labour should be too. Here as on other occasions, he also called for the separation of industrial organisation from politics.[92]

It was in this plea to keep politics separate from trade unionism that Appleton revealed the main difference between his position and that of more influential trade union leaders. What he really meant by it was that trade unions should not be tied to the Labour Party, and it was precisely this link that the party's new constitution of 1918 renewed and strengthened. There was an element also of the old industrial unionist – or even guild socialist – thinking in Appleton's view. He consistently opposed unnecessary intervention by the state in industrial policy, and where he supported union co-operation seems to have done so on the ground that the unions must seize every opportunity to keep the reins of administration in their own hands. His attitude to unemployment insurance exemplified this: he wanted insurance to be administered on a voluntary basis exclusively through trade unions.[93] Labour Party policy, however, was now turning in the direction of handing power over the means of production to the state; and the old hostility to state socialism, which had characterised some of the more radical trade unionists before the war, was no longer a force.

Other factors added to the general view of Appleton and the GFTU as a conservative force and a potential brake on the progress of the trade union movement. The Management Committee certainly seems to have been more wholehearted in its support of Lloyd George's coalition than most trade unionists. Appleton himself very clearly preferred a policy of industrial co-operation to one based on class warfare, even though he had a clear vision of the dichotomy of interests between capital and labour. This was the time when most trade union leaders were rejecting or at most receiving with suspicion the new proposals of the Whitley Committee for Joint Industrial Councils and other machinery for co-operation between employers and workers.[94] The tone of the era as far as the unions were concerned was set not by 'Whitleyism' but rather by the great railway strike of 1919.[95] And yet Appleton chose to write,

> Sympathy and intelligence can solve most of the imminent industrial difficulties if these qualities are exercised by employers and trade unionists who have each experience and ability. If these problems drift for solution wholly into the hands of the political visionary or the civil servant – God help all of us![96]

He compounded sins like this by fighting back hard against the criticisms levelled at the General Federation, and when he turned *The Federationist* into *The Democrat* in 1919 he published in it some rather objectionable personal invective against Robert Smillie.[97] Delegates to the GFTU's own meetings took exception to some of Appleton's views and at the 1919 annual general council meeting *The Democrat* came in for severe criticism. It was no longer the official organ of the General Federation; Appleton personally had taken it over together with a deficit of £185 and was using it to express opinions quite at variance with those of most trade unionists within the federation. John Hill, with whom he had crossed swords before, censured him particularly for an article on prices in which he had said that the purchaser was responsible for forcing the seller to sell at a reasonable price; a view not in keeping with current attacks by other trade unionists on profiteering.[98] At the TUC in 1920 *The Democrat*'s support for Liberal Party policies and its sustained attacks on the strategy of 'direct action', especially those comments directed at Smillie and the miners, figured prominently in the debate before the vote to exclude the GFTU entirely from international affairs.[99]

William Appleton, therefore, was personally to blame for much of the unpopularity of the General Federation. He seemed to lack judgement about when to keep his mouth shut, and had no inkling of how to make himself liked in the trade union world at large. There was little room for his qualities in a world of which Beatrice Webb could write, 'what the delegates [to the TUC] enjoy is a joke, it matters not what sort of joke' and 'the leading men have grown fatter in body and more dully complacent in mind than they were twenty years ago' and whose leaders she could describe as 'fatheads ... buffoons, simpletons and corrupt persons'.[100] A sense of bitterness and personal impotence tinged her cruel judgement; nevertheless the weaknesses which she exaggeratedly described were the very opposite of Appleton's weaknesses. Nor was it only his personality that made things difficult. He *was* becoming more right-wing in terms of current political alignments, perhaps pushed in that direction by his complete failure to win a place in the mainstream of the labour movement. The General Federation could not fail to be identified with him, especially when he insisted on publishing his views as he did, and the reports of the GFTU's annual meetings at the end of the decade reflect the membership's growing disquiet about their general secretary.

The views and personal failings of William Appleton, however important, must not be allowed to obscure other reasons for the General Federation's decline. Prominent among these was its changed character after about 1913 as a shelter for smaller craft unions, just at a time when the larger general and industrial unions were gaining decisively in size and strength. Whatever opportunities may have existed for a new centralised trade union structure in Britain and however desirable that might have been, it was not the direction in which the leaders who mattered wanted to go. The General Federation, it is true, lacked suitable leadership to make the trade union world look seriously at the possibilities it offered, but we can be almost certain that no kind of leadership would have been able to coax the unions as a whole into a federal fold. Arthur Henderson attempted something of the sort, with a limited representative type of federation in mind, after the national industrial conference that took place in London in February 1919, and he was rebuffed.[101]

The debate over the formation of the TUC General council in 1920–2 also shows how far from ready the British trade union movement was for the sort of unity that the General Federation of Trade Unions might have offered. This attempt to form a central body which was able to intervene more positively in disputes and broadly to guide and unify the policies of organised labour was only partially successful.[102] Ironically it was G. D. H. Cole, former champion of the GFTU, who was asked to draw up the outlines of the TUC reorganisation. From the beginning of discussions, which opened at Congress in

1920, it became clear that the new General Council would have to guarantee the autonomy of individual unions, a theme reminiscent of the GFTU's early years.[103] In 1921 a motion to allow for a period of consultation in the labour movement as a whole before any union went on strike was defeated by a large majority with three of the largest unions[104] objecting that it would have interfered with their freedom of action. Further proposals that the TUC General Council should be kept informed of all disputes and empowered to intervene, even to raise levels for the support of unions involved in strikes, were given short shrift. Frank Hodges of the Miners' Federation wrote in a newspaper article:

> The assumption that it [the TUC General Council] can succeed where the trade unions severally and separately would fail is altogether without foundation. Fundamentally the conflicting differences as between craft and industrial unions will make it impossible for the General Council ever to function uniformly for the movement as a whole . . . [It] cannot assume a perfection which is not a reflection of the state of affairs in the movement itself. I venture the view that the British trade union movement is so arranged that the General Council will never be more than a bureau of information, plus a court of appeal for quarrelling trade unions as to poaching of members or lines of demarcation.[105]

Sir David Shackleton, the former leader of the weavers' amalgamation and Labour MP, now permanent secretary at the Ministry of Labour, observed with the scepticism born of experience that the proposal to form a General Council of the TUC 'is a case of history repeating itself. The General Federation of Trade Unions was started 22 years ago to do these very things'.[106] The failures and achievements of the TUC General Council since its formation have been chronicled by others.[107] But we may observe that if it in fact did not 'assume a perfection' that was not possessed by the trade union movement as a whole, the same was true of the General Federation. If one factor more than any others caused the GFTU to disappoint the hopes of its founders and then to dwindle into relative insignificance after 1920, it was the unshakeable independence of the main trade unions and their leaders.

Notes: Chapter 5

1   For example, Churchill's dealings with the TUC over unemployment insurance, and so on. See above, pp. 84–5. During the war this tendency was manifest

again in consultations over the Munitions of War Act and after the war when it was the TUC leaders whom Lloyd George and George Barnes invited to discuss the labour implications of the peace proposals in Paris in 1919.

2 GFTU, *Annual Report*, 1919.
3 GFTU, *Proceedings and Reports*, 1918–19, report of 1918 agcm.
4 GFTU, *Annual Report*, 1919.
5 Arnot, *The Miners*, Vol. 2, *Years of Struggle*, pp. 94–5.
6 Sassenbach, *Twenty-Five Years of International Trade Unionism*, pp. 31–2.
7 TUC, *Report*, 1913.
8 TUC Parliamentary Committee minutes, 8 July 1914.
9 The summary of this paragraph and the next is based on Sassenbach, *Twenty-Five Years of International Trade Unionism*, *passim*, and on Lorwin, *International Labor Movement*, pp. 30–41.
10 Tillett's motion to found a trade union information bureau was passed at the agcm of 1911. Owing to pressure of other work, it was never fully implemented (GFTU, *Proceedings and Reports*, 1917–18; pamphlet of autumn 1917 on the functions of the GFTU compared with those of the TUC).
11 The Webbs (*History of Trade Unionism*, pp. 555–6) blame the declining popularity of the GFTU partly on Appleton's 'almost continuous negotiations' with Gompers and Jouhaux during the war.
12 The long French report on international labour legislation which formed the basis for discussion at the conference was printed as a pamphlet, *Conference of Delegates from the General Federations of Trade Unions of the Allied Countries* (June 1916). A copy is bound in the British Library's volume of GFTU pamphlets (WP 4743).
13 GFTU, *Proceedings and Reports*, 1916–17, circular entitled *International Labour Charter* (September 1916) including text of a letter from the Management Committee to Asquith, 30 August 1916.
14 ibid.
15 The main precedent, as the Leeds conference of 1916 was aware, was the Franco-Italian treaty of 1904 which had provided for reciprocation in accident and unemployment insurance, the free transfer of savings bank deposits between the two countries and common protection of minors working in industry.
16 For example, see H. Pelling, *A Short History of the Labour Party*, 4th edn (London: Macmillan, 1972), pp. 41–2; McKibbin, *Evolution of the Labour Party*, pp. 92–111.
17 GFTU, *Proceedings and Reports*, 1917–18, report of conference of 10 and 11 September 1917.
18 The International Metal Workers, National Sailors' and Firemen's Union (led by Havelock Wilson), Textile Workers' Factory Association, General Union of Textile Workers and Amalgamated Operative Cotton Spinners were all represented, in addition to the GFTU.
19 TUC, *Report*, 1917, quoted in Roberts, *The TUC*, p. 294.
20 Harvey, *Samuel Gompers*, p. 242. Gompers, *Seventy Years of Life and Labor*, Vol. 2, p. 384.
21 For the fluctuations in this proportion, see table of membership, Appendix A.
22 For one contemporary comment on the difficulties caused by divided British representation, see Webb, *History of Trade Unionism*, pp. 555–6.
23 See above, pp. 105–6, 109–10, 111.
24 Labour Party, *Manifesto on War Aims* (London: Labour Party, 1918). The process of peacemaking after the First World War has received the attention of many historians. A convenient summary may be found in A. J. P. Taylor, *English History 1914–1945* (London: Oxford University Press, 1965), pp. 110–14, 132–6; p. 119 contains a summary of the Fourteen Points. Webb,

History of Trade Unionism, pp. 695–6, discusses the contribution of British labour.

25   Webb, *History of Trade Unionism*, p. 696 n., 'It is difficult not to be struck with the greater breadth of vision, the higher idealism, and . . . the larger statesman-ship of the Labour Party . . . [than that of the politicians who framed the eventual treaty]'. Fair comment, no doubt, but a little startling in view of Sidney Webb's own large part in Labour policy-making.

26   GFTU, *Proceedings and Reports*, 1915–16, report of 1915 agcm.

27   Lorwin, *International Labor Movement*, p. 55.

28   Harvey, *Samuel Gompers*, p. 268.

29   ibid., ch. 16.

30   Gompers, *Seventy Years of Life and Labor*, Vol. 2, p. 419. Stephen White, 'Soviets in Britain. The Leeds Convention of 1917', *International Review of Social History*, vol. 19, pt 2 (Amsterdam, 1974), pp. 165–93, concludes that pacifism not Bolshevism was the moving force behind the left wing of British labour.

31   Roberts, *The TUC*, pp. 300–3.

32   TUC Parliamentary Committee minutes, 19 July, 16 September and 8 October 1918.

33   TUC, *Report*, 1918; Roberts, *The TUC*, pp. 300–3.

34   TUC, *Report*, 1918, p. 213.

35   Gompers, *Seventy Years of Life and Labor*, Vol. 2, pp. 420–1; GFTU, *Annual Report*, 1919.

36   Meeting between the Parliamentary Committee and GFTU Management Committee, 8 October 1918, recorded in the minutes of both.

37   TUC Parliamentary Committee minutes, 19 December 1918.

38   GFTU, *Annual Report*, 1919.

39   All those first appointed were MPS who pleaded pressure of other work but probably also disliked the association with the Socialist International almost as much as did the GFTU Management Committee. The three delegates who did attend were Margaret Bondfield, R. Shirkie and T. Greenall. See TUC Parliamentary Committee minutes, 8 January 1919.

40   GFTU, *Annual Report*, 1919.

41   Roberts, *The TUC*, pp. 327–8.

42   Lorwin, *International Labor Movement*, p. 56.

43   ibid. See also Labour Party, *International Labour and Peace*, Report of the Berne Conference of 1919 (London: Labour Party, 1919).

44   TUC Parliamentary Committee minutes, 15 May 1919.

45   ibid., 11 June 1919.

46   The TUC delegates were Stuart-Bunning, Thorne, J. B. Williams, Hill and Greenall. Appleton, Tillett, J. Asquith and Crinion represented the GFTU.

47   Brief accounts of the Amsterdam conference may be found in Lorwin, *International Labor Movement*, Sassenbach, *Twenty-Five Years of International Trade Unionism*, Roberts, *The TUC*, and elsewhere. The account given here is based mainly on Appleton's report to the Parliamentary Committee and GFTU, dated 10 August 1919 and bound in GFTU, *Proceedings and Reports*, 1919–20.

48   Roberts, *The TUC*, p. 300, does Appleton an injustice by lumping him with Havelock Wilson. See, for example, GFTU, *Annual Report*, 1918; *Proceedings and Reports*, 1915–16, report of 1915 agcm, pp. 122–3; ibid., 1917–18, report of international conference, 1917.

49   GFTU, *Annual Report*, 1920.

50   TUC Parliamentary Committee minutes, 10 May 1920.

51   McKibbin, *Evolution of the Labour Party*, pp. 91–106. As he points out, however, only in Britain did the left wing of the labour movement emerge from

the war weaker than before, despite the more left-wing position adopted by the mainstream of the Labour Party.

52 TUC Parliamentary Committee minutes, 8 October 1919, undated copy of letter from Appleton to J. B. Williams, the committee's vice-president of the IFTU.
53 W. A. Appleton's, *America and International Labour Problems* (London: GFTU, 1919), a report of his visit with Alderman Gwynne of the GFTU Management Committee to Washington in October–November 1919.
54 Roberts, *The TUC*, pp. 327–31, briefly considers the final round in the TUC's exclusion of the GFTU from international affairs. See also the preamble to Appleton's report in GFTU, *Proceedings and Reports*, 1919–20; and TUC Parliamentary Committee minutes, 11 December 1919.
55 TUC Parliamentary Committee minutes, 19 February, 10 March, 21 April and 17 August 1920.
56 ibid., 10 May 1920.
57 Appleton to Fimmen, 4 June 1920, reporting a meeting of the TUC/GFTU joint international committee on 3 June; letter entered in GFTU Management Committee minutes, 17 June 1920.
58 ibid.
59 TUC Parliamentary Committee minutes, 17 November 1920, For their reluctance to hold this conference, see minutes of 3 June and 17 August 1920.
60 Harvey, *Samuel Gompers*, p. 266.
61 TUC Parliamentary Committee minutes, 29 March 1921.
62 G. D. H. Cole, *Organised Labour. An Introduction to Trade Unionism* (London: Allen & Unwin, 1924), praised the postwar IFTU for this work but did less than justice to the prewar federation, whose growing functions especially in 1913–14 have been neglected by historians.
63 Cole, op. cit., pp. 158–9.
64 Harrison, 'The WEWNC', has drawn attention to the influence of the WEWNC in this direction.
65 Webb, *History of Trade Unionism*, pp. 554–6.
66 PRO, RECO 1/462, Ministry of Reconstruction papers, minutes of meetings of committee on financial risks, meeting of 14 October 1918.
67 TUC, *Report*, 1902; Davis, *The British Trades Union Congress. History and Recollections,* 2 vols (London: TUC Parliamentary Committee, 1910 and 1916), Vol. 2, p. 236.
68 See article by Appleton in GFTU, *Quarterly Report*, March 1903; *Who Was Who*, 1929–40, lists his membership of educational committees, and so on, starting with the Nottingham School Board in 1898.
69 GFTU, *Quarterly Report*, March 1906, article on 'The causes and consequences of war'.
70 See above, Chapter 4, p. 124.
71 Appleton was born on 31 December 1859.
72 *Who Was Who* (London: A. & C. Black, 1929–40).
73 GFTU, *Proceedings and Reports*, 1918–19, report of 1918 agcm.
74 ibid.
75 Management Committee minutes, 11 June 1919.
76 Pelling, *History of British Trade Unionism*, p. 157.
77 Webb, *History of Trade Unionism*, p. 556.
78 See above, Chapter 4.
79 The departmental committee on juvenile education in relation to employment after the war, set up by the Ministry of Reconstruction. Appleton was the only labour representative among sixteen members. The committee's findings were well received by the ministry. Its recommendations included a uniform compulsory school-leaving age of 14, provisions for safeguarding the health of young

people and compulsory provisions for some form of further education between the ages of 14 and 18 (PRO, ED 24/1175, Ministry of Education, Private Office Papers).

80   *Who Was Who*, 1929–40.
81   BLPES, Beatrice Webb's diary, p. 3509, entry for 7 June 1917. See also p. 3372, entry for September 1915.
82   See above, Chapter 4.
83   ibid.
84   For example, in 'The causes of unrest among workpeople', paper for the London Economic Society, reprinted in GFTU, *Proceedings and Reports*, 1910–11.
85   This claim was made with particular force when the ASE seceded.
86   See, for example, *The Federationist*, December 1913; GFTU, *The General Federation of Trade Unions. What It Is. What It Seeks to Accomplish. Can There Be Unity?* (1918).
87   BLPES, Beatrice Webb's diary, p. 3371, entry for September 1915.
88   James Hinton, *The First Shop Stewards' Movement* (London: Allen & Unwin, 1973), ch. 2.
89   Appleton, *Trade Union Organisation*.
90   ibid.
91   GFTU, *Proceedings and Reports*, 1916–17, leaflet of 3 November 1916 issued to affiliated societies, and return of votes.
92   GFTU, *The General Federation of Trade Unions. What it is . . .*
93   See, for example, Appleton's book *Trade Unions: Their Past, Present and Future* (London: Philip Allan, 1925).
94   See Rodger Charles, *The Development of Industrial Relations in Britain, 1911–1939. Studies in the Evolution of Collective Bargaining at National and Industry Level* (London: Hutchinson, 1973), on the development of this machinery.
95   See Roberts, *The TUC*, pp. 331–9, for a brief consideration of this strike.
96   *The Federationist*, March 1918.
97   *The Democrat*, 1919–20, *passim*.
98   GFTU, *Proceedings and Reports*, 1919–20, report of 1919 agcm.
99   Roberts, *The TUC*, p. 329, gives a description of this debate.
100 BLPES, Beatrice Webb's diary, pp. 3368, 3360–1, entries for September 1915 and 10 January 1919.
101 Rodney Lowe, 'The failure of consensus in Britain: the national industrial conference 1919–1921', *Historical Journal*, vol. 21, no. 3 (1978), pp. 649–75.
102 V. L. Allen, 'The reorganization of the Trades Union Congress, 1918–1927', *British Journal of Sociology*, vol. 11, no. 1 (1960), pp. 24–43, describes the debate. See also Roberts, *The TUC*, chs IX and X and app. 4.
103 This summary of the arguments is based on the one compiled by the Ministry of Labour at the time (PRO, LAB 2/1149/IR1592/1921). I am indebted to Dr Lowe for drawing my attention to this file.
104 The Miners' Federation, boilermakers, and National Union of General Workers (formerly the gasworkers).
105 PRO, LAB 2/1149/IR 1592/1921, quoting an article in an unspecified newspaper.
106 ibid., minute dated 24 January 1922.
107 See J. C. Lovell and B. C. Roberts, *A Short History of the TUC* (London: Macmillan, 1968).

6

Between the Wars

Organisation and Debate in the Early 1920s

The General Federation of Trade Unions fought hard to re-establish itself in the changed world of the 1920s. Appleton and the Management Committee were constantly on the lookout for chinks in the armour of the TUC and the new big battalions of the trade union movement. There had to be some way of rebuilding the federation's influence, re-entering the international trade union community and winning back disaffiliated trade unions. Not until after the General Strike in 1926 did it become unmistakably clear that the GFTU from then on would be known as a shelter for small craft and medium-sized industrial unions. And it was some time after that before the federation adapted to and actually embraced this altered role.

At the beginning of the 1920s the General Federation embarked on two new plans to increase membership: it drew up a scheme for district committees and appointed a new organiser, the ironfounder George Bell. The district committee scheme never came fully into effect, but Bell's appointment in 1921 brought about some important changes. He took over much of the work formerly undertaken by the Management Committee, travelling around the country to negotiate between unions and help them in disputes with employers. His report appeared separately from the secretary's in the GFTU annual reports and recorded an active programme of travel, organising meetings, lectures at working men's institutes, and so on. Increasingly Bell's name rather than Appleton's appeared as signatory to special reports. He was to stay with the GFTU for more than thirty years, becoming general secretary after Appleton's retirement in 1938 and eventually retiring at the age of 76, in 1953.

The arrival of George Bell did not bring about the rise in membership for which the federation had hoped; nor did he stem the tide of secessions by large unions and by smaller ones absorbed into larger amalgamations. But this would probably have been a hopeless task even for the team of six organisers which the Management Committee had wanted to appoint in the past. For one young and little-known trade union organiser with the whole country to cover and the support of only five staff members altogether at head office,[1] it was impossible. Some of the new organiser's work involved trying to persuade the separate branches of seceding unions to remain affiliated to the GFTU in their own right.[2] For the most part, however, he busied himself with the smaller unions, many of which now served declining industries and vanishing memberships. Bell's organising activities helped to establish personal contact between many such unions and the GFTU, and he was to win praise for a quantity of successful negotiations. But he did also contribute to the general federation's very marked and rapidly growing reputation for craft-based conservatism. Quite early in his career the federation reports printed a letter from one union that he had visited, expressing pleased surprise at his moderation, and this caused raised eyebrows at the annual general council meeting in 1923.

Most of the delegates to GFTU annual meetings were beginning to agree, certainly after 1926, that these were not the place for important discussions of trade union policy which properly belonged to the TUC. The Management Committee, however, continued to put forward general motions and throughout the years between the two world wars, these gave rise to some interesting debates. Several annual meetings in the early 1920s were enlivened by a clash of views between the young communist Harry Pollitt, a delegate from the boilermakers, and the veteran MP John Ward, now a 'Liberal Unionist' whose old navvies' union was now known as the Public Works and Constructional Operatives' Union. Ward was a forceful speaker and one of the most colourful personalities who ever graced the meetings of the GFTU. He had been a member of the Management Committee since 1901, and some of his early clashes with the socialist Pete Curran have already been noted. He had courage, daring and a taste for adventure which in his youth had taken him to the Sudan as a railway construction worker for the British army and led him into court charged with unlawful assembly and assaulting the police at a demonstration of the unemployed.[3] At the outbreak of the First World War Ward exchanged the sombrero hat and generally bandit-like appearance which had disturbed some of his fellow MPs for the uniform of an army officer. He raised a 'Navvies' Battalion' and four other labour battalions and became a lieutenant-colonel. His appearance in uniform at the 1915 annual meeting of the GFTU was greeted with a hero's welcome.

At the end of the war Ward served in the interventionist force against the Bolsheviks in Siberia and developed a deep hatred of communism as a result of his experiences there. Always an influential member of the GFTU Management Committee, he persuaded his fellow members to meet a delegation of anti-Bolshevik trade unionists from the Urals at the beginning of 1920, and to publish their support for them.[4] His strong opposition to communism and to the Bolsheviks in particular won little sympathy from his fellow trade unionists. At about the same time as he was cementing his friendship with the White Russian Admiral Kolchak and receiving the honoured title of Cossack *hetman*, the TUC was considering whether to use direct action to force the British government to withdraw its troops from Russia. In May 1920 one example of such direct action against the government's anti-Bolshevik policy actually took place: dockers in London, encouraged by Harry Pollitt and with the official blessing of Ernest Bevin, refused to load weapons on board the *Jolly George* for use by Poland against Soviet Russia. Feeling on the subject ran so high in the summer of 1920 that even such Labour moderates as J. R. Clynes and J. H. Thomas supported the move to call a general strike if necessary to prevent the government from intervening on the side of Poland.[5] In this context Ward's opinions, both on the Russian question and on domestic issues, made him an outcast at the TUC, a position he shared with his friend Appleton.

Ward's opinions were equally at odds with those of a large number of people within the GFTU. To Harry Pollitt and some other militant left-wingers, they were anathema. Pollitt had joined the Communist Party of Great Britain, formed in 1920, in its very early days; he was already one of its leading lights and would eventually become chairman. Although the GFTU might seem an unlikely place for him to air his views, Pollitt was not a man to let any opportunity slip. He and the boilermakers' general secretary, John Hill, together launched several attacks on Appleton for the pro-capitalist tone of the federation's reports. It became an annual event for Pollitt to move the reference back of the report and for John Ward to spring to its defence. In this context in 1922, Ward dealt scathingly with the TUC's campaign for a 44-hour week when the 48-hour week had not even been achieved in this country despite its acceptance at the international conference in Washington in 1919. At the 1923 annual general council meeting there was a row because Appleton and Alfred Short, the boilermakers' representative on the Management Committee and its chairman that year, had attended an international conference of trade unions which were not affiliated to the International Federation of Trade Unions, and which Pollitt claimed were financed by capitalists. 'With the growth of international knowledge and international trade-unionism it is now too late in the day, Mr Appleton, for you to think you can make any alliance in the name of this Federation with reactionaries in this country or any other', declaimed Pollitt. Ward pointedly inquired what was the difference between the various trade union internationals, and observed that while Pollitt might be fierce in defence of the Amsterdam-based IFTU, the Moscow-based 'red international' of trade unions actually condemned it. Russia remained a source of division. In 1923 Appleton wrote to *The Times* supporting the British government's renewed intervention on behalf of the White Russian forces;[6] and at the annual meeting that year Pollitt objected strenuously to Appleton's letter. The next year, he and Ward had an argument about the economic stability of Russia, before Pollitt proceeded to his main task of pulling apart the annual report, which in that year had condemned unofficial strikes.

At the annual general council meeting of 1925 Ward and Pollitt had the last of their public skirmishes. Pollitt was arrested, tried and imprisoned soon afterwards with eleven other communists for incitement to mutiny, and by the time he was released after the General Strike, the boilermakers had seceded from the GFTU. John Ward was no longer in the best of health and his own appearances at the GFTU were to become less frequent. The encounter in 1925 arose, as usual, over Pollitt's motion to refer back part of the annual report. He objected to those sentences which said that the General Federation still aimed at industrial peace and saw 'more virtue in negotiation than in war'. In Pollitt's opinion:

> It would be utter Folly for this Council to endorse this sentence at this particular moment when in the railways and mines and the engineering trade the capitalists have themselves declared war and have not only resisted the most moderate demands of the unions but have put forward a set of conditions which represent a standard of life lower than anything which has obtained in this country since 1905 . . . There is a war, a class war, and I consider it is our duty to refer this paragraph back and do it with the knowledge that we want to see the General Federation tell the workers of the country that the Federation is not merely a financial instrument but is something that is going to take its definite place in helping the workers to overthrow capitalism and establish Socialism in its place.

In reply to this, John Ward did not go as far to the opposite extreme as Kean of the Wallpaper Workers' Union who, to cries of 'nonsense!' from the floor, asserted that all strikes were bad. Ward knew that strikes could often be the only way to force negotiations, but he condemned Pollitt for not wanting negotiations at all: 'he wants industrial war to the knife, and to the death of somebody – not himself of course – but others.' Later, in the debate on the Management Committee's rather weak resolution on unemployment, Pollitt and Ward crossed swords again. Pollitt suggested that the way to revive Britain's trade was to recognise the communist government of Russia. Ward: 'But Russia is suffering from bad government, disorder, Sovietism and anarchy generally.' Pollitt: 'Rats!' During this debate Ward was taken ill and had to leave the platform. He had over-exerted himself, and Appleton decided to leave the conference early in order to escort him back to London by the next train.

The General Strike and Its Aftermath

The background to these debates at the General Federation's annual meetings was a growing malaise in British trade unionism in general, and persistent depression in industry. The high unemployment that followed a short, immediate postwar boom of 1919–20 had been foreseen; but few had imagined that industry would remain depressed for so long, and the government's unemployment relief schemes showed a complete failure to understand how deeply rooted the problem had become. Trade union membership was falling by millions from the peak it had reached at the end of the war, but at the same time the new generation of leaders included some notable militants. Trade union strategy was still much influenced by the 'direct action' school of thought, and the tone of the TUC by 1925–6 was more radical than it had been before the First World War or would be again until after the Second. One important factor in this militancy was a general disappointment with the first Labour government in British history, which came to power in a fragile minority in January 1924, heavily dependent on the support of the Liberals, and resigned less than ten months later. Ramsay MacDonald as Prime Minister fell short of the hopes of trade unionists. Not only did he keep their representatives in a minority in his Cabinet, but he took action against striking dockers and transport workers as stern as any that might have been taken by the Conservatives under their new leader, Stanley Baldwin. The inclusion of the railwaymen's leader, J. H. Thomas, in MacDonald's Cabinet also removed the most influential of moderate trade unionists from the General Council of the TUC, until he rejoined it at the Congress of September 1925.

Amongst all the industrial problems of the early 1920s, that posed by the coalmines seemed to be the most intractable.[7] During the war the mines had been under government control but they were returned to the owners after Lloyd George's Conservative-dominated coalition rejected the recommendation of the Sankey Commission in 1919 that coalmining ought to be nationalised. In 1921, just after decontrol took effect, a miners' strike went ahead without the support of the other members of the Triple Industrial Alliance, the transport workers and the railwaymen, which was withdrawn at the eleventh hour on 'Black Friday', 15 April 1921, after the miners refused J. H. Thomas's plea that they should resume negotiations. 'Black Friday' sounded the death knell of the Triple Alliance and demonstrated a fact of life which the General Federation could and did point out to the trade union world at large: that without some central authority in charge of negotiations, even the strongest of unions would not support each other in a struggle over which they felt they had no control.[8] The lesson of this experience persuaded trade union leaders in 1925 to place arrangements for the General Strike in the hands of the only body that was in any way equipped for the task, the General Council of the TUC.

The General Strike arose out of the renewed crisis in the mining industry when, facing further recessions and a drop in exports, the mine-owners demanded a reduction in wages and increased working hours. The hastily assembled Samuel Commission, which reported on the industry early in 1926, included no representative of the miners' interests, unlike the earlier Sankey Commission of which Robert Smillie and three other Miners' Federation appointees had been members along with the eminent socialists Sidney Webb and R. H. Tawney. The report of Sir Herbert Samuel and his colleagues contained some pungent criticisms of the mine-owners and the chaotic organisation of the industry. It recommended the nationalisation of royalties and mineral rights, a substantial measure of state finance and control, and improvements in industrial relations which were to include profit-sharing and paid annual holidays. But it also called for some wage cuts in order to restore profitability, it stopped short of recommending complete nationalisation without which the Miners' Federation believed no real reform was possible, and its support for the miners' dearly held principle of national rather than district wage negotiations was ambiguous. Neither miners nor employers were prepared to accept Samuel's recommendations, the employers continued to insist on heavy wage cuts, and the Miners' Federation called on the TUC for support. The government subsidy which had kept the miners' wages at their old level while the Samuel Commission reported came to an end on 30 April 1926, and after that the miners were locked out for refusing to accept wage cuts. On May Day a special conference of trade union executives voted by a majority of more than $3\frac{1}{2}$ million to less than 50,000 to authorise the TUC to conduct a general strike in support of the miners.

The strike began on 4 May despite last-minute attempts at negotiation and lasted for nine days. Unlike the government, which had begun preparations for this eventuality months before, the General Council had only a week in which to lay its plans. Nevertheless its organisation under the guidance of Ernest Bevin was highly effective. The strike began with workers in particular industries, including printing, iron and steel and power, and after a week further industries were called out on strike. Local strike committees or 'councils of action' throughout the country were mainly based on trades councils. They co-ordinated the strike at local level, communicating with the TUC's strike organisation committee through a network of couriers on motorcycles.

The response to the strike call was impressive. There could be no doubt of the TUC's success in disrupting normal life and bringing the nation's industry virtually to a standstill. No one who lived through those nine days could ever forget the experience, whether they were strikers, volunteers on the government side who helped to run essential services, or simply non-participants who found themselves without newspapers, electric light, or transport and witnessed the parades of troops and special constables through city streets, at docks and railway stations. But in the end the TUC's negotiating committee agreed to accept the compromise put forward by Sir Herbert Samuel, who had rushed home from the continent to intercede in the negotiations. The 'Samuel Memorandum' proposed a complete reorganisation of the coal industry but also acknowledged the need for some wage cuts in the short term; and it was on the understanding that the government would do its best to carry out Samuel's suggestions that the negotiating committee visited Baldwin on 12 May to call off the strike. The miners, however, could not accept these terms and Baldwin's vague assurances did not augur well for the future of their dispute. The face-saving announcements at the end of the General Strike could not disguise the fact that the miners remained locked out until the winter, when they were obliged to return to work in complete surrender to the mine-owners' terms.

Although the General Strike was a magnificent display of trade union solidarity and powers of organisation, it had no overriding theme or purpose beyond support for the miners. The concept of a general strike for revolutionary political ends had long inspired some militants in British trade unions, but this was not the aim of the TUC in calling the General Strike of 1926. It was precisely because they could go no further that the members of the General Council were ready to find a formula for calling off the strike when they did, even though they were none too happy with Baldwin's evasiveness. Their action was responsible and realistic, perhaps inescapable, in the circumstances and, as Beatrice Webb remarked, 'the failure of the General Strike shows what a *sane* people the British are'.[9] But it left an aftermath of terrible bitterness, and its memory colours industrial relations even today. Although the struggle undoubtedly strengthened the solidarity of trade unionists, it seriously damaged the position of trade unions in the country. The Prime Minister followed up what was widely seen as an outstanding victory for him personally with the Trade Disputes and Trade Unions Act 1927. This struck at the unions by limiting picketing, outlawing most sympathetic strikes and prohibiting civil servants from joining unions affiliated to the TUC. And it struck at the Labour Party, which in fact had offered only lukewarm support to the unions during the strike, by changing the rules on political levies so that union members who wanted to contribute through their union to Labour Party funds now had to 'contract in' rather than contributing automatically with an option to 'contract out', which had been the case since 1913.

So came and went the great crisis of British trade unionism which in earlier days might have been thought a fitting challenge for the General Federation of Trade Unions. The response of the GFTU, and in particular of its secretary, to the events of 1926 was decidedly different from the energetic spirit in which Appleton had greeted the challenges of syndicalism and industrial unionism before the First World War. Before 1914, as we have seen, the Management Committee strove to be a force for unity among British trade unions: it fostered amalgamations, established strong links with trades councils, encouraged the unions to turn unemployment and health insurance to their advantage. Time and again it put before an unresponsive membership schemes that would have turned the General Federation into a strongly organised central authority and a real fighting force. By 1926 little more than pious lip-service remained of these ideals.

The GFTU's annual general council meeting of 1926, just two months after the General Strike, debated at some length the Management Committee's refusal to grant dispute benefit to any unions which had not been facing a direct threat to their own members' pay and conditions. The committee had issued a report giving exhaustive detail of previous occasions when benefit had been refused for disputes in which the claimant union was not directly involved. John Hill nevertheless made a strong plea for benefit to be paid this time, claiming that workers in the collieries, steelworks, on the railways and elsewhere had been striking in effect to preserve their own pay and conditions. He described the straits in which the boilermakers found themselves, a story only too familiar to many of the other delegates. For the past five years an average of one-third of the boilermakers' membership had been out of work, the union had been forced to spend all of its reserve funds and to borrow from the bank; and when the TUC called upon them to join the General Strike they were not in a position to pay benefit. In 1925 they had changed their rules in order to levy individual members for contributions to the GFTU, as the union's central funds could no longer bear the cost. Now they found that the 5 shillings a week benefit that they had led their members to expect from the General Federation was not available. This was causing grave disquiet, and Hill foresaw that the whole future of the federation was endangered unless some payments could be made.

Other speakers supported Hill's point of view. The Ship-constructive and Shipwrights' Union, for example, had an agreement with the National Union of Railwaymen whereby 'when they stop working we automatically stop'. Such defensive alliances, in fact, were increasingly common in postwar trade unionism. They really made a nonsense of the federation's stand against sympathetic strikes. This limited policy had never made sense in an organisation specifically founded for mutual insurance and defence; but, on the other hand, given the persistent refusal of the affiliated unions to enlarge their contributions, the Management Committee simply did not have the resources to meet a crisis of this magnitude. Except for unions like some craft unions with workers in the collieries and indeed some branches of the boilermakers, which were directly involved in the miners' dispute, it could not pay benefit to all those who had participated in the General Strike and hope to remain solvent. Appleton pointed out the financial realities to the delegates, and also commented with some justice that the federation could not be expected to bear the brunt of a policy decided by the TUC, in which it had had no say. He received support from one of the weavers' delegates, who asserted that 'as the TUC pledged themselves to support every organisation affected, the claim for benefit should be made upon the TUC'. The debate made very clear that several of the largest remaining unions would disaffiliate if the Management Committee did not change its policy, but none of the speakers volunteered any extra contributions and John Hill's motion to widen the payment of benefit for the General Strike was defeated on a show of hands by 41 votes to 6.

There was little point in many of the unions still affiliated to the GFTU keeping up their membership after this; for, if the federation did not provide insurance against the most dire emergency that most of them had ever faced, what could it offer that the well-staffed and far more prestigious TUC did not give? There might have been more sympathy for the federation's stand, however, if Appleton had not offered in print some typical and quite gratuitous observations on the general folly of the proceedings of May 1926. In his quarterly report for June he wrote that the federation 'frankly aims at peace and when compelled to fight never sets out with the intention, avowed or otherwise, of ruining the industry by which its members live'. In September he printed his angry defence against the charges made by the National Union of Tailors and Garment Workers that he had been indulging in anti-working-class propaganda. 'What I have opposed has been the stupid policies which involved Trade Unions in troubles with which they ought never to have been concerned, and in activities altogether outside their natural and possible functions.' In December he was still at it, condemning the many conferences that had been held since May, mainly in order to apportion blame for 'this flagrant piece of foolishness'. He pleaded for strength through federation and boasted of the GFTU's financially sound position, a soundness which many of its members would surely have exchanged for just a little help when they so badly needed it.

The proceedings of the 1927 annual general council meeting emphasised how isolated the General Federation had become. By that time the tailors and garment workers, the boilermakers, the shipwrights, the London Society of Compositors and the stevedores had all seceded even though some, like the compositors, roundly condemned the General Strike.[10] That year's chairman, Hutchison of the stove grate makers, defended the Management Committee's record and, interestingly, stated that 'we are in being as an insurance body'. He believed that the committee had discharged faithfully its duties in that capacity, but it was the first time that a presidential speech at the GFTU had presented so limited a view of its functions. Some other speakers were much more forthright. Alex Gossip, a militant leader of the Furnishing Trades Association, moved to dissociate the GFTU from its secretary's 'reactionary statements' in the quarterly reports, which had assumed the permanence of the capitalist system and criticised the miners for demanding sacrifices of other workers. His colleague Alfred Tomkins, a member of the Communist Party, told the meeting that the rank-and-file members of the furniture union regarded the GFTU as 'a centre of Trade Union reaction'. A delegate from the weavers, who were more often supporters of the Management Committee line, agreed with Gossip and Tomkins, even though he did not think the committee as a whole deserved to be associated with Appleton's extreme conservatism.

The real disgust that some trade unionists now felt with the General Federation and its policies was vividly illustrated in the secession of the National Union of Tailors and Garment Workers in the summer of 1926. That year they held in Leeds the third of their biennial general conferences since the union was founded by an amalgamation of several garment workers' unions in 1921. As Appleton later reminded their general secretary, the union had actually come into being under GFTU auspices, with Appleton convening several conferences, drafting rules, conducting the ballot of the separate unions' membership and acting as honorary treasurer until the newly formed union elected its own officials.[11] At Leeds, however, the conference unanimously carried a resolution to secede from the federation. This had been suggested twice previously but rejected.[12]

One consideration was the 'bad investment' that membership of the General Federation represented. In a peaceful industry with new agreements with the manufacturers' federations which would virtually bind them, at least for the next year, not to strike, there seemed no point in paying out for strike insurance. Some speakers considered the possibility of a few branches or a small proportion of the whole membership remaining affiliated, but the debate really turned on the principle involved in affiliation to the GFTU. The union's Midlands organiser declared that 'from a propaganda stand-point it [the federation] has been absolutely detrimental . . . if the mouthings of . . . Mr Appleton are an indication of the feelings of the Committee . . . the sooner we disaffiliate the better'. Then a delegate named Elsbury, one of the leading militants at a meeting that seemed generally to be in militant mood, delivered a shattering broadside:

I think we should leave the Organisation even if it paid us financially to be there for at the head of it you have a man the name of Appleton who has proved himself to be one of the worst lick-spittles of the capitalist class that we have in this country today.

A watered-down version of Elsbury's remarks appeared in the *Sunday Worker* on 15 August and provoked Appleton to write to the general secretary of the tailors and garment workers detailing some of the help that he had given the union at its foundation and afterwards. He bitterly resented being told that his words caused trade unions to lose members and declared that he would continue to speak out against what he saw as stupid policies, because these would 'have one-third of the British workers on the scrap heap, another third on the dole and the remainder sweating their hearts out in efforts to earn subsistence for the whole'.[13] In the history of recriminations and reappraisals that went on throughout British trade unionism after the General Strike, the row between the tailors and garment workers and the General Federation was a trifling episode. But it was symptomatic, for the GFTU, of the low regard in which trade unionists in general now held it.

The unions that were still affiliated to the General Federation in 1927 were now almost all craft or small-scale industrial unions, many of them with only a few hundred members. They were dominated within the federation by the Lancashire textile unions and the hosiery, pottery and furniture workers, with a cluster of small Yorkshire textile unions forming another distinct group. For several years longer the foundry workers kept up their membership despite a public quarrel over benefits in 1927,[14] and a number of smaller unions in the engineering industry stayed within the federation. Apart from these the membership was scattered among many different industries, generally represented by unions under threat from some of the big general unions. From time to time one of the General Federation's affiliates would disappear into the eager embrace of the Transport and General Workers, the General and Municipal Workers or the Amalgamated Engineering Union. Poaching of members by these big battalions was a constant cause of complaints during the 1930s.[15] The GFTU, which in its heyday had been the champion of amalgamations, now cautioned its members against losing their identity in inappropriate mergers with big general unions, and condemned the trend towards 'one big union'. George Bell's reports as organiser dealt with unions that seemed to be on the point of extinction, like the silk workers based in Macclesfield, who had once boasted 14,000 members and were now reduced to about 270.[16] Occasionally he intervened at a union's request to take over the work of a sick general secretary or to try to rebuild membership in districts where one of the big unions had been poaching with particular success. More often he addressed meetings in towns with potential members for several affiliated unions; and in 1927 the GFTU tried again to revive its district committee scheme with a view especially to increasing the membership of its affiliated unions. Rochdale, an important centre of textile trade unionism, became a focal point for the federation's more general educational work; and both Bell and Appleton regularly gave lectures at the adult education institute in the town.

Perhaps the most important event in the federation's history between the General Strike and the outbreak of the Second World War was the opening in 1930 of the building that still houses its headquarters, Central House in Upper Woburn Place, London WC1, near Euston Station. Central House now consists of seven floors plus a basement but was built originally to a height of six floors. It constituted an extremely shrewd investment of the federation's funds. Office space had often presented problems in the past, especially when the insurance section was set up with its own staff, and the federation's headquarters had moved several times. In 1930 its tenancy of Hamilton House, Bidborough Street, ran out and the National Union of Teachers who owned the building planned to take over the space occupied by the federation. Now, worrying searches for accommodation in a business-dominated area of London, where trade unions were often not welcome, were a thing of the past. The General Federation became its own landlord and also itself landlord to a large area of lucrative office space, although some members of the Management Committee continued to hope that the GFTU's own functions and membership would expand again to fill the building.[17] It is quite appropriate that Central House should appear these days on the cover of the GFTU reports, for it represents the bedrock of the federation's finances. At the time of its opening it had cost £85,095 which, with the federation's reserves standing at £209,410, was a very reasonable sum. At a modest ceremony on 17 December 1930 Thomas Mallalieu, a founder member of the Management Committee and then a trustee, performed the official opening. The staff presented Appleton with an inscribed desk stand and pen and pencil set, reported in terms that suggest that, within headquarters at any rate, the atmosphere of the GFTU was cosy and congenial. Those present included Isaac Haig Mitchell, now principal conciliation officer at the Ministry of Labour, who made a short speech in which he referred to Central House as 'a monument to the constructive side of trade unionism', and the veteran Ben Tillett who, when his dockers' union seceded on the formation of the Transport and General Workers' Union in 1922, had remained on the board of the GFTU's health insurance society. The proceedings concluded with tea provided by the staff in the new boardroom.

Unemployment Insurance in the 1920s and 1930s

The top floor of Central House housed both the small headquarters staff of the GFTU industrial section and the staff of its friendly society and insurance section. Although the federation's non-industrial insurance functions dwindled like its industrial side during the 1920s, these were the basis of its most constructive work in that decade. Before the First World War, as we have seen, unemployment insurance had seemed to offer great opportunities to the trade unions. The chimera of 'total trade unionism' had danced before the eyes of Appleton and his committee and for a short time they foresaw a world in which trade unions, acting in concert through the General Federation, would safeguard the workers' well-being throughout life. The GFTU had not stopped short with unemployment insurance as many unions did. By 1913 it was also offering a health insurance scheme under part I of the National Insurance Act 1911 and was venturing into life assurance as well.

In 1920 Parliament passed a new Unemployment Insurance Act as part of its plans for reconstruction in the aftermath of the war. This Act extended the right to insurance to all workers earning less than £250 a year. But it came just when the postwar boom was ending, and the country was poised on the brink of a period of unemployment far longer and more serious than any it had previously experienced. The provisions of the 1920 Act, actuarially based on figures from before the war, turned out to be completely inadequate. They soon had to be supplemented by the hated 'dole', handouts of money which bore no relation to the old insurance principle of 1911 whereby a working man was entitled to benefit in proportion to the amount of contributions he had made and the whole procedure was removed from the Poor Law and its humiliating implications. Appleton criticised the financial premises of the 1920 Act and thought it clumsy and unworkable in other ways.[18] But the TUC at a special Congress went further; it condemned it utterly and advised unions to have nothing to do with it. This was because, as in 1911, the new Act enabled friendly societies and commercial insurance companies as well as the trade unions to administer unemployment insurance; it also imposed administrative requirements which would place any trade union insurance society at a severe disadvantage compared with the commercial ones.[19]

Appleton still regarded unemployment insurance as a great opportunity for trade unions. Like the majority of TUC leaders he deplored the inclusion of commercial companies in the Act, but as a second best he would have liked to see the unions make a bid to administer unemployment insurance in competition with them. It is difficult to judge whether he was right. During the extremely difficult years ahead, many unions were to find their resources severely stretched, and it is doubtful whether they could have coped with the new task of administering insurance in addition to the other problems that crowded in on them; the few that did make the attempt soon abandoned it. In 1920, however, these difficulties were scarcely beginning, union membership had barely begun to decline from its wartime peak, and the TUC objected not to the difficulty of making unemployment insurance work, but rather to the absence of any special advantages in it for them. Since trade union membership was only about one-third of the country's total workforce, such an attitude was quite unrealistic; no government would have granted a monopoly over administering unemployment insurance to a group of organisations that represented only a third of the possible recipients. The TUC, in refusing to co-operate with the Act, however, did save itself from many potential complications.

The TUC's rejection of unemployment insurance made the GFTU

pause for some time before deciding to try to continue with the scheme even under its new limitations. In September 1920 Appleton eventually recommended to the Management Committee that it should go ahead.[20] The GFTU insurance society already had branches in Birmingham, Manchester, Glasgow, Bristol, Hanley and Bolton. In order to comply with the 1920 Act, it would need to set up offices in other districts as well. It should aim to become a central organisation for all the trade unions that wanted to administer unemployment insurance, using branch officials of the affiliated unions and local union organisation as much as possible. The Management Committee accepted a modified version of the report and making it clear that it did not wish to interfere with unions that were already preparing their own schemes, it sent out a circular with a reply post-card to 1,198 unions.[21] Three weeks later only thirty-five had replied and several of them were hostile to the idea. The Management Committee therefore abandoned its scheme and withdrew altogether from the administrative sphere of national unemployment insurance, which it had entered upon so hopefully less than ten years earlier. It reported rather scornfully that some labourers' unions, especially the London dockers, were offering unrealistically high benefits, and predicted that unemployment in the future would be so high that all calculations based on figures for the past ten years would be invalid.[22] In this at least the committee was only too right. It was a sad appendix to the whole affair that in 1920–1 Appleton was a member of the Adkins committee on old age pensions which recommended that pensions should be made available to everyone over a certain age; the government decided to ignore the recommendations on the grounds that they would be financially impossible during the recession.[23] The 1920s, in other words, began as they were to continue with a reversal of the prewar circumstances in which the government had begun to extend social benefits to working people partly with the co-operation of the trade union movement.

Unemployment insurance remained very much a live issue throughout the interwar period. In the 1920s unemployment remained persistently high, around an annual average of 10 per cent of the total workforce, a rate unprecedented in Britain except for very short periods. It overturned all the calculations of trade union insurance societies and the government, and kept insurance problems on the agenda of both sides of industry. In February 1922 the committee which had been set up under Sir Eric Geddes to suggest economies recommended fierce cuts in all areas of government expenditure. The 'Geddes axe' took a swing at welfare spending by proposing, among other things, that unemployment insurance ought to be financed wholly by trade unions and employers, organised industry by industry; and the Ministry of Labour immediately began to look into the feasibility of such a plan.

On 1 March 1922 John Ward introduced an unemployment insurance Bill in the House of Commons on behalf of the GFTU Management Committee. It proposed: that employers' associations and trade unions should co-operate in administering insurance; that all liabilities incurred by unions which administered insurance during the experimental period of the 1920 Act should be eliminated; the creation of a common fund for unemployment purposes; a clearing-house arrangement for shifting employment between industries; and the provision of a 'residual group' to cover those occupations for which the Bill did not otherwise provide.[24] The Bill was given its first reading without a division, but it gave rise to a very interesting short debate between Ward and J. R. Clynes, who opposed it on behalf of the Labour Party. The episode showed amongst other things how defensive the GFTU's committee could be, even at this relatively early stage in its decline. For Ward saw fit to emphasise that his Bill was sponsored by 'the only great purely industrial and non-political organisation of workers in this country', a claim that the Labour members greeted with ironical cheers.[25] Clynes questioned whether Ward really represented the wishes of the GFTU. He opposed the Bill (although he did not wish to force it to a division) because he thought that it would cause administrative chaos, because it apparently made no provision for general labourers and because it excluded the state when in Labour's view the state ought to take more, not less, responsibility for unemployment.

This last objection was the nub of the matter. The GFTU's Bill, which was probably the brainchild of Ward and Appleton together, sought to remove unemployment insurance from the sphere of the state as a matter of principle. The federation's Management Committee had been considering such a policy since the annual general council meeting in Bangor in 1921, a fact that Ward was careful to mention in introducing the Bill, lest anyone should charge the GFTU with colluding with the government or with borrowing its policies from the Geddes recommendations. The aim of the Bill was to achieve 'the greatest benefit to the unemployed at the smallest administrative cost and with the least loss of moral fibre to the people themselves'.[26] In that respect it was a striking example of how far to the right Ward, Appleton, Wilkie (the Bill's co-sponsor in the House of Commons) and others were moving the General Federation. But, more than this, it was an interesting hangover from the days before 1920 when the GFTU threw its weight behind industrial unionism. Since the government clearly would not hand over the administration of insurance to the unions altogether, the preferable alternative from a trade union point of view was to share it with the manufacturing employers rather than with companies whose whole business was to make a profit out of insurance. Such a policy would have the effect of strengthening industrial unions *vis-à-vis* the large general unions, which would find themselves faced with administering any number of separate insurance arrangements for the benefit of their extremely diverse memberships. It also had the merit of following the industrial structure and discipline which the Whitley Committee and its offspring the joint industrial councils attempted to give to collective bargaining, and which flourished most in those industries where industrial unionism was strong. If the two sides of industry were forced to co-operate over unemployment insurance, they would find themselves meeting each other regularly outside the context of trade disputes, and this was bound to improve industrial relations.[27]

The GFTU's unemployment insurance Bill never got beyond its first reading, mainly because clause 17 called for a contribution from the Treasury to help set up the new scheme, and this would have required the government to move a financial resolution in Parliament. The Minister of Labour, Sir Montague Barlow, had received a disappointing response to his own circular letter on insurance by industries, sent out to trade unions and employers in February 1922; and although his officials gave the scheme a lot of attention during the year, by December they were beginning to suspect that it was impracticable.[28] Just before Christmas the GFTU Management Committee visited Barlow, both to press for implementation of the Washington Convention of 1919 on the 48-hour week and to discuss with him their plans for unemployment insurance.[29] Of three alternative insurance schemes which the Ministry of Labour officials themselves had drawn up, one closely resembled the GFTU's, and the Management Committee went away from the meeting rather pleased with their chances of success.[30] But there were snags. As Ward acknowledged, the 'political side of the trade union movement' was opposed to their scheme.[31] The element of compulsion which the GFTU thought necessary if the plan was to work did not appeal to the Minister of Labour. Appleton might argue that industry would manage its own affairs better than the state; but set against this was the enormous complexity of a scheme that called for separate employment exchanges for each industry in each town, with elaborate arrangements for workers who transferred between industries and for the large 'residue' who did not fall into convenient categories.[32] On the very day when the GFTU Management Committee was meeting Barlow, the *Daily Herald* reported 'an important statement' issued by the National Joint Council of Labour representing the TUC, Labour Party and Parliamentary Labour Party, which urged that no union should agree to the 'transfer of national responsibility for national disorganisation, whether due to unemployment, ill-health or old age to any special industry, until the movement as a whole has had the opportunity of considering the subject in its widest aspects.[33] Opposition to insurance by industries was hardening rather than diminishing as Ward had hoped.[34] At the annual general council meeting of the GFTU in 1923 a resolution calling for this policy was withdrawn after several speakers pointed out that most trade unions opposed it.

This was effectively the end for some years of any national debate about the role of government in insuring workers against the financial calamity of unemployment. The short-lived Labour government in 1924 extended insurance payments to all the unemployed for however long they remained out of work, but bowed to Liberal pressure to make this provision contingent on a review after two years.[35] In 1927 the recommendations of the Blanesburgh Committee set up by the Conservatives resulted in yet another Act, entitling the unemployed to an unlimited period of benefit after paying minimum contributions, with a new 'transitional benefit' to protect those who had not worked for long enough to contribute even the minimum. The only qualification for receiving benefit was to be (as it is today) the individual's ability to prove that he was 'genuinely seeking work'. Two years later the Local Government Act brought in by Neville Chamberlain as Minister of Health swept away the old system of Poor Law guardians and introduced local public assistance committees to administer benefits other than unemployment insurance. This succession of changes during the 1920s was designed to remove the welfare of the poor, the sick and the unemployed from the demoralising environment of charity and the old concepts of 'deserving' and 'undeserving' poor which had surrounded it in the nineteenth century; it placed responsibility for basic social welfare squarely in the domain of the state. In this respect the legislation of all governments in the decade was well intentioned. But it reflected a concern to palliate unemployment and all its attendant evils, rather than a will to attack the root of the problem by radical economic measures. Even at the end of the 1920s J. M. Keynes was still only developing the economic theories, published in full in 1936,[36] which would influence so profoundly the policies of governments in Britain and around the world after 1945. Keynes's idea that expansionist economic measures and large-scale public investment in industry and schemes of public work could help to conquer unemployment and reinvigorate the economy had a small following in all three main political parties. Among trade unionists its most notable exponent was Ernest Bevin. Within the Parliamentary Labour Party the economic radicals were led by the brilliant young aristocrat Sir Oswald Mosley, then tipped as a future Labour prime minister, who left the party in impatient disgust when his programme was not adopted and, after a few years as founder-leader of the 'New Party', became leader of the British fascists, one of the strangest metamorphoses in British political history.

The dominance of economic orthodoxy in all three parties combined with the new burdens which the social legislation of the 1920s had put on the public purse to store up disaster for Ramsay MacDonald's second Labour government (1929–31) when the worst of the international recession hit Britain in 1931. Philip Snowden, MacDonald's Chancellor of the Exchequer, had watched the number of unemployed receiving transitional benefit rise in two months from 140,000 to 200,000 as a result of Labour's decision that the unemployed should not have to prove any longer that they were genuinely seeking work in order to be eligible for benefit, and that the onus for proving they were not eligible lay with the officials. In other words, the number of people accepted as being genuinely un- employed, but who had not been in work for long enough to pay minimum insurance contributions, had doubled in eight weeks. This dramatic and costly demonstration of the intractable problem led Snowden to appoint a committee under Sir George May to advise him how to balance the budget. In July 1931 the May Committee reported that drastic cuts in benefit payments were essential in order to balance the national budget, preserve the parity of the pound and restore international confidence in Britain. The Labour Cabinet split and nine of its twenty members, led by Arthur Henderson, resigned rather than be responsible for cutting the dole. MacDonald formed a coalition National Government with himself, Snowden, Lord Sankey and J. H. Thomas as the only Labour members of the Cabinet along- side Liberals and Conservatives, and was quickly expelled by the Labour Party. The government carried out what the minority in the Labour Cabinet had been powerless to prevent: 10 per cent cuts in the dole, which was now limited to twenty-six weeks' duration; and a stringent means test for transitional benefit (now called 'transitional payment') which was to be administered by the public assistance committees. The means test with its humiliating inquisitions into family life and its rough-and-ready injustices, became an even more searing experience for many unemployed people than the 10 per cent cut in what was already barely a subsistence allowance.

The British trade union movement's opposition to the policies of the early 1930s was led most vocally by Ernest Bevin, one of the few individuals of national standing who could claim to have advocated a coherent alternative policy based on sound economic reasoning. But it is worth noticing that Bevin and his like-minded colleagues at the TUC had a tradition of constructive alternatives put forward by the unions on which they could draw. The provision of jobs for the unemployed in schemes of public works, labour colonies and other projects had been a policy of some charitable and labour organisations back in the nineteenth century.[37] By the early years of the twentieth century it had become a familiar demand at trade union conferences. The General Federation of Trade Unions had brought and kept the subject before the attention of the Joint Board and in 1908 offered one of the most fully thought-out schemes for the relief of unemployment. It pointed out that workers who could afford themselves to buy the products of industry were far more useful to the economy than unemployed workers reduced to the breadline or below.[38] Some despairing trade unionist observers in the 1930s must have felt that advanced economic theory was beginning to catch up with common sense at last, and wondered whether government policy would ever do so.

The Work of the General Federation in the 1930s

The GFTU in the 1930s continued to debate unemployment insurance and to pass resolutions against the various injustices that arose under the piecemeal and confusing legislation of the period. For instance, one condition for receiving unemployment benefit under the national insurance scheme was that the recipient must not be involved in a dispute at the time, or employed on the same grade and in the same place of work as others who were on strike. This provision left scope for some vindictive employers to manipulate circumstances so that sections of their workforce which had been thrown out of work by disputes elsewhere could be made to appear involved in the dispute, and so to forfeit their unemployment pay. Instances of this and other malpractices were described at GFTU annual meetings, but little could be done to prevent them.[39]

In some individual cases the GFTU intervened to help small unions to obtain justice for their members. In 1936–7, for example, the employment department of the Ministry of Labour gave a lot of time to the case of some unemployed chainmakers in Staffordshire, which had been brought to its attention by George Bell for the GFTU. The chainmakers concerned were outworkers, a category newly catered for in the Unemployment Insurance Act 1935; but these men needed to prove that they were in fact the employees of one firm and not self-employed, in order to qualify for unemployment benefit. The sworn statement of one of them brings to life the nature of work in this little documented industry before the Second World War:

I, Albert Homer, state that I work on my forge for Mr Southall. I have not worked for anyone else for some years as Mr Southall gives me sufficient. My wages are piece-work rates plus an allowance for firing utensils. Mr Southall notifies me either by letter or visit if he wants any different sizes made. He checks the work when it is returned. He could make me pay for loss of iron. I should ask Mr Southall if I wanted to take on any help before I did so.

I should not refuse Mr Southall entry into my shop, but it is my shop and I can please myself as to the hours I work. He does not interfere with the way I do it.[40]

The senior partner of another firm testified to the 'peculiarly independent and insubservient character of the persons engaged in the chain making trade'. 'From him I gather' wrote an inspector for the Ministry of Health, 'that the personal service aspect comes into prominence when the rod for making the chain is delivered for making up. . . .Mr Woodhouse claims to be able to detect each chain maker's work from the finished chain.'[41] The chainmakers' very independence, however, disqualified them from receiving unemployment benefit under the 1935 Act, for it could not be established that the employers had a right of entry to the outworkers' workshops, and in the event only two men were considered eligible. The GFTU had raised an important principle with implications throughout the chainmaking industry and for other occupations. The Ministry of Labour, in this instance at least, certainly took it seriously, and the federation was credited with having done its best for its affiliated members, though the outcome was not what they would have hoped.

Not all of the federation's dealings with unemployment insurance were so amicable, however. Appleton considered the subject very much his own, and held strong and increasingly conservative opinions about it. In 1931 he was quoted in the press as the only trade union leader who did not favour an extension of the dole. This report gave rise to angry scenes at the annual general council meeting that year, when Appleton answered his critics by insisting that it was not the business of the state to provide either employment or maintenance, and that unemployment pay was provided only at the expense of those who were in work. One delegate declared, 'We have listened to a statement from Mr Appleton which I consider a disgrace, the like of which I never want to hear again'. It was perhaps all to the good that unemployment insurance was not any longer a significant part of the GFTU's activities.

The least contentious and more successful work of the General Federation, taken over the whole period between the two world wars, went on in its health insurance and life assurance sections. The GFTU had set up an Approved Society administering health insurance under the terms of the National Insurance Act 1911 and had also taken on the administration of unemployment insurance. In 1913 it added a life assurance scheme to its other work in the field, partly to attract extra members to its other branches. Before the First World War the health insurance section built up a membership of 140,000. At one time it was obliged to shed some of its business to other unions under pressure from the insurance commissioners, but it continued to operate both health and life insurance successfully, and could claim with some justice to be one of the most efficient of the trade union Approved Societies.[42] In 1930 it was able to advertise benefits over and above the minimum laid down by the insurance Acts.[43] Apart from offering high cash benefits, it held out the additional offer of payments for dental treatment, treatment in a convalescent home or rheumatism clinic, and surgical appliances. The life and general insurance section of the GFTU offered both infant and adult insurance policies plus cover against fire and a scheme whereby trade unions could insure their own staffs against accidents and any other form of industrial risk. Conservatively managed by separate annual meetings and committees, the GFTU's insurance side operated very cheaply. By 1926, having rebuilt its membership to 100,000, it was the largest of the trade union Approved Societies,[44] and by 1930 it was increasing its staff of outside agents who called on members individually to collect their payments, spreading the gospel of trade unionism as they did so.[45]

The insurance activities of the GFTU led its Management Committee to take a close interest in problems of health. One scheme supported by the federation in the 1920s and 1930s was the Joseph Cross Memorial Convalescent Home in Poulton-le-Fylde, which commemorated the Lancashire weavers' leader who had been chairman of the Management Committee from 1918 to 1920.[46] On Appleton's initiative, the committee also took action on the problem of rheumatism, which accounted for between 6 and 10 per cent of the health insurance claims on the federation.[47] In 1926 Appleton joined a party of hydrologists on a visit to inspect continental spas and their methods of treating rheumatism, and after his return the Management Committee visited some British spas and issued a report. It concluded that spa treatment was the best then available for rheumatic ailments, recommended that the government ought to provide spa clinics, and offered financial support in the meantime to any other movement to provide such treatment for working people.[48] More closely connected with the industrial side of the GFTU's work was its concern with occupational diseases and workmen's compensation. It first took up the question of silicosis in 1921, and carried out inquiries into the disease until well into the 1930s. In 1928, acting on the instructions of that year's annual general council meeting, the Management Committee sent a deputation to the Home Secretary to ask for the extension of the latest Workmen's Compensation Act. It complained that hundreds of workers in the pottery and metal grinding industries were still getting no compensation, despite the fact that dermatitis and silicosis now came under the provisions of the Act; and it asked the Home Secretary to delete the provision whereby a lead worker suffering from poisoning could not claim compensation unless he had worked in the industry for at least twelve months.[49]

Compensation for industrial diseases was almost always on the agenda in one form or another at the federation's annual meetings in the 1920s and 1930s. The pottery workers, whose industry was notoriously unhealthy,[50] were among the most active campaigners for industrial safety at the GFTU. Lead poisoning from the glazes, silicosis caused by pottery dust and the debilitating disease of 'plumbism' caused by high levels of lead in the blood were all familiar enemies of the pottery worker: so much so that in 1920 a pottery worker aged 30 would be classified automatically as 35 for insurance purposes.[51] At the annual general council meeting in 1931, Mann of the coopers' union, a sympathiser of the potters', graphically described the dangers in the industry:

The chief ingredient of the trade, animal bones and flint stone, are worked to such an extent that they become liquid. They are, perhaps, not so dangerous in their liquid form, but during the transition from one department to another . . . the workers breathe the dust into their lungs.[52]

At one pottery that he knew of, 130 different people handled the raw material in the process of turning it into liquid.

Thomas Mallalieu added evidence of the need for the government to regulate industrial safety from his own experience in the felt hat making trade. Twenty-five years earlier he had taken a survey of one of his union's branches, where he 'never saw an old man'. His union negotiated with the Home Office and obtained an order to provide fans to remove the dust from the workshops. Now, some twenty years after the fans were introduced, the average lifespan of the workers in that branch had increased, almost unbelievably in so short a time, by

18 years and 9 months.[53] Later in the 1930s the General Federation turned its attention to the health of cardroom operatives who suffered incapacitation from inhaling cotton dust.[54] (A commission of inquiry reporting in 1931 had decided against scheduling this particular disease for compensation only because the doctors could not discover precisely which ingredient caused the damage.) But despite its continuous involvement in the problem of industrial health and safety, a motion at the 1938 annual general council meeting to improve the statutory provisions for workmen's compensation was referred back because it did not go nearly so far as the Bill then being sponsored by the Labour Party.[55] The contribution of the GFTU, even on a subject where it could be really effective, was not in the sphere of policy formation or propaganda, but in detailed fact-finding, campaigning on a small scale, and in patient visits to government departments, factory inspectors and industrialists.

Apart from the various forms of insurance that preceded the welfare state as we know it today, the GFTU turned its attention to most of the problems of industry between the wars. Prominent among these was the introduction of new work patterns based on time and motion study, a practice imported to Britain and other European countries from the United States. Among the GFTU's affiliated unions, the hosiery workers and the cotton weavers were the most affected, and at their behest the federation investigated the question in some depth.[56] They concentrated on the best known of the new time and motion systems, that introduced by the Bedaux Company of New York. Bedaux set out to measure the amount of energy contained in a given piece of work in the same way as one might measure electric power. They reduced output to units of 'Bs' which they defined as the amount of work reasonably done in a minute in any given operation. On this basis a minimum rate of pay was determined, and all workers would be paid this basic rate. On top of that, a premium was payable to workers who produced more than 60 'Bs' an hour. Foremen and overseers received a premium based on their department's weekly output of 'Bs'.

Predictably, the problems created by the Bedaux system were legion. As the GFTU's investigating team discovered, the premiums paid to foremen in practice came out of those due to the workers themselves. The introduction of the system into any factory involved theorists employed by Bedaux coming to judge the work of skilled craftsmen in industries of which they themselves had no experience. The period of weeks or months when the system was being tried out involved the workers in all the strain of being constantly watched and judged. There was a built-in tendency to sacrifice decent working conditions to higher productivity and the quality and craftsmanship of a product to sheer quantity. Union observers found that the amount of scrap or spoiled work increased as a result of Bedaux and similar schemes. Workers were often rather hastily stigmatised as inefficient and transferred to other jobs or sacked. On the other hand, when the system worked well, it could encourage workers to take more pride in their output, in some cases it did increase productivity, and it sometimes resulted in raising wages quite significantly. The unions' attitude to Bedaux was not therefore wholly hostile.

A good example of how a union might take advantage of time and motion methods came in the Wolsey hosiery factory in 1931–2.[57] Here an eight-week strike followed the management's attempt to introduce the Bedaux system in place of its traditional piecework rates. The main union negotiator involved was Horace Moulden, then general secretary of the Leicester hosiery union. He spent three days hammering out with management a compromise settlement that ended the strike. Wolsey had moved too fast for its workforce in introducing Bedaux, but under the new arrangements that followed the strike they kept the system and did in fact improve productivity. Moulden persuaded them to let him select a girl from among their employees to be trained in Bedaux methods and to work alongside the Bedaux personnel in the factory whenever a dispute arose between them and the workers. Combined with fairly close union supervision, this system worked well. Under the old piecework system it had been common for one inefficient girl to earn only half as much as the girl who worked beside her, no matter how much union officials or fellow workers might try to help her improve: hosiery work involves an innate dexterity which to some extent cannot be taught. But under the 1932 agreement at the Wolsey factory, union officials were enabled to find alternative work in the factory for the less dexterous workers and to eliminate far more of the discrepancies between individuals' earnings that had flourished in the days of piecework.

This episode is interesting, incidentally, for its illustration of Horace Moulden's style as a trade unionist. It would be less than justice to Moulden, who joined the GFTU Management Committee in 1934–5 and became one of the General Federation's most colourful and persuasive speakers, to call him 'typical' of his or any other generation of GFTU trade unionists. Nevertheless, his intervention in the Wolsey strike could almost have been a model for fellow members of the General Federation. Always a believer in strong, centralised industrial unionism, Moulden also firmly believed in negotiation and dialogue between the two sides of industry. He developed early in his career a well-informed understanding of business methods and a preference for solutions that would advance the interests of both sides, rather than winning short-term gains for the workers at the expense of the employers. He would probably agree that the most solid achievements of his career were those where both management and unions agreed to adopt new methods, leading to the closer involvement of the union in the firm's affairs and often to union recognition where it had not existed before. To a certain extent this would be true of almost all competent trade unionists, but the emphasis on a consultative and conciliatory approach is one that seems to have been particularly characteristic of GFTU trade unions, at any rate from the 1930s onwards. As officials of member unions of the General Federation have often claimed, both at annual meetings and elsewhere, the specialist nature of most of their unions gives them an intimate knowledge of the work about which they negotiate, and often helps them to influence the decision of management on a wide range of questions.

Discussion of the Bedaux and similar systems did not end with the Wolsey hosiery workers' strike. On the whole, such 'stop-watch' methods were strongly disliked. Horace Moulden himself moved a protest against them at the annual general council meeting in 1935. The textile workers spoke out against Bedaux on several occasions at GFTU meetings. Alex Gossip of the Furnishing Trades Association registered strong objections, based on the experience of a series of strikes which had been caused by firms' attempts to increase productivity by a work-measuring system.[58] Time and motion methods played some part in the deterioration of industrial relations in the woollen textile industry in Yorkshire, where a major strike in 1930 cost the GFTU more than £33,000 in benefit payments.[59] The problem of measuring work, in fact, hit the GFTU's unions especially hard because of the high concentration of craft working arrangements and therefore of piecework payments, as opposed to weekly wages, among their membership. A reading of the federation's disputes benefit ledger for the 1930s reveals changes in piece rates, often resulting from Bedaux and similar systems, as one of the main causes of strikes. Other recurrent grievances included the managers' attempts to replace skilled with unskilled labour or to introduce more than the agreed number of apprentices, and some hard-fought battles to win or maintain union recognition. In this it reflected the common experience of trade unions in general during the 1930s.

These problems all arose in one way or another out of the economic recession. Even though in the middle 1930s the British economy revived substantially and throughout the decade living standards improved for the great majority of the population, unemployment remained intractably at over 13 per cent.[60] Some 1·75 million or more individuals were out of work at any one time, and many of them suffered years of unemployment. This, in a period when unemployment and health insurance had not yet become universal, even though provisions for social welfare were improving, kept trade unions very much at a disadvantage. Union membership, which had declined almost continuously during the 1920s, began to increase appreciably in 1933 and continued to rise after that. But even at 6·25 million, which it had reached by the eve of the Second World War, it represented only 39 per cent of the nation's workforce.[61] The struggle to prevent hard-pressed employers from seeking recovery at the expense of their employees was an unequal one.

One further illustration of the industrial problems of the 1930s may be drawn from among the GFTU's affiliated unions. This was the Lancashire textile workers' fight over the 'more looms' system which culminated in 1932 in what has been called 'the last real mass strike by British workers for twenty-five years'.[62] The cotton textile unions were bedevilled by disunity, as the GFTU had learned to its cost back in 1908–9.[63] This weakness formed part of the background to the dispute but, much more important, there had been a contraction in demand for cotton textiles ever since the First World War, and this decline had become particularly alarming after about 1928.[64] By 1930 the trade had fallen off by more than 60 per cent from its 1914 level. In 1928 the masters' associations tried to improve business by introducing new working methods. They removed weavers from the ancillary jobs of oiling and sweeping, and carrying the weft and cloth, and they introduced larger cops to reduce the amount of work involved in reshuttling the looms. They then required each weaver to work eight looms instead of the previous four, in effect introducing a longer working week for less pay. The lockout and strike that followed forced the weavers to abandon the system then. But the recession in the textile industry was getting worse and that, combined with the failure of the cotton textile unions to agree on a common policy of their own, made a renewed confrontation inevitable. The weakness of the unions was highlighted by the fact that some workers were beginning to condone departures from the agreed price lists in order to save their jobs.[65]

There were lockouts in a number of cotton mills in 1929 and again in 1931, by which time unemployment in the industry had reached 47 per cent.[66] The industry-wide strike of 1932 arose out of the employers' attempt to introduce six-loom working and their abrogation of all existing wage agreements when the unions rejected this system. The cotton unions resisted fiercely: they drew a total of £163,407 in benefit payments from the GFTU and appealed for funds, though with only limited success, to the TUC during the September Congress.[67] Eventually they returned to work under the terms of a joint agreement to undertake six-loom working on a limited range of mainly plain cloths. They had exhausted their own resources and their entitlement to federation benefit, and they knew that they were fighting a losing battle against economic realities. But labour relations in the textile industry remained extremely disturbed. The six-looms agreement paid the worker less per piece than the old four-looms working arrangement, and some employers were quick to apply the six-loom rates outside their legitimate sphere – for instance, where a worker had been given only four looms to work. Thus, in the words of a board of inquiry set up by the Ministry of Labour, 'a vicious circle of wage cutting and price cutting was set up and the industry was faced with the possible collapse of the whole principle of collective bargaining'.[68]

In contrast to the long strike by Lancashire textile workers in 1908–9, the GFTU did not intervene directly in negotiations in 1932. Such interventions had become very clearly the preserve of the TUC. The federation was happy to point out, however, that large sums of GFTU benefit had been of material assistance to the unions and their members, whereas financial help from the TUC had come 'too little and too late'.[69] Textile workers by now formed nearly a majority of the GFTU's members and certainly faced problems as severe as any others. The hosiery and the furniture workers, for example, troubled though they were by the introduction of time and motion methods and (especially in the furniture industry) by problems of recognition, were shielded from the worst effects of the depression by changes in fashion. Hosiery was very much more in demand than it had been in the days of long skirts. And in the furniture industry new production techniques and the increased use of plywood had developed alongside a new mass market for inexpensive furniture, which was further encouraged by the boom in house-building and home-ownership that was transforming the lives of so many people in the 1920s and 1930s.

No such advantages developed to help the textile workers out; on the contrary, competition from growing textile industries abroad combined with that from new man-made textiles and even with the fashion for skimpier clothing to put cotton, woollen and silk textiles together among the most dramatically declining industries in the country. The GFTU, although it no longer intervened directly in the industry, did take a close interest in its misfortunes. As early as 1928, for example, it sent a deputation to the President of the Board of Trade to raise the question of 'inflation of capital'.[70] One of the industry's problems as the GFTU diagnosed it was that immediately after the First World War its American cotton section had been recapitalised by the purchase of firms at extravagant prices during the short postwar boom. These firms had then been refloated at lower prices, thereby necessitating much higher profits in order to keep up share dividends and repay loans. With no actual expansion of business to meet the problem, the burden fell upon the workers and there were disastrous reductions in wages. The federation urged the Board of Trade to intervene to prevent such wanton schemes of capitalisation in the future; but as usual its representations were unheeded. Nor did the GFTU's views on capital control command attention in the trade union movement as a whole. It is worth noting, however, that as far as Appleton was concerned, his investigation of problems of capitalisation in the textile industry formed the background to a firm belief in industrial co-partnership.[71]

Such views might win support today but they were alien and irrelevant to a trade union and labour movement which had yet to win the nationalisation and public ownership that it saw as the panacea for industrial problems. Opinions differed within the mainstream of the labour movement as to the form that nationalisation might take and there were significant distinctions of view about industrial structure, involvement of the workforce in company policy, and so on. But Appleton's opinions on industry really belonged outside the whole framework of the labour movement's debate. The same was true of most of the observations put forward in the name of the GFTU during the 1930s.

Relations with the TUC and the Big Unions

In 1932, acting on the instructions of the previous year's annual general council meeting, the organising subcommittee of the GFTU published a *Report on the Causes of the Failure to Increase Trade Union Membership*. The member of headquarters staff on this subcommittee was not Appleton but George Bell; but the report that he helped produce was as conservative as any that Appleton himself might have drafted. The subcommittee members paid some attention to bad employers, the growth of shop clubs and employees' associations, and so on, the undermining of moral fibre during the war and the existence of the 1927 Trades Unions Act as factors in the decline of trade unionism. But the main thrust of their report was an indictment of general unionism. They defended the old craft unions' restrictions on the numbers of apprentices and extolled the self-discipline, the 'old Trade Union spirit of service and fraternity' and 'strength of character' which in their view typified the craft unions. Large unions had neglected health and unemployment insurance, and so lost the chance to bind their members more closely together in times of need, a loss exacerbated by the public service unions' tendency to look to political solutions for all their industrial problems. Trade unionists in general were not making use of trade boards or fair contract clauses, after all the hard work that their predecessors had put into obtaining the Trade Board Acts of 1909 and 1918 and drawing up model fair contract clauses. (This latter policy was one in which the GFTU had been especially active from an early date.) The report complained also of poaching by the big unions, a problem that delegates often brought to the attention of GFTU meetings, and one that the anti-poaching agreement reached at the Bridlington TUC in 1939 would only partly remove. Poaching by the big unions lowered the dignity of the trade union movement, the GFTU report insisted, and 'unrestricted general organisation provide[d] an easy escape from real Trade Union discipline'. In its most damning sentence, the report condemned what it called the 'One Big Union policy' thus:

> Necessarily, [the One Big Union] is opposed to organisation by trade, occupation or industry; it involves interference with established Trade Unions; economically it is foolish; democratically it is impossible; socially it is disastrous, as its tendencies are in the direction of the despotic control of the lives of all workers by a central executive or head.[72]

As far as I can discover, the report attracted no attention or comment outside the ranks of the GFTU itself. The federation's importance had dwindled already beyond the point where other trade unionists felt obliged to pay it the courtesy of their notice. This complete insignificance in the eyes of the trade union world as a whole was underlined most humiliatingly at the Weymouth TUC in 1934. There the Typographical Association moved for an addition to TUC rules that would provide for a levy of up to $1d$ per member per week on all affiliated unions during the course of any strike sponsored by the General Council. Jack Jones, MP, of the General and Municipal Workers' Union, wanted to see a continuous contribution of $\frac{1}{2}d$ per week per member, into 'a common fund controlled by the general body of the Trade Union Movement'. 'We ought to be organised' he told Congress, 'so that when trouble really does come there should be some central body with central power of control whereby the Unions will act together.' Congress referred the resolution to the General Council to be reported on the following year, at the end of a short debate in which no speaker once mentioned the General Federation of Trade Unions.[73]

The GFTU Management Committee produced in a printed pamphlet a spirited rejoinder to the Typographical Association's proposal.[74] It poured scorn on the notion that a levy could be effective as anything other than 'a medium of self-advertising' and offered a very reasonable defence of the General Federation's methods of administering dispute benefit, which it did as a matter of course, quietly, effectively and without drawing attention to the financial plight of the unions concerned. In a practical spirit it also opened negotiations with the TUC over a possible closer working relationship.[75]

A long and patient correspondence ensued between Appleton and Sir Walter Citrine, general secretary of the TUC, and on 27 January 1937, after several postponements, eight members of the TUC General Council visited the GFTU Management Committee at Central House. It was the first time the two bodies had met since 1923.[76] The TUC delegation included Citrine, Vincent Tewson, who eventually succeeded him as general secretary, and Ernest Bevin. They had previously been presented with a long memorandum drawn up by Appleton which set out the sad history of relations between the two organisations. Appleton's tone in this document was if anything even more bitter than that of his printed broadsides. He charged that those people at the TUC who wanted to set up a new method of financing disputes without reference to the GFTU had 'neither constructive ideas nor apprehensions of what the Federation, often in the face of jealousy and hostility, has accomplished . . . '. He dwelt on the past omissions of the TUC in dealing with insurance and especially on its folly in not encouraging the unions to take up national health insurance in 1911. According to Appleton, the TUC's indecision on this, despite the GFTU's attempts to procure joint action, meant that commercial insurance companies had time to cream off the ablebodied trade union members who were 'good risks', leaving the unfortunate bad risks to the belatedly formed trade union Approved Societies. The catalogue of TUC sins continued with several further examples. Despite this unconciliatory document, the TUC General Council delegation tried to introduce a more peaceable note into its meeting with the GFTU Management Committee. As Bevin remarked, 'It is no good arguing about the past. We have to try and see the problem as we face it now.'

The TUC offered little in the way of practical proposals as to how a closer co-operation with the GFTU might be achieved. Two special subcommittees met again in June 1937, however, and during the year it emerged that the TUC might consider co-opting members of the GFTU Management Committee on to its own economic committee and committees on workmen's compensation, social insurance and organisation. At an early stage the two sides agreed that not all unions would ever agree to join a special benefit section of the TUC; the benefit organisation must remain separate, therefore, and might as well be based on the General Federation. The TUC representatives suggested that if they undertook to recommend membership of the federation to their affiliated membership, the GFTU should 'act reciprocally'. But it was not clear how the GFTU could reciprocate. The TUC suggested that with GFTU representatives on some of its own committees there would be no need for the GFTU to send separate deputations to govenment departments, and so 'one agreed point of view from the trade union movement' would be ensured.

But at GFTU headquarters Appleton and Bell were deeply suspicious of the TUC's motives. Appleton wrote to the chairman of the Management Committee, Joseph Frayne of the Card, Blowing Room and Ring Spinners' Association, that:

> Each day adds to our doubts and difficulties and brings us informa-
> tion of attempts by the Fascist Trade Unions – that is, those Trade
> Unions who, by hook or by crook, force other unions within the
> ambit of their control and authority – to break up or force into so-
> called amalgamations, Unions that have been with the Federation
> for a very long time, and who have taken very little in the way of
> money out of the funds. These unions have, it is true, asked for and
> received help and information from all of us in the office. But it
> becomes increasingly difficult to give them information which can
> be of real value . . . if the independence of the General Federation
> of Trade Unions is to be lessened by association with the big, and
> sometimes hostile unions who dominate the policy of the TUC.

He cited unscrupulous methods used by the big unions which seemed to amount to bribing officials to bring about mergers.[77]

Frayne replied sympathetically to Appleton's fears. In his opinion 'the whole business is mere sham, and . . . the TUC are simply flouting us in the hope that we will break off negotiations and so throw the onus on the Federation'.[78] By early 1938 negotiations had virtually broken down and in December of that year *The Times* reported that the TUC was thinking of creating a wholly new central dispute fund 'of much wider scope' than the GFTU.[79] The great majority of unions affiliated to the TUC, however, favoured the existing haphazard arrangements whereby unions in trouble could be helped out by a special levy. In a letter to Bell in June 1939, therefore, Citrine formally brought the whole question to an end. Appleton, Bell and Frayne almost certainly were justified in believing that the TUC General Council did not sincerely want to bring about closer relations between the two bodies. And the rather nebulous proposals for GFTU representation on certain TUC committees probably would not have safeguarded the interests of unions affiliated to the General

Federation at all effectively. Certainly in the eyes of the GFTU they were not a suitable compensation for giving up their own independent voice. It seems likely, even so, that some members of the Management Committee may have wanted some form of reconciliation with the TUC. Perhaps they may have seen the TUC's proposals as a dignified solution to the GFTU's own problems, even at the risk of eventually giving up the federation's independent identity. Certainly some committee members did not see eye to eye with Appleton on the matter,[80] though it is not clear exactly what their views were.

There were, however, general differences in attitude between the leaders of the GFTU as a whole and those of the TUC. In 1937 a GFTU subcommittee produced a *Report on Trade Union Organisation* in which it reaffirmed the federation's own special outlook, no doubt partly as a contribution to the controversy that was then going on between the two organisations in private meetings. In this pamphlet the GFTU attacked amalgamations of unions on any other than trade, craft, industrial or occupational bases and praised the personal attention and specialist skills offered by the officials of craft and industrial unions; and it claimed (not without justice) that such unions were better placed than general unions to achieve and enforce a closed shop. It extolled the courage of the early pioneering trade unionists and their commitment to the ideals of brotherly solidarity. It offered practical suggestions for attracting new members to the unions, and proposed that federations of industrial unions ought to affiliate to the General Federation.

A strong moral tone marked this report even more noticeably than earlier ones. The authors attacked the 'slack mentalities' of non-unionists and the 'easily accepted platitudes' with which the big general unions persuaded their members to see themselves as victims of an unjust fate, with little responsibility for their own betterment. We may doubt whether the authors of the *Report on Trade Union Organisation* really believed, in 1937, that they could yet rebuild the General Federation into an important national institution. But the last two paragraphs of their report, full of hope and impracticality, stand as a sort of epitaph to the first forty years of the federation's existence:

EARLY PRINCIPLES JUSTIFIED

The trade union movement must not turn too far away from the personal principles required by the early craft, trade and occupational trade unions. These principles are the natural development of Nature's richest gift to Man – intelligence to plan and build, and even to make sacrifice when called upon to defend an established economic and social brotherhood. There is no real reason why the

Trade Union Movement should not be organised by agreement so that each trade union would be well disposed toward the other. The psychological effect of such a disposition would enable all to reap the reward in a few years' time.

WHY NOT?

Mutual recommendation by organised workers to unorganised workers to join their correct organisation would be of tremendous service, and would popularise trade unionism throughout the country. Further, with our Trade Union Approved Society work, it would be possible to evolve a scheme for trade union approved societies, collectively to develop membership, and with unity of purpose, to become a great force in national insurance finance, in the economic education of our people, in the work of the government of our country, and the economic development of our Empire.

Notes: Chapter 6

1   GFTU, *Annual Report*, 1920.
2   GFTU, *Proceedings and Reports*, 1921–2, report of 1921 agcm.
3   See article on Ward in Saville and Bellamy, *Dictionary of Labour Biography*, Vol. IV.
4   GFTU, *Proceedings and Reports*, 1919–20, report of meeting of 1920, later published also as a pamphlet.
5   See Roberts, *The TUC*, pp. 341–3; Margaret Morris, *The General Strike* (Harmondsworth: Penguin, 1976), pp. 178–9.
6   *The Times*, 16 May 1923, p. 16, ccl. *e*.
7   It is impossible to give a brief account of the background to the General Strike without oversimplifying. For fuller treatment within the general context, see Pelling, *History of British Trade Unionism*, and Lovell and Roberts, *Short History of the TUC*. Detailed studies include Patrick Renshaw, *The General Strike* (London: Eyre Methuen, 1975). G. A. Phillips, *The General Strike: The Politics of Industrial Conflict* (London: Weidenfeld & Nicolson, 1976), Margaret Morris's *The General Strike*, from which much of my own account in the following five paragraphs is drawn and Jeffrey Skelley (ed.), *The General Strike, 1926* (London: Lawrence & Wishart, 1976).
8   GFTU, *Quarterly Report*, June 1927, written after the alliance finally wound up its affairs.
9   Diary entry for 18 May 1926, quoted in Pelling, *History of British Trade Unionism*, p. 180.
10 In the GFTU, *Quarterly Report*, for December 1926, Appleton quoted the LSC's view that trade unions 'exceed their functions . . . in seeking to create conditions akin to passive or violent revolution'.
11 Letter to A. Conley, 26 August 1926, quoted in GFTU, *Quarterly Report*, September 1926.
12 National Union of Tailors and Garment Workers head office, Milton Keynes:

NUTGW verbatim report of the third general conference, August 1926 (typescript), vol. 2, pp. 538 ff. The account given here is based on this document.

13 Letter to A. Conley quoted in GFTU, *Quarterly Report*, September 1926.
14 GFTU, *Annual Report*, 1927.
15 See, for example, report of the debate at the 1934 agcm.
16 GFTU, *Quarterly Report*, December 1926, article on the centenary of the Macclesfield silk-weavers' union. At the 1931 agcm the National Silk Workers' Association publicly thanked Bell for his work in the Macclesfield area, and said that they did not know what they would have done without it.
17 The opening is described in GFTU, *Quarterly Report*, December 1930. The proceedings included a speech by the architect J. M. Shepherd, who gave detailed specifications of the building. See also reports of the 1929 and 1930 agcms.
18 Report by Appleton to the Management Committee, 16 September 1920, printed in GFTU, *Annual Report*, 1921.
19 TUC, *Report*, 1920, pp. 241–7.
20 Appleton's report of 16 September 1920, printed in GFTU, *Annual Report*, 1921.
21 Management Committee report of 17 September 1920, GFTU, *Annual Report*, 1921.
22 Management Committee report of 7 October 1920, ibid.
23 GFTU, *Annual Report*, 1921.
24 Printed in GFTU, *Annual Report*, 1923.
25 *Hansard*, 5th series, vol. 151 (1 March 1922) cols 387 ff.; *The Times*, 2 March 1922, p. 6, col. *c.*
26 *Hansard*, loc. cit., col. 189.
27 PRO, LAB 2/903/IR 1633/1922, Ministry of Labour files: minutes of a meeting between GFTU Management Committee, Sir Montague Barlow and ministry officials, 21 December 1922, remarks by Appleton.
28 PRO, PIN 7/61, Ministry of Labour, employment branch, unemployment by industry, weekly summary of replies to the minister's circular letter of 22/2/22.
29 PRO, LAB 2/903/IR 1633/1922, meeting of 21 December 1922.
30 As reported in the *Yorkshire Post*, 22 December 1922 (cutting in PIN 7/61).
31 PRO, LAB 2/903/IR 1633/1922, meeting of 21 December 1922.
32 ibid.
33 PRO, PIN 7/61.
34 PRO, LAB 2/903/IR 1633/1922.
35 The history of unemployment during the depression is treated in some detail in Fraser, *Evolution of the British Welfare State.*
36 J. M. Keynes, *The General Theory of Employment, Interest and Money* (London: Macmillan, 1936).
37 Harris, *Unemployment and Politics*, chs II–IV, considers some of these schemes.
38 See above, p. 84.
39 See, for example, GFTU, *Proceedings and Reports*, 1931–2, report of 1931 agcm.
40 PRO, PIN 7/234.
41 PRO, PIN 7/234.
42 W. A. Appleton, *The TUC and the GFTU*, pamphlet dated July 1936 (London: GFTU).
43 GFTU, *Proceedings and Reports*, 1930–1 and afterwards, contain this advertisement.
44 GFTU Management Committee report on *Rheumatism*, issued as a pamphlet, January 1927.
45 GFTU, *Proceedings and Reports*, 1930–1, report of 1930 agcm.
46 GFTU, *Proceedings and Reports, Quarterly Report*, December 1924 (obituary); *Annual Report*, 1931.
47 GFTU Management Committee, report on *Rheumatism*, 1927.

48   ibid.
49   GFTU, *Proceedings and Reports*,1928–9, report of deputations to government departments (also published separately as a pamphlet).
50   As described in Burchill and Ross, *A History of the Potters' Union.*
51   ibid., p. 150.
52   GFTU, *Proceedings and Reports*, 1931–2, report of 1931 agcm.
53   ibid.
54   The issue was discussed at the agcms of both 1936 and 1938.
55   GFTU, *Proceedings and Reports*, 1938–9, report of 1938 agcm.
56   GFTU, *Report on the Bedaux and Kindred Systems* (March 1932), made by a sub-committee and issued as a separate pamphlet.
57   The account that follows is based on an interview with Mr Moulden in Edinburgh in May 1977.
58   GFTU, MS dispute benefit ledger, esp. for 1933–4.
59   GFTU, *Proceedings and Reports*, 1930–1, report of 1930 agcm.
60   According to Mitchell and Deane, *Second Abstract of British Historical Statistics*, p. 67, there was only one year (1937) when the percentage of insured people unemployed fell below 13·3 per cent before 1939. In the worst year of the decade, 1932, 22·5 per cent were unemployed. A survey of 'Industrial relations history and policy' prepared in the Ministry of Labour during the Second World War (PRO, LAB 10/434) gave 13 per cent as the sticking point for unemployment to the end of 1938 and estimated that full-time weekly wages rose by about 12 per cent between 1932 and 1939, while the cost of living rose by about 10 per cent.
61   Mitchell and Deane, *Second Abstract of British Historical Statistics*, pp. 60–1, 68.
62   H. A. Turner, *Trade Union Growth, Structure and Policy. A Comparative Study of the Cotton Unions* (London: Allen & Unwin, 1962), pp. 327–31.
63   See above, Chapter 2.
64   PRO, LAB 10/22, report to the Minister of Labour by the Board appointed under section 1(1) of the Cotton Manufacturing (Temporary Provisions) Act 1934.
65   ibid.
66   Turner, *Trade Union Growth, Structure and Policy*, pp. 327–31.
67   GFTU Management Committee, *Better Machinery. An Examination of the Resolution Moved at the Trades Union Congress, September 1934*, pamphlet (1935).
68   PRO, LAB 10/22, report to the Minister of Labour . . . , p. 18.
69   GFTU Management Committee, *Better Machinery. . . .*
70   GFTU, report of deputations to ministers in connection with resolutions passed at the Yarmouth annual general meeting, July 1928, published in *Proceedings and Reports*, 1928–9, and reprinted as a pamphlet (1929).
71   *The Times* obituary (21 November 1940, p. 7, col. *c*) singled out Appleton's belief in co-partnership as a leading feature of his philosophy.
72   GFTU *Report on the Causes of the Failure to Increase Trade Union Membership*, p. 6.
73   TUC, *Report*, 1934, pp. 220–4.
74   GFTU Management Committee, *Better Machinery. . . .*
75   TUC, *Report*, 1935, pp. 240–1.
76   The following account is based on an unlabelled file in the GFTU archives, containing the correspondence relating to the negotiations, copies of documents drawn up by Appleton in defence of the GFTU and transcripts of the meetings between TUC and GFTU officials.
77   GFTU unlabelled file, Appleton to Frayne, 8 June 1937 (carbon copy).
78   ibid., Frayne to Appleton, 9 June 1937.
79   *The Times*, 16 December 1938, cutting circulated on that date to members of the Management Committee.

80 GFTU unlabelled file, Frayne to Appleton, 9 June 1937: 'I am afraid that one or two of the Management Committee have not been very helpful in this matter, and . . . have been very discourteous to you.'

7
From the 1940s to the 1970s

In the Doldrums, 1939–49

At the end of 1938 William Appleton, approaching his 80th year, finally resigned as general secretary of the GFTU on grounds of ill-health. He retired to his home in a picturesque Hertfordshire village and there he died two years later, earning a short obituary in *The Times* which stated succinctly that 'his conception of the functions of the trade unions and his criticism of their political activities were not those which won acceptance'.[1] The obvious and unopposed choice as his successor was George Bell. Bell was widely respected among craft workers and their union officials, and felt a special sympathy for them. Before joining the GFTU in 1922 he had been first organiser and then assistant general secretary of the Friendly Society of Iron-founders (from 1920 the National Union of Foundry Workers), jobs which he must have earned partly through his spirited interventions at the society's conferences. (In 1911 he moved the resolution to appoint organisers, which was to result in his own first full-time job as a trade union official.)[2] As a young man he was active in local politics and first stood for Nottingham City Council in 1907 as the candidate of the Labour Party. His candidature on that occasion was endorsed by the Nottingham Trades Council on the motion of William Appleton. So when Bell became organiser for the GFTU fifteen years later, he was already well known to the general secretary.[3] A fluent, persuasive speaker and a man of obviously upright character, his working life as organiser for the General Federation was spent mainly in visiting unions around the country and helping them to recruit members; and he formed close friendships with some of their officials.[4] He showed much the same conservatism in his approach to national trade union policy as Appleton did during the years between the two world wars. Now in his early 60s, he moved to the head of an organisation that clearly felt itself cut off from and rather at odds with the main stream of industrial relations.

The General Federation of Trade Unions on the eve of the Second World War was a very different organisation from the General Federation on the eve of the First. It was by no means wholly demoralised or moribund. What had happened was that by degrees it had acquired a distinctive place as the representative of smaller-scale trade unionism in Britain. Despite an occasional grandiose call to action on the part of all unions, like that issued in 1937, the General Federation had little wish to take a front seat again in the national counsels of trade unionism. This was particularly true under the leadership of Bell who had joined the GFTU when this change was already taking place and who did not have personal reasons, as Appleton did, for feeling embittered by the past. Nevertheless, the federation's position on the eve of the Second World War was not easy. There was good reason for its Management Committee to feel that its particular brand of trade unionism was seriously threatened.

The agreement against poaching of members by rival unions, which the TUC reached at its Bridlington Congress in 1939, turned out to provide a surer safeguard for large unions against each other than it did for small unions against the large ones. Not only did trade unionists in general tend to consider the smaller unions a nuisance and an irrelevance, but this was the accepted view in industrial relations as a whole. A supplement to the Ministry of Labour's internally circulated handbook on industrial relations, prepared in 1944, stated that 'The strength and feeling of craft unions still constitute a severe obstacle to the advance in this country towards a more scientific and symmetical form of trade union organisation'.[5] The ministry's policy, following that outlined in a TUC report of 1927 which it quoted several times, was to encourage industrial unionism wherever possible. It defined craft unions as 'associations of workers employed on a single process, or on processes so nearly related that there can be interchange between them'. Industrial unions consisted of workers employed in the same industry 'irrespective of process, skill or any other principle', a framework within which it was possible for the workers to develop greater local autonomy at factory level. The officials of the Ministry of Labour found this form of 'workshop control' also highly desirable in the light of their wartime experience of local joint production committees, and again it was a development which in their view the craft unions obstructed.* Against this background, the grievances of craft unions got short shrift. The ministry almost always decided in favour of a larger union, for example, when

* In this they were only partly correct. Craft unions during the Second World War often did try to prevent 'dilution' of labour by the introduction of semi-skilled (often female) workers to skilled jobs. They also had to be treated as separate, often intractable, entities in any attempt to establish co-operation on essential production during the war. But on the other hand the 'craft ideal' often came closer to that informed and independent-minded bargaining on particular jobs which seemed to be what the Ministry of Labour valued especially in industrial unionism.

one or more small unions in a particular industry appealed against a big general union's being represented on the Joint Industrial Council dealing with skilled labour.[6]

One example from the reports of the GFTU illustrates the problems faced by small unions of skilled workers.[7] The National Gas Fitters' and Allied Workers' Union, founded in 1889, found itself being squeezed out of negotiations in the gas industry. By the beginning of the Second World War the problem had become acute; the employers informed the union that all wages questions in future would be decided by the Joint Industrial Council for the Gas Industry, which they advised the union to join. The gas fitters, on applying to the JIC, were advised to amalgamate with the larger union concerned but a ballot of their members turned down the proposal. The trade union side of the JIC then refused to admit the gas fitters; and despite the intercession of the GFTU Management Committee and at their request that of the Ministry of Labour, the other unions in the gas industry remained adamant. The gas fitters' union had been effectively destroyed, since its members were now forced to accept settlements negotiated by a body on which their union was not represented. But although the union itself dissolved, many of its members transferred to another skilled union which also was not part of the JIC group. The hostility of the larger unions to one long-established craft union, therefore, had not helped to rationalise industrial relations in the gas industry, but rather embittered and perpetuated an unsatisfactory state of affairs. It is precisely this sort of outcome that the GFTU in the present day tries to avoid when advising small affiliated unions on problems in their relations with other unions.

The problems of small unions versus the giants of the trade union world grew worse, if anything, during the Second World War and the GFTU had to record the disappearance of several of its smaller affiliated unions during the 1940s. In 1943 the TUC instructed its General Council to investigate the possibilities for amalgamations and other structural changes that would eliminate overlapping and competition between unions and 'ensure maximum trade union efficiency in the future'. This resolution was passed against a background of continuing pressure on the small unions to affiliate with larger ones. While the TUC General Council's investigation was still in progress, the GFTU reminded its members that small unions enjoyed exactly the same legal status as large ones, and advised them to look carefully (and by implication, suspiciously) at any terms that they might be offered with a view to amalgamation. The report presented by Citrine and his colleagues to the Congress of 1944, however, stopped short of recommending that the TUC should take any special powers; for the General Council members were only too well aware of the dangers of seeming to threaten the autonomy of the large unions. What they did recommend was that amalgamations should take place where possible; and that as a more feasible alternative, federations of unions should be strengthened. Within the organisation of the TUC itself, its system of advisory committees on particular industries was to be extended, and steps were taken to strengthen its research and educational services.[8]

From the TUC point of view, two of the most hopeful developments of the war period were the entry of the foundry workers and the Amalgamated Engineering Union into the Confederation of Ship-building and Engineering Workers in 1944 and 1946 respectively, and the formation of the National Union of Mineworkers in 1944. At its own end of the trade union scale, despite its dislike of amalgama-tions that involved small unions losing their identity completely, the GFTU welcomed mergers between its own members or unions of similar size. The war acted as a catalyst to two particularly welcome such amalgamations within the federation: the formation of the National Union of Hosiery and Knitwear Workers at the end of 1944 from the Hinckley, Ilkeston, Leicester, Loughborough and Notting-ham hosiery unions; and the amalgamation of three furniture unions in 1947 to form the equally successful National Union of Furniture Trade Operatives.[9] The hosiery workers having overcome their long-standing problems of separatism, succeeded in nearly doubling their membership in the first six years after amalgamation.[10] And NUFTO (which after some further mergers is now the Furniture, Timber and Allied Trade Union, FTAT) increased membership by 20 per cent in its first year. Whatever the General Federation's view of large and, in particular, general unions, it viewed the growth of skilled industrial unions within its own ranks with warm approval. For, as George Bell wrote in 1946 in a long statement in favour of the closed shop, 'to work in a mixed or open shop is to be in a state of insecurity'.[11] Industrial unionism facilitated the achievement of closed shops.

The internal development and growth of trade unionism during the Second World War took place in the context of growing co-operation and consultation between government and the TUC. In May 1940 Churchill appointed Ernest Bevin Minister of Labour and National Service in his new coalition government, and by the end of the year Bevin was a member of the small inner circle of the War Cabinet. Bevin's appointment and his conduct of the Ministry of Labour marked a great step forward in the relations between govern-ment and organised labour. As one historian has remarked, the years 1939 to 1951 became an era of 'power with responsibility' for the TUC.[12] As a former outstanding leader both of his own union, the TGWU, and on the General Council of the TUC, Bevin was in a position to persuade the unions to accept policies that might otherwise have seemed intolerable. He also had an instinct for just how much the unions would accept and, except in his dealings with the miners, seldom put a foot wrong. His own understanding of and trust in the union way of doing things led him to strengthen the channels of consultation as a means of carrying out policy, and this in turn greatly strengthened the unions' position *vis-à-vis* the employers. One of his first actions as minister was to secure the appointment of a joint consultative committee of seven employers and seven trade union leaders, which was small enough to act decisively when necessary. Soon afterwards this committee agreed to the establishment of a National Arbitration Tribunal as a compulsory last resort in negotiation, and an Order in Council (Order 1305) made the tribunal's decisions binding and outlawed strikes and lockouts. Other extreme measures which would never have been accepted in peace time included the progressive introduction of regulations on the movement of workers into and out of essential jobs. But Bevin stopped short of introducing outright national control of wages, and none of the measures he took interfered with the basic structure of collective bargaining. Under the Restoration of Pre-War Practices Act 1942, unions were guaranteed a return to prewar practices after the war if they so wished; and on the huge number of local and national committees on production, rationing, and so on, trade unionists and employers played an equal part.

In all of these changes the General Federation of Trade Unions played only a small part compared with its important role during the First World War. Most of its affiliated unions and their officials were deeply involved in local production committees and the various other organisations of the industrial war effort. Some, like the National Union of Hosiery and Knitwear Workers and especially its leader Horace Moulden, played a decisive part in wartime production in their industry and greatly strengthened the standing of their own unions as a result. But the GFTU itself had relatively little to offer to the national counsels of labour in wartime. Some problems were familiar from the experience of the First World War, and the Management Committee was quick to offer warnings and advice on these. The question of government contracts, for example, was raised at the annual general council meeting in 1939, where it was resolved that the fair wages clause inserted into government contracts should be brought up to date and that trade union conditions, including holidays with pay, ought to be a necessary condition before the government awarded a contract for the manufacture of wartime necessities to any firm. Other subjects on which the federation's advice was sought during the war included unhealthy workshops,

Sunday working, the legality of certain wage stoppages and various negotiations with employers. In 1941 the Management Committee successfully pressed the Ministry of Food for an increase in food rations for the chainmakers, because of their especially heavy work.[13]

Financially the General Federation was in a strong position to help the war effort. By September 1941 its accumulated funds had reached the highest point in its history to that date; and the Management Committee decided to reduce the proportion of a union's membership on which it paid dues from 90 per cent to $66\frac{2}{3}$ per cent, in addition to suspending contributions from members who were on active service. As the general secretary remarked with pardonable complacency, it was unprecedented for any kind of insurance body to 'suspend the contributions of members called up for active service in a war of the magnitude of the present one, and at the same time to preserve the right of those members to benefit on their return to their former peace-time occupations'.[14] Other examples of the federation's generosity included the gift of a fully equipped ambulance (cost, £550) to the Red Cross, an interest-free loan of £10,000 to the government for the duration of the war and the investment of £10,000 in $2\frac{1}{2}$ per cent war bonds. During the war it reported further grants to war charities.

Central House itself was also a substantial asset. Soon after the outbreak of war the government requisitioned the vacant parts of the building and for the first time it became fully tenanted. Although the GFTU headquarters staff remained in the building, which had its own large air-raid shelter, the federation's friendly and collecting society evacuated to Bletchley in Buckinghamshire. After the fall of Norway in 1941 the leader of the Association of Norwegian Trade Unions, Konrad Nordahl, took shelter in Britain and was given an office on the same floor of Central House as the GFTU's own headquarters. From there he endeavoured to serve an estimated 25,000 Norwegian trade unionists who had escaped from Nazi-occupied Europe.[15]

One concern that the General Federation took up with special interest during the war was the reform of company law. It had always been a handicap to trade union negotiators that whereas they were compelled to disclose their union's numerical membership and financial circumstances in annual returns to the Register General of Friendly Societies, the employers with whom they dealt were under no similar compulsion. Under the Companies Act 1929 public companies had obligations to their shareholders to disclose information, and this made it easier for the unions to assess what any given public company could afford to pay its workforce. Private companies, however, were not compelled to make any disclosure of their accounts. In certain industries where small private companies predominated, like cotton weaving, furniture manufacture or specialised engineering, the scarcity of information available to the unions often made any systematic or amicable conduct of industral relations almost impossible. The problem was made worse by the fact that large public companies often operated a large part of their undertakings through small private subsidiaries.[16]

The GFTU had a long history of interest in financial practice and company law. During the late 1920s and early 1930s it had paid close attention, for example, to the problems caused by over-capitalisation in the stricken cotton industry.[17] It was common practice among officials of many of its affiliated unions to take pains to acquire the commercial expertise relevant to the industries with which they dealt. Resolutions calling for reform of the Companies Act became almost an annual event at the annual general council meetings of the federation. And the general secretary took great pride in the service the GFTU performed on numerous occasions for its affiliates by obtaining details about a company in cases of dispute.[18] When the Board of Trade set up a committee on the amendment of company law under Mr Justice Cohen in 1944, the General Federation was quick to give evidence before it.

In two printed memoranda, as well as in oral evidence before the committee, the GFTU outlined the history of changes in negotiating procedure since before 1914. The decline of district-based negotiating after the end of the First World War and the growing separation of managerial functions from wage negotiation had increased the alienation of working people from management. It did not help to improve this state of affairs that trade union officials were so often in the dark about the true financial circumstances of the companies for which their members worked. The GFTU gave several examples, from the cotton industry, from metalworking and elsewhere. One engineering firm had tried to impose a 15 per cent wage cut on the grounds that it was close to insolvency, but the GFTU discovered that this company was in fact closely associated with another, much wealthier, firm in which the directors and shareholders of the first company were credited with shares to the value of nearly £150,000. When challenged with these figures the employers dropped their demand for any wage cut at all and the employees, who had been on strike, went back to work. The managing director had the face later to write to the GFTU reporting that industrial relations in the firm were now on a most satisfactory footing and commenting that 'the men are now behaving excellently'.[19] As the GFTU delegation told the Board of Trade committee, 'The Federation is conscious of the psychology of the working people, especially of those engaged in production and manufacture, who desire to know more of the economic facts which govern their lives'.[20]

The TUC also sent a delegation to the Cohen Committee, and much of its evidence coincided with the views and experience of the GFTU. Perhaps somewhat to the irritation of Sir Walter Citrine and his colleagues, the General Federation's evidence was quoted to them for comment and at one point Citrine felt it necessary to point out that the TUC was not only far more representative but that it had itself established the General Federation, 'with every respect', for a limited purpose. The TUC's recommendations on company law differed from those of the GFTU mainly in seeking greater publicity for the finances of all companies than the GFTU had dared to suggest. Where the General Federation merely pleaded that in the case of a dispute companies should be obliged to reveal certain financial details to the accredited union representatives of its employees, the TUC wanted a statutory obligation on all companies to register financial information. Failing a completely open registration of company accounts, Citrine told the committee that it might be satisfactory for companies to be obliged to give such information to the TUC, which was sufficiently representative to reconcile the interests of all the unions involved in any given dispute. Clearly such a solution would not have satisfied the GFTU, and it is doubtful whether many of the larger unions affiliated to the TUC would have favoured it either. In the event, not even the relatively modest suggestions of the GFTU were adopted. The *Report of the Committee on Company Law Amendment*[21] acknowledged the abuses of company law by private subsidiaries of public firms but still recommended that very small private companies (in practice, usually small-scale family firms) should not be required to disclose information that might be useful to their competitors. The thorny problem of the employees' right to know was shelved, in effect, for another twenty years.

The pressure to reform company law came to a head during the Second World War partly as a result of wartime conditions which made closer government scrutiny and control seem more acceptable to both sides of industry and at the same time strengthened the respect in which trade unions in general were held. Although in the case of company law only a few of the unions' demands were met, there were other more important developments arising out of the war that they could welcome wholeheartedly. Most notable of all was the publication in December 1942 of the Beveridge plan for national insurance. Implemented in stages by the Labour government after 1945, Sir William Beveridge's plan proposed comprehensive insurance for everyone in the country for the first time, against the hazards of ill-health, unemployment or abject poverty. His report was greeted with widespread public approval and there was an outcry when it seemed likely that the coalition government was going to shelve it.[22] In common with almost all trade unionists, the GFTU welcomed the Beveridge plan unequivocally, and warned against the dangers of permitting any system of opting out of the proposed national insurance schemes. The proposals for health insurance were especially welcome, for as the GFTU knew well, 'No system of insurance has revealed the ill-effects of part-time and unhealthy occupations, low wages and bad housing so poignantly as the Approved Society system of National Health Insurance'.[23]

The coming of a comprehensive welfare state along the lines of Beveridge's blueprint, however, spelled the end of the residual health and unemployment insurance schemes that the General Federation of Trades Unions still administered. Its role in insurance was now confined to insuring unions against the cost of strikes. And even in this sphere postwar Britain under Attlee's Labour government seemed likely, in the early flush of enthusiasm for the new regime, to inaugurate a period of more peaceful industrial relations. In the great programme of nationalisation and social reform that was implemented between 1945 and 1950, the leaders of the TUC and the large unions had greater opportunities for a constructive and advisory role in national affairs than had ever been offered before. Six union-sponsored MPs became members of Attlee's new Cabinet, including Ernest Bevin as Foreign Secretary. The government repealed the hated Trade Disputes Act 1927. Trade union leaders were consulted about the constitution and membership of the new boards of the nationalised industries and a number of them now took jobs on these boards, beginning with Ebby Edwards, general secretary of the National Union of Mineworkers, and Sir Walter (newly created Lord) Citrine on the National Coal Board. The TUC General Council managed, though with increasing difficulty, to obtain the co-operation of trade unionists as a whole in the government's policy of austerity and wage restraint.

But the brave new world that beckoned these national leaders left the General Federation of Trade Unions without a purpose. Most of the forms of insurance with which it dealt were no longer needed; and, as we have seen, most of its member unions tended to be regarded by both TUC and government as obstacles to the rational development of industrial relations which would sooner or later become part of larger units. It was not easy for the General Federation to function as their spokesman or defender if it did not provide necessary services to back up this position and if it did not carry weight in national trade unionism. To several members of the Management Committee it seemed that the time had come to wind up the federation's affairs.

It was leaders of two of the federation's largest and most flourishing unions, Clifford Groocock and Horace Moulden of the hosiery and knitwear workers and Alfred Tomkins of the furniture workers, who led the attempt to close down the GFTU. One of Tomkins's colleagues later recalled that his union's real reason for remaining in the GFTU was its hope of being entitled to a share of the federation's capital when it ceased to exist. Present officials of his union, however, would strongly disclaim such a view of the federation's usefulness either now or in the past. Moulden's chief reason for abandoning the campaign to close the federation down was that after taking legal advice the Management Committee discovered that the founding unions which had long since seceded might well be entitled to a share of the federation's assets. In his view the risk of so enriching the unions that had now become the AEU, TGWU and GMWU and others was quite unacceptable. It was partly this consideration that kept the GFTU alive when it was at its lowest ebb.

During the debates on the federation's future that took place at the annual general council meetings in 1947, 1948 and 1949, however, there was plenty of support for the services and other benefits that affiliated unions got from the GFTU. For officials of some of the smaller unions, even then, the GFTU would have been quite irreplaceable. It was the one meeting place where they felt they could be heard with the interest and respect to which their many years' experience entitled them. It was the only institution that they could trust to offer them appropriate advice without also pressuring them to join forces with some larger union. And small though the General Federation was in comparison with the TUC, unions that belonged to it could claim in their negotiations with employers that they had the support of a national organisation behind them. Before the outbreak of the Second World War approximately two-thirds of GFTU unions were not members of the TUC,[24] a proportion that has dwindled progressively since then. When at the annual general council meeting in 1948 delegates were asked to vote on a motion to test the opinions of their membership on dissolving the federation, the resolution was lost by the votes of 7 unions to 21, but in terms of aggregate membership the margin was much narrower: 143,795 to 125,575. It was quite clearly the smaller unions, therefore, that kept the General Federation in being. For several of them it was their only link with national trade unionism.

It was for such intangible benefits as these, far less important to the larger affiliated unions, that many members of the GFTU really valued it. Dispute benefits were low by comparison with what most of the unions themselves paid to each of their members. (As one delegate to the annual meeting of 1949 remarked, his union received only 3s 6d per member per week on the lower scale, whereas it paid out £3.) If the benefits were so nebulous, however, and yet the federation was not going to be wound up, some way had to be found of adding to its services and generally invigorating it. One interesting suggestion was made at the annual meeting of 1946 by T. M. Ferguson of the Dundee Jute and Flax Union, that the federation might yet build on the possibilities of national insurance. Since the new National Insurance Act required that in order to qualify for full benefits an individual must have made at least fifty weeks' contributions in the year, Ferguson suggested that GFTU benefit payments might be used by the unions receiving them to cover their members' insurance contributions while on strike. He saw this as a possible inducement to all unions in the country to join the federation; but he was tactfully dissuaded by Tomkins who pointed out that the trade union movement would prefer to obtain a change in the law, which harked back to the hated Blanesburgh Committee recommendations of 1927. Echoes of this debate may be found in the Thatcher government's intention in 1980 to withhold benefits from workers who are on strike, on the assumption that their unions would be paying them benefits.

In 1948, after the second of the general council debates at which the end of the GFTU was seriously contemplated,[25] a subcommittee set to work to make recommendations for its future. The most positive outcome, after much debate at the annual general council meeting in 1949, was an amendment in the rules which favoured the smaller unions by giving them a larger proportion of delegates to the general council than they had had before. The maximum number of delegates permitted was changed from six to eight and the numerical membership above which a union became entitled to this number was lowered from 50,000 to 35,000. In addition affiliation fees, which had been restored to 4*d* on the higher scale and 2*d* on the lower and made payable on 100 per cent of membership in 1946, were reduced, and the federation began to look at ways of increasing payments of dispute benefit while tightening up the rules for payment so that its funds would not be unduly depleted.

It was a matter of concern to the delegates that any possible new members of the federation should not be able to benefit from its accumulated wealth immediately or disproportionately, and perhaps act like cuckoos in the nest. This fear had been expressed when in 1947 the federation introduced a system of bonus payments to distribute some of the much increased revenue from Central House, hoping that 'the interest in insurance [and therefore by implication, in the GFTU's continued existence] can be kept alive if something is seen on the receipts side from the Federation'. It was decided then that no union should be entitled to share in the bonus until it had been affiliated for five years. And the rules as amended in 1949, which placed well-defined restrictions on the maximum amount of dispute benefit that any union or individual member could draw in one year, reflected the same fear. A further safeguard to the interests of the existing members of the GFTU was embodied in what had been rule 18, now numbered 23, which laid down a procedure for dissolving the federation. Although Alfred Tomkins, proposing the new rules on behalf of the Management Committee, no longer envisaged that the General Federation would be wound up there and then, he explained that the best legal advice available had been taken to make it possible for the federation to be dissolved in due legal form in, say, ten years' time or whenever the question might come up again.[26] The new rule provided for a postal ballot on dissolution in which not less than 50 per cent of the aggregate membership of the federation must vote and not less than 75 per cent of those votes must be in favour before the federation could be wound up. Despite some vocal objections to postal balloting, notably from Andrew Naesmith of the Amalgamated Weavers' Association, who ridiculed the idea of distributing ballot papers among all 72,000 of his members, the rule was approved. It built in another safeguard to the interests of the smaller unions and made the likelihood of the federation's winding itself up very remote. By the end of the 1940s, therefore, the General Federation of Trade Unions was still very much in business. It recognised itself more clearly now, both in spirit and by rule, as the organisation of small and medium-sized craft unions. And in some of its financial arrangements as well as in some of the attitudes expressed at meetings and in its reports, there was a distinct impression that these unions were closing ranks.

The General Secretaryship of Leslie Hodgson

The most important step forward for the General Federation of Trade Unions after the decisions of 1949 was a change in personnel. As always in its history, personalities played an important part and a great deal depended on the character and energies of the general secretary. When the question of the federation's future was discussed in the late 1940s, George Bell was in his 70s. There is some reason to suppose that he was already tired and demoralised when he took over the general secretaryship from William Appleton at the end of 1938. He had certainly had to wait long enough for the job; and the Second World War, through which he guided the federation with only a small staff and infrequent meetings of the Management Committee, did not present the opportunities to the GFTU that it did to the TUC. On the other hand, having come late in life to the job of general secretary and having succeeded a man who was not far short of 80, Bell probably did not see why he should give up the job in his early 70s.

In 1947 the General Federation changed the provisions for its staff on retirement, so that for the first time pensions would be paid and a specific retirement age enforced; women were to retire at 60, men at 65 and the general secretary not later than 70, which was Bell's age in 1947. After thirty years' service with the federation, staff became entitled to a pension of 30 per cent of their annual salary at the time of leaving, and the general secretary was to receive one-third of his annual salary as pension, regardless of how long he had served. These arrangements were not particularly generous by the standards then becoming common in industry. By trade union standards they were reasonable, however, as it was by no means universal practice then, or even twenty years later, for retiring union officials to receive pensions, and the smaller unions in particular had as a result a high proportion of elderly general secretaries. No doubt the GFTU Management Committee devised their pension scheme with the departure of George Bell in mind, although there were other long-serving employees to consider too. But 1947 was not a good time for appointing a new general secretary with the future of the federation still very much in doubt, and twice after that Bell was asked to defer his retirement by a year. By the summer of 1949, having weathered three annual meetings where delegates considered winding up the federation altogether, and having introduced its golden jubilee on a note of some relief and pride, he was understandably not in a hurry to leave immediately. Apart from personal and professional pride, he probably had heavier financial responsibilities than many men of his age. He and his wife had taken on the upbringing of a granddaughter, whose mother, the wife of one of their sons, had died very young.[27] For these various reasons, when the General Federation of Trade Unions entered the 1950s and its own second half-century, it had been run for nearly thirty years by general secretaries over the age of 60.

Bell's continuance as general secretary was not altogether a brake on the federation's progress, however members of the Management Committee may have seen it. He continued to visit unions that needed background help and information in negotiations with employers, and earned the warmly expressed gratitude of more than one general secretary during his last years in office.[28] There was work to be done on the defects of the National Insurance Act 1946, and here the GFTU and TUC co-operated in a series of meetings, deputations to and correspondence with the Ministry of Pensions and National Insurance. Clearly Bell had succeeded in mending fences with the TUC since the acrimonious days when Appleton had so bitterly resented the attitude of the larger body. Another sign of progress was the introduction of *Federation News* at the beginning of 1951. This quarterly publication, edited by Bell under the close scrutiny of the Management Committee, replaced the old quarterly reports which the GFTU had been publishing ever since it was founded. The idea behind the new journal, which still flourishes, was to spread news of the federation's work more widely both in trade union circles and on the shop floor. Distributed free of charge through union headquarters, more or less to anyone who asked for it, and in much larger numbers than the quarterly reports, it also included far more information of general interest to trade unionists, as well as useful statistical facts and figures. Under Bell's successor it became increasingly lively, well written and attractively produced, but the foundations were already there when Bell handed over.

In 1951 the Management Committee took definite steps to find a new general secretary. They invited written applications and held an oral examination and in April they decided to appoint Harry Earnshaw, JP, of Blackburn, the secretary of the Amalgamated Association of Beamers, Twisters and Drawers, to take over in twelve months' time. A month later, however, Earnshaw withdrew because of the difficulty of finding a house that he could afford in north-west London; and rather than select one of the other candidates, who seemed not to have impressed them very much, the Management Committee started again from scratch. This time they faced the fact, as their successors would do again twenty-six years later, that the terms they were offering were not attractive enough. A subcommittee therefore raised the salary on offer to £1,000 a year with £150 a year expenses allowance, and recommended that the Management Committee should consider appointing instead an assistant general secretary at £750 a year, who would be expected to take over from George Bell in two years' time.[29] This course was adopted in the end, and the man they chose was Leslie Hodgson, a 38-year-old Yorkshireman and secretary of one of the federation's smallest affiliated unions, the Card Setting Machine Tenters' Society. At the annual general council meeting in Morecambe in May 1952 he was duly elected and on 11 June he attended a subcommittee meeting at Central House for the first time as assistant general secretary of the GFTU, having taken a drop in salary in order to take up the job.

The son of a coachman-chauffeur, Hodgson had grown up in a mining district and learned both his working-class politics and his cricket from the miners who used to field a cricket team every year against the squire's team into which young Leslie Hodgson was sometimes co-opted.[30] His youth had fitted him in several ways for the conservative and craft-based traditions of the GFTU. He served his apprenticeship in one of the most specialised crafts of the highly specialised Yorkshire woollen textile industry and joined his union as a full member at the age of 20. Experience of the widespread unemployment in Yorkshire in the 1930s had taught him the importance of having a skill and had shown the benefits that a craft union could offer. He found that even on short-time working, as little sometimes as two or three days a fortnight, as a craftsman he could earn more than a week's unskilled labour would have given him. This was thanks, of course, to the rates of pay which the union had established and then fought to maintain. He also learned to value technical education, the first subject which he would write about in *Federation News* when he joined the GFTU; and among other qualifications he possessed the associate's diploma of the Textile Institute, which entitled him to teach on textiles at graduate rates of pay.

Hodgson brought great qualities to his new job, and his twenty-five years with the General Federation were to transform it. But when he first arrived he very nearly turned around and went straight home to Yorkshire. The Management Committee had assured him when he accepted the job that provided he gave satisfactory service he would become general secretary within two years; and privately he understood that George Bell, who was in failing health, would leave much sooner than that. The picture at Central House, however, was quite different. Bell resented Hodgson's presence, appeared to have no thought of leaving and gave him little to do. When the new assistant general secretary looked at the minutes and saw that the federation had actually considered winding itself up only a few years before, he almost despaired. But then the very bleakness of the outlook began to seem a challenge to him and he decided to stay.

One of the resolutions passed at the annual general council meeting in 1952 called for the GFTU to extend its services and during the debate a research service was mentioned several times. The main objection to this was that it was something the federation already provided informally. As Hodgson was to find, it would be twenty years before the federation accepted a formally constituted research service. A great difficulty for any official of the GFTU was precisely that independent spirit on the part of the small unions which made them value the federation as their own distinctive organisation, but which also made them most distrustful of any central body. The debates of the late 1940s over changes in the federation's rules showed that delegates were suspicious even of permissive clauses giving the Management Committee the power to help settle disputes when invited to do so by the unions involved. Similarly in 1952 some speakers objected that the Management Committee already had the powers to carry out research and other activities, and seemed to feel that it needed no further invitation to do so.

Whereas in its early history the General Federation had been mistrusted by the larger and stronger unions because potentially it had more authority than the TUC, in the 1950s there was a feeling that the federation now constituted a refuge from the overbearing policies of the TUC and the large unions that dominated it. This was as good a reason for limiting the activities of the GFTU as for keeping it in being. It was part of the same paradox that officials of the larger affiliated unions tended to regard any new activities taken on by the federation as merely justifications for its existence, ways of keeping the general secretary busy; while the smaller affiliates welcomed the federation's services but were quick to suspect it of unwarranted interference. This state of affairs was calculated to develop in Leslie Hodgson all his skills of patience and tact, and to call on the meticulous attention to correct procedure and the rather old-world style of courtesy that he had already found useful as the official of an old-fashioned craft union. In 1952 the resolution in favour of generally extending services eventually passed with only three dissentients, and this suggested that a gradual policy of building the federation up would win acceptance. But it would have to be a very gradual policy indeed.

Another year passed before Hodgson's position in the GFTU was resolved. It was eased somewhat when he was sent away on a course on industrial management with the firm of industrial consultants Urwick, Orr and Partners, which lasted for most of April and May 1953. Finally the Management Committee hit on the solution of giving Bell six months' leave of absence from the date of the 1953 annual general council meeting, officially to let Hodgson show whether he was qualified to become general secretary. This was agreed without debate at the annual meeting in Yarmouth and at the end of October 1953 Bell formally retired and Hodgson took over.[31] In that year he began to put his stamp on the General Federation by issuing *Federation News* in a new cover. Since his arrival at Central House each issue had contained an article signed by L. Hodgson; now it began to show also on occasions his relish for the lighter side of life –for instance, when in April 1955 it reprinted an article on 'Football and Culture' by the historian Asa Briggs. More substantially, Hodgson managed gradually to build up the journal into a widely respected quarterly for the trade union world. By the late 1960s it could claim (though it never did so in print) to be read by 'all sensible academic industrial relations experts'.[32] In 1971, to take one example of the influence it could have, *Federation News* was the first journal to publish a detailed legal analysis of the Conservative government's Industrial Relations Bill; and this source provided much of the ammunition for the parliamentary debate on the Bill.[33]

Hodgson also launched a new publication in 1953. *Abstracts,* issued monthly free of charge to affiliated trade unions, still provides essentially the same service for which he designed it. It contains abstracts or précis of important literature, including parliamentary business, in the fields of industry, commerce and industrial relations; and acts as a kind of monthly notice board for trade unionists who could not possibly hope to find and read for themselves the ever-growing mass of material relevant to their work. This quiet but immensely useful extension of the federation's work followed the direction that *Federation News* had begun in 1951. It also reflected the new general secretary's own emphasis on the need for trade union officials to approach their work as trained, well-informed professionals. Throughout his general secretaryship Hodgson compiled *Abstracts* himself, a job that he obviously found very satisfying. The journal has become so much a part of the scenery of the General Federation that commentators sometimes tend to forget it when they are evaluating the contribution of the GFTU to trade unionism. In fact, together with *Federation News*, it is the one regular service that all affiliated unions get out of the federation, including those which seldom call on GFTU headquarters for dispute benefit or legal advice, and which do not make use of the educational and other special courses that it now provides. With the inexorably growing complexity and speed of change in modern industrial relations, *Abstracts* represents a service that many officials of the GFTU unions, especially the smaller ones, must find indispensable.

Important though Hodgson's appointment was, the General Federation did not change suddenly or dramatically as a result of his arrival. When the chairman for his first full year in office, Cecil Heap of the Wallpaper Workers' Union, paid a generous tribute to the new general secretary at the annual general council meeting in 1955, it was as much as anything a tribute to his ability to fit in with an organisation which had its own traditions and which valued the long-standing comradeship that had grown up over the years. When asked to explain what sort of asssistance the federation had given to the unions in cases brought before the Industrial Disputes Tribunal, Hodgson's reply showed how much the federation was the servant of its affiliated unions and how careful he was that it should remain so.

The type of assistance which we like to give to organisations . . . is that we like to discuss with the secretaries and executives the problems they face or the claims they are putting forward. We do not make the claim for them and I want to dispel any idea that we do. We try to assist unions to put forward the points that will carry weight before the Tribunal. . . . It is not a Federation case. We certainly assist at every level as far as we can and would prefer to give that assistance in draft form. We like the statement which goes before the Tribunal, and even the statement which goes before the employers, to be the statement of the Union. It should, in my opinion, always be the statement of the Union. I think that is the main type of assistance we give.[34]

The other subjects discussed at the same annual meeting followed a pattern which had been familiar at the TUC for many years. The question of industrial injuries came up in two motions. The first pressed for help for injured workmen who had to take time off from work to attend hospital for follow-up treatment. The second reaffirmed the federation's concern that Raynaud's Disease, a disease contracted by people who worked with vibratory tools, should be pre-scribed as an occupational risk under the National Insurance (Industrial Injuries) Act 1946. Another resolution dealt with old age pensions, and the Management Committee also sought authority to repay one-fifth of contributions to the affiliated unions that year. So the federation was still as much concerned as ever with industrial health and safety, and it still had surplus wealth to dispose of.

Changes were taking place in the trade union world as a whole, however, of which the GFTU was keenly aware and which in turn brought about considerable, even if gradual, change within its own ranks. Most noticeably, during the 1950s it was becoming more and more unrealistic for unions to cling to apprenticeship or other craft regulations as a condition of membership. Officials of most of the unions now affiliated to the GFTU would date the breakdown of the old distinctions between skilled and unskilled labour in their industries to the late 1940s and the 1950s. In the small engineering unions the clearest demonstration of this change tended to come when the union admitted women to full membership for the first time (as the National Society of Metal Mechanics did in the mid-1950s). This was not an admission that women workers in their branch of the engineering industry were skilled, but simply that survival demanded a more flexible organisation. Among the garment workers' and textile trade unions, where women members had predominated for a long time, other but parallel adjustments had to be made to the levelling effects of new technology and the different patterns of people's work-ing lives. The need for a fresh approach to organising, and the charge that trade union officials were becoming alienated from their rank-and-file membership, cropped up together as related matters for concern at annual meetings throughout the 1950s. In this context the emphasis of the GFTU began to change. By degrees it was becoming less of an organisation to protect the practitioners of disappearing craft skills, and concentrated more on the benefits of small and close-knit unions whose officials knew their industries from their own experience, and remained approachable and in touch with the membership.

Another change profoundly affecting the GFTU was the continuing decline in the textile industry. Among the large and prestigious unions that remained loyal to the federation after the great wave of secessions ending in 1926–7, the cotton textile unions were the oldest and proudest. Their complex regional and federal structure, comprehensive organisation and tight discipline had aroused the admiration of the Webbs in an earlier generation.[35] They grew up with the industrial revolution and formed a pattern for many other unions in industries which came later to the factory system. The mule spinners' union, the Amalgamated Association of Operative Cotton Spinners and Twiners, embodied some of the best qualities of the traditional GFTU affiliates. It was unique within the industry in compelling attendance at its monthly branch meetings (with a maximum of two absences a year for specific reasons allowed). By this means it achieved a unity and degree of organisation similar to, though perhaps greater than, that of other unions in the GFTU. The spinners had a closed shop even in mills where other workers were less well organised. They also operated a carefully regulated craft structure whereby the spinners themselves paid the union dues of the less skilled piecers who worked for them. (It was only in the 1940s that this arrangement ceased to apply also to the piecers' wages.) Through this system the union obliged the spinners to be responsible for their piecers' membership and for inculcating a sense of union solidarity into the junior partners in the spinning process. Their full-time officials, chosen partly by written examination and almost always from the shop floor, were dedicated trade unionists with a highly professional approach to their job and a record of involvement in both local and national politics. It was also a characteristic of the spinners that the membership had a high rate of commitment to the Labour Party. Through the United Textile Factory Workers' Association (UTFWA) the spinners, the weavers, the cardroom workers and several smaller unions together worked for improvements in trade union and general industrial legislation. They pressed especially for tighter regulations on health (for instance, the designation as an industrial disease of the cardroom workers' scourge of byssinosis) and on unemployment insurance.

In 1950 the unions that made up the UTFWA had a combined membership of about 300,000. By January 1974, when they merged to form the Amalgamated Textile Workers' Union, their numbers were down to below 50,000 and since then they have dropped to below 40,000. This decline had already set in by the early 1930s. But its accelerated speed after 1950, due mainly to competition from the rapid growth of textile industries in the developing countries, shifted the balance within the GFTU. By the mid-1950s the more prosperous hosiery, furniture and pottery workers had become relatively large and dominant unions within the federation, although the weavers and the cardroom workers with 83,000 and 50,000 members respectively in 1955 were still the two largest individual unions, and textile workers altogether far outnumbered any other industrial group. Their declining strength meant that far from developing new functions such as research and educational services on their own behalf, as stronger unions were doing in the 1950s, they looked outside for this sort of support. And although they were not without a voice at the TUC, the GFTU with its concentration both on small unions and on the textile industry was a natural home. In the 1960s and 1970s, therefore, the general secretary was to find his attempts to extend the work of the General Federation increasingly supported by representatives of the Lancashire cotton unions.

The historians both of the TUC and of textile trade unionism, both writing in the 1950s, came to the conclusion that the GFTU was a spent force, or even a 'poker game' in which the member unions were sitting it out, waiting for their share of the federation's assets when it eventually dissolved.[36] Two other observers of the trade union scene have pointed out more recently that these critics failed to notice the underlying strengths which have formed the basis of a new vitality in the General Federation.[37] Decline in the membership of the textile unions, as we have noticed, while weakening them sadly in relation to other unions and reflecting their powerlessness to protect their members' jobs against overwhelming economic odds, has given them a greater stake in the resources of the General Federation than might have been the case if they had maintained their prewar levels. And meanwhile there has been a steady rate of new affiliations to the GFTU, with several unions showing a growing membership and, not least among its successes, several mergers between its affiliates and some others between affiliated and non-affiliated unions which have resulted in the whole organisation affiliating to the federation. Between 1945 and 1970, according to the calculations of Marsh and Speirs, more than 106,000 new members were brought into the federation by previously unaffiliated unions. More than double this number was to accrue in the 1970s with the reaffiliation of the National Union of Tailors and Garment Workers (with 116,000 members in 1980)[38] and National Society of Metal Mechanics (formerly the Amalgamated Society of Brassworkers, and with about 50,000 members in 1980)[39] which had both been lost to the GFTU for decades, and with the entry of the National Union of Lock and Metal

Workers, the National Association of Licensed House Managers, two carpet unions and a number of other, mainly smaller, unions. The momentum generated in the mid-1950s, therefore, proved to be sustainable and must surely confound those who say that there is nothing useful left for the General Federation to do.

It was in 1956 that the Management Committee formally adopted a policy of approaching small unions with a view to recruiting them into the federation, and the general secretary afterwards reported that he had made a start by approaching unions affiliated to the TUC that had less than 5,000 members. The definition of a 'small' union suitable for affiliation to the GFTU soon increased to any with a membership of under 30,000, and in the 1970s, with the affiliation of two much larger unions, this definition also went by the board. Thanks largely to the decimation of the cotton unions between 1950 and 1980, the aggregate membership of the GFTU actually fell slightly during the 1950s and 1960s, but the underlying picture was one of consolidation. This formed the background to a steady increase in the federation's activities under Hodgson's guidance.

In addition to *Federation News* and *Abstracts* (which drew on an increasing number of sources: seventy in its first year, seventy-five in 1955–6, plus parliamentary papers and reports) the GFTU maintained a library of agreements on wages and conditions of work for officials and other members of its affiliates to consult. The general secretary spent much of his time helping unions to prepare wage claims and cases for presentation to the Industrial Disputes Tribunal. He had also persuaded the Management Committee in 1955 to adopt a new structure consisting of three subcommittees dealing respectively with finance and organisation, wages and insurance, and education and publications. These took the place of the former system whereby a single subcommittee dealt with all matters arising in the course of each month, and reported to the full Management Committee at their monthly meetings. The new system reflected the increased amount of business and also had the advantage of giving more specific responsibilities to every member of the Management Committee. In 1965, when Hodgson tried again to introduce a full research service, a fourth subcommittee was set up, dealing with 'research and advice'.

In financial matters as well as administrative there was some change. In 1962 the federation established a pension scheme for trade union officials, to which affiliated unions could subscribe. The invidious position of George Bell (who died in 1959) at the end of his career with the federation may have been in Hodgson's mind when he proposed the scheme. But examples of ageing general secretaries who clung on to their jobs for lack of any prospect other than the state old age pension could be found among several of the federation's smaller affiliates; and even today there are general secretaries who can recall their own union's difficulties with their immediate predecessors in the not-so-distant past. For most of the 1950s, disputes were at a low level and trade unions in general were able to devote a relatively large proportion of their time to such matters as extending research and educational services, cultivating international links (another sphere in which the textile unions were especially active) and, above all, to dealing with the swelling volume of new legislation on unemployment, social security, and so on. Within the GFTU, as elsewhere, it was services rather than dispute benefit that most of the members valued, and from 1954 until 1962 the annual general council meeting voted for a return of one-fifth of contributions to the affiliated societies. In 1958 the rate of dispute benefit was raised to £1 on the higher and 10 shillings on the lower scale, following a year when the number of disputes reported to the General Federation rose from the usual four or five to twelve.* It remained, however, at the level of a useful financial back-up for most of the unions that drew on it and, as in the 1970s, few officials in the 1950s would have put dispute benefit at the top of their list of reasons for belonging to the GFTU. A more valuable financial benefit, even though almost unique, was the grant of £2,000 made by the federation to the Associated Metal Workers' Society in 1963 to help with the costs of the important case of *Cartledge and others* v. *Jopling*. The case concerned the right of workers suffering from an industrial disease (here it was pneumoconiosis) to sue the employer in whose factory he contracted it, after a lapse of some time. It was a subject with which the GFTU was always much concerned, and therefore it was appropriate that in this one case it broke its usual rule of leaving support for union litigation to the TUC.

The area in which the General Federation's services were expanding most usefully, apart from publications, was education. It had always supported Ruskin College, the WEA since its foundation and the National Council of Labour Colleges, and this support continued. In addition, an expanded programme of scholarships for members of affiliated unions to courses run by these and other institutions began and in 1954 new prizes were instituted for success in various trade examinations. In 1966 the prize system was overhauled to concentrate specifically on: boot and shoe manufacture, the dyeing of textiles, woollen and worsted manufacture, hosiery and knitted goods, cotton spinning, cotton weaving, silk and man-made fibres,

* According to figures given in the GFTU's evidence to the Donovan Commission in 1966 (for which, see below) the annual number of disputes in the ten years 1955–64 averaged 6·6, with none in 1964 and eleven in 1957, the year of a major engineering dispute. The GFTU annual report for 1958 refers to twelve disputes in the year up to June 1958.

foundry practice and the furniture industry. In that year for the first time the federation began to offer grants of up to £50 per year to nominated members of affiliated unions who were studying at college or university, and the first such grant went to a nominee of the National Union of Furniture Trade Operatives at the University of Sussex. The GFTU offered courses itself. Summer schools for trade union officials at Oxford became an annual fixture and weekend courses, which began in the early 1960s, attracted reasonable attendances. A number of day conferences on specific issues seemed to be particularly popular. In March 1962, for example, over one hundred delegates attended a day conference in Manchester on questions connected with wages and the vexed problem of wage differentials, an attendance that rivalled that at the annual general council meetings. The next November 140 representatives from thirty-five unions met for a day in Manchester to discuss accidents at work and the government's proposal to set up a National Incomes Commission, with the help of two expert speakers.[40]

Where the General Federation perhaps tried hardest but certainly had least success was in bringing its own views and activities to the attention of a wider public. As Marsh and Speirs commented in 1971, the federation's role is a modest one in relation to British trade unionism as a whole; and its very modesty may insulate it from the competitiveness of other organisations. Leslie Hodgson always knew this. He seemed even to cultivate an unobtrusive and diplomatic style and knew from both instinct and experience that in its relations with its affiliated unions a posture of unobtrusive helpfulness was what they liked. But such a policy, however successful in forwarding praiseworthy ends, is the enemy of public acclaim. It irked not only Hodgson but also those members of the Management Committee who backed up his approach, to see the General Federation and its work virtually unknown outside its own affiliates, and during the 1960s and 1970s various attempts were made not only to recruit new affiliates but to attract the attention of government, trade unionists generally and the press. It seems to have been sadly typical of these ventures that when in 1975 the federation launched its published research study, *Courtaulds. The Anatomy of a Multinational*, the press duly arrived and consumed a buffet lunch laid on especially for them but (at least to the knowledge of the general secretary) published not a word on the subject.

In the early 1960s this public neglect was irksome in particular because the GFTU had some reason to complain that the views of small unions were not only ignored but spurned. Debates over industrial relations focused now not only on the 'stop–go' economic and incomes policies of successive Conservative governments, but on the increasing number of disputes that were arising over wage differentials and the often related problem of demarcation between different jobs on the same shop floor, especially in engineering. The now familiar and perhaps outworn cliché about multi-unionism being the bane of British industrial relations developed as the affluent society in Britain began to become aware that others, and not only in the United States, were growing more affluent than themselves. The example of West Germany, whose trade unions had been rebuilt from scratch after the war along industrial union lines which owed a lot to the advice of British trade unionists, began to be invoked. In this context, even those unions which could claim to fit the industrial as well as the craft mould[41] came to be seen as not only outdated but even pernicious brakes on the industrial progress of this country. This view was often shared by officials of the large trade unions and, it is fair to assume, by those of the TUC. Writing of the still low membership of trade unions in general in 1963, Hodgson observed:

It is . . . of real importance if we are to continue to attract members into our movement that the view which is held of us is not one of outdated organisations clinging nostalgically to the ways of the past. We have failed in allowing an image to be built up of us as being more backward-looking and opposed to new ideas than the community of which we form a part.[42]

In October 1963, at the request of the executives of several affiliated unions and following a programme of visits to all affiliated executives by the general secretary, the Management Committee issued a special statement on trade union structure. 'It is high time', it declared:

that attention was drawn to the fact that bigness, powerful resources, and strong administration are not the standards by which trade unions should be assessed. It is rather the degree of personal service, contact, and interest, together with the loyalty which is engendered in groups of workers who in their work and workplace feel a community of interest.[43]

The GFTU concluded its paper on trade union structure by prophesying great changes in the trade union world. This view at least was widely shared, for in 1964 Harold Wilson's Labour government, the first Labour administration for thirteen years, announced the setting up of a Royal Commission on Trade Unions and Employers' Associations under the chairmanship of Lord Donovan. The written and oral evidence that the General Federation gave before the Donovan Commission in 1966 provides an excellent portrait of it as it was in the 1960s and deserves detailed consideration.[44] Despite some important changes and additions to its work in the 1970s, the General Federation is recognisable as the same organisation today.

In its written submission the federation presented itself as an organisation which encouraged its affiliates to see their work in a wider context. The officials of the affiliated unions themselves had a close relationship with their members and provided an exemplary service within their own context.

> They would generally claim to enjoy the best rates and conditions for their trade or industry; a high degree of organisation; a high ratio of officers to members; few instances of unofficial action; and, with the background of full employment which [had] been maintained in recent years, to have attitudes to new methods and techniques which are not restrictive.

It observed that no one form of union structure was ideal: 'diversification is a characteristic of our unions and of industry. We hope it will remain so.' The federation went on to voice its fear that a few strong groups would eventually dominate unionism completely, and stressed the importance of a structure involving active shop floor participation in union affairs. While there ought to be change in trade unionism, it 'must be of such a form that we are neither using outdated methods nor turning ourselves into a huge bureaucratic machine where the top is talking in a language which the shop floor does not understand'. In other words, it must remain possible in Britain for 'workers to form and run their own trade unions, however "inefficient" these may seem to outsiders'. The federation reinforced its position as a defender of British individualism in the trade union world by repudiating the role of legislation in most trade union affairs. In its defence of free collective bargaining it upheld a view that was and is widely held among trade unionists in this country, preferring a framework of law in which employers' organisations and trade unions could function with a minimum of outside interference. The state could help, however, in certain well-defined cases. It would be useful for the Registrar-General of Friendly Societies to draw up model rules for unions to consult when bringing their own rule books up to date to cope with modern legislation; some form of arbitration body was needed similar to the old Industrial Disputes Tribunal (or indeed, along the lines of the present-day ACAS); and it was essential that redundancy payments should be made compulsory by law (as they are today) if unions were to co-operate fully in the industrial changes that brought about redundancy.

The profile of the General Federation that emerged from its

affiliates' replies to a questionnaire appended to its written evidence supported the picture of a peaceable organisation in which industrial strife was the exception, not the norm. All forty-nine of the unions responding to the questionnaire had an established grievance procedure, and few of them recorded any serious difficulties with management, shop floor organisation or employers' associations. They attributed what difficulties there were to a resentment of trade unions in general or to ignorance of the established procedures. Disputes over recognition hardly existed. When they came to give evidence orally, however, this was one of the questions on which they were pressed. Hodgson told the commission that since the GFTU's affiliates were almost all long-established they had solved problems of recognition long since, and certainly did not want to see legislation for compulsory recognition. Nor should the law intervene in other matters of union business, such as unfair dismissal, where GFTU union officials were usually in such close contact with firms that there was a simple procedure for sorting out such problems. One member of the commission in particular challenged the GFTU delegation hard on these questions. So did other members, on the problem of restrictive practices. Hodgson insisted that the GFTU's affiliates were not bastions of restrictive practice as the commission seemed to think, though he did admit that 'when a man has been trained for a particular skill, it is obvious he is going to build up restrictive practices around it, if there is no opportunity for him to use the skill in a wider field'. The answer to this problem was a background of full employment and emphatically not legislation. Similarly, the closed shop was desirable and in many instances GFTU affiliates had achieved it; but it should be won by persuasion, not by law. Challenged several times to discuss principles on which the legislation might be based, the GFTU delegation to the commission insisted that the particular case must always be considered. In Hodgson's words, 'My answer is you should allow ... unions to organise and develop, and then they will in fact see there is suitable procedure'.

The Donovan Commission did not agree about 'allowing unions to organise and develop' without some attempt to impose reform on what it saw as national chaos in industrial relations. Nor does it appear to have been particularly sympathetic to the General Federation and its affiliates as institutions. At one point during its meeting with GFTU officials a member of the commission remarked (incorrectly) that the federation appeared to spend ten times as much on keeping itself going as it did on services for its members.* Later in

* This question was based on the figures for educational expenditure alone and did not take account of publications and other services, as the general secretary pointed out.

the meeting the GFTU's refusal to discuss principles of law in industrial relations apparently displeased the commission.

Nevertheless there was a considerable amount in the Donovan Report that coincided with the GFTU's point of view.[45] The commission found, for example, that the seat of power in the unions had almost always been close to the shop floor and that industrial relations depended above all on the relations between managers and trade unionists within the workplace. 'Multi-unionism' did not bother managers, shop stewards or rank-and-file members of trade unions nearly as much as it did the branch and national officials of trade unions, or employers at a higher level than middle management. On the contrary, there was considerable evidence that trade unionists in general were usually satisfied with the way the system worked. What concerned the Donovan Commission and the Labour government, however, was the problems that multi-unionism created for industry nationally. The incidence of unofficial, often wildcat, strikes had been growing since the mid-1950s and national agreements were increasingly difficult to enforce. The absence of structure and discipline in the system as a whole was seen, moreover, to be leading to the progressive disintegration of industrial relations which sooner or later would become unworkable at the workplace level, as they already were threatening to become at the national level. Multi-unionism was a main ingredient in this recipe for disaster; and the Donovan Commission recommended a thorough reform of negotiating procedures within factories and other workplaces, so that as far as possible only one union would represent each grade of worker within each workplace.

In so far as these recommendations affected the GFTU, or would have done if they had been carried out, they did not necessarily spell the end of small unions. In fact the recognition of the small local unit (and implicitly therefore of personal relations) as an irreplaceable element in any system of industrial relations was good news for the GFTU. It recognised the worth of what General Federation affiliates had always claimed was important.* But on the other hand the Donovan Commission's finding in this respect also showed that

---

* This was in contrast to the evidence submitted by Professor Allan Flanders (in the form of his paper, *Industrial Relations: What Is Wrong with the System? An Essay on Its Theory and Future* (London: Faber, 1965), in which he stated that 'personal . . . relations have their importance for management and workers, but they lie outside the scope of a system of industrial relations'. Any opinion of Professor Flanders on this subject deserves to be treated with the utmost respect but while GFTU officials would surely agree with his main emphasis on a 'system of rules', most of them would also emphasise that in their experience personal relations are just as central to the whole matter, and any system which ignores them must be incomplete.

workplace bargaining was strong among large unions as well, so that it did not in any way concede the special place that the GFTU claimed for the small trade union. The commission's findings on restrictive practices were similarly ambiguous as far as the General Federation was concerned, for the evidence on the protection of craft interests, whether or not this involved 'restrictive practices', showed that large unions like the AUEW played a large part in maintaining differentials for their skilled members. There were some less ambiguous points of contact between the Donovan findings and the views of the General Federation. The federation had recommended the setting-up of a new industrial arbitration service, with the possibility of compulsory arbitration held in reserve for particularly intractable cases. Donovan wanted a commission on industrial relations with power to recommend compulsory arbitration in certain cases affecting recognition; and this was in fact the only substantive recommendation that Harold Wilson's government put into effect. Again, Donovan wanted to see trade unions appoint more officers to cope with local problems, and it was already a feature of the GFTU style of trade unionism, as the federation had pointed out, to provide a high ratio of officials to membership. It would be wrong to suggest, however, that the General Federation by itself had much impact on the Donovan Commission; for it remained relatively insignificant in the world of British trade unionism, at least in the eyes of outside observers.[46]

The Donovan Report itself was destined to remain little more than an expensive and exceptionally authoritative analysis of British industrial relations in the 1960s. Barbara Castle's White Paper *In Place of Strife*, which built on many of the commission's recommendations, fell foul of the unions largely because of its proposals for some legal regulation of trade union activities, and the Labour government did not get round to implementing any modified proposals for industrial law reform before its own demise in the general election of 1970. By that time it had become accepted in political, and especially in Conservative, circles that radical reform of the trade unions was essential to Britain's industrial well-being, and the government of Edward Heath set out to achieve this in its own way. Much of the history of the Heath government of 1970–4 centres on its disastrous relations with trade unions. Industrial relations for the whole of the 1970s were profoundly conditioned by the failure of the Industrial Relations Act 1971 and by the showdown over the miners' strike, the three-day week and the fall of the Conservative government in the winter of 1973–4. The 1970s are still too recent for us to be able to see them in perspective, and this is especially true of industrial relations, where so many developments of the decade have yet to reach their resolution. But we must now turn, however sketchily, to glance at the history of the General Federation of Trade Unions in these last ten years and so complete the picture of its existence to date. .

New Developments in the 1970s

The gradual change of direction brought about during the 1950s and early 1960s had laid the groundwork for some very considerable additions to the services offered by the General Federation in the 1970s. It was in the 1970s that it really turned its face more positively towards the future and added more to its activities than it had done at any time in its history since the First World War. An attempt at a composite picture of the sort of trade unionism that the GFTU represents may be found in a series of articles (originally intended as appendices to this book) in forthcoming issues of *Federation News*. In the next few pages we shall concentrate more on the nature of the General Federation as an institution during the 1970s.

The decline of the textile industry had prompted Hodgson and the Management Committee to seek new recruits among unions in other industries, and in the early 1970s they achieved some success, with the affiliations of the Amalgamated Union of Asphalt Workers and the National Union of Lock and Metal Workers. The National Union of Furniture Trade Operatives amalgamated with a smaller, unaffiliated, union (the Woodcutting Machinists) and changed its name to the Furniture, Timber and Allied Trades Union, keeping its enlarged membership within the General Federation. Even more usefully, when the Waterproof Garment Workers' Union merged with the very much larger National Union of Tailors and Garment Workers in 1972, the small union's general secretary, Fred Henry, chairman of the GFTU in 1968–9, helped to persuade the larger union to affiliate to the federation. Other affiliations were to follow, most notably, perhaps, that of the National Society of Metal Mechanics in 1976. The emphasis of the federation therefore shifted, as it had been doing since the 1950s, gradually further from textile manufacturing to a more diverse membership, with growing links with specialised engineering. The textile unions and the garment unions together, on the other hand, now formed a more formidable group, and one with healthier membership figures, within the GFTU than the textile unions alone had done since the 1940s.

These were necessary developments. As the 1970s approached, officials of the GFTU were well aware that small unions continued to be regarded as anachronisms in British trade unionism.[47] Although in general they welcomed the Donovan Report, one criticism of it was that it neglected many of the older industries, such as textiles, treating them as unimportant examples of declining systems of industrial relations, and proposing remedies that were really only suitable for a few 'star' industries.[48] Research into small trade unions had been almost non-existent, but when two Oxford writers on industrial relations began work on this neglected subject at the end of the 1960s, they found every reason to support the GFTU affiliates' claims to efficiency and professionalism. They found that there was no relationship between the size of a union and the proportion of its finances that it spent on costs, nor did large unions provide a necessarily better or more expert service.[49] The results of a questionnaire sent out to twenty-six GFTU affiliates in 1972 showed that they valued the federation most of all for its services, which were geared to small unions, but that they wanted it to have a higher standing in the trade union movement and felt that it ought to 'do more to make its presence felt'.[50]

The difficulty of publicising the General Federation's separate identity in a wider world remained and perhaps even grew, as in some ways the GFTU became closer to the TUC. Its identity in fact is absolutely distinct and officials of the affiliated unions are quite clear about the value they place on its separate services. But in some important ways the GFTU has followed the same path as the TUC. In terms of membership, both have grown enormously in aggregate numbers while numbering fewer separate unions among their affiliates. The TUC's increase of 38·9 per cent in the eleven years 1968–79 brought it up to 12,128,000 members (in round figures) with a decrease in the number of affiliated unions in the same period from 160 to 112.[51] These figures of course dwarf those of the GFTU, but in percentage terms the General Federation's growth has been even more impressive. Aggregate membership virtually doubled between 1970 and 1980, when it reached over 490,000 with a decline in the number of affiliates, mainly due to mergers within the federation, from forty-seven at the end of 1971 to forty-one in 1980. On its own modest scale therefore, the GFTU has shared the experience of British trade unionism in general, whereby fewer unions are catering to more members than ever before. It is worth noticing also that there has been a steady decline in the number of GFTU unions that are not affiliated to the TUC, from twenty-three of the fifty-five in the federation when it prepared its written evidence for Donovan in 1966, to only three in 1980.

In terms of policy too, it has found itself working parallel to the TUC on the issue that dominated the 1970s: the place of legislation in industrial relations. At its annual meeting in Scarborough in 1969, the general council passed a resolution against the White Paper *In*

Place of Strife, condemning in particular its proposals for a compulsory secret ballot before taking strike action and its imposition of fiscal and other penalties on miscreant unions. There were many welcome features among the proposals, including the safeguards against unfair dismissal, provision for trade unions to have access to more commercial information and a rule that employers should register certain collective agreements with the Department of Employment and Productivity. The federation also welcomed proposal number 25 in the White Paper, which suggested a procedure for complaints against arbitrary action by trade unions; for there was much concern within the federation about unconstitutional actions by small groups of workers. Nevertheless, 'the GFTU, like the TUC, believe[d] that the finding of the Donovan Commission [was] much nearer a more sensible and harmonious system of industrial relations than the proposed Government Bill'. Or, to put it more strongly, 'This foul and most hateful Bill if passed in its entirety, will stand as an eternal and monumental indictment of a Government and a Cabinet wherever the English language may be spoken'.[52]

Similarly but with even more force, the General Federation condemned the Conservatives' Industrial Relations Act 1971 and at the annual general council meeting of 1973, which had been addressed by Len Murray, then assistant general secretary of the TUC, delegates followed the example set by the TUC in suspending (to be expelled the following year) the few remaining affiliates which had not removed themselves from the register of trade unions in protest against the Act. Neither decision was unanimous. As Fred Henry said in 1969 in his address as chairman of the federation,

> I have always accepted the sanctity of agreements, as I know delegates to this annual meeting do, and we have the responsibility to see that this is accepted by our membership. The few Trade Unions, and they are few, which are principally affected by this issue, must give urgent attention to rectifying a position which brings discredit on the whole of our movement.

There remained a body of opinion at the GFTU, even in face of the much more punitive Industrial Relations Act, which very much disliked flouting government or the law. What really persuaded the General Federation to take the extreme step of suspending and then expelling member unions was its commitment to the unity of the trade union movement. The resolution passed at a private session of the annual general council meeting at Southport in 1973 read:

> This Conference believes that opposition to the Industrial Relations Act can be most effective if the Trade Union Movement as a

whole acts in unison. It supports the action of the Trades Union Congress in suspending from Congress unions that have remained registered under the Act.

It believes that the General Federation of Trade Unions should mirror the action taken by the TUC by taking the same action against GFTU affiliates who refuse to de-register.

It was this theme of solidarity with the TUC that Leslie Hodgson emphasised afterwards in conversation, speaking as though there really could never have been any doubt about the matter. Nevertheless it was a sad day for the federation, with its special traditions of tolerance and friendliness, when it took this step. As the seconder of the motion said, 'this . . . is a friendly organisation, we are colleagues, and therefore I would not want to disrupt the meeting by saying some of the things I might say at a different meeting'. The Management Committee moved an amendment to the resolution (which had been moved by the textile workers) trying to give another year's breathing space to unions which had not de-registered, before they were suspended. And a future chairman of the federation, Margaret Fenwick of the jute and flax workers, supporting the amendment, pleaded for the 'friendly' and 'comradely' atmosphere of the GFTU to be preserved. Delegates from the National Union of Funeral Service Operatives and the Yorkshire Association of Power Loom Overlookers explained the particular difficulties of their unions, both of which were still on the register. The executive of the funeral workers had voted to de-register but had failed so far to persuade its members; and the Yorkshire loom overlookers were a federation of five tiny unions, which would remain registered even if the overall organisation were not.* But the motion to suspend the registered unions was passed unamended in an atmosphere of considerable bitterness, and those unions which were still registered were formally expelled in 1974. The permanent losses to the General Federation were not great in terms of numbers. They included its smallest union, the Teston Independent Society of Cricket Ball Makers, with eighteen members, and the National Union of Flint Glassworkers, with just over a thousand members.

In its changing membership patterns and in matters of major policy therefore, the General Federation of Trade Unions has tended to 'mirror' the TUC, as the motion of 1973 put it. Some of the services it provides are also parallel to those available through the TUC. But

---

* In the event the problems of both these unions were solved, and both remain in the GFTU today, the funeral workers having merged with FTAT during the year (1978–9) when their general secretary, D. R. Coates, was actually chairman of the federation.

what distinguishes it and gives it a special character that is highly prized by its affiliated unions is that it provides these services specifically for smaller unions, and does so in a friendly and approachable manner. Trade union officials who feel 'frustrated', 'swamped' or 'overwhelmed' at the TUC or who simply never attend Congress and never call on its services for similar reasons, value the friendship that they find at meetings of the GFTU. They know that they can drop in at Central House or pick up the phone to speak to the general secretary or one of the other full-time officials without a feeling that they must be intruding on more important business. It is in this context that we should look at the way the General Federation developed its services during most of the 1970s under the patient guidance of Leslie Hodgson and has continued to expand them since January 1978 under his successor, Peter Potts.

Once the federation as a whole was prepared to countenance a more formal expansion than it had allowed during the first seventeen years or so of Hodgson's term of office, there were good foundations on which to build. Quite apart from the organisational groundwork that Hodgson had laid, the General Federation's finances were in a good state. In 1972 work was completed on a new top floor for Central House, which now became the premises for GFTU headquarters, freeing more office space for rent on the lower floors of the building. Central House represented the federation's most valuable capital asset and enabled it to give exceptionally good value in return for contributions. Another piece of financial underpinning was the establishment of the GFTU educational trust, first set up in 1970 and then reconstituted so as to exempt a proportion of federation income from tax. Contributions also were raised modestly, and Hodgson persuaded the Management Committee to look regularly at the level of both contributions and benefits although it did not take up the suggestion made by two outside observers in 1971 that affiliation fees ought to be index-linked in some way.[53] With the great changes in the London office accommodation scene during the past ten years, which have reduced the relative value of rents in the Holborn district where Central House is, there may be some reason to regret that such a decision was not taken then. At the annual general council meeting of 1980 a resolution was passed to undertake a thorough review of the levels of contributions and benefits (not primarily for this reason but in view of current government policy). The General Federation in the 1980s, therefore, will not enjoy the financial solidity with which it faced the 1970s. But its progress in the last decade did take advantage of great financial strengths which previously had not been used as they could have been.

In October 1971, along with the TUC and some other organisations, the GFTU joined in sponsoring the new Trade Union Research Unit (TURU) at Ruskin College, Oxford. The GFTU educational trust was to pay £200 to the unit for its first five years and, in addition, for the first year of the unit's existence the federation paid £100 towards the cost of every research project that any GFTU affiliate commissioned it to undertake. Both the federation in its own right and a number of affiliated unions continue to draw on the services of TURU. This, however, now complements the GFTU's own research service. Leslie Hodgson liked to tell the story of how the idea of a research service finally won acceptance from a sceptical Management Committee and general council. The guest speaker at the annual general council meeting in 1971 was James Callaghan, and at lunch before he was due to speak he asked Hodgson whether there was any special point that he would like him to put across. Hodgson mentioned the project closest to his heart, and Callaghan duly inserted into his speech a plea that the GFTU's affiliates should 'create a central research organisation that will help to determine policy and to fight the employers on their own ground and in the most sophisticated ways possible'.[54] Backed by so eminent a speaker, the idea easily won agreement. The use of TURU was its first fruit, and in 1973 the GFTU appointed its own first full-time research officer.

The research service did not enjoy untroubled progress from the first. Affiliated unions, having voted to set it up, had to be persuaded to use it. The first research officer tried to move rather too quickly and without always consulting the general secretaries of the unions concerned before embarking on his fact-finding forays. But these were only teething troubles. Affiliated unions' answers to the questionnaire that they were sent in 1972 showed that in general they valued the GFTU more for its services and for an intangible sense of community with other small unions than for its benefit payments. Most of them wanted the federation to extend these services by providing more research and advice. A more impressionistic survey by the present writer, drawn from conversations at two annual meetings more than five years later and from some more extended interviews, suggests that the research and educational services, as they are now, stand together at the head of most general secretaries' reasons for valuing the GFTU. Staffed now by two full-time research officers and with the co-operation of a full-time education officer, the research service wins praise for its thoroughness and (from some quarters) for the speed with which it delivers the information required.

The general secretary of the Amalgamated Union of Asphalt Workers, with 3,000 members and affiliated for ten years, considers research by far the most important benefit that his union derives from affiliation. Its greatest service to his union so far has been the compilation of a long report on wages and conditions in the asphalt industry, for which a GFTU research officer visited workplaces all over England and Wales during a twelve-month period. This report will continue to be of use for as long as the measured day-work system of payment continues to operate in the asphalt industry. Its cost to the union concerned was nil, and to produce anything comparable would have been far beyond the union's own resources.

Another example of a large project undertaken by the GFTU's research service, but in this case jointly with TURU, is the study *Courtaulds. The Anatomy of a Multinational*, published by the GFTU in 1975. Courtaulds was an obvious choice for research, arising out of more general discussions about multinationals at GFTU meetings, since the company employs a very large proportion of the members of the textile unions affiliated to the General Federation. Co-operation from the company itself was not forthcoming but the research team managed nevertheless to produce a fairly penetrating study. They showed among other things how a tightly knit and surprisingly centralised management structure had the advantage over a diverse, overlapping and rather disunited pattern of unions with members in the company, and recommended the creation of some form of focal point for collective bargaining purposes. The TUC's Courtaulds working party, which supervised the research jointly with the GFTU Management Committee, was suggested as a possible starting point; but in fact the unions concerned in Courtaulds, all of which were given copies of the report, set up a special co-ordinating committee. This work, a rare but not unique example of good communications with the TUC, was followed up by a special conference at York in the presence of Courtaulds' chairman, Sir Arthur Knight.

Both the asphalt industry survey and the report on Courtaulds were large projects absorbing a large proportion of the GFTU research officers' time over a relatively long period. The bread-and-butter work of the research service is more varied. On the whole the larger affiliated unions, which employ their own research officers, draw on the GFTU for statistical information and for details about companies, mainly drawn from the Companies Registration Office. Here it is clearly useful to unions based outside London (like the Tailors and Garment Workers in Milton Keynes and the Hosiery and Knitwear Workers in Leicester) to have a London-based service to supplement their own research work. Other unions find a variety of aspects of the service useful. Many have received help in bringing their rule books up to date, a task that has become increasingly often necessary in order to negotiate the minefields of industrial and labour law in the 1970s. Help in preparing wage claims, both by carrying out research into the state of the industry or of particular companies and by analysing comparable wage patterns, forms another large part of the service. Often information is needed in a great hurry and the research officers are expected to perform the almost impossible. While some officials of affiliated unions praise them for the speed of their response, others have complained of having to wait too long for a reply to their inquiry; though in general those unions with some direct experience of the problems of research are less apt to complain of slow service.

Background services provided by the research officers include the maintenance of a library at Central House and the compilation of summaries of important recent legislation. Several affiliates would like to see more help on legal matters, and some have even suggested the appointment of a full-time officer with a legal training – a service that seems increasingly necessary as the employers make more and more use of barristers at industrial tribunals. At present the legal aspect of the federation's services consists mainly of the research officers' own expertise built up from experience, a series of courses designed to inform trade union members about their rights under recent legislation (for example, one on maternity benefits, held in 1980), and occasional references of thorny legal questions to the federation's unofficial legal adviser, Professor R. W. Rideout, who also takes at least one weekend school a year. There could well be scope for development while still retaining the essentially advisory nature of the GFTU's service.

The comments of affiliated union officials on the GFTU's research service are for the most part highly appreciative, even admiring. Criticisms tend to be in the direction of wanting an expanded service. It is noted, for example, that the officers can seldom spend as much time as union officials would like actually 'in the field' getting to know the union for which they are doing their research. If more officers were available they might be able to spend more time with the unions, even helping the hard-pressed general secretaries of some very small organisations with rudimentary problems such as analysing company balance sheets. This latter suggestion recalls the more leisured days of the federation, when Leslie Hodgson once spent two weeks with the new general secretary of a Scottish silk workers' unions, now defunct, training him in his job; and almost certainly such a function formed part of George Bell's regular work as organiser in the 1920s and 1930s.

Until recently the research officers were responsible for running the GFTU's educational services which, with a growing number of courses each year, absorbed a great deal of time. In 1978, however, at the suggestion of the new general secretary, another full-time officer was appointed, officially to the research service but in fact to take over education duties. The two research officers still arrange courses too, but more of this work is now taken off their shoulders. The GFTU's educational work has an unbroken tradition going back to the early years when it first supported Ruskin College, the WEA and the National Council of Labour Colleges. From the early 1960s onwards, the federation offered one-day and weekend courses regularly, with a summer school for trade union officials and an annual weekend school on labour law. It now offers a range of courses of varying length, ranging from introductory ones on a range of subjects to an advanced course every November which is attended mainly by general secretaries and assistant general secretaries and is particularly designed to keep them abreast of legislative developments. In the past the attendance at such courses has varied widely, and the Management Committee sometimes felt it necessary to admonish its colleagues in the annual report for not making more use of what was offered. With the appointment of a full-time education officer, however, with more time to devote to publicity and administration, over-subscription is now more often the problem.

The educational services of the GFTU have also received their share of praise from members of affiliated unions. The larger unions in particular subscribe to them because they can better afford to add to the subsidy which the GFTU already gives to rank-and-file members who attend. Even the largest of the GFTU's affiliates are relatively small by TUC standards, and their members bring back 'glowing' reports (in the words of one official) of how well suited the courses are to the special needs of their own work. Only a few of the very small unions, or those with a very different industrial basis from the majority, either cannot afford to send members to the courses or find that their members feel at sea when they do attend. For most, it is here that the GFTU's special qualities of comradeship and friendliness are most apparent. The present general secretary takes some pride in the fact that cliques of course-attenders do not develop at GFTU courses as they tend to do within the TUC. Many union members may only attend one or two GFTU courses during their career but, when they do, some pains are taken to see that the atmosphere is congenial. Since those who attend all share the fact of being members of small unions and very often have a common industrial background, it is possible for them to participate knowledgeably and not to feel swamped by the more political environment which a larger organisation almost un-avoidably generates. At the same time it is noticeable that GFTU affiliates' general secretaries and other full-time officials frequently attend the federation's courses, a phenomenon that would not be found among larger unions. The traditional GFTU emphasis on training and education, in other words, continues to apply to all levels within the trade union structure.

The 1970s saw further developments in the federation which fell outside the defined scope of research or educational services. Throughout the decade it continued to show a close interest in health and safety. The trade unionist Bill Simpson, chairman of the Health and Safety Commission under the Health and Safety at Work Act 1974, was one of the two main speakers at the annual general council meeting in Edinburgh in 1977; and several GFTU courses have concentrated on the practical application of the Act within the industries most represented in the federation. Among specific issues taken by the GFTU earlier in the 1970s was the problem of occupational deafness. The National Union of Hosiery and Knitwear Workers, with GFTU support, commissioned a piece of research into the problem by Dr Jean Stone, and her findings were published jointly by the union and the federation and circulated to all affiliated unions in 1972.[55] The federation meanwhile backed up the union's campaign to get occupational deafness prescribed as an industrial disease, failing in an attempt to persuade the TUC to act jointly with it. Although provisions to deal with noise were made under the Health and Safety Act in 1974, workers in many noisy occupations still were not covered and the GFTU continued to press for a review. Another example of the federation's vigilance on safety was its campaign to protect workers who suffered injuries while on industrial retraining schemes. Both the Ceramic and Allied Trades Union and the National Union of Lock and Metal Workers undertake responsibility for people introduced into their factories on job retraining. The ceramic union discovered after one very minor accident that there was no protection for such workers by law, and asked the General Federation to pursue the matter. The Manpower Services Commission, when approached, had never heard of the GFTU before. The TUC, at a joint meeting with the GFTU, was happy for the smaller organisation to pursue what was, in the overall scale of trade union business, a relatively trivial matter. It is one example from many that could be cited to show how the GFTU takes up problems and injustices affecting the lives of individuals, which otherwise might well be ignored because they only apply to small minorities or in other ways lack the 'sex appeal' that might lead to a major campaign.

Health and safety at work have been long-standing preoccupations of the GFTU, dating back to the days of the National Insurance Act 1911 and William Appleton's campaigns for trade union insurance. Similarly, all matters affecting pensions and social security are traditional concerns of the federation, which it continued to pursue in the 1970s – for example, in pressing for the abolition of the waiting period before payment of unemployment insurance. In 1972 the Employers' Liability (Compulsory) Insurance Act 1969 came into effect and the GFTU noted with satisfaction that this legislation was largely due to the efforts of the Furniture, Timber and Allied Trades Union. Some of the union's members had suffered tragically in a fire at an upholstery factory in Glasgow where the employers had been unable to meet their liabilities to pay compensation. Other issues which arose regularly at the General Federation's meetings during the 1970s included the provisions of the Sex Discrimination Act 1975. Here, delegates from the GFTU participated in a TUC conference on the subject and the federation subsequently included it in some of their courses. Women are attracting growing attention in the trade union world in general, and the subject is far from being peculiar to the GFTU. Nevertheless, women workers form an especially high proportion of the GFTU membership, traditionally in the textile and garment industries, and now figure increasingly in the recruitment drives of unions in other industries (for example, the National Society of Metal Mechanics); and this fact is reflected in the number of courses for women that the GFTU provides.

The catalogue of the General Federation's growing activities in the 1970s could extend indefinitely, but one further development ought to be singled out. This is the inauguration in 1976 of a series of annual lectures, to be given to an invited audience of members of GFTU affiliated unions, employers and others from the wider world of industry. The speakers so far have been: Professor J. C. Wood, Francis Cripps and Frank Wilkinson of the Cambridge Economic Group, Sir Arthur Knight, the chairman of Courtaulds, Joel Barnett, MP, the former Labour Cabinet minister, and Sir Richard O'Brien, chairman of the Manpower Services Commission. Each year the lecture is preceded by a buffet supper at University College, London, where the GFTU again has an opportunity to demonstrate its friendly atmosphere. Officials of some of the smallest organisations attend these lectures, sometimes bringing employers with them, when they could not manage to attend the more expensive and time-consuming meetings or even to send members on educational courses. The venture may be seen as another attempt to bring the General Federation into the public eye and to demonstrate its practical concern with the wider issues of industrial society. So far, although members of the press are always invited, they have shown no signs of interest; but to those who attend the occasions have always seemed worthwhile.

This indeed may be the fate of the General Federation of Trade Unions: that to its members it is an immensely worthwhile organisation, one well worth developing and well worth shouting about; but from outside, mainly because of its small size, it appears incorrigibly modest and insignificant and, to the incurious, even hopelessly out-dated. It was a fate that worried Leslie Hodgson, and it may even be seen as a personal tragedy that the recognition that he strove to win for the General Federation obstinately eludes it still, after his retirement and death.

Hodgson determined to retire early and, as he put it, to enjoy himself. Mindful of his own experience waiting in the wings for George Bell to retire, he thought it was of paramount importance that he should not cling on to the general secretaryship. In 1976 he therefore informed the Management Committee that he intended to retire the following year, at the age of 63. By that time he would have completed twenty-five years with the federation, and it was enough. Plans accordingly were set in motion for the choice of a new general secretary from among officials of the affiliated unions. Following the example of the textile unions, candidates were to sit an examination, and this closely reflected Hodgson's own perception of his job. Question 1 called on the candidates to summarise the main features of a lease put before them and then to calculate the costs of heating the building in question on the basis of some complicated sets of figures. Question 2 dealt with publications and included an article on trade unions in Germany, of which the candidates had to make an abstract. Question 3 consisted of outlining some new services to be introduced into the GFTU, with the case for and against reducing any one existing service. The first six nominees did not meet the standard, partly on medical grounds. To Hodgson's disappointment and un-doubtedly to their own chagrin, the whole procedure had to be repeated. In the interim the Management Committee improved the terms it was offering in order to attract more competition. Trade union general secretaries are not usually well paid, and the general secretaryship of the GFTU was no exception. At the second attempt, however, more candidates were found and a special meeting of the general council in September 1977 elected from among those whom the Management Committee considered eligible the national organiser of the National Union of Tailors and Garment Workers, Peter Potts. He joined Leslie Hodgson almost immediately at Central House for a three-month takeover period. Hodgson retired at the end of December 1977 in a round of parties and presentations. The following month he went into hospital, cancer was diagnosed and a year later, after a painful illness and several operations, he died. A small group of friends gathered on one of the iciest days for many years at Golders Green crematorium. There was no memorial service, and no obituary in the national press.

The General Federation of Trade Unions today is substantially Leslie Hodgson's creation. He always remembered that he was the servant of his membership and he cherished the values that his members stood for. Quiet, unfussy, highly professional in his approach to industrial problems and always ready to be swayed by professional advice, he worked by patience and persuasion. He was a fluent and even stylish writer, he had a shrewd sense of humour and, as many colleagues of his on the Management Committee would testify, he and his wife had a gift for friendship. His instinct for 'doing things properly' showed itself in every detail of the federation's business, not least in the meticulous planning of the lavish dinner-dances that were the high point of every annual general council meeting. Two qualities Hodgson lacked which stand any trade unionist in good stead: those of rhetoric and personal flamboyance. At Management Committee meetings he preferred to introduce new ideas as the scheme of one of the other committee members, and in his dealings with affiliated unions he followed the same policy, knowing that the union itself must take credit with its members for any success in which the GFTU might have helped. His diplomacy with a committee made up mainly of officials much older than himself may have been the only course that he could pursue for many years. When, in the late 1960s, the composition of the Management Committee changed noticeably, his years of diplomacy paid off and he was able to steer the General Federation towards more rapid change. Perhaps it was too much for him to expect of himself that he could also turn into a publicist and gain wider recognition for the organisaiton as it remoulded itself in a world where size and muscle are still the more eye-catching qualities. But whatever his private disappointments may have been, Leslie Hodgson left behind a record of solid achievements. Not the least of them was the skill with which he had husbanded the traditional virtues of the GFTU and its affiliated unions and turned them to good account in the modern world.

The General Federation of Trade Unions entered the 1980s with an enlarged professional staff and a general secretary whose contacts at the TUC and among larger unions may help to win a more prominent place for it in the trade union world. Among the changes that are already taking place are an increased educational role and a likely increase in contributions which affiliated unions may need to use, if benefits are also increased to meet the shortfall in social security payments to workers involved in industrial disputes, under the Thatcher government's policy. In the very much longer term, some quite different future could be in store. Might there be a role for the General Federation (it has been suggested) as a large textile and garment industry union? Although a *rapprochement* between its two largest unions and perhaps thereafter between them and some of the textile unions is not impossible, it is difficult to see how the federation as a whole could develop along these lines. In the past ten years especially, its tendency has been to diversify outside the textile and garment industries, and there are also sizeable unions of long-standing affiliation, such as the ceramic and furniture unions, which would stand to lose much by such an exclusive development. Another prospect has been suggested whereby the General Federation might affiliate to the TUC as the representative of smaller unions in general, with a seat on the General Council but continuing to provide the special services that its affiliates value. But in view of the present structure of the TUC, whose constitution represents unions by industry rather than by size, all such speculation is idle.

It is more to the point to observe that the General Federation of Trade Unions meets a need in its present role. Just as its affiliated unions continue to exist and in many cases to prosper because their members want them to, the General Federation continues at the will of its members. The late 1970s have witnessed some changes in public opinion in favour of smaller units which are more responsive to the wishes of the individual, and these changes have had their repercussions in trade unionism. The words of the General Federation's annual report of 1969 are still relevant:

> There is an area between a movement composed of small isolated and parochial trade unions . . . and one with just a few large unions dominating the movement and seeking constantly to reduce the number of trade unions. . . .
> A trade union's value lies in the work it does in pursuing its purpose of improving wages and seeking to regulate the conditions under which its members are employed; in the services it effectively and efficiently provides; and in the degree of participation, loyalty and responsibilities it calls forth from its members.

Notes: Chapter 7

1 *The Times,* 21 November 1940, p. 7, col. *c.*
2 *Report of the Ironfounders' Society Conference, 1911* (London: FSI, 1911), and *Annual Reports* of the Friendly Society of Ironfounders, 1913–18. Bell's own set of these reports is kept at GFTU headquarters.
3 GFTU, unlabelled file containing correspondence between George Bell and Leslie Hodgson after Bell's retirement, Bell to Hodgson, 27 May 1957.
4 I am indebted to Mr Sydney Allen of Bromsgrove, historian of the chainmakers' unions, for helping me to form a picture of George Bell's character, through his

tape-recorded conversations with Mrs Gladys Head, widow of Albert Head who was the last general secretary of the Chainmakers' and Strikers' Association and a personal friend of Bell, and with Mr Wesley Perrins, former MP and regional official of the General and Municipal Workers' Union, who also knew Bell and attended some of the meetings that he addressed.

5   PRO, LAB 10/465.
6   PRO, LAB 10/462, wartime file on the intrusion of unions into new industries.
7   GFTU, *Quarterly Reports*, December 1929 and September 1941; GFTU, *Jubilee Souvenir 1899–1949* (1949), p. 62–3.
8   See TUC, *Reports*, 1943 and 1944; Pelling, *History of British Trade Unionism*, pp. 219–20; Lovell and Roberts, *Short History of the TUC*, pp. 152–5; GFTU, *Quarterly Report*, June 1944.
9   GFTU, *Quarterly Report*, December 1944; *Annual Report*, 1948.
10 See R. Gurnham, *A History of the Trade Union Movement in the Hosiery and Knitwear Industry, 1776–1976* (Leicester: National Union of Hosiery and Knitwear Workers, 1976), pp. 160–1.
11 GFTU, *Quarterly Report*, September 1946.
12 Pelling, *History of British Trade Unionism*, ch. 11, title. For Bevin's time at the Ministry of Labour, see Alan Bullock, *The Life and Times of Ernest Bevin*, Vol. 2, *Minister of Labour 1940–1945* (London: Heinemann, 1967).
13 GFTU, *Quarterly Report*, June and September 1941.
14 ibid. September 1941.
15 ibid., December 1941.
16 GFTU, *Quarterly Report*, September 1944; PRO, BT 146/8, pt 11, evidence of the GFTU and TUC to the Board of Trade, Insurance and Companies Department, Committee on the Amendment of Company Law, 1944–6.
17 See above, pp. 196–7.
18 GFTU, *Quarterly Report*, June 1942.
19 GFTU, *Quarterly Report*, September 1944.
20 ibid, and PRO, BT 146/8, pt 11.
21 *Report of the Committee on Company Law Amendment*, Cmnd 6659 (London: HMSO, 1945).
22 In fact, the bulk of the report was accepted in principle by Churchill's Cabinet. See Bullock, *Life and Times of Ernest Bevin*, Vol. 2, ch. 8; Harris, *Beveridge*, ch. 17.
23 GFTU, *Quarterly Report*, December 1942.
24 See GFTU, unlabelled file on relations between GFTU and TUC, Miss D. Golding (Appleton's secretary) to Appleton, 2 February 1938, stating that two-thirds of the unions affiliated to the GFTU were not members of the TUC. Appleton used Miss Golding's remarks in a letter to Citrine, 22 February 1938. Citrine retorted (12 April 1938) that only about 36,000 aggregate members of the GFTU were in organisations not affiliated to the TUC.
25 A. I. Marsh and M. D. Speirs, 'The General Federation of Trade Unions 1945–70', *Industrial Relations Journal*, Autumn 1971, p. 31, mention only two attempts at dissolution, in 1948 and 1949. The procedure for dissolving the federation was, however, discussed in private session at the 1947 agcm.
26 Much was made in this debate of the fact that GFTU had taken advice from the same lawyer who helped the TUC to change its rules.
27 Tape-recorded interview between Mr Sydney Allen and Mrs Gladys Head, 21 April 1980.
28 For example, speeches by C. D. Stanier and H. J. Sharp, of the National Union of Flint Glassworkers and the London Glass Workers' Trade Society respectively, at the 1952 agcm.
29 GFTU Management Committee minutes, 31 October 1951.
30 The information in this and the next paragraph is based on a series of interviews

with the late Mr Leslie Hodgson in 1977, on *Federation News*, July 1952, p. 2, and on remarks made in interviews with several other individuals.

31 GFTU Management Committee minutes, 1953, *passim.*
32 The opinion of Professor R. W. Rideout in a letter to the author, 25 July 1980.
33 ibid.
34 GFTU, *Proceedings and Reports*, 1955–6, proceedings of agcm 1955, speech on first afternoon by the general secretary.
35 Webb, *History of Trade Unionism, passim*. A detailed analysis of trade unionism in the cotton textile industry can be found in H. A. Turner, *Trade Union Growth, Structure and Policy*. I am indebted for most of the information in this paragraph to an interview in 1977 with Mr Jack Brown and Mr Joseph Richardson, respectively general secretary of the Amalgamated Textile Workers' Union and retired general secretary of the Amalgamated Association of Operative Cotton Spinners and Twiners.
36 B. C. Roberts, *Trade Union Government and Administration in Great Britain* (London: London School of Economics/Bell, 1956), pp. 397–401; Turner, *Trade Union Growth, Structure and Policy*.
37 Marsh and Speirs, 'The General Federation of Trade Unions 1945–70'.
38 GFTU, *Annual Report*, 1980, statement of contributions, benefits and membership.
39 ibid.
40 These were Professor Allan Flanders and Mr C. W. Hewlett, deputy superintending inspector of factories in Manchester.
41 The Donovan Report remarked that one of the problems in analysing British trade unionism was the inadequacy of the 'craft', 'industrial' and 'general' labels under which unions in this country are habitually categorised. This is certainly a difficulty in writing about the GFTU.
42 GFTU, *Annual Report*, 1963.
43 Reprinted in GFTU, *Annual Report*, 1964.
44 Minutes of evidence before the Donovan Commission at its 58th meeting, 15 November 1966, published by HMSO, 1967. The GFTU was represented before the commission by the chairman and vice-chairman, E. D. Sleeman and R. Doyle, and by the general secretary.
45 *Report of the Royal Commission on Trade Unions and Employers' Associations* (London: HMSO, 1967), esp. ch. III, paras 112–22. A useful summary of Donovan's terms of reference and findings is given in H. A. Clegg, *The System of Industrial Relations in Great Britain*, pp. 445–52. Professor Clegg, later chairman of the standing Comparability Commission, was a member of the Donovan Commission.
46 See, for example, Clegg's one-paragraph summary of its origins and modern functions in *The System of Industrial Relations*, p. 397.
47 See, for example, GFTU, *Annual Report*, 1969.
48 ibid., summary of letter from GFTU Management Committee to Harold Walker, first Secretary of State for Industry, December 1968.
49 Article by Arthur Marsh in *Federation News*, October 1969.
50 Malcolm Speirs, 'The GFTU and the future', *Federation News*, January 1972.
51 TUC, *Yearbook*, 1979, article on 'Trade Union growth: the past 10 years'.
52 The words of E. Tullock, of the Associated Metalworkers' Union, one of the more forceful and colourful speakers at the GFTU in the past ten years (GFTU, *Proceedings and Reports*, 1969–70, report of 1969 agcm).
53 Marsh and Speirs, 'The General Federation of Trade Unions 1945–70'.
54 GFTU, *Proceedings and Reports*, 1971, report of 1971 agcm; information from the late Leslie Hodgson.
55 See GFTU, *Annual Report*, 1972.

Appendix: Membership of the General Federation of Trade Unions 1899–1980

A.1 List of affiliated trade unions in 1900

The names of the unions are given here as printed in the first *Annual Report* of the GFTU. Where 'etc.' appears in the name it has not been possible positively to ascertain the missing words, since some of these unions frequently changed their titles.

National Union of Boot and Shoe Operatives
National Amalgamated Society of Brassworkers
Federal Union of Bakers
Barge Builders' Trade Union
Midland Counties Bleachers', Dyers', etc., Federation
Britannia Metal Workers
United Operative Cabinet and Chairmakers
Alliance Cabinetmakers' and Furniture Trades' Association
Amalgamated Card and Blowing Room Operatives
Amalgamated Society of Card Setting Machine Tenters
Amalgamated Operative Cotton Spinners
London Society of Compositors
Perseverance Carpenters and Joiners
National Society of Drillers
London and District Drillers
Dock, Wharf, Riverside and General Labourers
National Union of Dock Labourers
Electrical Trades' Union
Amalgamated Society of Engineers
National Amalgamated Society of Enginemen, Cranemen, Firemen and Boilermen
Amalgamated Society of French Polishers
Floor Cloth and Linoleum Trade Protection Society
Firemen, Dippers, etc., Society
Amalgamated Engine and Iron Grinders
Table Blade Grinders
London Society of Glass Blowers
National Union of Gasworkers and General Labourers
Amalgamated Society of Gasworkers, Bricklayers and General Labourers
National Plate Glass Bevellers
Amalgamated Society of Journeymen Felt Hatters
Amalgamated Felt Hat Trimmers and Wool Formers
National Hosiery Federation

Holloware and Sanitary Pressers' Trade Protection Society
Holloware Stampers' Trade Protection Society
Holloware Buffers' Trade Protection Society
Friendly Society of Ironfounders
Jet and Rockingham Workmen's Association
Heywood and District General Labourers
National Amalgamated Union of Labour
Lancashire and Adjacent Counties Labour Amalgamation
Fancy Leather Workers
Lace Pattern Readers, etc.
Amalgamated Operative Lacemakers
National Amalgamated Labourers
United Machine Workers' Association
Midland Counties Trades Federation
Amalgamated Plate and Machine Moulders
Amalgamated Musicians' Union
Navvies', Bricklayers' and General Labourers' Union
Amalgamated House Decorators and Painters
Tobacco Pipe Makers
British Plate, Spoon and Fork Filers
South of England Block Printers' Trade Society
Printers and Transferers' Trade Protection Society
Scottish Block Printers' Society
Packing Box Makers' Society
Pocket-Book and Leather Case Makers
North Wales Quarrymen
National Stove Grate Workers
Shipwrights' Provident Society
Associated Shipwrights
UK Society of Amalgamated Smiths and Strikers
Silversmiths' Trade Protection Society
Amalgamated Shuttle Makers
Hull Seamen and Marine Firemen
Silver and Electro-Plate Finishers
National United Smiths and Hammermen
London and Provincial Hammermen
Amalgamated Society of Tailors
Amalgamated Jewish, etc. Tailors
Burnley Textile Operatives
Upper Mersey Watermen and Porters
Weavers' and Textile Workers' General Union
Amalgamated Society of Wood Turners, Sawyers, etc.

A.2   List of affiliated trade unions in 1980

Amalgamated Union of Asphalt Workers
Lancashire Box, Packing Case and General Woodworkers' Society
Rossendale Union of Boot, Shoe and Slipper Operatives

Amalgamated Association of Beamers, Twisters and Drawers
National Society of Brushmakers and General Workers
Northern Carpet Trades Union
Power Loom Carpet Weavers' and Textile Workers' Union
Amalgamated Society of Textile Workers and Kindred Trades
Card Setting Machine Tenters' Society
Manchester and District Caretakers' Association (NUPE)
Tobacco Mechanics' Association
Cloth Pressers' Society
Hosiery and Textile Auxiliary Association
SLADE (Wallpaper and Textile Section)
Furniture, Timber and Allied Trades Union
Amalgamated Textile Workers' Union
Pressed Glassmakers' Society
National Union of Hosiery and Knitwear Workers
Amalgamated Society of Journeymen Felt Hatters
Amalgamated Felt Hat Trimmers' and Wool Formers' Association
National Union of Lock and Metal Workers
National Association of Licensed House Managers
Associated Metalworkers' Union
The National Society of Metal Mechanics
London Jewel Case and Jewellery Display Makers' Union
National Union of Dyers, Bleachers and Textile Workers (Jute and Flax Branches)
General Union of Associations of Loom Overlookers
Scottish Union of Power Loom Overlookers
Yorks Association of Power Loom Overlookers
Ceramic and Allied Trades Union
Screw, Nut, Bolt and Rivet Trade Union
Society of Shuttlemakers
National Union of Tailors and Garment Workers
Lancashire Amalgamated Tape Sizers' Association
National Union of Dyers, Bleachers and Textile Workers (Craftsmen/Staff Branch)
Scottish Lace and Textile Workers' Union
Nelson and District Association of Preparatory Workers

A.3 Graph Showing Membership of All Trade Unions in Britain, Aggregate Membership of the TUC and Aggregate Membership of the GFTU, 1900–80

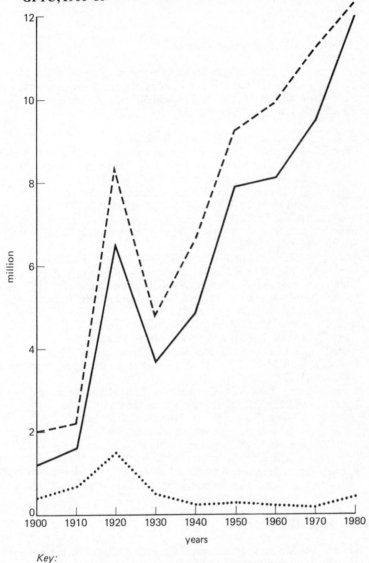

Key:
------- total membership of trade unions in Britain
——— aggregate membership of the TUC
············· aggregate membership of the GFTU

Sources: Mitchell and Deane, *Second Abstract of British Historical Statistics*; TUC *Reports* and *Yearbooks* 1979 and 1980; GFTU, *Proceedings and Reports.*

Sources and Select Bibliography

1 Interviews with trade union officials

Apart from informal meetings with many members of trade unions affiliated to the GFTU, I have benefited from a number of visits to union headquarters and elsewhere, to speak to past and present officials of some of the affiliated unions. The following list gives details:

Amalgamated Textile Workers' Union (Rochdale)
  Interview with Mr Jack Brown, general secretary of the ATWU, and Mr Joseph Richardson, retired general secretary of the Amalgamated Association of Operative Cotton Spinners and Twiners, 1977.
Amalgamated Union of Asphalt Workers (Peckham, London)
  Interview with Mr H. M. Wareham, general secretary, 1977.
Ceramic and Allied Trades Union (Hanley)
  Interview with Mr L. R. Sillitoe, OBE, JP, general secretary, and Mr J. K. W. Arnold, organiser, 1978.
Furniture, Timber and Allied Trades Union (Kingsbury, London)
  Interviews with: Mr D. R. Coates, former general secretary of the National Union of Funeral Service Operatives and now an official of FTAT; Mr R. S. Shube, former general secretary of FTAT; and Mr B. Rubner, present general secretary of FTAT, 1977 and 1978.
National Society of Metal Mechanics (Birmingham)
  Interview with the late Mr J. H. Wood, general secretary, 1977.
National Union of Lock and Metal Workers (Willenhall)
  Interview with Mr J. Martin, JP, general secretary, and several of his colleagues, 1977.
National Union of Tailors and Garment Workers (Milton Keynes)
  Interview with Mr Alec Smith, now general secretary, 1977.
Pressed Glassmakers' Society of Great Britain (Gateshead)
  Interview with Mr A. de Vere, central secretary, 1977.
SLADE, Wallpaper and Textile section (Salford)
  Interview with Mr D. Hill, formerly general secretary of the United Society of Engravers and now assistant branch secretary of the Manchester branch of SLADE, and secretary of the Wallpaper and Textile section, 1978.

2 Archives of the GFTU

The unprinted archives of the General Federation are kept in the basement of its headquarters building, Central House, Upper Woburn Place. London WC1H 0HY. I have consulted the following:

MS minute book of Management Committee meetings, 1899–1900. (From mid-1900 the Management Committee printed its minutes.)

Dispute benefit ledgers: a running account of claims made and benefit paid, kept in longhand and including claims that were disallowed, with reasons.

Correspondence files. Files have survived from at least the 1920s, but in many cases they are unlabelled. Those dating from before 1953 are not in any particular order. Each file, however, relates to a particular subject or organisation and generally appears to contain a complete record of the GFTU's side of the business in question.

3 Publications of the GFTU

The General Federation's publications include a great many ephemeral pamphlets, broadsheets, and so on. Most of these are bound with the federation's own set of its *Proceedings and Reports*, which are kept in the library at Central House. Many appear in other sets – for instance, at the British Library and the British Library of Political and Economic Science. Neither of these two libraries has a complete set, the BL series having a number of gaps and the BLPES series ending in 1950. There is one bound volume of miscellaneous pamphlets published by the GFTU, mainly in the period 1912–18, in the BL under the reference WP 4743. Only a selection of the federation's publications is given here. In all cases the place of publication is London and the publisher the GFTU itself.

Code of Rules (1899).
Proceedings and Reports, 1899 – in progress. Also known as *Reports etc.* These include:
    Annual Reports;
    Quarterly Reports, 1899–1950;
    other special reports and printed minutes of Management Committee meetings.
The Federationist, monthly, 1913–19. Later published as *The Democrat*, weekly, 1919–20.
High Prices of Food, pamphlet (27 January 1915).
The Management Committee and the General Situation, pamphlet (27 May 1915).
Soldiers' and Sailors' Pay. Report of a Conference at the House of Commons, pamphlet (1917).
Report of the Special General Council Meeting Held in the Queen's College, Birmingham, on Thursday, October 11th, 1917, to Consider Sailors' and Soldiers' Pay, National Reconstruction and Organisation, Organisation of the Federation, pamphlet (11 October 1917).
Rheumatism, pamphlet (1927).
Report on the Bedaux and Kindred Systems, pamphlet (1932).
Report on the Causes of the Failure to Increase Trade Union Membership, pamphlet (1932).
Better Machinery. An Examination of the Resolution Moved at the Trades Union Congress, September 1934, pamphlet (1935).
Report on Trade Union Organisation, pamphlet (1937).

Jubilee Souvenir 1899–1949 (1949).
Federation News, quarterly, 1950 – in progress.
Abstracts, monthly, 1953 – in progress.
Courtaulds. The Anatomy of a Multinational (1975).

4   Other Unpublished Sources, Listed by Location

Amalgamated Union of Asphalters headquarters, Jenkin House, 173A Queens Road, Peckham, London SE15 2NF:
  MS minutes of the union's executive committee meetings.
British Library Reference Division, Department of Manuscripts, London, WC1
  John Burns papers, ADD MS 46287.
British Library of Political and Economic Science, London School of Economics, Houghton Street, London WC1:
  Beveridge Collection, Coll. B, printed but unpublished minutes and reports of the Central (Unemployed) Body for London;
  Passfield Papers.
  Beatrice Webb's diary, typescript version, amended by Mrs Webb from her own longhand;
  Webb (Trade Union) Collections A, B and E.
John Rylands University Library of Manchester, University of Manchester, Oxford Road, Manchester M13 9PP:
  Judith P. Fincher, 'The *Clarion* movement: an attempt to implement the cooperative commonwealth in England', MA thesis, Manchester University, 1971.
National Union of Tailors and Garment Workers headquarters, Radlett House, West Hill, Aspley Guise, Milton Keynes MK17 8DT:
  typed verbatim reports of biennial general conferences.
Public Record Office, Ruskin Avenue, Kew, Richmond, Surrey TW9 4DU:
  BT 146/8 Board of Trade, Insurance and Companies Department, evidence before the Committee on the Amendment of Company Law, 1944–6;
  CAB 37 Cabinet papers (photographic copies);
  ED 24 Ministry of Education private office papers;
  LAB 2 Board of Trade and Ministry of Labour files;
  LAB 10 Ministry of Labour Industrial Relations papers;
  PIN 7 Papers of the Ministry of Labour (employment department) taken over by the Ministry of Pensions and National Insurance;
  PRO 30/69 Ramsay MacDonald papers;
  RECO 1 Ministry of Reconstruction files;
  T 1 Treasury In-letters.
SLADE Manchester Branch, Slade House, 297/9 Chapel Street, Salford M3 5JT:
  United Society of Engravers, typed and printed reports.

Trades Union Congress, Congress House, Great Russell Street, London
WC1:
    TUC Parliamentary Committee, manuscript and typed minutes,
    1888–1922. (A microfilm copy is in the British Library.)
University of London Library, Senate House, Malet Street, London WC1:
    Logie Barrow, 'The socialism of Robert Blatchford and the *Clarion*',
    PhD thesis, London University, 1975.

5 Published Works

V. L. Allen, 'The reorganization of the Trades Union Congress, 1918–1927',
British Journal of Sociology, vol. 11, no. 1 (1960), pp. 24–43.

Amalgamated Association of Card and Blowing Room Operatives, *Annual
Reports* (Rochdale: published by the union, no starting-date known).

Amalgamated Association of Operative Cotton Spinners and Twiners,
Annual Reports, new series (Manchester: published by the union,
1878–1975).

Amalgamated Society of Engineers, *Monthly Reports*, later *Monthly
Journal*, new series (London: ASE, February 1897–July 1920).

Amalgamated Union of Asphalt Workers, *Asphalters* (journal) (London:
AUAW, 1934–).

W. A. Appleton, 'The causes of unrest among workpeople', talk to the
London Economic Society, reprinted in GFTU, *Proceedings and Reports*,
1910–11.

W. A. Appleton, *The Future of Trade Unionism* (London, 1916).

W. A. Appleton, *Trade Union Organisation: How to Make the Movement
More Effective* (London: GFTU, 1916).

W. A. Appleton, *America and International Labour Problems* (London:
GFTU, 1919).

W. A. Appleton, *Trade Unions: Their Past, Present and Future* (London:
Philip Allan, 1925).

W. A. Appleton, *The TUC and the GFTU*, pamphlet dated July 1936
(London: GFTU).

R. Page Arnot, *The Miners*, Vol. 1, *A History of the Miners' Federation of
Great Britain, 1889–1910*, and Vol. 2, *Years of Struggle: A History of the
Miners' Federation of Great Britain from 1910 Onwards* (London: Allen &
Unwin, 1949 and 1953).

G. R. Askwith (Lord Askwith), *Industrial Problems and Disputes* (London:
John Murray, 1920).

F. Bealey and H. Pelling, *Labour and Politics, 1900–1906. A History of the
Labour Representation Committee* (London: Macmillan, 1958).

R. H. Best, W. J. Davis and C. Perks, *The Brassworkers of Berlin and of
Birmingham*, 2nd edn (London: 1905, no publisher named).

W. H. Beveridge (Lord Beveridge), *Power and Influence. An Autobiography*
(London: Hodder & Stoughton, 1953).

Robert Blatchford and P. J. King, *Trades Federation*, Clarion Pamphlet 17
(London: Clarion, 1897).

Asa Briggs and John Saville (eds), *Essays in Labour History 1886–1923* (London: Macmillan, 1971).

British Funeral Workers' Association, *The Funeral Workers' Journal.*

E. H. Phelps Brown, *The Growth of British Industrial Relations. A Study from the Standpoint of 1906–14* (London: Macmillan, 1959).

Kenneth D. Brown, *Labour and Unemployment 1900–1914* (Newton Abbot: David & Charles, 1971).

Alan Bullock (Lord Bullock), *The Life and Times of Ernest Bevin*, 2 vols (London: Heinemann, 1960 and 1967).

Frank Burchill and R. Ross, *A History of the Potters' Union* (Hanley: CATU, 1977).

Rodger Charles, *The Development of Industrial Relations in Britain, 1911–1939. Studies in the Evolution of Collective Bargaining at National and Industry Level* (London: Hutchinson, 1973).

The Clarion, ed Robert Blatchford (Manchester: Clarion, 1891–3; London: Clarion, 1893–1932).

H. A. Clegg, *General Union in a Changing Society. A Short History of the National Union of General and Municipal Workers, 1889–1964* (Oxford: Blackwell, 1964).

H. A. Clegg, *The System of Industrial Relations in Great Britain* 3rd edn (Oxford: Blackwell, 1978).

H. A. Clegg, A. Fox and A. F. Thompson, *A History of British Trade Unions since 1889, Vol. 1: 1889–1910* (London: Oxford University Press, 1964).

G. D. H. Cole and W. Mellor, *The Greater Unionism* (London and Manchester: National Labour Press, 1913).

G. D. H. Cole, *Labour in War Time* (London: Bell, 1915).

G. D. H. Cole, *Organised Labour. An Introduction to Trade Unionism* (London: Allen & Unwin, 1924).

Dame Margaret Cole, *The Life of G. D. H. Cole* (London: Macmillan, 1971).

Norman H. Cuthbert, *The Lace Makers' Society. A Study of Trade Unionism in the British Lace Industry* (Nottingham: Amalgamated Society of Operative Lace Makers and Auxiliary Workers, 1960).

Darlington Labour Representation Committee, *Report of a Meeting Held in the Assembly Hall, Darlington, on April 8th 1903, and an Address Delivered by Mr Isaac H. Mitchell* (Darlington: Darlington LRC, 1903).

W. J. Davis, *The British Trades Union Congress. History and Recollections*, 2 vols (London: TUC Parliamentary Committee, 1910 and 1916).

Allan Flanders, 'Collective bargaining – a theoretical analysis', *British Journal of Industrial Relations*, vol. 6, no. 1 (1968), pp. 1–26.

Allan Flanders, *Industrial Relations: What Is Wrong with the System? An Essay on Its Theory and Future* (London: Faber, 1965).

Allan Flanders, *Trade Unions*, revised edn (London: Hutchinson, 1968).

Derek Fraser, *The Evolution of the British Welfare State: A History of Social Policy since the Industrial Revolution* (London: Macmillan, 1973).

Friendly Society of Ironfounders, *Report of the Ironfounders' Society Conference*, 1911 (London: FSI, 1911).

Friendly Society of Ironfounders, *Annual Reports*, new series (London: Hansard Publishing Union, [1890]–).

Furniture, Timber and Allied Trades Union, *Rules* (London, FTAT, published periodically).

Furniture, Timber and Allied Trades Union, *Annual Reports* (London: FTAT, 1972–).

Bentley B. Gilbert, *The Evolution of National Insurance in Great Britain. The Origins of the Welfare State* (London: Michael Joseph, 1966).

S. T. Glass, *The Responsible Society: The Ideas of the English Guild Socialists* (London: Longman, 1966).

Samuel Gompers, *Seventy Years of Life and Labor*, 2 vols (New York: E. P. Dutton Co., 1925).

R. Gurnham, *A History of the Trade Union Movement in the Hosiery and Knitwear Industry, 1776–1976* (Leicester: National Union of Hosiery and Knitwear Workers, 1976).

José Harris, *William Beveridge. A Biography* (Oxford: Clarendon Press, 1977).

José Harris, *Unemployment and Politics. A Study in English Social Policy 1886–1914* (Oxford: Clarendon Press, 1972).

Royden Harrison, 'The War Emergency Workers' National Committee 1914–1920', in A. Briggs and J. Saville (eds), *Essays in Labour History 1886–1923*.

Rowland Hill Harvey, *Samuel Gompers, Champion of the Toiling Masses* (Stanford, Calif.: Stanford University Press, 1935).

R. Y. Hedges and A. Winterbottom, *The Legal History of Trade Unionism* (London: Longman, 1930).

M. A. Hickling (ed.), *Citrine's Trade Union Law*, 3rd edn (London: Stevens, 1967).

James Hinton, *The First Shop Stewards' Movement* (London: Allen & Unwin, 1973).

E. J. Hobsbawm, 'British gas-workers, 1873–1914', in E. J. Hobsbawm, *Labouring Men* (London: Weidenfeld & Nicolson, 1964).

Bob Holton, *British Syndicalism 1900–1914: Myths and Realities* (London: Pluto Press, 1976).

James B. Jefferys, *The Story of the Engineers, 1800–1945* (London: Amalgamated Engineering Union, 1946).

Joint Board (of TUC, Labour Party and GFTU), *Report on Unemployment* (London: Joint Board, 4 June 1907, repr. in GFTU, *Proceedings and Reports*, 1907–8).

J. M. Keynes, *The General Theory of Employment, Interest and Money* (London: Macmillan, 1936; repr. 1963).

P. J. King, *Good and Bad Federation*, Clarion Pamphlet 24 (London: Clarion, 1898).

P. J. King, *Federation in a Nutshell*, Clarion Pamphlet 28 (London: Clarion, 1898).

P. J. King, *Trades Federation. The Official Scheme. A Crushing Criticism*, Clarion Pamphlet 33 (London: Clarion, 1899).

The Labour Leader (London: Independent Labour Party, 1891–1922).

Labour Party, *International Labour and Peace*, Report of the Berne Conference of 1919 (London: Labour Party, 1919).

Labour Party, *Manifesto on War Aims* (London: Labour Party, 1918).

Emmet Larkin, *James Larkin, 1876–1947: Irish Labour Leader* (London: Routledge, 1977).

London Trades Council, *Report of the National Trade Union Conference Held on Saturday 1 January 1898* (London: LTC, 1898).

Lewis L. Lorwin, *The International Labor Movement. History. Policies. Outlook* (New York: Harper, 1953).

J. C. Lovell and B. C. Roberts, *A Short History of the TUC* (London: Macmillan, 1968).

Rodney Lowe, 'The failure of consensus in Britain: the national industrial conference 1919–1921', *Historical Journal*, vol. 21, no. 3 (1978), pp. 649–75.

Ross McKibbin, *The Evolution of the Labour Party 1910–1924* (London: Oxford University Press, 1974).

Tom Mann (ed.), *Industrial Syndicalist* [London, 1910–11] reissued with an introduction by Geoff Brown (Nottingham: Spokesman Books, 1974).

Tom Mann, *Tom Mann's Memoirs* (London: Labour Publishing, 1923).

Paul Mantoux and Maurice Alfassa, *La Crise du Trade-Unionisme* (Paris: Bibliothèque du Musée Social, 1903).

David Marquand, *Ramsay MacDonald* (London: Cape, 1977).

A. I. Marsh and M. D. Speirs, 'The General Federation of Trade Unions 1945–70', *Industrial Relations Journal*, vol. 2, no. 3 (Autumn 1971), pp. 22–34.

Ross M. Martin, *TUC: The Growth of a Pressure Group 1868–1976* (Oxford: Clarendon Press, 1980).

B. R. Mitchell and Phyllis Deane (eds), *Second Abstract of British Historical Statistics* (Cambridge: Cambridge University Press, 1971).

Margaret Morris, *The General Strike* (Harmondsworth: Penguin, 1976).

National Union of Lock and Metal Workers, *Annual Reports* (Willenhall: NULMW, in progress, starting date unknown).

The Northern Echo, Darlington, 1903–6.

Henry Pelling, *A History of British Trade Unionism* (Harmondsworth: Penguin, 1963).

Henry Pelling, 'The labour unrest 1911–14', in H. Pelling, *Popular Politics and Society in Late Victorian Britain. Essays* (London: Macmillan, 1968).

Henry Pelling, *A Short History of the Labour Party*, 4th edn (London: Macmillan, 1972).

G. A. Phillips, *The General Strike: The Politics of Industrial Conflict* (London: Weidenfeld & Nicolson, 1976).

Pressed Glassmakers' Society of Great Britain, *Quarterly Reports* (Gateshead: Pressed Glassmakers' Society, 1900–10).

Bill Purdue, 'Isaac Mitchell and the "Progressive" Alliance', in North East Group for the Study of Labour History, *Bulletin*, no. 11 (1977), pp. 1–12.

Railway Review (London: Amalgamated Society of Railway Servants, 1900–10).

Patrick Renshaw, *The General Strike* (London: Eyre Methuen, 1975).

Report of the Committee on Company Law Amendment, Cmnd 6659 (London: HMSO, 1945).

Report of the Royal Commission on Trade Unions and Employers' Associations, Cmnd 3623 (London: HMSO, 1967–8).

B. C. Roberts, *The Trades Union Congress 1868–1921* (London: Allen & Unwin, 1958).

B. C. Roberts, *Trade Union Government and Administration in Great Britain* (London: London School of Economics and Political Science/Bell, 1956).

Johannes Sassenbach, *Twenty-Five Years of International Trade Unionism* (Amsterdam: International Federation of Trade Unions, 1926).

John Saville and Joyce Bellamy (eds), *Dictionary of Labour Biography* (London: Macmillan, 1972–).

Sir James Sexton, *Sir James Sexton, Agitator. The Life of the Dockers' MP. An Autobiography* (London: Faber, 1936).

Jeffrey Skelley (ed.), *The General Strike, 1926* (London: Lawrence & Wishart, 1976).

Robert Smillie, *My Life for Labour* (London: Mills & Boon, 1924).

A. J. P. Taylor, *English History 1914–1945* (London: Oxford University Press, 1965).

Malcolm Totten, *Founded in Brass. The First Hundred Years of the National Society of Metal Mechanics* (Birmingham: NSMM, 1972).

Trades Union Congress, *Reports* (Manchester, later London: TUC, 1868–).

Trades Union Congress, *Yearbook* (London: TUC, 1979).

Ben Turner, *About Myself, 1863–1930* (London: Cayme Press, 1930).

H. A. Turner, *Trade Union Growth, Structure and Policy. A Comparative Study of the Cotton Unions* (London: Allen & Unwin, 1962).

War Emergency Workers' National Committee, *Minutes* (London: WEWNC, 1915–18).

War Emergency Workers' National Committee, *Labour After the War* (London: WEWNC, 1916).

Sidney and Beatrice Webb, *The History of Trade Unionism*, revised edn, extended to 1920 (London: Longman, 1920).

Stephen White, 'Soviets in Britain. The Leeds Convention of 1917', *International Review of Social History*, vol. 19, pt 2 (Amsterdam, 1947), pp. 165–93.

Noelle Whiteside, 'Welfare legislation and the unions during World War I', *Historical Journal*, vol. 23, no. 4 (1968), pp. 857–74.

Who Was Who (London: A. & C. Black, various dates).

J. M. Winter, *Socialism and the Challenge of War* (London: Routledge, 1974).

Index

ACAS (Advisory, Conciliation and Arbitration Service) 230
AF of L *see also* Gompers, Samuel
  affiliated to IFTU 143-4
  article in *The Federationist* on 131
  membership of 134
  president of 64, 93
  relations with TUC of 91
  representation at international conferences of 93, 147, 150, 154
  Trades Union Congress, at 143
AEU 136, 180, 209, 215
ASE
  accused of blacklegging 21
  arrogance of 21
  disaffiliation from TUC 21, 131
  district committees of 25
  Eight Hours Committee and 4
  Federation of Engineering and Shipbuilding Trades and 21, 40, 131
  formation of 1
  founder member of GFTU 11
  funds of 4, 10
  lock-out (1897–98) 4-5, 9-10, 20
  membership of 3, 18, 132
  militancy of 9
  organisation of 3-4
  outvoted by smaller unions 26
  parliamentary representation 3
  refusal to contribute to costs of Osborne case 132
  representation on Management Committee 23, 26, 132
  secession from GFTU 108, 131-2, 134
  strength of 3-4
  strike by (1908) 54
  threat to expel Mitchell 88
Abstracts 2, 21-2, 226
Adkins Committee (on old age pensions) 183
Advisory, Conciliation and Arbitration Service (ACAS) 230
Aesop's fable 24
Alfassa, Maurice 72, 96
amalgamations of unions 2, 24, 34, 41-45, 60, 65, 107, 135-6, 160, 161, 176, 208-9
America, *see* USA
American Federation of Labor, *see* AF of L

Anderson, James 105
Appleton, William Archibald
  Adkins Committee member, as 183
  admired by Gompers 94
  alliances advocated by 42
  appointed secretary of GFTU 49
  awarded CBE 159
  blacklegging and 53, 121
  character of 113, 124, 157-63
  craft unions and 160
  criticism of 162, 189
  Democrat, The 162
  disputes and 39, 43, 52-6, 60-2
  education and 180
  General Strike and 177
  German contacts of 54, 143
  gradualism of 116
  health of 158
  IFTU and 144, 152-3, 155-6, 171
  industrial co-partnership and 197
  Labour Congress Hall and 112
  Labour Party and 61, 120, 161
  Lacemakers and 49-50, 158
  NUT & GW and 178-9
  pension for 159
  politics and 64, 111, 113, 123, 127-30, 142, 145, 157-63, 171-2, 206
  presentation to 181
  procedures tightened by 50
  resignation as secretary of GFTU 50, 206
  resigned as secretary of Joint Board 121
  rheumatism and 190-1
  Smillie attacked by 162
  soldiers' employment 62
  soldiers' pay 129-30, 159
  TUC and 120-3, 155-8, 169, 199-200
  trade union organisation and policy 160-2, 177-9, 206
  USA visited by 147, 154-5
  unemployment insurance and 117-20, 123, 158, 161, 182-5
  VAF and 39, 61
apprenticeship 44, 142, 194, 223
Armstrong-Whitworth Ltd 4
Arrandale, Matthew 23, 27, 36, 53-4, 59, 61
Ashton, Thomas 9, 23, 27, 53, 54, 56, 58
Askwith (Sir) George, later Lord 39, 48, 55, 104
Asphalt Workers, Amalgamated Union of 234, 239

Asquith, Rt Hon H. H., MP, later Earl of Oxford and Asquith, 73, 80, 84, 127, 145
ASRS 8, 11, 18, 72-3, 83, 87
Attlee, Rt Hon Clement, MP, later Earl 214
ATWU 224-5
Australia 101, 131
Australian Labour Party 101
Austria 92-4, 124
Austro-Hungarian Empire 93

Baldwin, Rt Hon Stanley, MP, later Earl 130, 175-6
Balfour, Rt Hon A. J., MP, later Earl 75, 77
Barlow, Sir Montague, MP 185
Barnes, Rt Hon George, MP 3, 10, 28, 37, 65, 72-4, 96, 146, 154
Beamers, Twisters and Drawers, the Amalgamated Association of 52, 134, 219
Beaumont, Wentworth, MP 73
Bedaux system 192-4
Belgium 123-4, 144, 152
Bell, George 169-70, 180, 188, 197, 200, 206-7, 217-19
Bell, J. N. 23, 27, 44-5
Bell, Richard 72-5, 112
Beveridge Report (on social services) 213-14
Beveridge (Sir) William, later Lord 21, 47, 80, 213
Bevin, Rt Hon Ernest, MP 129, 148, 171, 175, 186-8, 199, 209-10
Billposters, Amalgamated Society of 11
'Black Friday' 174
Blanesburgh Committee (on unemployment insurance) 186, 216
Blastfurnacemen, National Federation of 109, 121
Blatchford, Robert 7-12, 14
Board of Control for the Port of London 52
Board of Trade, The 21, 36, 39, 47-8, 61-2, 64, 196-7, 212
Boilermakers and Iron and Steel Shipbuilders, United Society of 2, 4, 16, 18, 40-4, 51, 66, 107, 110, 170, 171, 176-7
Bolton Spindle and Fly Makers 11
Boot and Shoe Operatives, National Union of 18, 23, 89
Bower, Frederick 104

Bowerman, C. W. 82, 110, 121, 123, 143
Bowman, Guy 104
Brace, W. A. 125
Brassworkers, Amalgamated Society of 23, 109, 134, 143, 225
  see also NSMM (National Society of Metal Mechanics)
Bridlington agreement, 1939 207
Briggs, Asa 221
British Iron, Steel and Kindred Trades Association, The 136
British Labour Amalgamation, The 67, 134
Broadhurst, Henry 5, 9
Browne, Edmund 39, 76
Brownlie, J. 132-3
Building Workers' Industrial Union, The 104
Burns, Rt Hon John, MP 2-3, 9, 12, 20, 46, 79, 84
Burton, Sydney 48

CATU 243
Callaghan, Rt Hon James, MP
Canada 143, 146
Card and Blowing Room Operatives, Amalgamated Association (or Union) of, later the Card, Blowing Room and Ring Spinners' Association 23, 53, 56-58, 63, 191, 200
Card Setting Machine Tenters' Society, The 219
Carpenters and Joiners, Amalgamated Society of 80
carpet unions 226
Carters, United Association of 28
Cartledge and others v. *Jopling* 227
Castle, Rt Hon Mrs Barbara, MP 233
Catchpole, G. P. 111-12
'Caxton Hall concordat', the 75, 77-8
Central House 180-1, 211, 216, 238, 241
Central Society of Ironmoulders 52, 54, 62
Central (Unemployed) Body for London 21, 79-81
Ceramic and Allied Trades Union, *see* CATU
Chainmakers' and Strikers' Association, The 64
  see also Cradley Heath chainmakers
Chamberlain, Rt Hon Neville, MP 186
Chandler, Francis 80
Churchill, Rt Hon (Sir) Winston, MP 84, 98, 209

Citrine (Sir) Walter, later Lord 199-200, 208, 213-14
Clarion, The 4, 7-11, 14, 17-18, 29
Clarke, A. 14
Clémenceau, President Georges 154
Cleveland and Durham Blastfurnacemen's Association, The 121
Cleveland miners 10
closed shop 224, 231
Clyde Shipbuilders' Association, The 40
Clynes, Rt Hon J. R., MP 14, 28, 44-5, 114, 171, 184
Coach Builders, United Kingdom Society of, The 55-6, 61, 68-9
Coal Mines (Minimum Wage) Act (1912) 103
Coates, D. R. 237
Coates, T. Wilson 119
Cohen Committee (on Company Law Amendment) 212-13
Cole, G. D. H. 115-16, 126, 130-1, 163
Combination Acts 1
Communism 131
Communist Party of Great Britain 171, 178
Companies Act (1929) 211-12
Companies Registration Office 240
Contributions to the GFTU 17-18, 27, 28, 68, 95, 106, 108, 114, 134, 211, 223, 238, 246
Confédération Générale du Travail, La 101, 107, 145
Confederation of Shipbuilding and Engineering Trades Unions, The 21, 40-1, 64, 131, 209
Connolly, James 103
Conservative Party 75
Consolidated Bookbinders, The 25
Conway v. *Wade* 105
Cooper, Ben 125, 127, 150
Co-operative Movement 13, 125
Co-operative Printers, The 24
Co-operative Smiths' Society, The 21
Co-operative Wholesale Bank, The 64
cop packers' association 61
Cotton Spinners and Twiners, Amalgamated Association of Operative, The 23, 53, 56-9, 64, 224
Courtaulds Ltd 240
Courtaulds, The Anatomy of a Multinational 228, 240
Cradley Heath chainmakers 62, 188-9
Crane, Walter 24, 87
Crinion, James 23, 37, 53-4, 56-9

Crise du Trade-Unionisme, La, see Alfassa, Maurice; Mantoux, Paul
Cross, Joseph 190
Cummings, D. C. 78
Curran, Pete, MP
  chairman of GFTU, as 19, 52, 56, 62, 85, 89, 106
  character of 19-20, 62, 89
  co-operation with Mitchell 47
  death of 89
  district committees and 25
  enters Parliament 19, 48-9, 89
  Gasworkers' and General Labourers' Union and 19, 106
  Joint Board and 20
  LRC and 19-20, 75-6, 79, 87
  Labour Party and 19-20, 83, 85
  negotiation, in 46, 61, 64
  Parliamentary Committee and 19
  politics and 10, 19, 47, 76, 87, 89
  unemployment insurance and 61, 81
  vice-president of national labour conference 73

Daily Citizen 82
Daily Herald, The 121, 185
Danish Federation of Trade Unions 38
Davis, W. J. 2, 23, 36, 57, 75, 89, 143
deafness, occupational 243
  see also industrial diseases and injuries
Decorators' and Painters' Union (of uncertain title) 23, 33
Democrat, The 131, 162
Denmark 91-2, 94, 131
Department of Employment and Productivity 236
Dipper, A. T. 14
disputes 16, 27, 34-37, 43, 50-65, 83, 114, 121-2, 163-4, 193-4, 229, 231
  engineering dispute 1897-98 3-5, 9-10, 20
  Clyde shipbuilding 1905-06 40-1
  Penrhyn quarrymen 35-6, 97
  cotton industry 1908 34, 56-60
  cotton industry 1932 195-7
  variety artistes and musicians 1906-08 38-9, 59
district committees of the GFTU 25-6, 112, 169
Dock Labourers, National Union of, The (the Liverpool dockers) 10, 18, 27, 52, 55, 107, 109, 114, 134
Dock, Wharf, Riverside and General Workers' Union, The 2, 18, 23, 63, 67, 148

Don't Shoot 104
Donovan Commission and Report 227, 229-34, 249
Donovan, Lord 229
Dundee Jute and Flax Union 216
Durham miners 28
Dutch Federation of Trade Unions 150-1
see also Fimmen, Edo; Oudegeest, Jan
Dyer, Colonel 4, 10

Earnshaw, Harry 219
education service of the GFTU 225, 227-8, 231, 238, 239, 241-2, 246
Edwards, Clement, MP 73
Edwards, Ebby 214
Eight Hours Committee 4
Elsbury (of the National Union of Tailors and Garment Workers) 179
Employers' Federation of Engineering Associations 4
Employers' Liability (Compulsory) Insurance Act (1969) 244
Engineering Union, Amalgamated, The, *see* AEU
Engineers, Amalgamated Society of, The, *see* ASE
Enginemen, Cranemen, Firemen and Boilermen, National Amalgamated Society of, The 28, 114

FTAT 209, 234, 244
Fabian Society, The 19
Federal Labour Parliament 10
Federation News 219-22, 226, 234
Federation of Cotton Spinners' Associations, The 57
Federation of Engineering and Shipbuilding Trades, The 21, 40-1, 64, 131, 209
Federationist, The 130-1, 133, 144, 160, 162
Felt Hatters, Amalgamated Society of Journeymen, The 23, 191
Fenwick, Mrs Margaret xi, 237
Ferguson, T. M. 216
Fimmen, Edo 151-2, 155
Flanders, Allan 34, 232
Flint Glassworkers, National Union of, The 237
Foundry Workers, National Union of, The 206
see also Ironfounders, Friendly Society of

'Fourteen Points' 148
France 12, 92-4, 102, 124, 130, 143-4, 146
Frayne, Joseph 200
French Polishers, Amalgamated Society of, The 54
frost cog and screw makers 63
Funeral Service Operatives, National Union of, The, *see* NUFSO
Furnishing Trades Association, National Amalgamated, The 54-6, 61, 178, 194
Furniture Trade Operatives, National Union of, The 209, 234
Furniture, Timber and Allied Trades Union, *see* FTAT

Gardner, David 53-4, 56, 59-60
Gas Fitters' and Allied Workers' National Union 208
Gasworkers', Brickmakers' and General Labourers' Society or Union, Amalgamated, The 23, 67, 109, 134
Gasworkers and General Labourers, National Union of, The 13-14, 18-19, 26, 44, 67, 105-6, 109, 114, 123, 134
Geddes, Sir Eric, MP 183
Gee, Alderman Allen 23, 52-5, 60-3, 79, 86, 107, 112
General Commission of Trade Unions, *see* Generalkommission
General Council of the GFTU 17-19, 28, 51, 64, 73, 94, 104-6, 108, 109, 112, 113, 114, 134-5, 148, 158, 162, 170-3, 178, 186, 192, 215-17, 220, 235-6
General Federation of Trade Unions (GFTU), *see* contributions; district committees; education service; General Council; insurance section; Management Committee; pension scheme; research service; rules
GFTU Approved Society, *see* insurance section of the GFTU
General Labourers' National Council, The 44-5
General and Municipal Workers' Union, The, *see* GMWU
General Secretaries of the GFTU, *see* Appleton, William Archibald; Hodgson, Leslie; Mitchell, Isaac Haig; Potts, Peter
General Strike, The (1926) 169, 174-9

Generalkommission 93-94
Germany 54, 92-4, 99, 123-4, 131, 139, 143, 157, 229
Giblan v. *Williams* 73
Gill, A. H. 57, 83
Gladstone, Herbert 89
Gladstone, Rt Hon William Ewart, MP 5
Glasier, J. Bruce 9
Glassworkers' Federation, The 43, 53, 67
GMWU 180, 198, 215
    see also National Union of General and Municipal Workers
Gold, Silver and Kindred Trades' Union, The 134
Gompers, Samuel 64, 93-4, 144, 147-51, 154-5
Gossip, Alex 178, 194
Greater Unionism, The 115-16, 131
Gregory (of the Amalgamated Gasworkers', Brickmakers' and General Labourers' Union) 28
Groocock, Clifford 215
Guild Socialism 115-16, 160, 161

Haldane, Lord 73
Hamilton House 180
hammermen's societies 43
Hardie, Keir, MP 5, 9, 80, 84-5, 110
Health and Safety at Work Act (1974) 243
    see also industrial diseases
health insurance 116, 120, 176, 181, 190-1, 195, 214
Heap, Cecil 222
Henderson, Rt Hon Arthur, MP
    calls conference to form WEWNC 125
    central building for labour movement and 109-10
    formulates labour's war aims 147-9
    joins coalition government 125
    Joint Board and 86
    labour newspaper report by 82-3
    Labour Party and 113, 147, 187
    'oneness of the movement' and 105-6, 111, 113, 163
    re-elected MP 90
    represents ironfounders 62
    resigns from Cabinet 146-7, 187
    resigns from GFTU 125
    Russian visit by 146
Henry, Fred, JP 234, 236
Hill, John 110, 113, 121, 162, 171, 176-7
Hinckley Hosiery Union 209
Hodge, John 161

Hodges, Frank 164
Hodgson, Leslie x, 100, 229-34, 237
    appointed to GFTU 219
    background 219-20
    extends GFTU services 221-2, 226, 238
    personal style 221, 228, 246
    professionalism 222
    retirement and death 245-6
    subcommittees introduced by 226
    views on trade union structure 229-30
Holland 92, 94
    see also Dutch Federation of Trade Unions
Holmes, James 23, 36-7, 53-5
Home Office 191
Hornidge, W. B. 23, 28, 35, 73
Hosiery Federation, National, The 23, 53
Hosiery and Knitwear Workers, National Union of, The 209-10, 243
hours of work 4-5, 79, 97, 151, 185
House of Commons 73, 80, 110, 113
House of Lords 91, 105
Hudson, Walter 83
Hueber, Anton 152
Hungary 94
Hutchison (of the Stove Grate Makers' Union) 178
Hyndman, H. M. 5

IFTU 93, 144, 150, 152, 154, 156, 171
Ilkeston Hosiery Union 209
Independent Labour Party (ILP) 5, 19-20, 46, 76, 80, 124, 149
industrial diseases and injuries 191-2, 223, 243
    see also deafness, occupational
    Health and Safety at Work Act
    Raynaud's Disease
    Workmen's Compensation Acts
Industrial Disputes Tribunal 222-3, 226, 230
Industrial Relations Bill 221
Industrial Relations Act (1971) 221, 233, 236
Industrial Syndicalist Education League, The 104
Industrial Syndicalist 104
Industrial Workers of the World, The 101, 143
In Place of Strife 233, 236
insurance, general 63, 108, 116-23, 131, 160, 181-8, 190-1, 199, 213, 216, 243
insurance section of the GFTU 116-123, 131, 181-8, 190-1, 202

International Federation of Trade Unions, *see* IFTU
'International Labour Charter' 145, 151, 155
International Labour Office 155
International Lacemakers' Federation, The 50
International Miners' Federation, The 143
International Secretariat of National Trade Union Centres 93
   see also IFTU
Iron and Steel Trades Confederation, The 150
Ironfounders, Friendly Society of, The 2, 18, 23, 36-7, 59-60, 106, 206,
   see also Foundry workers, National Union of
Ironmoulders of Scotland, Associated and Central 52, 66
Italy 92, 144

Jet and Rockingham Workmen's Association, The 42
Jewish Bakers' Union, The 121
Jewish Tailors' Association, Amalgamated, The 11
Joint Board (of the TUC, Labour Party and GFTU)
   amicable relations on 65
   blacklegging and 94, 121-2
   complaint against Salvation Army referred to 52
   constitution of 83
   demobilisation and 127
   dissolution of 122
   division of workers in same industry opposed by 44
   employment of disabled and 127
   formation of 21
   fusion of constituent bodies of 109-10
   GFTU proposals presented to 63-4, 86
   international labour movement and 78
   Irish transport strike and 131
   Labour Party and 84-5, 123
   membership of 20-1, 78
   Miners' Federation and 122
   office for constituent bodies 82, 112
   Osborne case and 83, 85-6, 108, 132
   Parliamentary Committee and 84-5
   pay dispute intervention by 83
   political activity of 78-84, 90, 117
   Right to Work Bill and 81-4

Royal Commission on Poor Law and 79, 84
   secretary of 21, 121
   set up (in 1905) 20-1, 78
   Tillett's criticism of 121
   unemployment and 55, 61-2, 79-82, 85-6, 117, 188
Joint Committee of Trade Unionists and Co-operators 131
Joint Committee on Labour Problems After the War 127
Joint Industrial Council for the Gas Industry 208
Jones, Jack, MP 198
Joseph Cross Memorial Convalescent Home 190
Jouhaux, Léon 101-2, 144, 148, 154, 158
Justice 9

Kean, J. (of the Wallpaper Workers' Union) 172
Keynes, J. M. 186
King, P. J. 7-8, 10-14, 17-18, 29
Kitchener, Lord 140
Knight, Sir Arthur 240, 244
Knight, Robert 16, 40, 110
Knowles, Nigel xi
Kolchak, Admiral 171

LRC ix, 6, 19-22, 70, 73-9, 87-90
Labour After the War 127
'Labour Congress' proposal 110-12
Labour Convention in the Treaty of Versailles 145, 151, 155
labour exchanges 81-2, 84, 91, 95, 98
Labour Exchanges Bill 84
Labour Government 173, 186, 213-14, 229, 232-3
Labour Leader, The 9
Labour Party, The, *see also* Joint Board and LRC
   Appleton's views on 161
   constitution of 154, 161
   disenchantment of workers with 103
   election results (1906) 79
   Henderson's leadership of 147-8
   hostility to trade unions in 111
   Joint Board and 84, 98, 122
   Joint Committee on Labour Problems after the War 127
   Mitchell's relationship with 46, 88
   'oneness of the movement' and 106, 109-11, 113, 120

Labour Party (*continued*)
  Osborne case and 85
  Parliamentary Committee and 82-3,
    86, 95, 115-16
  separation from LRC of 19, 76
  socialism of 154, 157, 161-2
  Taff Vale case and 74
  theoretical climate of 46
  trade union support for 157, 224
  Trades Union Act (1927) and 176
  unemployment insurance and 184-5,
    187
  WEWNC and 125
  war aims of 148
  war-time support for recruiting 124
  workmen's compensation and 192
Labour Representation Committee, *see*
  LRC
Labour Temperance Fellowship 21
Lacemakers' Society (or Union), Amalga-
  mated Operative, The 45, 49, 158
Lace Pattern Readers' Association, The
  64
Lancashire and Cheshire Miners' Federa-
  tion 9
Lansbury, The Rt Hon George, MP 46,
  88
Larkin, James 55, 103
League of Nations 148, 154
leatherworkers' societies 43
Legien, Carl 92-4, 139, 143-5, 157
Leicester and Leicestershire Amalga-
  mated Hosiery Union 193, 209
Liberal Party, The 5, 27, 75, 79, 146, 162,
  186
Licensed House Managers, National
  Association of, The 226
Lloyd, Marie 39
Lloyd George, David, MP, later Earl 53,
  84-5, 90, 116-20, 126-9, 146, 162
Local Government Act (1929) 186
Local Government Board 77-9, 84
Lock and Metal Workers, National
  Union of, The, *see* NULMW
London County Council 21, 46, 80, 89
London Entertainments Protection Asso-
  ciation, The 39
London Provident Shipwrights' Society,
  The 60
London Society of Compositors, The 178
London Trades Council, The 10, 30, 94
Long, Rt Hon Walter, MP 77
Longuet, Jean 99, 149-50
Loughborough Hosiery Union 209

Lyons v. *Wilkins* 72

Macarthur, Mary 62, 126
McCarthy, Tom 14
MacDonald, Rt Hon James Ramsay, MP
  articles in GFTU report by 75
  Central (Unemployed) Body member-
    ship of 79
  distrusts trade union politics 76
  fusion of GFTU, Labour Party and TUC
    opposed by 110
  joint secretary of Joint Board 21, 84
  LRC secretary, as 76, 78
  Mitchell criticised by 88
  National Government formed by 187
  Prime Minister, as 173, 187
  refuses to support war 124
  Right to Work Bill and 81-2
  Royal Commission on Poor Law and
    84
  secret election pact made by 89
Macdonnell, Lord 52
Machine and General Labourers, Amalgamated Union of, The 67
Machine Workers' Association, United,
  The 23, 59-60, 134
Macready, General 103
Maddison, Joseph 23-4, 36-7, 52
Mallalieu, Thomas 23, 27, 51-3, 59-63,
  135, 181, 191
Management Committee of the GFTU xi,
  21-2, 27-8, 35-43, 49-64, 70-1, 73-4,
  91, 94-5, 116-123, 134-5, 142, 145,
  150, 157-62, 169-71, 176-8, 183-5,
  190-1, 207, 210-11, 219-23, 229,
  237, 238, 245-6
  arbitration, and 36, 68-9, 72, 233
  constitution 17, 19, 22-4
  conciliation, and 21, 95, 112
  debates on winding up GFTU 214-17
  negotiations with TUC 75, 77-8, 151-6,
    198-201
  recruitment of small unions, and 226,
    228, 235
  soldiers' and sailors' pay, and 128-30,
    134, 159
  sympathetic strikes, and 28-9, 105, 114
  syndicalism, and 105-114
Manchester Dispatch, The 62
Mann, Tom 2-3, 10, 24, 101-7, 118-19,
  132, 191
Manpower Services Commission, The
  243, 244
Mantoux, Paul 72, 96

Marx, Eleanor 4
Marx, Karl 149
Maxton, James, MP 149
May Committee (on National Expenditure) 187
May, Sir George 187
Mellor, William 115-16, 130
Merrie England 7-8
Mertens, Cornelius 144, 155
Metal, Engineering and Shipbuilding Amalgamation Committee, The 132
Metal Mechanics, National Society of, The, *see* NSMM
Metal Workers' Associated Society, The 227
Middleton, J. S. 125-6
Midland Counties Trades Federation, The 64
Miners' Federation of Great Britain, The
  campaign to remove GFTU from national movement 121-3, 142, 157
  eight-hour day sought by 2
  federation with TUC opposed by 10, 14, 17-18, 22
  GFTU's politics defended against 135
  Joint Board and 122
  membership of International Miners' Federation 142-3
  minimum wage fight by 143
  Munitions of War Act resisted by 123
  national collective bargaining sought by 122
  national strike by (1912) 103
  refusal to meet NAUL 122
  representatives on Sankey Commission 174
  Samuel Commission without representation of 174
  strength of 3, 22
  WEWNC levy contribution refused by 122, *see also* Cleveland miners, Durham miners, Lancashire and Cheshire Miners' Federation, National Union of Mineworkers, Scottish miners
Mineworkers, National Union of 209, 214
Ministry of Health 189
Ministry of Labour 181, 184-5, 188-9, 196, 204, 207-9
Ministry of Pensions and National Insurance 218
Ministry of Reconstruction, departmental committee on juvenile education and employment 167-8
Mitchell, Isaac Haig 19-26, 29, 37-42, 45-50, 74, 78-82, 87-92, 98, 99, 181
Monthly Journal (of ASE) 132-3
'more looms' problem in Lancashire cotton industry 195-6
Morning Leader, The 39
Morris, William 15, 131
Mosley, Sir Oswald 187
Mosses, William 64
Moulden, Horace 193-4, 210, 215
Mule and Ring Spindle Makers' Society, Operative, The 53
Municipal Employees' Association, The 44
Munitions of War Act (1915) 123, 126, 132, 165
Murray, Len 236
Music Hall Dispute Conciliation Board, The 38
Musicians' Union, The 38-9, 134
Mutiny Act (1797) 104

NAUL 18, 23, 41, 67, 73, 105, 121, 123
NSMM 225, 234, 244
NUFSO 237
NULMW 225-6, 234, 243
NUT & GW 178-9, 225, 234, 245
Naesmith, Andrew 217
National Amalgamated Union of Labour, *see* NAUL
National and International General Federation of Trade and Labour Unions 11
National Anti-Sweating League, The 62
National Arbitration Tribunal 210
National Coal Board 214
National Council of General Labourers' Unions, The 61, 94
National Council of Labour Colleges 227, 242
National Democratic League, The 88, 101
National Federated Association of Employers of Labour 3
National Federation of General Workers, The 45, 135
National Free Labour Association 3
National Government 187
National Insurance Acts 19, 109, 116-19, 121, 181-2, 243
National Insurance Act 1946 216, 218
National Insurance (Industrial Injuries) Act (1946) 223

National [Insurance] Weekly 120-1, 123
National Joint Council for Labour, The 185
National Labour Advisory Council 140
National Society of Metal Mechanics, The, *see* NSMM
National Temperance League, The 47
National Transport Workers' Federation, The 104, 134
National Union of Funeral Service Operatives, The, *see* NUFSO
National Union of General and Municipal Workers, The 136
see also GMWU
National Union of Lock and Metal Workers, The, *see* NULMW
National Union of Tailors and Garment Workers, The, *see* NUT & GW
Navvies' Battalion, The 170
Navvies', Bricklayers' and General Labourers' Union, The (also known as the Navvies', Builders' Labourers' and General Labourers' Trades Union) 14, 67, 170
see also Public Works and Constructional Operatives' Union
Netherlands *see* Holland
New Statesman, The 131
Newell, H. 23, 33
Nordahl, Konrad 211
North Wales Quarries Ltd 36
North Wales Quarrymen's Union, The 29, 35-6
North-West Coast Engineering Trades Employers' Association, The 40
Norway 92, 94
Norwegian Trade Unions, Association of 211
Nottingham Hosiery Union 209
Nottingham Trades Council 49, 98
O'Grady, Councillor (Sir) James, MP
'ante-Taff Vale' position favoured by 74
chairman of National Federation of General Workers, becomes 135
disputes and 53-4, 64
federation advocated by 15
GFTU chairman, as 135, 157
'German military machine' and 146
'great Congress Hall' sponsored by 112
Joint Committee on Labour Problems after the War 127
political activity of 15, 89, 99, 113, 157
presidential address by 15

soldiers' pay and 129-30
unemployment insurance and 117
WEWNC vice-chairman, as 125

old age pensions 53, 87, 223
'One Big Union' 180, 198
Osborne Judgement, The 70, 83, 85, 108, 132
Oudegeest, Jan 144, 151-2, 155
Oxford and Asquith, Earl, *see* Asquith, Rt Hon H. H., MP

Painters and Decorators, National Union of House and Ship, The 134
Palmer, Sir Charles, MP 89
Parliament Act (1911) 116
Parliamentary Committee (of TUC)
Appleton's annoyance of 159
arbitration and 97
blacklegging and 21, 97, 121
confusion in 115
criticisms of 10-11, 19, 75, 121, 150
federation and 7, 11, 16, 82-3
GFTU's relations with 16, 19, 73, 76-7, 121, 123, 125, 135, 149-50, 155-7
inertia of 70, 133, 150, 156
international activity of 143, 149-51, 155-6
labour newspaper and 76
Labour Party and 95, 116
levy on unions and 122
Right to Work Bill and 82
Royal Patriotic Fund and 126
secretary of 22, 121
Trade Disputes Bill and 80
trade union law and 73, 80
unemployment insurance and 118
voting and 7
WEWNC and 126
war-time support of government by 127
Workmen's Compensation Act and 27
see also Joint Board, LRC, Labour Party and TUC
Parliamentary elections
Clitheroe, 1903 75
general, 1906 88-90, 97-98
general, 1910 89, 91
Jarrow, 1907 48, 89
Parliamentary Reform Acts 5
Passfield, Lord, *see* Webb
Patternmakers' Association United, The 4, 64, 109, 134
Pease, Pike, MP 89-90

Penrhyn, Lord 35-6
pension scheme of GFTU 226
Pickard, Ben, MP 14
plasterers 63
Plate and Machine Moulders, Amalgamated Society of, The 59
plumbism, *see* industrial diseases
Pollitt, Harry 170-3
Portugal 144
Pottery Workers, National Amalgamated Society of Male and Female, The 42-3
Pottery Workers, National Society of, The 43, 191
Potts, Peter xi, 238, 245
Pratt, Edwin 70-1
Pressed Glassmakers' Society of Great Britain 67
Printing Machine Managers' Society, The 25
Professional Football Players' Association, The 64
Prudential Insurance Company 120
Public Works and Constructional Operatives' Union, The 170
   see also Navvies', Bricklayers' and General Labourers' Union, The
Pugh, Arthur 150

Quarrymen, National Union of 61

Railway Servants, Amalgamated Society of, The, *see* ASRS
Railway Workers' General Union, The 14
Railwaymen, National Union of, The 104, 122, 134, 177
Raynaud's Disease 223
Red International of Labour Unions 157
reelers and winders in the cotton industry 57-8
Registrar General of Friendly Societies 230
Reid, Sir Robert 73
Report of the [May] Committee on National Expenditure 187
Report of the Committee on Company Law Amendment (Cohen Committee) 212-13
Report of the Departmental Committee on Unemployment Insurance (Blanesburgh) 186, 216
Report of the Departmental Committee on Old Age Pensions (Adkins Com-

mittee) 183
Reports of the Royal Commissions on the Coal Industry 173-4
Report on Social Insurance and Allied Services (Beveridge) 213-14
Report on the Causes of the Failure to Increase Trade Union Membership 197
Report on Trade Union Organisation 201
Report on Unemployment 82
research service of GFTU 220, 225, 226-7, 239-41
Restoration of Pre-War Practices Act (1942) 210
Richards, T. F., MP 54, 61, 63-4, 89, 128
Rideout, Professor Roger xi, 241
'Right to Work Bill' 81-4
Rollermakers' Operative Trade Union (or Society), The 59-60
Rosebery, Lord 5
Royal Commission on the Poor Laws, The 46, 70, 79-80, 84
Royal Commission on Trade Combinations and Trade Disputes 75
Royal Commission on Trade Unions and Employers' Associations 229, 231-3, 235-6
Royal Patriotic Fund, The 126
rules of the GFTU 16-18, 24, 25, 28-9, 33, 51, 52, 69, 121, 216-17, 220
Ruskin College 227, 239, 242
Russia 144, 146, 154, 170-3

SDF 5, 7, 9, 19, 77, 81
Samuel Commission (on the coal industry) 174
Samuel, Sir Herbert, MP 174-5
Samuel Memorandum 175
Sanders, W. S. 131
Sankey Commission (on the coal industry) 173
Sankey, Lord 187
Sassenbach, Johannes 152
Scandinavian trade unionism 38, 152
   see also Denmark, Norway, Sweden
Scottish Amalgamated Society of House and Ship Painters 109, 121, 134
Scottish bakers' union, The 10
Scottish Co-operative Wholesale Society, The 56
Scottish Labour Party, The 5
Scottish miners 10
Scottish Railway Servants, The 20

Scottish TUC, The 8
Seddon, J. A. 125
Serbia 146
Sex Discrimination Act (1975) 244
Sexton (Sir) James 10, 27, 55, 74, 107, 110, 114
Shackleton (Sir) David, MP 75, 80, 83, 84, 85-6, 164
Shaw, Tom 135
Sheffield Table Blade Grinders 18
Ship-constructive and Shipwrights' Association, The 56, 177
Shipping Federation, The 3
Shipwrights, Associated Society of, The 7, 18, 23, 53, 56, 60
Shipwrights' Provident Union, The 53, 56
shopworkers' trade union 109
Short, Alfred 171
silicosis, *see* industrial diseases
Silk Workers' Association, National (Macclesfield) 180, 203
silver workers' unions 43, 53-4
Simpson, Bill 243
Smillie, Robert 10, 122-3, 125, 127, 138, 162, 174
Smith (Sir) Hubert Llewellyn 48
Smith, J. E. 105
Smith, Rod xi
Smiths, Co-operative Society of, The 21
Smiths and Strikers, United Kingdom Society of Amalgamated, The 28, 134
Snowden, Rt Hon Philip, MP 187
Social Democratic Federation, *see* SDF
Socialist International, The 151
Socialist Labour Party 20, 46
Socialist Party of America 150
South Metropolitan Gas Company 3
Steadman, W. C. 21, 38-9, 78-81
Steelworkers, Engineering and Labour League 134
Stevedores' union 105
Stockholm conference on peace, 1917 146-7
Stone, Dr Jean 243
Stuart-Bunning, G. H. 155
Sunday Worker, The 179
Sutton, Roger xi
Sweden 94
Swiss Federation of Labour 148
Switzerland 94
Syndicalism 12, 31, 46, 93, 101-7, 115, 132-3, 160

TGWU 45, 136, 180-1, 215
TUC, *see also* Joint Board, LRC and Parliamentary Committee
amalgamation of unions and 208
'ante-Taff Vale' vote 74
Clarion and 8-11, 14, 29
company law and 213
'conscription of riches' proposed by 128
disaffiliation of engineers from 21
dividing workers in the same industry 44
division within 115
engineers' lockout and 4-5
federation and 6-7, 11-16, 22, 78, 109-10, 113, 120, 163
foundation of 1
GFTU's relations with 22, 35, 52, 74-8, 85-6, 95, 121-3, 147-51, 155, 177, 199-200, 235-7
General Council of 163-4, 174, 198, 208, 214
General Strike and 174-7
Gompers at meetings of 64, 149
Industrial Relations Act (1971) and 236
international relationships of 91, 142-3, 146-7, 155-6
levy on unions by 105, 122, 198
membership of 3, 18, 75, 95, 107, 215, 235
militants in 2
national conciliation board proposed by 36
National Joint Council of Labour and 185
politics and 15, 70, 75-7, 86, 95, 107, 122, 135, 142, 173, 209, 214
presidency of 23
rules of 7, 9, 12, 73
Russia and 171
secretary of 5, 38, 199
textile workers' strike (1932) and 196
unemployment insurance and 182
WEWNC and 125
wage restraint and 214
war aims of 148
war-time recruiting supported by 124
TURU 239-40
Taff Vale Railway Company v. *Amalgamated Society of Railway Servants* 5, 70-5 80, 83
Tailors, Amalgamated Society of, The 18, 28, 35, 134

Tailors and Garment Workers, National Union of, The, *see* NUT & GW

Tawney, R. H. 174

Teachers, National Union of, The 180

Teston Independent Society of Cricket Ball Makers, The 237

Tewson (Sir) Vincent 199

Textile Workers, Amalgamated Union of, The *see* ATWU

Theatrical Employees' Association, The 39

Theosophical Society of New York 20

Thomas, Rt Hon J. H., MP 86-7, 156, 171, 173-4, 187

Thomas v. *Amalgamated Society of Carpenters and Joiners* 73

Thorne, Will, MP 2, 26, 68, 105, 114

Tillett, Ben
Appleton's conduct investigated by 50
arbitration believed in by 47, 68, 101
blacklegging investigated by 53
Central House opening, at 135
cotton industry dispute and 57
dockers' leader, as 2, 23, 52, 63, 103, 112, 181
health insurance society board, on 181
ironfounders' dispute reported on by 37
Joint Committee on Labour Problems After the War, on 127
'oneness of the movement' and 105, 110, 112-13
political activity of 52, 63-4, 135, 159
punches fellow trade unionist 115
soldiers' pay rise urged by 129
unemployment insurance and 61, 63, 118
WEWNC membership of 125

Times, The 70-2, 172, 200

Tolpuddle Martyrs 1

Tomkins, Alfred 178, 216-17

Tonypandy 103

Toyn, J. 10

Trade Boards Act (1909) 198

Trade Disputes Act (1906) 80, 91

Trade Disputes and Trade Unions Act (1927) 98, 176, 214

Trade Disputes Bills 73, 74, 80

Trade Union Act (1913) 86

Trades Unions Act (1927) 197

Trade Union Act (1871) 5

Trade Union Acts 72

Trade Union and Labour Officials' Temperance Fellowship, The 47

Trade Union Organisation 160

Trade Union Research Unit, *see* TURU

Trade Union Review 155

trades councils 107, 108, 110, 112, 125
see also London Trades Council
Nottingham Trades Council
Weardale and Tow Law District Trades Council

Tramway and Vehicle Workers, Amalgamated Association of, The 67

Transport and General Workers' Union, The, *see* TGWU

Transport Workers' Federation, The 122

Triple Industrial Alliance, The 104, 122, 134, 173-4

Tullock, E. 249

Turner, Ben 10, 138

Typographical Association, The 198

UTFWA 75, 224

Unemployed Workmen Act (1905) 78-81, 91

Unemployed Workmen Bill 77

unemployment insurance 61, 63, 77, 84-5, 95, 116-23, 142, 149, 165, 176, 181-8, 189, 195, 244

Unemployment Insurance Act (1920) 182-3

Unemployment Insurance Act (1935) 188

Unemployment Insurance Bills 84-5, 184-5

United Association of Carters, The 28

United Textile Factory Workers' Association, The, *see* UTFWA

USA 12, 38, 45, 93, 102, 146, 192

University College, London 244

VAF 39, 59, 61, 63

Variety Artistes' Federation, *see* VAF

Versailles, Treaty of 148, 151, 154-5, 165
see also Labour Convention

WEA 227, 242

WEWNC 122, 124-7

Wallpaper Workers' Union, The 172, 222

Walton, Sir John 80

War Emergency: Workers' National Committee, *see* WEWNC

Ward, John, MP
anti-capitalist views of 171
anti-socialist views of 76, 88
committee memberships of 14, 50,

Ward, John, MP (*continued*)
  53-4, 60, 64, 83
  debates with Harry Pollitt 170-3
  election to Parliament of 88
  LRC membership of 79
  Labour Party declared hostile by 111
  poor health of 172
  Russia, on 171-3
  strikes, on 172
  Taff Vale controversy, on 74
  TUC criticised by 171
  unemployment insurance bill introduced by 184-5
  unpopular opinions of 171
Washington Hours Convention 185
Waterproof Garment Workers' Union, The 234
Watson, John Christian 101
Watson, W. F. 132-3
Weardale and Tow Law District Trades Council 119
Weavers, Amalgamated Association of 18, 22, 51, 57, 135, 190, 195, 217
Webb, Sidney and Beatrice
  Appleton, on 157, 159
  GFTU, on 34, 49, 157
  Joint Committee on Labour Party Problems After the War suggested by 127
  Labour foreign policy admired by 148
  Mitchell and 46-7, 88
  Royal Commission membership of 46
  Sankey Commission membership of 174
  TUC, at 126
  Taff Vale, on 74
  WEWNC membership of 125
Whitley Committee for Joint Industrial Councils 162, 185
Wholesale Co-operative Society 112

Wilkie, Alexander, MP
  'ante-Taff Vale' position taken by 74
  anti-socialist views of 88-9, 123, 184
  committee memberships of 7, 23, 50, 83
  disputes, on 28
  election to Parliament 88-9
  mediation favoured by 7, 64
  sectionalism of 110
  withdrawal from parliamentary candidacy by 76
Wilkins, T. H. 132
Wilson, Havelock 149, 152
Wilson, Philip Whitwell, MP 82
Wilson, T. 10
Wilson, Woodrow, President 148, 151
Women's Trade Union League, The 126
women workers 53-4, 62, 126, 151, 218, 223, 244
  see also Macarthur, Mary; Sex Discrimination Act 1975; Women's Trade Union League; Women Workers, National Federation of
Women Workers, National Federation of 62
Woodcutting Machinists' Union 234
Woods, Sam 22, 31
Workers' Educational Association, *see* WEA
Workers' Union, The 67, 101
Workmen's Compensation Acts 15, 27, 91, 191
workmen's compensation 199
  see also industrial diseases and injuries; Workmen's Compensation Acts

Yorkshire Association of Power Loom Overlookers, The 237
Yorkshire Textile Workers' Federation, The 23
Young, Robert 132-3